CIPS STUDY MATTERS

DIPLOMA IN PROCUREMENT AND SUPPLY

COURSE BOOK

Contexts of procurement and supply

Printed and distributed by:

The Chartered Institute of Procurement & Supply, Easton House, Easton on the Hill, Stamford,
Lincolnshire PE9 3NZ
Tel: +44 (0) 1780 756 777
Fax: +44 (0) 1780 751 610
Email: info@cips.org
Website: www.cips.org

First edition September 2012
Reprinted with minor amendments June 2016

Contents

Preface

Welcome to your new Study Pack.

For each subject you have to study, your Study Pack consists of two elements.

- A **Course Book** (the current volume). This provides detailed coverage of all topics specified in the unit content.
- A small-format volume of **Revision Notes**. Use your Revision Notes in the weeks leading up to your exam.

For a full explanation of how to use your new Study Pack, turn now to page xi. And good luck in your exams!

A note on style

Throughout your Study Packs you will find that we use the masculine form of personal pronouns. This convention is adopted purely for the sake of stylistic convenience – we just don't like saying 'he/she' all the time. Please don't think this reflects any kind of bias or prejudice.

The Office of Government Commerce

The Course Book refers several times to the UK's Office of Government Commerce (OGC). The OGC no longer functions in its original form and its responsibilities have been allocated to different areas within the UK Government, principally the Crown Commercial Service (CCS). However, the OGC's publications remain an authoritative source of guidance on best practice in procurement and definitions of terminology. It is perfectly valid to cite the work of the OGC in these areas when answering exam questions.

June 2016

The Unit Content

The unit content is reproduced below, together with reference to the chapter in this Course Book where each topic is covered.

Unit purpose and aims

On completion of this unit candidates will be able to:

(a)   Offer advice and guidance to main stakeholders on the application of the sourcing process.

(b)   Understand supply chains which organisations operate in.

Learning outcomes, assessment criteria and indicative content

Chapter

1.0   Understand the added value that can be achieved through procurement and supply chain management

1.1   Explain the categories of spend that an organisation may purchase

• Definitions of procurement and purchasing and supply	1
• Typical breakdown of organisational costs represented by procurements of goods, services or constructional works	1
• Stock and non-stock procurements	1
• Direct and indirect procurements	1
• Capital purchases and operational expenditures	1
• Services procurements	1

1.2   Analyse the different sources of added value in procurement and supply

• The five rights of procurement	2
• Achieving the right price for procurements from external suppliers	2
• Defining total lifecycle costs or the total costs of ownership	2
• Achieving quality, timescales, quantities and place considerations in procurements from external suppliers	2
• Other sources of added value such as innovation, sustainability and market development	2
• Defining value for money	2

1.3   Compare the concepts of procurement and supply chain management

• Definitions of procurement, supply chains, supply chain management and supply chain networks	3
• The length of a supply chain	3
• Definitions of logistics and materials management	3
• Comparisons of supply chain management with procurement	3

1.4   Differentiate the stakeholders that a procurement or supply chain function may have

• Defining stakeholders	4
• Examples of stakeholders for a procurement or supply chain function	4
• Mapping of stakeholders for a procurement or supply chain function	4

How to Use Your Study Pack

Organising your study

'Organising' is the key word: unless you are a very exceptional student, you will find a haphazard approach is insufficient, particularly if you are having to combine study with the demands of a full-time job.

A good starting point is to timetable your studies, in broad terms, between now and the date of the examination. How many subjects are you attempting? How many chapters are there in the Course Book for each subject? Now do the sums: how many days/weeks do you have for each chapter to be studied?

Remember:

- Not every week can be regarded as a study week – you may be going on holiday, for example, or there may be weeks when the demands of your job are particularly heavy. If these can be foreseen, you should allow for them in your timetabling.
- You also need a period leading up to the exam in which you will revise and practise what you have learned.

Once you have done the calculations, make a week-by-week timetable for yourself for each paper, allowing for study and revision of the entire unit content between now and the date of the exams.

Getting started

Aim to find a quiet and undisturbed location for your study, and plan as far as possible to use the same period each day. Getting into a routine helps avoid wasting time. Make sure you have all the materials you need before you begin – keep interruptions to a minimum.

Using the Course Book

You should refer to the Course Book to the extent that you need it.

- If you are a newcomer to the subject, you will probably need to read through the Course Book quite thoroughly. This will be the case for most students.
- If some areas are already familiar to you – either through earlier studies or through your practical work experience – you may choose to skip sections of the Course Book.

The content of the Course Book

This Course Book has been designed to give detailed coverage of every topic in the unit content. As you will see from pages vii–ix, each topic mentioned in the unit content is dealt with in a chapter of the Course Book. For the most part the order of the Course Book follows the order of the unit content closely, though departures from this principle have occasionally been made in the interest of a logical learning order.

Each chapter begins with a reference to the assessment criteria and indicative content to be covered in the chapter. Each chapter is divided into sections, listed in the introduction to the chapter, and for the most part being actual captions from the unit content.

All of this enables you to monitor your progress through the unit content very easily and provides reassurance that you are tackling every subject that is examinable.

Each chapter contains the following features.

- Introduction, setting out the main topics to be covered
- Clear coverage of each topic in a concise and approachable format
- A chapter summary
- Self-test questions

The study phase

For each chapter you should begin by glancing at the main headings (listed at the start of the chapter). Then read fairly rapidly through the body of the text to absorb the main points. If it's there in the text, you can be sure it's there for a reason, so try not to skip unless the topic is one you are familiar with already.

Then return to the beginning of the chapter to start a more careful reading. You may want to take brief notes as you go along, but bear in mind that you already have your Revision Notes – there is no point in duplicating what you can find there.

Test your recall and understanding of the material by attempting the self-test questions. These are accompanied by cross-references to paragraphs where you can check your answers and refresh your memory.

The revision phase

Your approach to revision should be methodical and you should aim to tackle each main area of the unit content in turn. Read carefully through your Revision Notes. Check back to your Course Book if there are areas where you cannot recall the subject matter clearly. Then do some question practice. The CIPS website contains many past exam questions. You should aim to identify those that are suitable for the unit you are studying.

Additional reading

Your Study Pack provides you with the key information needed for each module but CIPS strongly advocates reading as widely as possible to augment and reinforce your understanding. CIPS produces an official reading list of books, which can be downloaded from the bookshop area of the CIPS website.

To help you, we have identified one essential textbook for each subject. We recommend that you read this for additional information.

The essential textbook for this unit is *Purchasing and Supply Chain Management* by Kenneth Lysons and Brian Farrington.

Examination

This subject is assessed by completion of four exam questions, each worth 25 marks, in three hours. Each exam question tests a different learning outcome.

CHAPTER 1

Categories of Procurement

Assessment criteria and indicative content

 Explain the categories of spend that an organisation may purchase

- Definitions of procurement and purchasing and supply
- Typical breakdown of organisational costs represented by procurement of goods, services or constructional works
- Stock and non-stock procurements
- Direct and indirect procurements
- Capital purchases and operational expenditures
- Services procurements

Section headings

1   Procurement and purchasing and supply
2   The scale and scope of procurement
3   Direct and indirect procurements
4   Stock and non-stock procurements
5   Capital procurements
6   Services procurements
7   Segmenting external expenditure

Introduction

The first section of the syllabus is designed to give you a broad introduction to the roles of procurement and supply chain management in a variety of organisations. We start by defining 'procurement' (the term used in the syllabus title) and distinguishing it from 'purchasing and supply'. We highlight the importance of procurement's role, in a business environment in which an increasing proportion of organisational costs is accounted for by external spend: that is, expenditure on goods, services and works 'bought in' from external suppliers.

We then go on to explore the various categories of procurements that organisations make, and some of the distinctive features of procurement in each context. We include the procurement of production materials; maintenance, repair and operating (MRO) supplies; capital assets (such as plant and machinery); and services.

Finally, we look briefly at another way of 'categorising' procurements: segmenting the procurement portfolio in order to prioritise and support procurement decisions.

1   Procurement and purchasing and supply

1.1   Doesn't everyone know the meaning of 'purchasing'? We all do it every day: purchasing food, newspapers, clothes, petrol, life assurance, transport services and a thousand other things. What's more, many readers of this Course Book will already be doing it in a professional capacity in the course of their jobs: purchasing materials, components, services and other requirements for the organisation that employs them.

1.2   All this may be true – but it skims over an important point. There is a big difference between doing something in everyday life and doing it as a professional. And there is even a difference between doing something as a professional and understanding it in the way that professional education requires. Organisational purchasing is a professional discipline based on a foundation of study and research, and proceeding according to systematic guidelines on best practice.

Purchasing and supply

1.3   **Purchasing** can be defined in various ways, depending on perspective.

- The purchasing *function* of an organisation involves the acquisition of supplies or inputs (raw materials, components, goods and services) to the organisation's activities (conversion, consumption or resale).
- In some organisations, there is a purchasing *department* or *unit* which has responsibility for carrying out this function, while in others, it may be carried out by individuals and teams in other departments (such as finance or production), or as part of a larger, more integrated cross-functional (organisation-wide) structure, such as materials management, logistics management or supply chain management. (We will look at these terms in Chapter 3.)
- The basic *objective* or purpose of purchasing is 'to buy materials of the right quality, in the right quantity, delivered to the right place at the right time at the right price.' These are sometimes known as the 'five rights' of purchasing. (We will look at the five rights in Chapter 2.)
- The purchasing *process* is a set of stages, or a chain of events, required to make a purchase or acquisition on behalf of the organisation. A typical purchase process might include receiving a purchase requisition, negotiating with suppliers, placing an order, receiving the ordered supplies, and making a payment. (We will look at this process in detail in Chapter 5.)

1.4   **Supply** may be defined simply as the act (or process) of providing something or making something available, often in response to buyers' or customers' requirements. It involves the transfer or flow of goods, services and information from one party (a supplier) to another (a customer).

1.5   In practice, as we will see in Chapter 3, supply often happens in a longer 'chain' of activity by which the outputs or products of one supplier become inputs to its customer's production processes – the outputs of which become the inputs of *its* customer, and so on. So, for example, raw materials are supplied to a manufacturer of components; the finished components are supplied to a maker of sub-assemblies or modules; the finished sub-assemblies or modules are supplied to a manufacturer or assembler of equipment; the finished equipment is supplied to wholesalers, who supply retailers, who supply the end users or consumers of the equipment.

1.6   The term 'purchasing and supply' is often used in recognition of the fact that the purchasing function has a role not just in 'buying inputs', but in 'securing supply': that is, ensuring the consistent, reliable, cost-effective flow of goods and services into the organisation from the supply market and supply chain. At the 'upstream' end of the supply chain, suppliers are regarded as an important factor in quality, because they influence the quality of the inputs that go into the making of products and the delivery of services. At the 'downstream' end, customers' needs are the driving force behind all organisational activities.

1.7   The role of purchasing and supply is thus to help to secure and convert inputs from suppliers into outputs that will satisfy customers.

1.8   Some definitions of purchasing emphasise its key role at the *interface* between internal customers and the external supply market. Its objective, in this role, is 'to provide the interface between customer and supplier in order to plan, obtain, store and distribute as necessary, supplies of materials, goods and services to enable the organisation to satisfy its external and internal customers'.

Procurement

1.9   Lysons & Farrington *(Purchasing & Supply Chain Management)* argue that traditional definitions of purchasing and supply – such as those outlined above – are inadequate and outmoded, when it comes to describing what organisational buyers actually do.

- They imply that purchasing is 'reactive': obtaining inputs in response to requests or instructions from user departments. In fact, modern purchasing is increasingly 'proactive': often taking the initiative in developing purchasing policies and working with users to define requirements.
- They imply that purchasing is 'transactional': concerned with processing purchase orders and contracts, in order to secure the best deal on a one-off or case-by-case basis. In fact, modern purchasing is increasingly 'relational': recognising that long-term best value is often obtained by developing long-term, collaborative relationships with selected suppliers: working *with* suppliers in a way that supports ongoing, mutually-beneficial business.
- They imply that purchasing is 'tactical': focused on short-term buying processes and goals. In fact, modern purchasing is increasingly 'strategic': focused on contributing to the achievement of long-term, high-level organisational objectives such as profitability, competitive advantage, innovation or corporate social responsibility.
- They imply that purchasing is always about 'buying' goods and services in return for some form of payment. In fact, there are a number of ways in which goods and services can be 'obtained', of which purchasing is only one. Goods and services are increasingly obtained via more complex processes such as hiring or leasing, borrowing from other organisations, sharing with other organisations (eg in a 'consortium' or business network), or gaining access or usage rights to resources owned by other firms (eg through strategic alliances, partnerships, subcontracting or outsourcing arrangements).

1.10   For some years, therefore, it has seemed desirable to find a less limited term than 'purchasing' for what organisations do to secure inputs to their activities. The terms 'procurement' and 'purchasing' are often used interchangeably and imprecisely in many organisations, and in much of the academic literature, according to preference. However:

- Procurement is a *wider* term than purchasing. Procurement may be defined as 'the process of obtaining goods or services in any way, including purchasing, hiring, leasing and borrowing'. (It would theoretically also include obtaining goods or services by means such as coercion, stealing or fraud – but we will leave these out of the discussion as incompatible with CIPS ethical procurement guidelines!) Procurement is therefore a more *accurate* term for what organisations actually do: hence its adoption in the title of this module (which in a previous syllabus was titled 'purchasing contexts').
- Procurement embraces a broader *process* than 'purchasing'. A purchase is sometimes described in terms of the 'purchase to pay' or P2P cycle: purchase order, expediting (monitoring and chasing delivery), receipt of delivery into stock, and payment of the supplier. Procurement, on the other hand, generally includes activities *prior* to the act of purchase, such as: identification and definition of a business need; surveying the market to identify potential suppliers and gather intelligence (eg on availability, price and technology developments); sourcing (identifying and selecting suppliers); and the negotiation and development of contracts. It also includes activities *after* purchase, including ongoing contract management (ensuring that both parties fulfil their obligations under a contract), supplier relationship management, dispute resolution, contract review and so on.
- Procurement reflects the more *proactive, relational, strategic and integrated* role of the function in modern organisations. (You may come across equivalent terms such as 'proactive purchasing' or 'strategic purchasing' in your wider reading.) Procurement is therefore a more *strategic* and *high-status* term than 'purchasing': hence its adoption in many organisation charts and job titles, reflecting either the reality or the aspirations of the function's role.

1.11   Lysons & Farrington retain the term 'purchasing', but suggest a more developed definition. We would propose that this definition can be effectively applied to the term 'procurement'.

'Procurement is… the process undertaken by the organisational unit that, either as a function or as part of an integrated supply chain, is responsible for procuring or assisting users to procure, in the most efficient manner, required supplies at the right time, quality, quantity and price, and the management of suppliers, thereby contributing to the competitive advantage of the enterprise and the achievement of its corporate strategy.'

We will be unpacking various terms and concepts from this definition throughout the Course Book.

What does the procurement function do?

1.12   Another way of looking at the definition of procurement is to consider what it is that procurement staff actually do. This may vary widely according to departmental organisation, specific role descriptions and organisation types, but in general, the task of procurement at an operational level includes the following activities.

- Supply market monitoring, and identifying potential sources of supply
- Supplier evaluation and selection
- Processing procurement or stock replenishment requests (requisitions)
- Providing input to the preparation of specifications (definition of requirements) for new purchases
- Negotiating, buying and developing contracts (settling terms and conditions of trade between the buyer and the seller)
- Expediting or contract management (ensuring that suppliers deliver according to the purchase order or contract)
- Clerical and administrative tasks: record keeping, report generation and processing of documentation through all of the above activities.

1.13   We will look at procurement as a *process* or chronological sequence of activities in Chapter 5 of this Course Book.

2 The scale and scope of procurement

Changes in the cost base of business

2.1   In recent decades, the cost structure of manufacturing firms has been transformed. Previously, the largest expense borne by a typical manufacturer, by far, was the cost of wages. Most manufacturing industry was heavily labour intensive, because most manufacturing processes were carried out manually by skilled and unskilled workers. The result was a large workforce and a large wages bill – and in this area of expenditure, procurement staff had little or no role to play.

2.2   Today the situation is very different. Many industries have seen a huge investment in automated production processes – and in many cases this has been accompanied by painful cuts in manufacturing work forces. From being labour intensive, such industries have become *capital intensive*: the sums invested in plant and equipment, often computer controlled, are high in relation to the sums paid in wages, salaries and benefits.

2.3   A related trend is for businesses to focus on their core activities – what Peters and Waterman (*In Search of Excellence*) call a 'stick to the knitting' approach. Many businesses now concentrate strategically on the 'core competencies' *(*Hamel and Prahalad) which they believe give them an advantage over their competitors: things they do distinctively well, which customers value, and which competitors would find difficult to imitate or match.

2.4   As a result, many support activities, which previously would have been provided by in-house functions, are now 'outsourced' – handed over to specialist external suppliers who provide the required service in exchange for a fee. (In some cases, this trend has been accentuated by regulatory pressures; for example, in many public sector concerns a regime of market testing – where in-house service provision must prove its competitiveness against external providers – has been imposed.)

2.5 Manufacturing businesses have similarly been increasingly ready to specialise in just one part of the manufacturing process. Where previously they might have made Product X entirely from scratch, nowadays they are more likely to buy subassemblies or modules for Product X from external suppliers, and confine themselves to the assembly process.

2.6 One effect of these trends is, again, to shift the balance of organisational costs away from internal labour costs – and *towards* external expenditure with suppliers and subcontractors. Organisations spend a much greater proportion of their budgets on buying in goods, services and works than they used to do.

2.7 This has a crucial impact on the scope of the procurement function. Where previously its responsibility may have extended only to a small proportion of the organisation's total expenditure, the proportion has now increased dramatically.

Goods, services and works

2.8 The syllabus refers to the procurement of 'goods, services or constructional works', as the main components of external expenditure. It is important to procurement operations to distinguish clearly and correctly between these three types of procurement: not least, because they are dealt with differently in contract law, and in category management (where responsibility for procurement, and procurement budgets, is allocated according to different categories or types of procurement).

- *Goods* are tangible or material items, which can be consumed. 'Consumer goods' are items people purchase to satisfy their needs and wants: such as clothing, food and electronic goods. 'Industrial goods' or 'producer goods' refer to the inputs or resources that producers utilise, such as cotton, steel, parts or subassemblies.
- *Services* are actions individuals or organisations perform which confer a benefit, but do not result in the 'ownership' of anything. Examples include: educational services, communication services, transportation/logistics services, health services and entertainment services.
- *Constructional works* includes projects such as the construction, alteration, repair, maintenance or demolition of buildings or structures (eg walls, road works, power-lines, pipelines, bridges or industrial plant); the installation of fittings (eg for power supply, ventilation, water supply, fire or security protection); and so on. This may involve the use of 'related goods' (such as materials and components, plant and equipment) and 'related services' (such as architectural, design, surveying, building, engineering, decoration and so on).

Typical breakdown of costs

2.9 The situation will vary, according to the size and type of organisation, what business sector or industry it is operating in, and what kinds of goods, services and works it procures. However, a broadly typical view of the proportion of organisational costs represented by external procurements for a modern manufacturing company (Lysons & Farrington) may be as follows: Figure 1.1.

Figure 1.1 *Typical proportion of organisational costs represented by procurement spend*

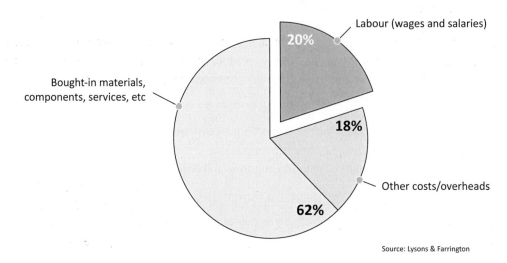

Source: Lysons & Farrington

2.10 Baily *et al* (*Purchasing Principles and Management)* depict the trend towards the growth of external spend in relation to internal costs such as wages and overheads (again, in a manufacturing setting) as follows: Figure 1.2.

Figure 1.2 *The proportion of external to internal costs*

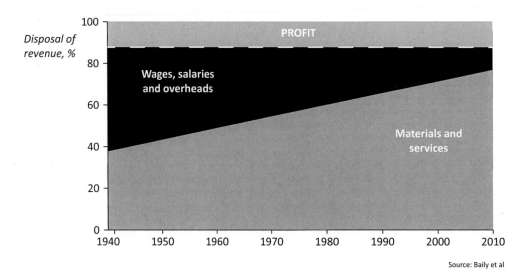

Source: Baily et al

2.11 In the public sector, a survey carried out on UK central government procurement in 1998 (Erridge & Hutchinson) found that average percentage spend by departments and agencies was 34% on goods, 41% on services, 13% on capital works and 12% on 'other' items (research, property rental and telecommunications). Over half of respondents stated that their procurement spend had increased over a three-year period: the principal reason being growth in large service contracts.

2.12 A 2004 UK National Audit Office report identified that half the expenditure of UK central government departments and agencies is accounted for by accommodation (19%), IT (14%), professional services such as management consultancy (11%) and financial services (5%).

2.13 In regard to local government, the English Audit Commission estimated in 2002 *(Competitive Procurement)* that more than 50% of spending by English local authorities went to external providers: up 10% over a ten year period. The most significant change was a substantial increase in spend on services, as services previously provided by the public sector became increasingly 'commissioned' or bought in from private or third sector providers.

2.14   One of the key implications of these trends for procurement is that, as the proportion of external expenditure rises, the potential *impact* of effective procurement activity on the costs, financial health and (in the private sector) profitability of the organisation is correspondingly greater.

3   Direct and indirect procurements

Classifying direct and indirect procurements

3.1   A manufacturing business generates a constant requirement for production materials. These may take various forms: raw materials, parts and components, subassemblies and so on. Without adequate supplies of these materials when they are needed, production operations may be disrupted with expensive consequences. The procurement of these items – direct inputs to the production process – is often referred to as 'direct procurement'.

3.2   Manufacturing businesses also require consumable supplies, sometimes referred to as maintenance, repair and operating (MRO) supplies. And all businesses spend money on general 'running' expenses: travel, stationery, telecommunications and so on. The procurement of these items – indirectly supporting the production process – is often referred to as indirect procurement.

3.3   In the procurement literature, this distinction is often made in the context of manufacturing businesses alone. However, as procurement disciplines have been developed more widely in the non-manufacturing sector, the distinction has broadened. In more general current terminology:

- **Direct procurement** refers to a range of situations when the items procured are either for resale (eg the goods purchased by a retailer), or for incorporation in goods for sale (eg raw materials and components purchased by a manufacturer).
- **Indirect procurement** refers to the purchase of any other, ancillary items (including MRO supplies, services and other operating expenses).

3.4   A slightly different (but overlapping) way of looking at the distinction between direct and indirect purchasing is provided by Professor Michael Porter's value chain model: Figure 1.3.

Figure 1.3 *Porter's value chain*

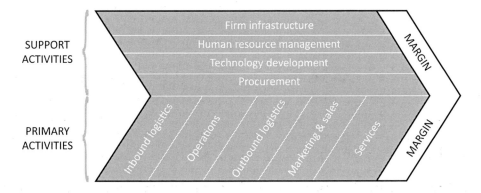

3.5   This model distinguishes between the *primary* activities of an organisation and the *secondary or support* activities.

- Primary activities are concerned with bringing resources into the organisation, transforming them by means of a 'production' process, moving finished products to customers, and marketing them.
- Secondary activities are concerned with supporting the primary business functions.

3.6 We will encounter the value chain again in Chapter 2, when we discuss the concept of 'added value', but in this context:

- Direct procurement refers to the procurement of inputs and consumables for the primary revenue-earning activities of the enterprise.
- Indirect procurement refers to the procurement of inputs and consumables for the support activities.

In effect, we are distinguishing two supply chains: a primary (direct) one and a secondary (indirect) one.

What difference does the distinction make?

3.7 A number of practical implications arise from the distinction between direct and indirect procurement.

- The quality of *direct* procurements has a direct impact on the quality of goods produced: poor quality will lead to increased quality costs, increased waste, scrap and rejects, and possibly reduced customer satisfaction. By contrast, the quality of *indirect* procurements does not generally impact on the production process.
- *Direct* procurements frequently need to be held in stock, in order to maintain service levels: to ensure that there is no disruption to production operations or availability for re-sale. By contrast, *indirect* procurements are usually made as and when required, minimising the amount of stock held, with its associated costs.
- *Direct* procurements are more likely to be made via longer-term, more collaborative supplier relationships, since the priority will be the security and continuity of supply. By contrast, *indirect* procurements are frequently made on the basis of one-off, transactional relationships, in order to take advantage of price competition, since the priority will be cost efficiency.
- *Direct* procurements are more likely to be carried out by the procurement and supply chain function, because of their specialised nature, the need for complex contract and supplier management, and the potential impact of supply disruptions or quality problems on production operations. By contrast, *indirect* procurements are more likely to be carried out by end users, as they represent relatively straightforward 're-buys' of standard supplies, often supported by approved supplier lists or framework agreements for supply (against which orders can be 'called off' as required).

3.8 In accounting terms, the cost of *direct* procurements is included in the organisation's 'cost of goods sold': if this cost can be reduced, the company's gross profit (and as a consequence, net profit) will be improved. By contrast, the cost of *indirect* procurements is included in the organisation's 'overheads' or indirect costs: if these can be reduced, net profit will be improved, but there will not be any effect on gross profit.

3.9 In many organisations, especially manufacturers, the cost of direct procurements is a very high proportion of total external spend. Opportunities for the procurement and supply chain function to improve the bottom-line profit of the organisation are therefore that much greater.

3.10 For example, if a manufacturing company's cost of sales is 60% of its sales revenue (ie it makes a gross profit of 40%), and 2% can be trimmed from the cost of direct procurements, this translates into a 1.2% increase in gross and net profit. The same organisation might typically spend 10% of its revenue on indirect procurements; the opportunity to improve bottom-line profit is only one-sixth of what it is in the case of direct purchases.

3.11 We will now look in a little more detail at some key categories of direct procurements: production materials, commodities and goods for re-sale.

Production materials

3.12 Materials used in manufacturing are often classified under the three headings of raw materials, components and assemblies, and work in progress.

- *Raw materials* include items extracted from the ground, such as minerals, ores and petroleum. The term also includes agricultural and forestry products: dairy products, fruit, vegetables, timber etc. Often these are sold to manufacturers in an unprocessed state, though in some cases a degree of processing may already have taken place before the manufacturer receives them.
- *Components and assemblies* are the finished output of other manufacturers upstream in the supply chain, which the buying organisation incorporates into its own outputs. The modern trend is towards purchasing more assemblies, thus taking advantage of supply chain technology and expertise, and enabling the final manufacture simply to complete the assembly – potentially, in response to customer demand. This is the basis of 'late customisation': many PCs, for example, are assembled to consumer specification (based on modularised assemblies) – without the need to hold stock.
- *Work in progress* refers to part-finished output, which is not yet ready for sale to customers.

3.13   Failure to obtain timely and secure supply of high-quality production materials can lead to disruption in manufacturing operations, incurring significant costs. The role of procurement professionals is therefore critical: we will discuss this further when we look at the manufacturing sector as a context for procurement in Chapter 11.

3.14   Here are some of the considerations that procurement staff must bear in mind in relation to production materials.

- The 'make or buy' decision: to what extent should we manufacture internally, as opposed to sourcing from outside? The modern trend has been towards reducing the amount of internal manufacture.
- The need for cross-functional collaboration (with functions such as design and engineering) to produce effective specifications for materials procurements
- The need to involve potential suppliers early in the procurement process, in order to take advantage of supply chain expertise. There may also be particular issues to negotiate with suppliers, eg the cost of developing specialised tooling to produce the items required.

Commodity procurements

3.15   Primary commodities are items that occur in nature and provide raw materials for businesses to incorporate in their products. They include crops such as cotton, coffee, tea, wheat and soya; and also minerals such as coal, iron ore and bauxite. In many cases such items are sold locally much as any other product might be, but there is also an international demand from companies worldwide who need such raw materials. To satisfy such demand a complex market has grown up in the form of commodity exchanges.

3.16   From a procurement viewpoint, these are the main challenges of sourcing commodities.

- They are unequally distributed, geographically: they often involve procurement in international sourcing – which brings a complex set of costs and risks (including currency exchange risk, transport risk, differences in legal jurisdictions, language and cultural barriers and so on).
- They are subject to significant and unexpected fluctuations in price. For example, if production is damaged by weather conditions or industrial action (or supply is disrupted because of war, civil unrest or government policy), the commodity will be scarce on the world markets, and prices will rise for the limited supplies that are available.

3.17   It is important for buyers to monitor relevant factors very carefully: these can include weather conditions, natural disasters, political instability etc. Often a solution may be to adopt a policy of forward buying, which means that buyers deliberately overstock in order to take advantage of a low price. If prices then rise, the existing stocks make it unnecessary to purchase until conditions become more favourable. Of course, the benefits of this policy must be weighed against the costs of storing and insuring the additional stock.

3.18 The main markets in which commodities are traded are in the United States. They include the market for precious metals (Comex) in New York, the New York Mineral Exchange (Nymex) and the Chicago Board of Trade, where grain, rice and soya are traded. There are also major markets in the UK, including the London Metal Exchange, with dealings in metals such as copper, zinc, tin and aluminium, and the International Petroleum Exchange.

3.19 Four groups participate in these markets: producers, buyers, traders, and speculators.

- Producers (eg farmers with a crop to sell) are interested in securing a good price for their produce.
- Buyers are interested in guaranteeing the price they will pay for commodities to be used in their businesses.
- Traders make the trading process function. They are both buyers and sellers, and make a small commission on trades in either direction.
- Speculators are also both buyers and sellers, but their aim is usually to make a substantial profit from their expertise in forecasting price movements. Speculators play a valuable role in that they foster the liquidity of the market by, in effect, introducing a greater number of both buyers and sellers.

3.20 Commodity markets offer a number of methods to dampen price fluctuations and enable sensible forecasting and budgeting, notably 'futures contracts'. A futures contract is essentially the right to purchase or sell a specified quantity of a commodity in the market. Any price fluctuation that is bad for a *buyer* (ie the price has gone up) will equally *benefit* him as a *seller*: 'hedging' the contract by making sure that the movement in price has a self-cancelling or off-setting effect on his financial position.

3.21 To illustrate this, suppose a buyer *purchases* 5,000 bushels of wheat on 1 January, when the price stands at $3 per bushel, for incorporation in products for sale on 1 March. If by 1 March the price of wheat has fallen to $2 per bushel, the buyer may be forced to sell those products to customers for $5,000 less than expected: bad news.

However, our buyer could enter a futures contract on 1 January, under which he agrees to *sell* 5,000 bushels of wheat on 1 March. He can purchase 5,000 bushels of wheat at the March price of $2 per bushel, knowing that he has a guaranteed customer for this quantity at a price of $3. (The 'forward price' of wheat for delivery in two months time will not in practice be exactly the same as the 'spot price' at the time, but we are illustrating the perfect hedge.) By gaining $5,000 on the futures contract, he offsets his loss on the physical purchase of wheat.

3.22 This is a complex area of procurement, and the detail is beyond the scope of this syllabus, but the point about price volatility in commodity procurement is worth bearing in mind.

Goods for re-sale

3.23 In businesses such as retail, wholesale and brokerage, buyers are purchasing finished goods for sale onwards to customers – with little or no work done on them by the intermediate organisation.

3.24 Retailers, wholesalers and brokers primarily buy the goods they intend to sell. This may include a wide range of different goods (as in a supermarket or department store); or a smaller range of speciality goods (as in a greengrocer, toy shop or consumer electronics store, say). The 'package' sought from suppliers may also include added value or service elements, such as sale-or-return arrangements; training for retail staff in the demonstration and handling of goods; or contribution to display and advertising costs.

3.25 Issues such as quality control, service levels and supplier relations will be important in the procurement of goods for re-sale – as they are in the purchase of production materials – but some of the procurement or supply chain function's priorities will be different. Arjen van Weele (*Purchasing Management: Analysis, Planning and Practice*) summarises some distinctive features of the procurement of goods for re-sale as follows.

- *Bottom line thinking.* Wholesalers and retailers are not in general adding much value to the products they sell, and their margins are therefore somewhat tight. Buyers must focus on buying what will sell at good profit margins.
- *Broad assortment.* One of the functions performed by wholesalers and retailers is to make available to customers a wide range of goods offered by many different manufacturers. The number of stock lines and the number of suppliers is typically very high – and this has implications for buyers attempting to monitor prices, quality and supplier terms and conditions.
- *Buying against supplier specifications.* In general terms, a manufacturing company specifies the materials and parts it requires for production, and sources suppliers who can meet its specifications. Retailers, on the other hand, will generally buy what is available on the market, as described by the suppliers. Changing suppliers is therefore easier for the retailer, and supplier relations tend to be less durable.
- *Short feedback loop.* In resale contexts, buying a product and selling it are close together in time. It very quickly becomes apparent which lines are selling and which are not: fast response to such information is a key requirement for procurement.
- *Technical complexity.* In retail organisations, the items purchased are usually of low technical complexity, whereas in industrial buying a procurement officer's technical knowledge may be indispensable.

3.26 Let's now look at a key category of *indirect* procurements: MRO supplies.

Maintenance, repair and operating (MRO) supplies

3.27 MRO supplies have been defined as 'all goods and services (other than capital equipment) necessary to transform raw materials and components into end products'. They include such items as paint, lubricants, packing materials, cleaning products and industrial clothing.

3.28 All manufacturing plants use MRO supplies regularly, and the number of MRO items may be very large. Some estimates suggest that a reasonably large manufacturing plant will carry in excess of 10,000 MRO stock lines. Although usage of any particular part may be relatively low, the potential for incurring high procurement and stockholding costs is clearly high, especially if stock 'proliferates': that is, if the range and variety of items, models or brands increases over time, as different users specify different items – without considering whether an item already in stock, or a generic item, would do the job.

3.29 In addition, the real value of MRO items may not be fully reflected in their purchase price. Their absence, or defective quality, may in some cases cause costly disruption to production – and it would be more appropriate to measure their value in terms of the additional costs or lost revenue that might result.

3.30 Despite the lower value and complexity of MRO items compared to direct procurements, it is therefore important for organisations to exercise sound commercial disciplines in their procurement. However, this is not always recognised: firms may lack defined policies and procedures for MRO purchases. It is often left to user departments to order MRO items without input from procurement specialists – and with little control over expenditure, value for money or supplier selection.

3.31 There are particular difficulties in establishing appropriate stock levels for MRO items.

- In many cases the actual usage of the item will be very low, or zero in some periods: the purpose of stocking it is to obtain relatively cheap insurance against a hazard that is unlikely to occur, for example a fault in a particular machine.
- The numerous items of MRO supplies are subject to a very wide range of demand levels. Determining a stock level separately for each is a daunting prospect, and may not seem cost-effective if the total cost of such items is not fully appreciated.

3.32 A systematic approach to inventory management is therefore essential.

- Each item of MRO supplies must be accurately described and a comprehensive catalogue developed.
- Opportunities for rationalisation – reducing duplication and variation – should be investigated.
- Stock movements must be recorded accurately, preferably on a computerised system (as discussed in Chapter 9).
- Slow-moving stock should be monitored with particular care as this problem is common with MRO items. Clearly items that remain on storage shelves for long periods are prone to deterioration.

3.33 Another issue in the procurement of MRO supplies used to maintain equipment – and especially spare parts – is that equipment manufacturers often recommend their own MRO items. While these may be the best buy, it makes commercial sense to consider alternatives, particularly if items are needed for multiple applications. The buyer may be able to buy larger quantities of generic/transferable items: benefiting from discounts, lower transaction costs, and less stock proliferation.

3.34 Ideally, maintenance and repair issues should be addressed with suppliers when procuring capital equipment, enabling the buyer to plan preventive maintenance and standardise MRO specifications.

4 Stock and non-stock procurements

4.1 Most organisations need to hold a certain level of stock of items to meet customer needs and production requirements. Buyers will procure *items for stock* on the basis of formal or informal estimates of demand: historic usage rates, forecasts of customer demand and so on. However, there are costs associated with holding stocks (eg the cost of capital tied up in stock, the cost of storage space and insurance, the cost of stock wastage due to deterioration or obsolescence, and so on) – and modern 'lean' thinking emphasises the need to minimise stock levels.

4.2 This has led to a trend towards *procurement for production*. In other words, materials are purchased with a view to immediate incorporation into the manufacturing or service delivery process.

Procurement for production

4.3 Non-stock procurements dominate in sectors such as construction, where most of the organisation's outputs consist of 'products' made in direct response to customer orders. (The products, in this case, may be a hospital, bridge or housing development, say.) The major supplies required by such a business are devoted to a particular project, and are therefore procured when the project requires them (on demand) rather than being procured for stock.

4.4 Non-stock procurement is also a feature of just in time (JIT) manufacturing and supply environments. JIT supply is a radical approach which has been widely adopted in factories in recent decades. It is based on the idea of minimising or eliminating 'buffer' stock: materials are procured so as to arrive at the factory only 'just in time' to go into the production process.

4.5 The philosophy of JIT is that 'inventory is evil': every effort is made to minimise stock holding, by securing demand-driven late delivery of required quantities of supplies. At the same time, given such 'tight' time and quantity parameters, the buyer cannot afford any defects in the supplies delivered: significant effort is also put into 'zero defects' quality management. Such a philosophy and practice requires strong integration and co-operation with suppliers. It is advantageous in reducing waste, minimising stock and lead times, and improving supply chain flexibility. But it comes at a risk: there are no time or stock buffers, if the supplier or the system fails...

4.6 Few companies take JIT principles to their ultimate conclusion, and a shift in emphasis towards 'agile' supply (the ability to respond swiftly and flexibly to changes in customer demand) has emphasised the benefit of procuring some stock (eg of assemblies and work in progress, to facilitate late customisation).

4.7 To minimise the costs of stockholding, a number of techniques have emerged in stock procurements.

- The use of economic order quantities (ie calculating the optimum size of order for each material so as to minimise the combined cost of acquiring and holding stocks)
- Improving the process of demand forecasting, so that stock procurements are more accurately related to requirements. (Where an organisation is prepared to procure for stock, issues of forecasting are less critical, but in procurement for production systems such as JIT, demand forecasting must be accurate in order to avoid stockouts and disruption to production.)
- The use of vendor managed inventory, whereby suppliers hold and manage stock on the buyer's behalf (sharing the costs and risks of stockholding) and release stock as and when required for production
- The use of management information systems to support inventory management (as discussed in Chapter 9).

Stock to order

4.8 Stock to order is a non-stock procurement policy whereby the organisation only procures materials as required to fulfil orders received from customers. Examples of industries where this might be the case include 'jobbing' manufacturers (such as bespoke furniture makers), construction projects, tailors or couture houses, and providers of services which require specific supplies (eg caterers).

4.9 A major challenge with this approach is the need to ensure reliable, swift performance from the supply chain against tight delivery schedules.

Stock to forecast

4.10 A stock to forecast policy is based on forecasting or estimating demand for finished products (for sale to customers) and for supplies (for operations), and planning inventory quantities and timing on this basis. Forecasting is particularly important in the retail sector where there may be wide seasonal variations in demand.

4.11 Although future demand may not be exactly known for purchased inputs, estimates can be made based upon past experience, statistical techniques or computer simulations and modelling.

Stock procurements

4.12 Under a 'stocking for inventory' (or procuring for stock) policy, items are procured and placed into storage in advance/anticipation of future need or demand.

4.13 There are many circumstances where this policy would be appropriate.

- In situations of *independent demand*: where the demand for a stock item exists *independent* of, or in isolation from, the demand for any other item. Examples include consumables and maintenance items, and finished goods sold in the retail sector
- In situations of *stable/predictable demand* for low-value, non-perishable items (especially if these do not take up too much warehouse space)
- Where there is a *long lead time* for obtaining stock from suppliers: the buyer may need to keep sufficient stock to meet customer orders
- Where items are *critical for operations*, and running out of them (or not obtaining them in time) would cause disruption to production
- Where there is a *legal requirement* to hold stocks (eg of health and safety equipment)
- Where inventory *appreciates in value* over time (eg wine, art works or timber)
- Where prices are *expected to rise*, and it will be more cost-effective for the organisation to buy or stockpile items while prices are still low

- Where *demand is seasonal*, and the organisation lacks the capacity to cope with peaks of demand: finished stocks will have to be made in advance

4.14 The benefits of such a policy include: the ability to respond to seasonal or unexpected peaks in customer demand; the availability of buffer/safety stock to maintain customer service and operations (in the event of supply disruptions); cost efficiencies from bulk ordering and transport (rather than multiple smaller deliveries); the securing of low prices while available; legal compliance (where relevant); and potentially, appreciation in the value of stock over time.

Perishable goods

4.15 Perishable goods are those that are subject to deterioration over time: once they have deteriorated, they are no longer fit for their intended purpose. A simple example is food products.

4.16 It is critical that such products are studied carefully so as to determine their useful life. In the case of food products it is usual to display this information in the form of 'sell-by dates' or 'use-by dates'.

4.17 This kind of product creates a need for specialised transportation and storage, without which the process of deterioration may be accelerated. The priorities of the procurement function will be attention to careful planning of logistics and storage, and rigorous testing to ensure product quality at the time of receiving the goods and afterwards.

4.18 In some cases, the process of deterioration creates significant risk: for example, in the case of foods, and certain chemicals. In such cases the storage and control of materials is usually tightly regulated, eg in the UK by the UK Control of Substances Hazardous to Health Regulations (COSHH).

5   Capital procurements

5.1 Another important classification of procurements is between capital procurements and operational procurements, generally referred to as 'cap ex' (capital expenditure) and 'op ex' (operational expenditures).

Capital goods

5.2 Two main features distinguish capital goods from other items procured by an organisation.

- *Length of lifecycle.* A capital item is one which the procuring organisation will use for a long time, usually several years – in contrast to operational items, which are mainly purchased for short-term consumption, production use or re-sale.
- *High acquisition cost.* A capital item is a large-value asset – in contrast to operational items which are comparatively inexpensive.

5.3 Typical examples of capital goods procured from external suppliers include buildings, manufacturing plant, computer hardware and vehicles. Other possibilities include certain internal projects, such as the design and installation of a new computer system. We will usually refer to capital equipment, as the procurement of manufacturing equipment is probably most common: 'equipment' could include plant and machinery, motor vehicles, computers etc.

Distinctive features of capital procurements

5.4 The procurement of capital goods differs in important ways from that of other goods.

- The basic purchase or leasing price is only one element, and sometimes not the most important element, in the total costs of owning a capital asset. Other costs (such as installation, maintenance, operating cost, 'down time' and disposal) are also relevant and may arise at any time over the life of the asset. The concept of 'whole life costing' or 'total cost of ownership' is discussed in Chapter 2.

- The monetary value of the asset is high. This generally requires specialised techniques of investment evaluation and control, asset maintenance (to preserve the asset's value) and so on. It also raises procurement and financing issues such as the decision of whether to purchase, lease, hire or acquire by other means (eg joint venture or alliance with the asset owner).

- Negotiations are usually more extended and complex than in other procurements, because of the high value and complexity of the total 'package' of benefits being sought over the asset's lifecycle. A team approach is usually needed in which the contributions of other departments, and not just procurement, must be effectively coordinated and managed.

- The procurement of a capital item tends to be non-recurring: there may not have been a similar purchase in the recent past, on which to base procurement decisions. The 'straight re-buy' orders that take some of the strain from raw materials and MRO purchases are not usually an option with capital assets: each new acquisition must be evaluated afresh.

- Specifications for capital equipment are usually more difficult to draft because of the technical complexity of the item; and the service elements which are usually included: pre-purchase research by the vendor, installation, operator training, after-sales service and so on.

- The benefits to be obtained from the procurement are often difficult to evaluate. For example, a machine may be replaced by a superior model in order to secure improvements in quality or ease of use. How can the value of such improvements be measured in financial terms?

5.5 A comparison between the main procurement considerations for MRO items and capital equipment may be summarised as follows, to illustrate the key differences: Table 1.1.

Table 1.1 *Considerations in the procurement of MRO and capital items*

CONSIDERATIONS IN MRO PURCHASES	CONSIDERATIONS IN CAPITAL PROCUREMENT
Availability	Total costs over life of asset
Cost	Asset utilisation: lifespan, flexibility
Ability to use standard/generic substitutes	Space/access requirements
Ability to minimise stockholding	Training, health and safety requirements
Supplier service levels	Cost/availability of spare parts through the life of the equipment
	Post-contract maintenance service
	Options (buy, lease or hire)

Evaluating and justifying capital procurement options

5.6 The benefits and costs of any capital procurement should be analysed in advance, in order to present a business case or justification for the exercise. This is often part of a formal feasibility study.

5.7 A capital asset is expected to be used for a number of years, and over that time it will give rise to many costs, in addition to the cost of purchase, lease or hire. There will also be costs of delivery and installation, maintenance and repair, operator training, supplier support, energy and labour, time lost to inefficiency or break down, decommissioning and disposal. In choosing between one asset and another, procurement staff must take into account the costs arising over the whole life of each.

5.8 The relatively long time period involved, combined with the subjectivity of estimates for most of these elements of cost, make it difficult to assess lifetime costs. One technical difficulty is that the relevant cashflows occur in years to come: such cashflows are not easy to evaluate in today's terms, even if they were known with certainty. The process of evaluating future cashflows in today's terms is referred to as 'discounted cashflow' (DCF): by applying this technique to all the costs and benefits associated with capital assets we can calculate, compare and evaluate the 'net present value' (NPV).

5.9   As well as estimating the costs of ownership, it is also important to estimate the benefits – although this is even trickier than estimating the costs of ownership, partly because of the conceptual difficulties involved in valuing intangible benefits such as improvements in quality.

5.10   The essence of cost/benefit analysis is that if benefits exceed costs, the procurement can be justified as worthwhile – while if costs exceed benefits, the procurement proposal will be rejected. It is possible to express this in the form of a benefit/cost ratio.

- If the ratio is significantly less than 1, benefits are less than costs. Conclusion: reject the project.
- If the ratio is significantly greater than 1, benefits are greater than costs. Conclusion: proceed with the project.
- If the ratio is close to 1, benefits and costs are approximately equal. Conclusion: further investigation is needed into the non-financial factors that might influence a decision.

5.11   Another approach is to calculate the 'payback period' (or 'recovery period') of the investment: calculating how many years it will take for the benefits to 'pay back' the initial total outlay. (If a machine is being bought for $1 million, say, and it is estimated that it will generate annual revenues or cost savings of $150,000 for 10 years, the payback period is calculated as $1 million *divided by* $150,000 = 6.6 years.) In general, an investment that pays back in a relatively short period is preferable to one that takes many years to pay back, but the basic question is whether the payback period is acceptable to the organisation.

5.12   Once the benefits and costs have been assessed, it is often necessary to present the business case for procurement. A structured justification of the proposal will be prepared and presented eg to a group of senior managers.

Lease or buy?

5.13   Leasing is a contract between a leasing company (or 'lessor') and the customer (or 'lessee'), under which the leasing company buys and owns the asset, and the lessee hires it: paying regular instalments (which can be regarded as rental payments) over a pre-determined period, in order to use the asset. Often, the buyer has the right to secure outright ownership once sufficient payments have been made under the agreement.

5.14   The advantages and disadvantages of outright purchase and leasing can be compared: Table 1.2.

5.15   As a compromise between straight purchase and leasing, an organisation may seek a hire purchase agreement, under which, after all the rental payments have been made, the user has the option of becoming the outright owner of the equipment. This enables the latest technology to be hired, but interest rates on the financing may make this a less financially effective approach than either leasing or purchase.

5.16   There may be other options which avoid capital expenditure altogether, in order to minimise large up-front investment and protect cashflows.

- Equipment could be *rented* for the duration of a particular project: this would be operating expenditure, rather than capital expenditure. It would not make sense to purchase an expensive asset if we plan to use it for a short fraction of its useful life.
- An IT system might be upgraded one unit or application at a time, over an extended period, as opposed to commissioning a large-scale project to replace the entire system.

Table 1.2 *The lease or buy decision*

ADVANTAGES OF OUTRIGHT PURCHASE	DISADVANTAGES OF OUTRIGHT PURCHASE
Total cost is low, compared to rental	High initial expenditure ties up capital: impact on cashflow, and opportunity cost of capital (what the purchase price would earn if used for other purposes)
The user has total control over the use of the asset	User bears all costs and risks of maintenance, operation and disposal
The asset may have residual re-sale value at the end of use	Risk of technological obsolescence (especially in rapidly changing environments): eroding value, requiring upgrade expenditure
Capital allowances may be set against tax, and government grants may be available	Wasteful, if equipment is needed only for a short period (eg a particular project)
ADVANTAGES OF LEASING	DISADVANTAGES OF LEASING
No initial investment to tie up capital	Long-term commitment to pay instalments: may be difficult in recession
Protects against technological obsolescence: ease of upgrade and replacement	User does not have total control of asset: lacks flexibility (and prestige) of ownership
Costs are known and agreed in advance	Total cost may be higher than purchase
Fewer complex tax and depreciation calculations	Large organisations may get better terms by securing their own finance to purchase (benefiting from capital allowances)
Hedge against inflation, as payments are made in 'real' money terms	Contract terms may favour the lessor (eg limitations to use, liability for risks/costs)

Procurement's role in capital decisions

5.17 Many functions are likely to have a voice in decisions about capital assets, including: engineering, user departments, top management and finance. In many cases, it will be appropriate to adopt a formal team approach to the procurement decision. The contribution of procurement specialists in such a team may be as follows.

- Performing research to identify potential vendors and to obtain relevant data about them
- Requesting quotations and evaluating bids, including consideration of price, lead time, operating characteristics, expected useful life, performance criteria, operating costs, recommended spares and maintenance schedules, warranty and payment terms and so on
- Organising and managing discussions and negotiations with suppliers, and finalising agreed terms and conditions
- Awarding the contract and placing the order
- Checking supplier's compliance with agreed terms
- Monitoring installation and post-installation performance
- Working with the manufacturer and maintenance service providers to extend the useful life of the asset, and to maintain its value.

5.18 We will elaborate on some of these concepts in Chapter 5, when we explore the procurement process in detail.

Operating expenditure (opex)

5.19 Operating expenditure benefits the organisation just briefly (unlike capital expenditure, where the purchase of an office building, say, may be an asset to the organisation for many years). Numerous items of expenditure fall into the opex category. Here are some examples.

- Expenditure on current assets (eg stock)

- Expenditure relating to running the business (eg administration expenses, selling expenses, telephone bills, stationery etc)
- Expenditure on maintaining the earning capacity of fixed assets (eg repairs and renewals). This of course contrasts with the cost of *acquiring* the fixed assets, which is capital expenditure.

6   Services procurements

What are services?

6.1   A service has been defined as 'any activity or benefit that one party can offer to another that is essentially intangible and does not result in the ownership of anything' (Philip Kotler). Some obvious examples include call-centre, cleaning, transport/logistics and IT services: something is 'done for you', but there is no transfer of ownership of anything as part of the service transaction. (It is also worth remembering that some form of service is part of the 'bundle of benefits' you acquire when you purchase materials and goods: sales service, customer service, delivery, after-sales care, warranties and so on.)

6.2   A wide range of services are offered by providers: financial services, banking and insurance; transport; entertainment, hospitality and catering; hairdressing; plumbing; education; healthcare; and so on. Some of the most common services utilised by business organisations include: banking, consultancy, advertising and design, catering, cleaning, security, maintenance, warehousing, transport/distribution and IT support.

Distinctive features of services

6.3   The distinctive features of services – as opposed to physical products – have been analysed primarily in the marketing literature. However, the following concepts also raise unique challenges for procurement.

- *Intangibility* (or in procurement terms, 'lack of inspectability': Baily *et al*). A service cannot be measured, weighed, chemically analysed or otherwise 'inspected' before it is purchased, or when assessing satisfaction (or conformance to specification) after purchase. The procurement function will have to look for other evidence of a service's attributes and quality, such as promised or agreed service levels, price, convenience, the efficiency of processes and the qualities of the people who deliver the service.
- *Inseparability*: services are produced and consumed at the same time. The efficiency and effectiveness of the processes and people involved in 'producing' (delivering) the service are crucial to the customer's experience of it, and will be crucial to the procurement function's selection and evaluation of the service.
- *Heterogeneity* or variability. Goods emerging from a manufacturing process generally have a high degree of uniformity, which simplifies their evaluation. In contrast, every separate instance of service provision is unique, because the personnel and circumstances are different. This makes it difficult to 'standardise' service specifications so that customers can be sure what they will get, or that they will get the same thing every time.
- *Perishability* (or in procurement terms, 'impracticability of storage'). A service cannot be stored or stockpiled for later use, so the timing of supply is difficult to control. The procurement function has to plan ahead, in collaboration with suppliers, so that the service is available when it is needed. (This does not apply to all services: Baily *et al* cite the examples of cleaning services, which are usually not time-critical, and insurance, which may be provided continuously in return for an annual premium.)
- *Ownership* (or in procurement terms, 'uncertainties in contractual agreements'). Services do not result in the transfer of ownership of anything, making it difficult to define when a contract for services has been properly fulfilled, and when risk and liability have passed from one party to another. (Baily *et al* use the example of an architect who submits a design which meets all the client's stated criteria – but which the client simply doesn't 'like'. Who, if anyone, is at fault – and who pays for the architect's second attempt?) Buyers will have to define their requirements very clearly, in detailed service specifications, service level agreements and an agreed basis for charges: an area often fraught with difficulties!

6.4 In addition:

- The exact purpose for which a tangible product is used will usually be known, and its suitability can therefore be assessed objectively. It is harder to assess the many factors involved in providing a service: what weight should be placed on the friendliness or smart appearance of the supplier's staff, say, compared with the efficiency with which they get the job done?
- Goods are usually purchased for more or less immediate use, such as incorporation in a larger product, or onward sale. A service may be purchased for a long period, during which requirements may change from the original specification.

6.5 These kinds of challenges present a strong argument for purchasing to be involved in sourcing services – rather than users, who may lack expertise in demand forecasting, negotiation, specification, contracting and ongoing supplier management.

Key features of service procurements

6.6 The more work that can be done at the pre-contract stage the better. Service levels, schedules, and the basis for charges should be agreed in as much detail as possible before the final agreement is signed: disputes often stem from differing expectations on the part of buyer and supplier.

6.7 This is particularly vital if the organisation is outsourcing service functions currently performed by in-house staff. The organisation will typically close down its own internal service provision, disposing of equipment, redeploying or shedding staff and so on. Once this has been done, the supplier is in a strong position – and shouldn't be given the opportunity to renegotiate the contract on the basis that the original agreement was vague on details of the service to be offered.

6.8 The procurement of services requires professional input, but it is equally important to involve user/ beneficiary departments in the specification of the service. For one thing, they are ideally placed (as customers) to help determine the level of service they require or expect; for another, involvement will help to secure 'buy in' and minimise later disputes.

6.9 Supplier management is an important ingredient in successful service buying. Often the level of service agreed upon is expressed in terms which are difficult to measure: it is not like purchasing steel rods which definitely are, or definitely are not, of the diameter specified. It is vital that from the earliest stages, the supplier is made aware of what the customer regards as satisfactory performance, and exactly what will be regarded as unsatisfactory.

6.10 Certain legal and technical considerations must also be addressed in the procurement of services. For example, staff employed by the contractor may work on the buyer's premises (eg in the case of catering, cleaning or security), and this may raise issues such as:

- Indemnity insurance, to cover the buyer's liability in case of accidents or other events in which contracted staff suffer injury or loss
- Confidentiality and protection of intellectual property, since contractors may gain access to information or designs which are commercially sensitive or valuable.

Measures of service quality

6.11 General performance criteria for service levels have been developed as part of an assessment tool called SERVQUAL (Zeithaml, Parasuraman & Berry).

- *Tangibles*: appearance of physical facilities, equipment, personnel, communications. For example: does the service provider have smartly-dressed staff and well-maintained equipment? Is its feedback documentation user-friendly?
- *Reliability:* ability to perform the promised service dependably and accurately. For example: is the service always delivered to specification, on time, within budget?

- *Responsiveness*: willingness to help customers and provide prompt service. For example: do service staff respond positively to urgent or non-routine requests?
- *Assurance*: customer confidence in the service provider, based on demonstrated competence, courtesy, credibility and security.
- *Empathy*: customer confidence that the service provider will identify with the customer's needs and expectations in relation to ease of access, communication and co-operation.

6.12 More specifically, key performance indicators (KPIs) can be drawn up to suit the needs of a particular service contract. KPIs are specific, standard measures of the performance of a unit or organisation, against which progress and performance can be evaluated.

- Where possible, such standards will be *quantitative:* that is, numerical or statistical. They may, for example, be expressed in terms of cost (eg cost per service delivery, amount of cost savings), time (eg hours per service delivery), quantity of outputs (eg offices cleaned per hour, number of deliveries made on-time-in-full, number of cost reduction initiatives proposed) or other statistics (eg the number of customer complaints per review period).
- Some targets, however, will be more *qualitative:* that is, subjective and pertaining to qualities or attributes that cannot readily be quantified. For example, you may want to evaluate user satisfaction, the effectiveness of the supplier's account management, its flexibility/responsiveness or commitment to quality. Even so, KPIs in these areas should be expressed as quantitatively as possible: the proportion of services rated satisfactory/non-satisfactory by customers; the degree of satisfaction expressed by customers (eg using rates scales or points scores); the proportion of requests/proposals responded to, and how quickly; scores on commitment to quality obtained via attitude surveys; number of 'critical incidents' illustrating professional or non-professional conduct; and so on.

6.13 The KPIs for services will be specific to the nature of the service contract. Using the example of a cleaning service, for example, there might be KPIs covering:

- Time taken to complete designated cleaning tasks
- Thoroughness of cleaning (perhaps specified as amount of dust or number of stains identified in spot checks, or proportion of litter bins left un-emptied)
- Number of re-cleans (or customer complaints/requests for re-cleans)
- Customer satisfaction with overall cleaning service (eg on the basis of feedback reports, or specified as number of complaints, or proportion of complaints to approvals).

Monitoring service levels

6.14 A wide range of techniques is available for monitoring – keeping an eye on – service provision and service levels, and feeding back the data in order to identify 'service gaps' which need to be addressed. Depending on the nature of the service and the data collection mechanisms in place, examples of such techniques include the following.

- *Observation and experience*: that is, seeing and experiencing the service. It may be obvious, for example, that an office has (or has not) been cleaned to a promised standard, or that a commitment to deliver goods on time has (or has not) been met. Customers may log or report service failures as and when they occur.
- *Spot checks and sample testing*: performance may be periodically tested or measured in some way. In the case of our cleaning service, a 'spot check' would involve an unannounced inspection of the offices with a checklist of measures (bins emptied, windows clean, toilets disinfected, carpets vacuumed), while 'sampling testing' might involve analysing the number of dust particles present in selected areas of the carpet, say.
- *Business results and indirect indicators:* services have a purpose – so good/poor quality service has a knock-on effect on customers' activities. So, for example, feedback from the customers' customers might indicate dissatisfaction with the cleanliness of the premises, late transport deliveries, or lack of courtesy by call centre staff.

- *Customer/user feedback:* customers and users of the service should periodically be invited to complete feedback surveys on the quality of the service they have received. In addition, mechanisms should be in place to facilitate customers and users in making complaints, to notify the service manager (and/or the service provider) promptly of specific service failures.
- *Electronic performance monitoring:* in some cases, service performance can be monitored using measuring or tracking devices. Examples include clocking-in-clocking-off devices to record hours worked; 'black box' journey recorders used by transport providers to track delays and routes; and computer programmes recording the number of transactions processed, telephone calls made/taken, cost and schedule variances from plans; and so on.
- *Self-assessment by the service provider:* service providers may require reports by their own staff or supervisors. This may range from a checklist signed off by the cleaners' supervisor at the end of a shift (with notes on where service could not be satisfactorily provided, and why, where relevant), to periodic, systematic self-review reports. (How did we do? How could we do better? What do we need from the customer to support improvement?)
- *Collaborative performance review.* Periodically, all the above information should be gathered and shared by customer and service provider, with a view to evaluating the success of the service contract.

6.15 Whichever method of monitoring and review is used, the information will have to be fed back to service or account managers on both sides, who will in turn disseminate the information to those responsible for performance.

Outsourcing

6.16 Although there is nothing inherent in the term 'outsourcing' to refer to the purchase of services, it is normally used in the service context. Outsourcing may be defined as the process whereby an organisation delegates non-core tasks, under contract, to external service providers, on a long-term relational basis. Organisations now routinely contract with specialist external suppliers to provide services such as cleaning, catering, security, facilities management, IT, recruitment and training, accounting, legal, transport and distribution – and procurement.

6.17 Lysons and Farrington (*Purchasing and Supply Chain Management)* explain the difference between outsourcing and subcontracting as a long-term strategic versus a short-term tactical approach: 'If you want a beautiful lawn in the neighbourhood and you hire someone to take responsibility for every aspect of lawn care, it's strategic sourcing. But hiring someone to cut your lawn is subcontracting.' Outsourcing is thus the ultimate expression of a buyer's attitude to the supply chain as an extension of in-house resources: functions performed in-house are delegated to external contractors, typically working very closely with the buying organisation.

6.18 In many cases, the same personnel may carry out the outsourced tasks, but instead of being employed by the buyer they work for the contractor. There are instances where the original staff remain *in situ*, and even work on the same equipment: the only difference is in the status of the staff (working for the contractor) and the ownership of the equipment (transferred from buyer to contractor).

6.19 Modern outsourcing practice emphasises the need for long-term collaborative relationships with the service provider, and expert contract and relationship management. Zenz (*Purchasing and the Management of Materials)* highlights several key issues in outsourcing.

- The need to deal with possible reductions in staff, or transfers of staff (under employment protection regulations)
- The need to closely integrate external suppliers
- The need to establish appropriate communication channels

6.20 Here are some other key issues for procurement and supply chain functions.

- The need for the outsource decision to be based on clear objectives and measurable benefits, with a rigorous cost-benefit analysis
- The need for rigorous supplier selection, given the long-term partnership nature of the outsource relationship to which the organisation will be 'locked in'. In such circumstances, as we will see in later chapters, selection should not only involve cost comparisons but considerations such as quality, reliability, willingness to collaborate, and ethics, sustainability and corporate social responsibility (since the performance of the contractor reflects on the reputation of the outsourcing organisation).
- Rigorous supplier contracting, so that risks, costs and liabilities are equitably and clearly allocated, and expected service levels clearly defined
- Clear and agreed service levels, standards and key performance indicators, with appropriate incentives and penalties to motivate compliance and conformance
- Consistent and rigorous monitoring of service delivery and quality, against service level agreements and key performance indicators
- Ongoing contract and supplier management, to ensure contract compliance, the development of the relationship (with the aim of continuous collaborative cost and performance improvement), and the constructive handling of disputes. This is essential if the organisation is not to gradually surrender control of performance (and therefore reputation) to the contractor.
- Contract review, deriving lessons from the performance of the contract, in order to evaluate whether the contract should be renewed, amended (to incorporate improvements) or terminated in favour of another supplier (or bringing the service provision back in-house).

6.21 Clearly a major reason for outsourcing is the possibility that it will be cheaper to procure the services from external providers than to perform them in-house. This is not necessarily an easy matter to establish, and assessing value for money in outsourced services is a delicate process.

- The first step is to learn as much as the supplier is willing to disclose of his cost and profit structure. This will facilitate comparison with alternatives.
- The overall cost of the service would obviously be compared with prices offered by alternative suppliers, and possibly with the costs of in-house operation if these are known. (They may not be if it is a new type of service that is being bought.)
- More crucially, the effectiveness of the supplier must be evaluated by a comparison of actual outputs achieved with the original objectives specified. This of course implies that the buying organisation starts with a clear idea of what it needs and what it expects to get, and the involvement of procurement professionals in the early stages can be of great assistance here.

6.22 Some of the potential advantages and disadvantages of outsourcing can be summarised as follows: Table 1.3. (You should be able to convert this data into the corresponding arguments for and against *internal* service provision or in-sourcing.)

Table 1.3 *Advantages and disadvantages of outsourcing*

ADVANTAGES OF OUTSOURCING	DISADVANTAGES OF OUTSOURCING
Supports organisational rationalisation and downsizing: reduction in the costs of staffing, space and facilities	Potentially higher cost of services (including contractor profit margin), contracting and management: compare with costs of in-house provision
Allows focused investment of managerial, staff and other resources on the organisation's core activities and competencies (those which are distinctive, value-adding and hard to imitate, and thus give competitive advantage)	Difficulty of ensuring service quality/consistency and corporate social responsibility (environmental and employment practices): difficulties and costs of monitoring (especially overseas)
Gives access to specialist expertise, technologies and resources of contractors: adding more value than the organisation could achieve itself, for non-core activities	Potential loss of in-house expertise, knowledge, contacts or technologies in the service area, which may be required in future (eg if the service is in-housed again).
Access to economies of scale, since contractors may serve many customers	Potential loss of control over areas of performance and risk (eg to reputation)
Adds competitive performance incentives, where internal service providers may be complacent	Added distance from the customer or end-user, by having an intermediary service provider: may weaken external or internal customer communication and relationships
	Risks of 'lock in' to an incompatible or under-performing relationship: cultural or ethical incompatibility; relationship management difficulties; contractor complacency etc.
	Risks of loss of control over confidential data and intellectual property

6.23   We will discuss outsourcing further in the context of procurement outsourcing, in Chapter 8.

7   Segmenting external expenditure

Procurement portfolio segmentation

7.1   Segmentation is an approach to analysing expenditure with external suppliers by categorising the procurement portfolio (items procured) or suppliers according to their priority, value or importance to the organisation. The segment to which a procurement or supplier is allocated determines the procurement resources and approaches that will be used in each case.

7.2   Both inventory and supplier management have become a focus for procurement organisations. Most procurement operations face increasing pressures to sustain and extend cost savings while assuring the quality and continuity of supply. Portfolio and supplier segmentation allows the procurement function to focus its resources, in order to maximise the cost effectiveness of the operation whilst minimising supply market risk exposure.

7.3   The approach to segmentation will vary from business to business. Whichever approach is used, it is essential to ensure there is a clear linkage between the segmentation rationale and key business objectives such as cost rationalisation, risk reduction and so on. We will look at two key segmentation tools: Pareto analysis (or ABC analysis) and the Kraljic procurement portfolio matrix.

Pareto (ABC) analysis

7.4   Italian economist Vilfredo Pareto formulated the proposition that: 'In any series of elements to be controlled, a selected small factor in terms of number of elements (20%) almost always accounts for a large factor in terms of effort (80%).'

7.5   The Pareto principle (or '80/20 rule') is a useful technique for identifying the activities that will leverage your time, effort and resources for the biggest benefits. It is a popular way of prioritising between tasks or areas of focus.

7.6   In a procurement context, the Pareto principle can be interpreted as 80% of spend being directed towards just 20% of the suppliers. This elementary form of segmentation can be used to separate the critical few suppliers (who supply important, high-value, high-usage items, which can only be sourced from a limited supply market) from the trivial many (who supply routine, low-value supplies which can easily be sourced anywhere). Most procurement effort and energy needs to be focused on the critical or category 'A' suppliers and the products procured from them.

7.7   Emmett *(Supply Chain in 90 Minutes)* summarises the implications of segmentation.

- Category A items. Because of the high value, stock must be minimised – but because of the high usage, continuity in supply is important: procurement methods such as just in time supply will therefore be used to replenish stock only for known requirements, with low buffer stocks. In general, most procurement and managerial control effort will be focused here.
- Category B items. Regular stock review and replenishment will be required, with ordering against demand forecasts (based on historical demand), and some buffer stock held to maintain continuity of supply. A moderate level of control will be exercised in this area.
- Category C items. High in number, but with low usage value. In general, the least procurement and managerial control effort will be focused here: the organisation may use low-maintenance or automatic replenishment methods, such as a 'two-bin' system or vendor managed inventory (VMI), where responsibility for managing stock is delegated to the supplier. Larger levels of safety stock are typically held, to minimise transaction costs.

The Kraljic (procurement positioning) matrix

7.8   The Pareto or ABC approach to segmentation is based on the value and volume of business we do with each supplier. However, this is not the only factor that a procurement or supply chain function should consider when segmenting suppliers.

7.9   Peter Kraljic (1973) developed a tool of analysis that seeks to map two factors.

- The importance to the organisation of the item being purchased (related to factors such as the organisation's annual expenditure on the item, and its profit potential through enabling revenue earning or cost reductions)
- The complexity of the supply market (related to factors such as the difficulty of sourcing the item, the vulnerability of the buyer to supply or supplier failure, and the relative power of buyer and supplier in the market).

7.10   The matrix therefore has four quadrants, as follows: Figure 1.4.

Figure 1.4 *The Kraljic procurement portfolio matrix*

Complexity of the supply market

	Low		High	
High	**Procurement focus** Leverage items	**Time horizon** Varied, typically 12-24 months	**Procurement focus** Strategic items	**Time horizon** Up to 10 years; governed by long-term strategic impact (risk and contract mix)
	Key performance criteria Cost/price and materials flow management	**Items purchased** Mix of commodities and specified materials	**Key performance criteria** Long-term availability	**Items purchased** Scarce and/or high-value materials
Importance of the item	**Typical sources** Multiple suppliers, chiefly local	**Supply** Abundant	**Typical sources** Established global suppliers	**Supply** Natural scarcity
	Procurement focus Non-critical items	**Time horizon** Limited: normally 12 months or less	**Procurement focus** Bottleneck items	**Time horizon** Variable, depending on availability vs short-term flexibility trade-offs
	Key performance criteria Functional efficiency	**Items purchased** Commodities, some specified materials	**Key performance criteria** Cost management and reliable short-term sourcing	**Items purchased** Mainly specified materials
Low	**Typical sources** Established local suppliers	**Supply** Abundant	**Typical sources** Global, predominantly new suppliers with new technology	**Supply** Production-based scarcity

7.11 At a strategic level, the Kraljic matrix is used to examine an organisation's procurement portfolio and its exposure to risk from supply disruption. For the purposes of this syllabus, it can be seen more simply as a tool for assessing what procurement approaches and types of supplier relationships are most appropriate for different types of procurements, and how a procurement function can add value by leveraging the potential of each.

- For *non-critical or routine items* (such as common stationery supplies), the focus will be on low-maintenance routines to reduce procurement costs. Arm's length approaches such as vendor managed inventory, blanket ordering (empowering end users to make call-off orders against negotiated agreements) and e-procurement solutions (eg online ordering or the use of purchasing cards) will provide routine efficiency. Procurement management is achieved by monitoring expenditure against regular reports received from vendors, end-users or e-procurement systems.
- For *bottleneck items* (such as proprietary spare parts or specialised consultancy services, which could cause operational delays if unavailable), the procurement priority will be ensuring control over the continuity and security of supply. This may suggest approaches such as negotiating medium-term or long-term contracts with suppliers; developing alternative or back-up sources of supply; including incentives and penalties in contracts to ensure the reliability of delivery; or keeping higher levels of buffer or 'safety' stock.
- For *leverage items* (such as local produce bought by a major supermarket), the procurement priority will be to use its power in the market to secure best prices and terms, on a purely transactional basis. This may mean taking advantage of competitive pricing; standardising specifications to make supplier switching easier; and using competitive bidding and/or buying consortia to secure the best deals.
- For *strategic items* (such as core processors bought by a laptop manufacturer), there is likely to be mutual dependency and investment, and the focus will be on the total cost, security and

competitiveness of supply. There will therefore be a need to develop long-term, mutually beneficial strategic relationships and relationship management disciplines (eg cross-functional teams, vendor/ account management and so on).

7.12   We will discuss supplier relationships, and the procurement approaches that maximise the effectiveness of different relationship types, in later chapters of this Course Book.

Chapter summary

- A modern emphasis on more strategic and proactive elements of the buyer's role has led to the use of 'procurement' rather than 'purchasing'.
- Changes in the cost base of many businesses – typically away from heavy costs of labour towards heavy costs of automation – have widened the scope of procurement activities. This has been reinforced by an increased readiness to outsource non-core activities.
- Direct procurement concerns supplies for resale or for incorporation in goods for resale; indirect procurement concerns ancillary and operating supplies.
- There are particular challenges associated with the purchase of commodities, particularly the risk of price fluctuations.
- Some organisations purchase items for stock; others stock to order or to forecast.
- Purchase of capital items gives rise to distinctive features, such as the need for whole life costing, the difficulties of estimating long-term benefits etc.
- Service purchases are also subject to particular challenges, arising from the intangibility and perishability of services.
- It is useful to segment and prioritise the various categories of external expenditure by an organisation. Pareto analysis and Kraljic's matrix are two tools that can be used for this.

 ## Self-test questions

Numbers in brackets refer to the paragraphs where you can check your answers.

1   Define (a) 'purchasing' and (b) supply. (1.3, 1.4)

2   What shortcomings to Lysons & Farrington identify in the traditional definitions of purchasing? (1.9)

3   Distinguish between goods, services and works. (2.8)

4   Distinguish between direct and indirect procurements. (3.3)

5   What are the practical implications of the distinction between direct and indirect procurements? (3.7)

6   What are the four groups who participate in commodity markets? (3.19)

7   What are MRO supplies? (3.27)

8   What is meant by (a) stock to order and (b) stock to forecast? (4.8–4.11)

9   List distinctive features of capital procurements. (5.4)

10 List advantages and disadvantages of leasing capital goods. (Table 1.2)

11 List distinctive features of service purchases. (6.3)

12 List techniques for monitoring service levels. (6.14)

13 List advantages and disadvantages of outsourcing. (Table 1.3)

14 Explain the implications of segmenting stock items using Pareto analysis. (7.7)

CHAPTER 2

Adding Value in Procurement and Supply

Assessment criteria and indicative content

 Analyse the different sources of added value in procurement and supply

- The five rights of procurement
- Achieving the right price for procurements from external suppliers
- Defining total lifecycle costs or the total cost of ownership
- Achieving quality, timescales, quantities and place considerations in procurements from external suppliers
- Other sources of added value such as innovation, sustainability and market development
- Defining value for money

Section headings

1. The operational objectives of procurement
2. Added value
3. The five rights of procurement
4. The right price
5. The right quality
6. The right quantity at the right time
7. The right place
8. Other considerations

Introduction

In this chapter, we focus on the core topic of this learning outcome: the ways in which procurement and supply chain management can 'add value' to an enterprise.

We start by considering some of the operational objectives of procurement: what it is broadly seeking to achieve. We then go on to explore the concept of 'value' and 'added value', and discuss the contribution procurement can make.

The bulk of the chapter is devoted to the so-called 'five rights of procurement': the traditional view of what procurement is designed to achieve. We begin with an overview of the 'five rights' model; the importance of achieving the five rights; and how, in practice, there are frequently trade-offs between them. We then go on to discuss each of the five rights in turn; how they can be achieved; and the key procurement considerations involved.

Some of this may be familiar to you from your work practice or earlier CIPS studies: if not, you may find this chapter fairly intense! Take the topics step by step, at your own pace...

1 The operational objectives of procurement

Obtaining the right inputs

1.1 The general objective of purchasing is to obtain the 'inputs' required by an organisation for its operations. As we have already suggested in Chapter 1, different types of organisation will require different types of inputs: a manufacturing organisation may require raw materials or components to make into products; a retail organisation may require finished goods to sell on to consumers; while a service organisation may require equipment, information and people to provide services to customers. But the principle is the same in each case.

1.2 The organisation can be seen as an open system which takes in inputs from the environment (including those obtained by the procurement function on its behalf) and processes them in some way to create outputs to the environment: Figure 2.1.

Figure 2.1 *The organisation as an open system*

1.3 The primary task of a procurement function is therefore to provide the 'right' inputs for the organisation's processes. The 'right' inputs are traditionally described as:

- Inputs of the right quality
- Delivered in the right quantity
- To the right place
- At the right time
- For the right price.

These are often called the 'five rights of procurement', and we will introduce them in Section 3 of this chapter.

Other general objectives

1.4 Meanwhile, it is possible to identify a number of other general objectives of procurement operations – or other ways of looking at the primary task of procurement.

- **Internal customer service**. Procurement provides inputs to organisational processes. The units responsible for those processes (such as the production or operations function) can therefore be seen as internal 'customers' of the procurement function. One of procurement's overall objectives is to service internal customers: ascertaining and satisfying their input needs (by the five rights); giving them advice and information about the best inputs, sources and prices available; and so on.
- **Risk management**. The organisation cannot function without inputs, particularly those which are essential to its production or service provision processes. If inputs become scarce, or a source of supply fails suddenly (eg a major supplier goes out of business), the organisation will be faced with problems and losses: production delayed or shut down, customers lost, extra costs incurred to get 'emergency' supplies and so on. One of procurement's overall objectives is therefore to ensure that

risks of supply failure or disruption are minimised and/or 'covered' by contingency plans. This means monitoring the supply market; anticipating demand; avoiding over-dependency on single suppliers; developing relationships with dependable suppliers; and so on.

- **Cost control and reduction**. In order to make a profit (the primary objective of commercial organisations) or to provide services cost-effectively (the primary objective of not-for-profit organisations), an organisation will need to control its costs – and a significant proportion of any organisation's overall costs will be the inputs it buys in: that is, its expenditure with external suppliers. One of procurement's overall objectives is therefore to control, reduce and/or minimise costs, by consistently buying the right quantity at the right price, and reducing or eliminating wastage in purchasing and supply procedures.

- **Relationship and reputation management**. Procurement is an important 'interface' or touch-point between the organisation and the outside world. One of its overall objectives is therefore to maintain constructive relationships with suppliers; and to conduct its activities in an ethical, socially responsible and environmentally friendly way, so as to promote and protect a positive reputation for the organisation.

1.5   You will be exploring these core functions of procurement and supply chain management throughout your CIPS studies. In this chapter, we will focus on some of the typical objectives of procurement operations – which are also likely to be the objectives of any specific procurement exercise or project – mentioned by the syllabus.

- Adding value
- Achieving the 'five rights' of procurement
- Achieving value for money

2   Added value

What are 'value' and 'added value'?

2.1   The influential writer on competition Michael Porter *(Competitive Strategy, 1980)* argued that an organisation's competitive advantage ultimately comes from the 'value' it creates for its customers. Value can be seen simply as the 'worth' of the product or service, which may be measured in two ways: what it costs the organisation to produce or provide, and what customers are willing to pay for it. In other words:

- An organisation creates value – by performing its activities more effectively or efficiently than its competitors.
- Customers purchase value – by comparing an organisation's products and services with those of its competitors.

2.2   The term 'added value' thus essentially refers to the addition of greater value or worth to a product or service, as a result of all the processes that support its production and delivery to the customer: marketing, design, production, customer service, distribution, maintenance and so on.

The value chain or value system

2.3   In Chapter 1, we briefly mentioned Porter's 'value chain' model, which depicts the various primary and secondary activities of an organisation through which value is created. Every organisational activity can be seen as part of the value chain: the sequence of activities by which value is successively added to organisational resources as they 'flow' towards the customer: Figure 2.2. (Note that value adding 'activities' are *not* the same as the *functions* of a business or business unit: they may be carried out across departments.).

Figure 2.2 *Porter's value chain*

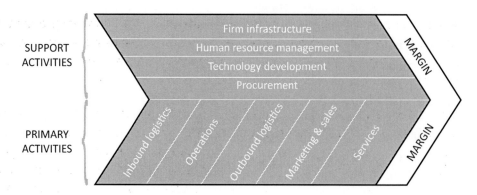

2.4 **Primary value activities** are grouped into five areas.

- Inbound logistics are the activities concerned with receiving, storing and disseminating inputs: materials handling, warehousing, inventory control etc.
- Operations are concerned with the transformation of inputs into finished goods or services. In manufacturing, these activities include assembly, testing, packing and equipment maintenance; in service industries, basic service provision.
- Outbound logistics are concerned with storing, distributing and delivering the finished goods to customers: warehousing, materials handling, transport planning, order processing and so on.
- Marketing and sales are responsible for communication with the customers to provide a means by which they can purchase the product (as well as an inducement to do so): market research, new product development, advertising and promotion, sales force management, channel management, pricing and so on.
- Service covers all of the activities which occur after the point of sale to enhance or maintain the value of the product for the customer: installation, repair, training, parts supply and maintenance.

2.5 The **secondary, or support, activities** operate across the primary activities, as in the case of procurement where at each stage items are acquired to aid the primary functions.

- Firm infrastructure refers to systems and assets for planning, finance, quality control and management.
- Human resources are all the activities involved in recruiting, deploying, retaining and developing people in the organisation.
- Technology development activities relate to equipment, systems and methods of work organisation: product design and improvement of production processes and resource utilisation.
- Procurement – as you know – involves all the activities required to acquire inputs for primary activities.

2.6 The key points of the value chain model can be summarised as follows.

- 'Each activity within a value chain provides inputs which, after processing, constitute added value to the output received by the ultimate customer in the form of a product or service or as the aggregate of values at the end of the value chain.' (Lysons & Farrington)
- Activities within the value chain are interdependent: each element can affect the costs or effectiveness of another in the value chain, forming what Porter called 'linkages'. These require co-ordination in order to optimise the flow of value. So, for example, improvement of product design or quality management might reduce the need for after-sales services – while on-time delivery requires the integration of procurement, operations, outbound logistics and service activities.
- One of the most important aspects of adding value along the supply chain is concerned with eliminating *waste:* non-value-adding activities and processes.

Procurement's contribution to added value

2.7 According to Porter, the ultimate value a firm creates is measured by the amount customers are willing to pay for its products or services *over and above* the cost to the firm of carrying out all its value-creating activities. A firm is profitable if the realised value to customers (what they are prepared to pay) exceeds the cost of value creation.

2.8 From an accounting perspective, therefore, added value is total revenue *minus* total cost of all activities undertaken to develop and market a product or service. This expresses the amount of economic value that has been added to the organisation's resources: how efficiently they are being used and how effectively they are being leveraged. From this perspective, an organisation can add value either by inducing customers to pay more (eg by providing additional features or services which attract a premium price) – and/or by reducing costs or increasing the efficiency of processes. Emmett *(Supply Chain in 90 Minutes)* offers some pithy advice for adding value: 'make it faster, move it faster, get paid faster'!

2.9 The procurement function can contribute significantly to the latter form of value addition, for example, by streamlining procurement operations and developing a well-managed supply chain to minimise wastes and costs.

2.10 From a marketing perspective, adding value means enhancing the offering to customers: 'augmenting' the core product or service with elements that customers value, and that differentiate the firm's offering or brand from competing offerings in customers' eyes (Kotler & Armstrong, 2003). Organisations can thus add value through enhancing product quality or design; value for money; delivery/availability; brand appeal; exclusivity; service levels; and so on. Porter and others have emphasised that value is effectively 'in the eye of the customer', and organisations must seek to understand exactly what aspects of their offering customers will place value on.

2.11 The procurement function can also contribute to this form of value addition: for example, by securing good quality materials and innovative suppliers, ensuring reliable delivery, supporting value-for-money pricing by keeping input costs down – and so on.

2.12 The main focus for procurement is that value can be added either by cutting costs (without loss of quality or product features) *or* by securing operational efficiency (enabling superior quality or features at no additional cost). Ideally, we might aim to achieve both of these objectives: improved output at reduced cost. Procurement can contribute to these objectives by means such as the following.

- Selecting and managing suppliers, in order to improve the quality of inputs, with consequent improvement in the quality of outputs
- Negotiating and managing procurements effectively in order to reduce the cost of inputs
- Managing procurement activities efficiently to reduce the cost of transactions
- Communicating effectively with user departments to improve procurement specifications, so that business needs are fulfilled more efficiently and at lower cost
- Managing inventory effectively, to minimise the costs of acquiring and holding stock
- Working with key supply chain partners to eliminate wastes (non-value adding activities) wherever they are found in the supply process: an approach sometimes referred to as 'lean' supply.

2.13 We will discuss procurement's contribution to quality later in this chapter. We will also have an opportunity to explore the value added at each stage of the procurement process, in Chapter 5.

3   The five rights of procurement

3.1   The five rights are a traditional formula expressing the basic objectives of procurement, and the general criteria by which procurement performance is measured. Even if they are not called 'five rights', they are often covered in procurement and supply chain management literature as 'key purchasing variables' (as in Baily et al) or 'purchasing factors' (as in Lysons & Farrington).

3.2   The five rights (or five Rs) of procurement, and the importance of achieving them, are summarised in Table 2.1. Don't worry if you don't understand all the points or terminology yet: we will be discussing these matters in more detail in the rest of the chapter.

Table 2.1 *The five rights of procurement*

RIGHT	DESCRIPTION	IMPORTANCE
Quality	Obtaining goods which are of satisfactory quality and fit for their purpose (suited to internal and external customer's needs), by: • Accurate specification of requirement and quality standards • Supplier- and buyer-side quality management	If not achieved: • Stock may have to be rejected or scrapped • Production machinery may be damaged • Finished products may be defective and have to be scrapped or re-worked • Defective products may reach customers, resulting in recalls, returns, compensation claims, lost goodwill, damaged reputation • The firm will incur high costs
Quantity	Obtaining goods in sufficient quantity to meet demand and maintain service levels while minimising excess stock holding (which incurs costs and risks), by: • Demand forecasting • Inventory management • Stock replenishment systems	If not achieved: • Insufficient stock may be held to meet demand. Stockouts may cause bottlenecks or shutdowns in production; costs of idle time; late delivery to customers; lost credibility, goodwill and sales • Excess stock may be ordered and/or held: tying up capital in 'idle' stock; wasting storage space; risking deterioration, theft or damage; risking obsolescence or disuse; incurring 'holding costs'
Place	Having goods delivered to the appropriate delivery point, packaged and transported in such a way as to secure their safe arrival in good condition, by: • Distribution planning • Transport planning • Packaging	If not achieved: • Goods may be delivered to the wrong place, creating delay and correction costs • Goods may be subject to unnecessary transport and handling (and related costs) • Goods may be damaged, contaminated or stolen in transit • Transport may cause unnecessary environmental damage
Time	Securing delivery of goods at the right time to meet demand, but not so early as to incur unnecessary inventory costs, by: • Demand management • Supplier management	If not achieved: • Goods may be too late, causing production bottlenecks (and associated costs) and/or delays in delivery to customers (with costs of damages, lost business) • Goods may be too early, causing undue risks and costs of holding inventory
Price	Securing all of the above at a price which is reasonable, fair, competitive and affordable. Ideally, minimising procurement costs in order to maximise profit, by: • Price analysis • Supplier cost analysis • Competitive pricing and negotiation	If not achieved: • Suppliers will be free to charge what they like, without check • Supplier profit margins will be 'squeezed' unfairly, leading to insecurity of supply • Materials and supply costs will rise • Profits will fall – or prices charged to customers will have to rise (losing sales) • There will be less profit to motivate shareholders and reinvest in the business

Interrelationships and trade-offs between the five rights

3.3   It is important to realise that the five rights are interdependent and interlinked, in all sorts of ways. Sometimes you can't get one without the other, and sometimes you can't get both at the same time! Here are some examples.

- If you don't get the right quality, you aren't getting the right quantity (because some items will be rejected or scrapped), at the right time (because delays will be caused by inspections and re-works), or the right price (because poor quality does not represent value for money, and incurs costs).
- On the other hand, high quality goods take a longer time to specify, produce and inspect (to manage the quality) – and if you don't get goods at the 'right time', high quality may be irrelevant: you may already have disrupted production and disappointed customers. Some corners may need to be cut on quality for 'urgent' requirements.
- The concepts of right quantity and right time are highly interdependent. You can have large quantities delivered early, in order to be sure to have sufficient items in stock – or you can have small 'top up' quantities delivered late, when you have a more accurate idea of demand (or even in response to demand, in a just in time system).
- There is often a trade-off between the right price and the other rights. Higher quality specifications cost more, as do short lead times (or 'urgent' orders) and complex delivery requirements (eg multiple deliveries). Quantity is a more complex trade-off. In terms of acquisition costs, frequent small orders may actually cost more (because of the extra transaction and transport costs) than fewer, large orders (subject to bulk discounts). However, fewer, larger orders will incur higher stockholding costs (such as storage and insurance). So the quantity/time factor will also have to juggle price considerations.
- Failure in any one aspect will impact on the others – and on procurement's overall performance.

3.4   We will now explore each of the five rights in more detail. The learning outcomes focus on your being able to explain the *objectives* of procurement, in terms of the five rights – but we will also briefly survey some of the principles and methods by which the five rights can be achieved (as appears to be the intent of the syllabus 'indicative content'). This makes for a long chapter, with some detailed technical content: take it one section at a time, at your own pace...

4   The right price

What is the 'right price'?

4.1   Price may be defined as 'the value of a commodity or service measured in terms of the standard monetary unit' (Lysons & Farrington). In other words, price is what a supplier charges for goods or services – and if two suppliers quote different prices, a procurement officer can readily compare the relative value offered by each.

4.2   So what does it mean to buy at the 'right' price? The procuring firm will be seeking to make a profit. It may also be seeking specifically to control or reduce its costs – and may expect the procurement function to play a major part in this by reducing the cost of obtaining materials, goods and services from external suppliers. So the 'right' price may simply be the lowest price available.

4.3   However, we have already established the need to buy goods of the right quality, in the right quantity, at the right time, delivered to the right place. You can probably get your goods faster, but at a higher price. You can probably get your goods cheaper, but at a lower quality. If you buy in higher quantities, you may get a bulk discount on the price – but you will also incur higher costs of holding stock. The 'right' price will therefore be the best or lowest price available, *consistent with* ensuring the right quality, quantity, timing and delivery.

4.4   In fact, there are a number of other requirements for the 'right price', seen from the supplier's point of view as well as from the buyer's point of view.

4.5   The 'right price' for the supplier or seller to charge (the right sales price) will be:

- A price which 'the market will bear': that is, a price that the market or a particular buyer will be willing to pay.
- A price which allows the seller to win business, in competition with other suppliers (according to how badly it needs the business, and the prices being charged by its competitors).
- A price which allows the seller at least to cover its costs, and ideally to make a healthy profit which will allow it to survive in business and to invest in growth.

4.6   The 'right price' for the buyer to pay (the right purchase price) will be:

- A price which the buyer can afford: allowing it to control its costs of production and make a profit on sale of its own goods or services
- A price which appears fair and reasonable, or represents value for money, for the total package of benefits being procured
- A price which gives the buyer a cost or quality advantage over its competitors, enabling it to compete more effectively in its own market
- A price which reflects sound procurement practices: requiring suppliers to price competitively; negotiating skilfully; recognising the difference between strategic/critical and non-critical/routine procurements; and so on.

Supplier pricing strategies

4.7   Suppliers may determine their prices in various ways, according to two basic models (Lysons & Farrington).

4.8   **Cost-based pricing** seeks to cover the supplier's costs (calculated in various ways) while allowing for an extra sum to secure a reasonable profit for the owners, or to reinvest in the business. The supplier may seek to cover its 'direct costs' (raw materials and labour used to produce the product) and/or its 'indirect costs' (or overheads); its 'fixed costs' (incurred regardless of the volume of sales or production) and/or its 'variable costs' (which vary as the volume of sales or production increases) – depending on the approach used.

4.9   **Market- or demand-based pricing** seeks to stimulate demand for the product. For example, market *share (or penetration) pricing* involves setting low introductory prices that will win customers and/or discourage or eliminate competition (because of the low profit margins available in the market). The aim may be (a) to stimulate the growth of a market, by getting people to try a new product or (b) to increase the supplier's share of the market (a strategy of 'marketing penetration'). Market-based pricing essentially aims to charge the maximum that the market will bear.

Factors in buyers' decisions on price

4.10 So far, we have talked about how suppliers go about deciding what prices to charge. But how do buyers go about deciding what prices to accept? Here are some of the factors in such a decision.

- The buying organisation's relative bargaining power in the market and the relationship. (A monopoly supplier may have power to set prices as it wishes – but if a buyer represents a large proportion of a supplier's business, it will be in a strong position to negotiate favourable prices.)
- The number of suppliers in the market and the possibility of substitute products (enabling the buyer to exploit competition to force prices down)
- The type of procurement. For non-critical or routine products, for example, a buyer will want to secure best price by competitive procurement, while for critical or strategic products, it may pay more for service and security of supply.
- The prices paid by competitors (if this information is available), so that the buyer keeps its materials costs competitive
- The total package of benefits offered for the price, and whether 'value' is better at a higher price (given the need for quality, delivery, supplier relationship and so on)

- What the buyer can afford, given the quantities likely to be involved over a given period
- What is a 'reasonable' price, based on price and cost analysis (discussed below). It is important for buyers to understand that suppliers are entitled to make a profit: that is, they are entitled to set or quote prices on goods which allow them to cover their costs and make a reasonable profit margin. This is important to protect the security of supply (not creating financial instability for suppliers); to protect the quality of supply (allowing suppliers to maintain standards and develop their business); and in the interests of corporate social responsibility (supporting sustainable supply chains).
- What is a 'fair' (ethical and sustainable) price from the buyer's and supplier's point of view.

Analysing quoted prices

4.11 When considering the prices quoted by a supplier, or offered in negotiation, there are two basic approaches that a buyer can use to decide whether 'the price is right'.

4.12 **Price analysis** is the process of seeking to determine if the price offered is a fair and appropriate price for the goods. The 'right' price in this sense may be one which is advantageous or reasonable compared to: the prices offered by other suppliers (competitive tenders or quotations); the prices previously paid by the buyer for the same goods or services; the market or 'going' rate; and/or the price of any alternative or substitute goods.

4.13 **Cost analysis** is a more specialised technique, often used to support price negotiations where the supplier justifies its price by the need to cover its costs (an approach called 'cost-based pricing'). Cost analysis looks specifically at how the quoted price relates to the supplier's costs of production. Suppliers may be asked to include cost breakdowns with their price quotations, to support this analysis.

4.14 Not all suppliers will be willing to share their detailed cost information with buyers (an approach called **cost transparency**). However, if they can be persuaded to do so – often, as part of a trusting buyer-supplier relationship – there are several benefits to cost analysis. It can keep prices realistic (ie no unreasonably large profit margins), in the absence of competition – for example, where there is a preferred supplier. It focuses attention on what costs ought to be involved in producing the goods or services, which acts as an incentive for cost control and reduction, and which may in turn lead to cost savings passed on to the buyer.

Beyond price: total cost of ownership

4.15 The modern procurement view is that 'cost' and 'value' are far broader concepts than just the purchase price of an asset. Current thinking emphasises the 'total costs of ownership' (TCO), 'total acquisition costs' (TAC) or 'total lifecycle costs' which includes a package of costs not immediately apparent from the purchase price, and which may be incurred throughout the lifecycle (or useful life) of the asset. (This is particularly relevant to the procurement of capital items, such as constructions, equipment and vehicles, which typically have long working lives.) In this way of thinking, the 'right price' is one which represents value for money for the 'total package of benefits' being purchased over the whole life of the asset.

4.16 There is a vital difference between the purchase price of an asset (the sum paid to the supplier to secure access or ownership) and its total cost of acquisition or ownership. The total costs of ownership can be categorised under six headings, as follows.

- *Pre-acquisition costs* such as research, sourcing, preparation of tenders and structural changes to allow for the asset
- *Acquisition costs* including the purchase price, the cost of finance (if borrowing is required to finance the procurement), delivery, installation and commissioning (starting operation)
- *Operating costs* such as labour, materials, consumables, energy usage, and environmental costs (eg disposal of wastes)
- *Maintenance costs* such as spares and replacement parts, servicing, repair, periodic overhauls, and reduced output with age

- *Downtime costs*, such as lost production, extra labour etc if the asset stops working or fails to perform as it should
- *End of life costs* such as disposal, ongoing liabilities, decommissioning, sale for scrap or resale.

4.17 Baily *et al* (*Purchasing Principles and Management*) suggest that there is a 'price/cost iceberg', of which purchase price is only the most obvious or visible 'tip': Figure 2.3.

Figure 2.3 *The price-cost iceberg*

Source: Baily et al

4.18 Looked at from the point of view of the lifecycle of an asset, there may be costs associated with each stage of its working life:

- Procurement
- Delivery, installation and 'commissioning' (putting into action)
- After-sales support from the manufacturer
- Operational costs (including user training, consumables, energy and so on)
- Regular maintenance, repairs and periodic overhauls or upgrades
- De-commissioning (winding-down)
- Disposal (including any 'negative costs' – or revenue – available from sale of the asset, if it has any remaining value).

4.19 Some or all of these costs may be included in the price quoted by a supplier, and a purchaser will need to bear this in mind when comparing two quotations: does a lower price reflect competitive pricing – or a lesser total package of benefits?

4.20 More generally, there is a *trade off* between the purchase price and the total package of benefits. 'It is an obvious fact, yet a commonly ignored one, that a low price may lead to a high total acquisition cost' (Baily *et al*). A lower price may reflect poorer quality, for example, and this will not necessarily be better value for money: the purchase price may be lower, but the total cost of acquisition and ownership may be higher, because of the need for more rigorous quality inspection, the number of rejects and reworks due to poor quality, lost sales through customer disappointment, and so on.

4.21 The procurement of capital assets illustrates the difference between purchase price and total costs particularly clearly. Such assets by their nature have a long life in use, and will give rise to many costs in addition to the original cost of purchase. CIPS therefore consider whole-life costing (or lifecycle costing) as a best practice tool for evaluating options for any substantial procurement: establishing the total cost of ownership, and annual spend profile, over the entire anticipated lifespan of the product.

4.22   'In whole-life costing, all costs over the life of goods and services are taken into account. This enables savings in running costs to offset any increase in capital costs. The savings are calculated for each year of the equipment or service contract life. It shows either a simple payback time or the payback during the life of the equipment or service contract. It can be applied to most situations to justify extra expenditure.' (CIPS Knowledge Works Document on Whole-Life Costing)

5   The right quality

Definitions of quality

5.1   Quality is, to an extent, 'in the eye of the beholder'. Garvin (*Competing in eight dimensions of quality*) identifies eight generic dimensions of product quality.

- *Performance*: the operating characteristics of the product
- *Features*: value-adding characteristics and service elements (such as warranties and after-sales service)
- *Reliability*: the ability of the product to perform consistently over time
- *Durability*: the length of time a product will last (and stand up to normal usage) without deterioration or damage
- *Conformance*: whether agreed specifications and standards are met
- *Serviceability*: the ease and availability of service support
- *Aesthetics*: how appealing or pleasing the product is to the senses of the user
- *Perceived quality*: the subjective expectations and perceptions of buyers.

5.2   However, quality will mean something different for a consumer buying clothes than it will for an industrial buyer of clothing material – or industrial safety wear, say. 'Quality' will mean something different for the purchase of computer equipment, engineering components, building materials, cleaning supplies, accountancy services or catering services.

5.3   Definitions of quality have therefore focused on a range of different dimensions.

- *Excellence*: the degree or standard of excellence of a product; the design, workmanship and attention to detail put into it; and the extent to which finished products are free from defects.
- *Comparative excellence*: how favourably a product is measured against competitive benchmarks (other products), best practice or standards of excellence
- *Quality of design*: the range of potential customer satisfactions built into a product
- *Fitness for purpose or use*: that is, the extent to which a product does what it is designed and expected to do; or, more generally, the extent to which it meets the customer's needs. (Garvin called this the 'user-based' approach to quality.)
- *Conformance to requirement or specification*: that is, the product matches the features, attributes, performance and standards set out in the specification. Conformance therefore also implies lack of defects, and therefore reflects on the quality of the producer's processes. (The 'product-based' or 'manufacturing-based' approach to quality.)
- *Acceptable quality and value for money*: buyers may be willing to sacrifice some performance and features in order to pay a lower price for a product, as long as it is still fit for purpose. (A 'value-based' approach to quality.)

5.4   For a buyer looking to procure materials, components or other supplies in a commercial setting, the most important definitions of 'right quality' are likely to be fitness for purpose and conformance to specification. Note that both of these criteria are essentially focused on the supplier's ability to satisfy the needs and expectations of the customer or buyer. Van Weele argues that: 'Quality is the degree in which customer requirements are met. We speak of a quality product or quality service when supplier and customer agree on requirements and those requirements are met.'

Fitness for purpose

5.5 The BSI definition of quality is: 'the totality of features and characteristics of a product or service that bear on its ability to satisfy a given need.'

5.6 Fitness for use or purpose was the focus of quality guru Joseph Juran, whose work you may come across in your later CIPS studies. It is also one of the key legal definitions of quality: the UK Sale of Goods Act 1979, for example, states that where a seller supplies goods in the course of a business, he is bound to provide goods:

- Of *satisfactory quality*: working and in good condition (so far as may be reasonably expected) and free from 'minor defects' (unless these are drawn to the buyer's attention or obvious to any reasonable pre-purchase inspection)
- *Fit for the purpose* for which they are commonly used, or for any specific purpose made known by the buyer to the seller.

5.7 So an industrial grinder of the 'right quality' is one that grinds. And if the buyer requested a grinder that would tackle a particular material, and grind it to a specific degree of fineness – that is what it should do. In the same way a bucket of the 'right quality' should hold water – and if the buyer asks for a 5-litre bucket, it should hold up to 5 litres of water.

Specifications and quality

5.8 As we will see in Chapter 3, a 'specification' is simply a statement of the requirements to be satisfied in the supply of a product or service. The role of a specification is to define and communicate the buyer's requirements, in terms of either:

- *Conformance*: the buyer details exactly what the required product, part or material must consist of, and a 'quality' product is one which conforms to the description provided by the buyer – or
- *Performance*: the buyer describes what he expects the part or material to be able to achieve, in terms of the functions it will perform and the level of performance it should reach. A 'quality' product is then one which will satisfy these requirements: the buyer specifies the 'ends' (purpose) and the supplier has relative flexibility about the 'means' of achieving them.

5.9 The specification can then provide a means of evaluating the quality or conformance of the goods or services supplied, for acceptance (if conforming to specification) or rejection (if non-conforming).

5.10 The first step for buyers in securing the 'right quality' will therefore be clear and accurate specification of exactly what is required. Essential though this is, however, conformance to specification is not sufficient to secure 'the right quality'. Indeed, it is possible to envisage a situation in which a product conforms to the buyer's specification (is of 'specified quality') – but doesn't do what it is supposed to do, or doesn't perform efficiently, or is difficult to maintain and operate – and is therefore, arguably, not of 'right quality' overall.

Costs of quality

5.11 A definition of the cost of quality is given in British Standard 6143, as: 'The cost of ensuring and assuring quality, as well as the loss incurred when quality is not achieved'. In other words, quality-related costs (Figure 2.4) include *both*:

- The cost of appraisal and prevention activities, designed to try and minimise poor quality products entering the production process and/or reaching the customer – *and*
- The cost of 'failure': losses incurred because of poor quality products entering the production process and/or reaching the customer.

Figure 2.4 *Costs of quality*

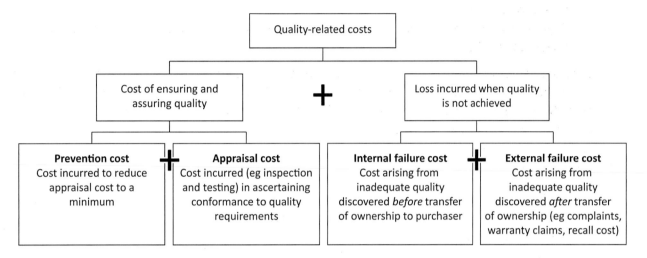

5.12 **Appraisal costs** are the costs incurred as part of the inspection process, in order to ensure that incoming materials – and outgoing finished products – are of the 'right quality'. Examples include: the cost of inspection processes and machinery, and quality audits.

Prevention costs are those incurred in order to *reduce* appraisal costs, by preventing or reducing defects or failures produced by the process. Examples include the cost of building quality into design and specifications; running 'quality circles' (quality problem-solving groups); and setting up defect prevention processes.

5.13 These costs are obviously substantial. Wouldn't it be more cost effective to spend less on such measures, and simply deal with a few defects now and then? Or won't there come a time when the benefits of improving 'that little bit more' will be outweighed by the costs of doing so? The answer generally given these days is: no. The costs of getting quality wrong may well be higher than the costs of getting it right – and the law of diminishing returns may not apply, because there will always be some benefit to improvement.

5.14 **Internal failure costs** are those that arise from quality failure, where the problem is identified and corrected before the finished product or service reaches the customer. Examples include: the scrapping or re-working of faulty items; re-inspection of re-worked products; the holding of contingency stocks (to allow for scrapped work and delays); and time and cost of activities required to investigate the causes of the failure.

5.15 **External failure costs** are those that arise from quality failure identified and corrected after the finished product or service reaches the customer. Examples include: the costs of 'reverse logistics' to collect and handle returned products; the costs of repairing or replacing defective products; the cost of customer claims for compensation; the administrative costs of handling complaints; the cost of lost customer loyalty and future sales; and reputational damage arising from 'word of mouth' by dissatisfied customers.

5.16 Since the costs of 'getting it wrong' are generally perceived as being higher (and further-reaching) than the costs of 'getting it right', there has generally been an increased emphasis on quality management, with the aim of 'getting it right first time'.

Quality control

5.17 Although you may come across a wide variety of techniques for managing supply and supplier quality, they generally fall into two basic categories or approaches: quality control (QC) and quality assurance (QA).

5.18 Systems for the detection and correction of defects are known as **quality control**. This is an essentially reactive approach, focusing on:

- Establishing specifications, standards and tolerances (parameters within which items can vary and still be considered acceptable) for work inputs and outputs
- Inspecting delivered goods and monitoring production processes, often on a 'sampling' basis (although '100% inspection' may be used on critical features, or where zero defects are required).
- Identifying items that are defective or do not meet specification
- Scrapping or re-working items that do not pass inspection – and passing acceptable items on to the next stage of the process.

5.19 You may already be able to see that a quality control approach, based on inspection, has certain limitations.

- A very large number of items must be inspected to prevent defective items from reaching production processes or end customers. Deming argued that this ties up resources – and does not add value (or indeed 'improve' quality).
- Defective items may slip through without being spotted or even inspected, in unacceptable numbers, owing to budget and schedule pressures (especially if the buyer is operating a strategy of just in time supply).
- The process aims to identify and reject defective items once they have already been made. By this time, however, they may already have incurred significant – wasted – costs (of design, raw materials, processing, overheads and so on). You are 'locking the door after the horse has bolted'.
- Inspection activity tends to be duplicated at each stage of the supply process – magnifying the inefficiencies and wastes.

Quality assurance

5.20 Systems for the *prevention* of defects are known as **quality assurance**. This is a more proactive and integrated approach, building quality into every stage of the process from concept and specification onwards. It includes the full range of systematic activities used within a quality management system to 'assure' or give the organisation adequate confidence that items and processes will fulfil its quality requirements. In other words, quality assurance is a matter of 'building in quality' – not 'weeding out defects'.

5.21 From the buyer's point of view, you are seeking to ensure that your buying processes, and your suppliers' quality management processes, work together to prevent defective products or materials ever being delivered. Quality assurance programmes may build quality measures and controls into:

- Product designs
- The drawing up of materials specifications and contracts
- The evaluation, selection, approval and certification of suppliers
- Communication with suppliers, feedback mechanisms and quality record-keeping
- Supplier training and development (where required to integrate the two organisations' quality standards and systems)
- Education, training, motivation and management of employees and suppliers to maintain required levels of performance

All this would normally be in addition to inspection, sampling, testing and other quality control techniques.

Quality management

5.22   The term quality management is given to the various processes used to ensure that the right quality inputs and outputs are secured: that products and services are fit for purpose and conform to specification; and that continuous quality improvements are obtained over time. Quality management thus includes both quality control and quality assurance.

5.23   A **quality management system** (QMS) can be defined as: 'A set of co-ordinated activities to direct and control an organisation in order to continually improve the effectiveness and efficiency of its performance'. The main purpose of a QMS is to define and manage processes for systematic quality assurance.

5.24   A QMS is designed to ensure that:

- An organisation's customers can have confidence in its ability reliably to deliver products and services which meet their needs and expectations
- The organisation's quality objectives are consistently and efficiently achieved, through improved process control and reduced wastage
- Staff competence, training and morale are enhanced, through clear expectations and process requirements
- Quality gains, once achieved, are maintained over time: learning and good practices do not 'slip' for lack of documentation, adoption and consistency.

5.25   There are several international standards for measuring and certifying quality management systems of various types, including the ISO 9000 standard developed by the International Organisation for Standardisation (ISO). Organisations can use the framework to plan or evaluate their own QMS, or can seek third party assessment and accreditation.

Total quality management (TQM)

5.26   The term total quality management (TQM) is used to refer to a radical approach to quality management, as a business philosophy. TQM is an orientation to quality in which quality values and aspirations are applied to the management of all resources and relationships within the firm – and throughout the supply chain – in order to seek continuous improvement and excellence in all aspects of performance.

5.27   Laurie Mullins (*Management and Organisational Behaviour*) synthesises various definitions of TQM as expressing: 'a way of life for an organisation as a whole, committed to total customer satisfaction through a continuous process of improvement, and the contribution and involvement of people'. From the buyer's point of view, the provision of 'the right quality' inputs is only one part of a total quality picture, which also embraces excellent supply chains; continuous collaborative improvement; cross-functional co-operation on quality; and so on.

Purchasing's contribution to quality

5.28   While the role of the procurement function in many organisations has shifted from 'buying materials' to 'managing suppliers', both of these activities have a significant influence on quality. Dobler et al (*Purchasing and Materials Management*) argue that: 'Quality must be built into a product. It is the buyer's responsibility to ensure that suppliers possess the ability, the motivation, and adequate information to produce materials and components of the specified quality, in a cost-effective manner. In fulfilling this responsibility, a buyer can exert positive control over the quality and attendant costs of incoming material.'

5.29   Quality guru W Edwards Deming, in his analysis of Japanese companies, similarly found that such companies were able to maintain high production standards primarily because of their ability to control the *quality of input materials* through close supplier relations, characterised by co-operative quality assurance, the training of supplier personnel and the incentive of long-term relationships. He also argued that considerations such as quality and reliability should be at least as important as price when choosing suppliers.

5.30 The procurement or supply chain function can thus help to provide 'the right quality' by a wide range of means.

- Selecting suppliers with third party approved or accredited quality management systems (eg ISO 9000).
- Appraising the quality management systems and 'track record' of suppliers, as part of the supplier appraisal and selection process
- Preparing preferred or approved supplier lists, to ensure that user departments only buy from suppliers with appraised quality management.
- Influencing the quality of product design, by working with design and production departments (and participating in quality circles, where used); keeping up to date with material developments; recommending alternative materials where appropriate; and involving suppliers early in the product development process, to gain their materials expertise in design decisions (an approach called 'early supplier involvement').
- Translating design requirements into clear, accurate materials and service specifications, reflecting users' needs (fitness for purpose) and specifying required quality standards, measures, inspections and tests.
- Developing goods inwards procedures for quality inspection and testing (where necessary in addition to supplier's quality assurance).
- Managing relationships with suppliers: developing a realistic mutual understanding of quality standards and procedures; providing incentives and rewards for high quality and continuous improvement; and so on.
- Monitoring and controlling suppliers' quality performance over time (eg using vendor rating); providing suppliers with feedback; and developing closer relationships with reliable quality performers.
- Working with suppliers to resolve quality disputes, solve quality problems and/or make ongoing quality improvements: eg by providing consultancy, training, access to technology and so on (supplier development).

5.31 The concept of approved supplier lists and supplier certification arises from the recognition that the quality management systems of a supplier and buyer are really part of the same process. If the buying organisation can be assured that the supplier has already done all the quality control required to supply 'the right quality' inputs, it won't have to duplicate the effort by monitoring or re-inspecting everything on delivery: it can merely check, from time to time, that the supplier's quality management systems are working as they should, by sampling outputs or inspecting procedures and documentation. Integration may be as simple as a getting a 'quality guarantee' from suppliers – or there may be detailed formal systems for responsibility sharing, in areas such as specification, inspection, process control, training, reporting and adjustment.

6 The right quantity at the right time

6.1 We have grouped these two 'rights' together, because quantity and time are inextricably linked in a buyer's decision-making. Issues such as 'demand' and 'stock levels' are as much a feature of time decisions as they are of quantity decisions.

- If you are procuring supplies to cover demand over a long time period, you will need a larger quantity.
- If you purchase in small quantities, you will need to re-order more frequently.
- If you think you might need stocks of an item at short notice (because customer demand might peak unexpectedly), you might buy a large quantity well in advance, so that you have extra stock available.

- Alternatively, you might wait and only top up with a small quantity when you need to – but then, the turnaround time for the order will need to be short.
- If you buy in large quantities, there is a time dimension: it will take longer to use up the stock – and this means higher costs of storage, and more risk of damage or deterioration.
- If you buy in small quantities, there is a time dimension: you are more likely to run out of stock in the face of unexpected demand – and then the 'right time' will be 'yesterday'!

6.2 We will look at these interrelationships and issues systematically, in brief.

What determines 'right quantity'?

6.3 What is the 'right quantity' to buy in a given situation? Of course, it varies. If you receive a requisition from the operations manager to replace one worn lathe, say, the 'right quantity' is one. If a bill of materials for a customer order specifies 2,000 subassemblies, the 'right quantity' is 2,000 subassemblies. But what if your company produces cars: how many components will it need in a given period? How much oil will it need to lubricate its assembly line? How much toilet paper will it need for the factory and offices? And what if you receive that requisition for one lathe – but you know that another lathe will become worn out shortly: is it more advantageous to buy one lathe now, or two? Buyers will have to work with users and inventory managers to establish the optimum quantity (and timing) of purchases for a given situation.

6.4 Lysons & Farrington suggest that the most important factors determining the 'right quantity' to procure in a given situation are as follows.

- *Demand for the final product* into which the procured materials and components are incorporated (dependent demand). The more cars you anticipate selling, the more wheels you are going to have to buy – and if you are planning on producing 1,000 cars in a given period, you will need 4,000 wheels in the same period.
- *Demand for procured finished items*, such as office equipment and supplies, computer hardware and software or maintenance services (independent demand). This may be based on past and average usage and replacement rates, for example. If your office gets through an average of 60 reams of paper per month, you will probably plan to purchase a similar quantity on a monthly basis.
- *The inventory policy of the organisation*: whether its main aim is to secure service levels by holding stocks (as a 'buffer' against unforeseen demand or supply difficulties) – or to minimise or eliminate stocks, to avoid the costs and risks associated with holding stock
- *The service level required*: whether an item must be available in full on demand 100% of the time (eg for critical production items or hospital supplies) or only 90–95% of the time (eg for routine supplies)
- *Market conditions*, affecting the price and security of supply, which dictate whether requirements must be 'stockpiled' to secure supply or take advantage of low prices, or can be bought on an *ad hoc* or opportunistic basis
- *Supply-side factors*, such as minimum order quantities/values, or price incentives for bulk purchases
- *Factors determining the economic order quantity (EOQ)* which balances the costs of acquiring stock (higher with frequent smaller orders) against the costs of holding stock (higher with fewer larger orders)
- *Specific quantities notified to buyers by user departments, according to identified needs*. For example, the operations function may indicate required quantities for a particular job or application via materials specifications or a bill of materials (BOM). Standard items, consumables and spares may be ordered by requisitions from user departments or stock control staff. Computerised inventory reports (or the electronic point of sale systems in a retail organisation) may specify re-order quantities when inventory gets down to a predetermined level, in order to 'top up' stock in line with anticipated demand.

How much stock should you hold?

6.5   There are many reasons why an organisation would want to hold stock or inventory.

- Stocks reduce the risks of disruption to production from unforeseen events. 'Safety' or 'buffer' stocks allow the organisation to keep working if supply is disrupted by strikes, transport breakdowns, supply shortages, supplier failure and so on. Stock 'buys time' for the procurement function to find alternative sources of needed materials. This is particularly important for items which are critical for operations: it would be disastrous if a firm ran out of such items, and some stock must be held in order to avoid this.

- Stocks reduce the risks of disruption to production from long or uncertain delivery lead times. Suppliers' production and delivery lead times cannot always be known accurately in advance, so stock in hand allows the organisation to keep working (and maintaining service to its customers) if replenishment takes longer than anticipated.

- Stocks allow rapid replenishment of goods which are in constant use and demand, such as maintenance and office supplies.

- Buyers may be able to take advantage of bulk discounts, lower prices or reduced transaction costs by placing fewer, larger orders, for quantities in excess of what is immediately required.

- Buyers may be able to protect against anticipated shortages, price increases, or exchange rate fluctuations, by buying (or 'stockpiling') goods at advantageous terms, or while available, in advance of requirement.

- Stocks of finished or almost-finished goods may be prepared ready for unexpected peaks in customer demand – or for the late customisation of products to customer specification. (A popular example is that of Dell computers, which builds up stock of finished computer models, which can simply be assembled swiftly and flexibly according to customers' requirements.)

- Stocks of finished goods may be prepared during periods of slow demand, ready to meet peaks of demand which are beyond the organisation's production capacity: in effect, 'smoothing out' peaks and troughs in production.

6.6   In particular, the organisation will want to avoid **stockouts**: that is, being out of inventory of a required item. Stockouts are costly because of: lost production output and idle time (due to the unavailability of materials or components); overhead costs still being incurred, with reduced production to cover them; loss of credibility, trust and customer goodwill through delayed delivery of finished items; non-delivery or late delivery penalties; and the costs of dealing with the stockout (such as high-priced 'emergency' purchases).

6.7   There are also good reasons for *not* holding stocks, or at least for *minimising* the level (quantity and value) of stocks. One of the most important reasons is that stockholding incurs costs.

- There are costs in *acquiring* stock: the cost of setting up and maintaining an information system for purchasing; and the cost of purchasing procedures each time an order is placed (preparing purchase requisitions, selecting suppliers, preparing purchase orders and other documentation, receiving and inspecting incoming deliveries; processing payment; and so on).

- There are costs in *holding* stock: the capital tied up in the stock (ie the purchase price); the 'opportunity cost' of having capital tied up in stock when it could be used to earn interest; the costs of storing inventory (rent and rates on warehouse space, insuring the stock, materials handling machinery, and the wages of warehouse or stores staff); and the cost of losses through damage, deterioration, pilferage and obsolescence while goods are being held.

6.8   *Acquisition costs* actually decrease as stock levels rise, because it is cheaper to make fewer, larger orders. But *holding costs* increase as stock levels rise. There is a genuine trade-off here. This has given rise to the concept of *economic order quantity (EOQ)*, which balances acquisition and holding costs to identify the quantity of a given item which should be regularly ordered in order to minimise its total cost to the firm. The general point, however, is that there is a fine line between the costs of holding stock – and the costs and risks of not having sufficient stocks to meet the firm's needs, and customers' requirements.

Forecasting demand

6.9   As we have already noted, the ability to forecast demand accurately is crucial for ascertaining what the 'right' quantity of stock will be at a given time.

6.10   Many stock items are subject to *dependent demand*: that is, the extent to which the item is used depends on the exact volume and nature of the production schedule for a larger item of which it forms a part. Dependent demand items are therefore typically subassemblies or components used during the production of the finished product. Demand is dependent on the specification and number of finished units being produced: it can thus be accurately measured on the basis of production schedules and materials requirements. For example, if 1,000 units are due to be manufactured, and each unit requires five sub-modules, then an order will need to be placed for 5,000 sub-modules.

6.11   Other stock items will be subject to *independent demand*: not linked to production of another finished item. The amount of oil required to keep a machine in working order does not depend on which products are being processed on that machine: it should simply be possible to identify that a certain (average) amount of oil is used each day, week or month. The same may be true of procurements such as office equipment and supplies, computer hardware and software, motor vehicles, marketing services, maintenance services and so on.

6.12   The distinction between dependent and independent demand is important because some inventory control systems are designed to meet dependent demand (forecasting the materials requirements for a specified type and level of production), while others are more suited to general *stock replenishment*, in response to independent demand.

Stock replenishment systems: periodic review

6.13   'Push' inventory management systems (for independent demand items) aim to set up a regular system for monitoring levels of stock, and planning to replenish them in time to meet forecast demand (the right quantity at the right time) – while generally carrying as little stock as safely possible. There are two main methods for doing this: periodic review systems and fixed order quantity systems.

6.14   Periodic review systems (also called 'fixed interval ordering or 'topping up' systems), are systems in which the stock level of an item is reviewed at regular or fixed intervals, and, depending on the quantity in stock, a replenishment order is placed for whatever quantity appears to be appropriate to 'top up' stock to the desired level. Replenishment quantities vary, being whatever is sufficient to bring stock levels up to a predetermined stock level – or whatever is needed to last through the next interval, or until the next delivery: Figure 2.5.

Figure 2.5 *Periodic review system*

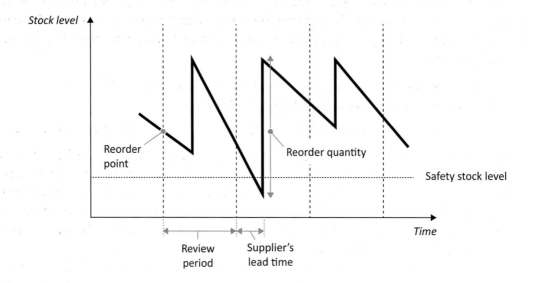

6.15 The length of the review period will be determined on a category-by-category basis, depending on usage patterns. The shorter the review period, the more effort and cost is involved, so it is usual to apply an ABC analysis: Category A items might be reviewed weekly, Category B items monthly and Category C items quarterly, say.

6.16 Once the current stock level has been established at a given review point (eg by a stocktake or electronic monitoring), the decision must be taken on how much to order to replenish the stock to a desired level. Take a monthly review system, for example. At the 1st January review point, an order will be made based on the quantities of the item likely to be required during January; *plus* enough stock to cover the lead time for delivery following a review and order on the 1st February; *plus* an appropriate level of safety stock.

Stock replenishment systems: fixed order quantity

6.17 In a fixed order quantity system (or 're-order point' system), stock of an item is replenished with a predetermined quantity when inventory falls to a predetermined minimum level (the re-order level or ROL). In other words – directly opposite to the periodic review approach – the timing of the order isn't fixed, but the quantity is: Figure 2.6.

Figure 2.6 *Fixed order quantity system*

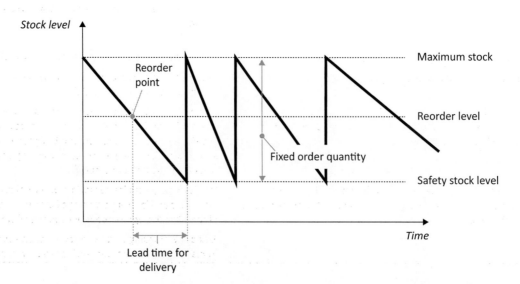

6.18 To determine the re-order point for a particular item, managers rely on past experience of demand and usage patterns for the item, taking into account any known factors which may lessen or increase demand and usage in the coming period. The aim is to fix on a stock level sufficient to keep the business in stock during the supplier's delivery lead time, plus a reserve of safety stock. In other words, a basic re-order level (ROL) should be equal to:

- Maximum amount used × maximum lead time for replenishment   *or*
- Average amount used × average lead time + safety stock

6.19 Once stock falls to this predetermined order point or ROL, the system triggers a replenishment order.

- A common manual method for doing this is a *two-bin system*. For each stock item, two bins are maintained. The first is immediate stock in use, while the second contains the amount of stock determined as the ROL. When the first bin is empty, you know automatically that you are down to the ROL, and it is time to re-order. While waiting for the order to be delivered, the contents of the second bin are used. Ideally, this bin will be down to safety stock level when the delivery comes in, and both bins are replenished from the order.
- Computerised perpetual inventory systems (using barcoding or RFID to record inputs and withdrawals of stock and maintain running totals) may be used to automatically trigger replenishment orders when inventory has fallen to the specified re-order point.

6.20 In either case, the re-order quantity is the same each time. For items of high value, it may be sensible to use a structured approach to determining what this should be, perhaps by using the economic order quantity (EOQ). For small-value items, simple decision rules (based on usage rates) may be more cost-effective.

6.21 The advantages and disadvantages of periodic review and fixed order quantity systems are summarised in Table 2.2.

Table 2.2 *Evaluating stock replenishment systems*

ADVANTAGES OF PERIODIC REVIEW	DISADVANTAGES OF PERIODIC REVIEW
Ease of administration and control, with predictable workload planning for purchasing and warehousing staff (at fixed review or replenishment periods)	The risk of unexpected stockouts, since the system assumes that there will be no review of stock other than at the fixed interval. This necessitates the use of safety stocks.
Orders may be placed at the same time for a number of items, enabling shipment consolidation, reduced transport costs, or quantity discounts from suppliers	Higher average stocks than with fixed order point systems, because of the need to provide for review periods, lead times and safety stocks
Ability to identify slow-moving or obsolete stock items, due to periodic stock review.	Re-order quantities not based on economic order quantities (EOQs)
	Waste of time reviewing stock levels which do not require action.
ADVANTAGES OF FIXED ORDER QUANTITY	**DISADVANTAGES OF FIXED ORDER QUANTITY**
Ability to use the EOQ, unlike periodic review systems	Acceptance of the holding cost (which may be expensive if the stock levels are set too high)
Lower average levels of stock than with periodic review systems, because of enhanced responsiveness to demand fluctuations	Assumption that stock usage patterns and lead times are predictable and stable. Parameters must be reviewed, to avoid risk of stockouts (if demand is higher, or lead time longer, than foreseen) – or excess stock (eg if replenished in full, despite fall-off of demand).
Automatic 'triggering' of replenishment by the system, without time being wasted on items where the stock level is satisfactory.	Inefficiencies, from inappropriate order points and quantities and/or from ordering of individual items at different times. Eg: frequent uneconomical small orders.
	Risk of overloading purchasing systems and staff, if multiple items reach their re-order levels at the same time.

Economic order quantity (EOQ)

6.22 As we have already seen, there are significant costs incurred in acquiring and holding stock.

- **Acquisition costs** are incurred when orders are placed: costs of management time, administration, paper work and transaction charges.
- **Holding costs** include the cost of working capital tied up in stock; the costs of storage; and the costs of damage, deterioration, pilferage and obsolescence while goods are being held.

6.23 The task of the purchasing manager is, ideally, to reduce these costs – but note that there is an inherent trade-off between them.

- You could seek to minimise *acquisition* costs by making fewer, larger orders – but this would increase your stock levels, and hence your holding costs.
- You could seek to minimise your *holding* costs by only purchasing stock in small quantities, as and when you need them – but this would increase the frequency of your orders, and hence your acquisition costs.

6.24 How is this dilemma resolved? There will be a certain order quantity at which holding costs will equal acquisition costs – and the total cost will be as low as possible: this is called the economic order quantity or EOQ. The EOQ can be computed mathematically or graphically, but this is beyond the requirements of your syllabus.

Pull inventory systems

6.25 'Pull' inventory management systems (for dependent demand items) are based on producing goods in response to actual demand (in the form of customer orders). Buyers place an order with suppliers as and when items are required for production. In such a system, demand is much more certain: inventory can therefore be relatively low – or even non-existent: for example, as in just in time (JIT) supply.

6.26 More strategic inventory management systems are an increasing part of the purchasing environment – and you will certainly encounter them elsewhere in your CIPS studies.

- **Just in time** (JIT) supply is a radical approach to inventory reduction which aims to ensure that goods only arrive at the factory 'just in time' to go into the production process. The philosophy of JIT is that 'inventory is evil': every effort is made to minimise stockholding, by securing demand-driven late delivery of required quantities of supplies. At the same time, given such 'tight' time and quantity parameters, the buyer cannot afford any defects in the supplies delivered: significant effort is also put into 'zero defects' quality management. Such a philosophy and practice requires strong integration and co-operation with suppliers. It is advantageous in reducing waste, minimising stock and lead times, and improving supply chain flexibility. But it comes at a risk: there are no time or stock buffers, if the supplier or the system fails...
- **Materials requirements planning** (MRP) is a set of logically related procedures, decision rules and records for managing dependent demand items. It is designed to translate a master production schedule (MPS) and a bill of materials (BOM: a breakdown of all the materials and components required for production) into time-phased 'net requirements' (taking into account existing stock levels) which trigger purchasing.
- **Manufacturing resources planning** (MRP II) draws on the master production schedule to develop materials planning plus personnel deployment, maintenance planning and financial analysis (for accurate costing of manufacture).
- **Enterprise resource planning** (ERP) consolidates materials, manufacturing, logistics, supply chain, sales/marketing, finance and HR planning information into one integrated management system: a single database able to offer 'real time' information for solving a range of business problems.

What is the 'right time' for delivery?

6.27   We have already seen that the 'right time' for delivery depends to a large extent on the buying organisation's policies about holding stock.

6.28   On the one hand, it is straightforward to say that goods must be 'on time': that is, not late for a production or delivery deadline. Late delivery deadlines set by a purchaser, or late deliveries by a supplier, may cause the following problems.

- Production 'bottlenecks' and stoppages, as machines or assembly lines wait for required supplies
- Costs associated with idle time (while waiting for delivery) and/or seeking out alternative 'emergency' supplies
- Late delivery of finished goods to the organisation's end customers, with attendant loss of trust, credibility and goodwill (and potentially, therefore, loss of future business), and possibly also late delivery penalties.

6.29   On the other hand, as we saw above, it is not necessarily a good thing for purchasers to set 'early' delivery deadlines (that is, to secure supplies before they are required for use) – because of the costs of holding stock, the risk of obsolescence and deterioration of goods in stock, and the difficulty of accurately forecasting demand in advance. The 'right time' may be 'just in time' for requirement.

6.30   Moreover, as our brief outline of 'just in time' supply suggests, there is an increasing emphasis on 'responsiveness' to customer demand – essentially, a 'time' factor – as an important source of competitive advantage. Organisations that can respond swiftly to customer orders, or to changing environmental factors, by getting hold of supplies at short notice, are able to offer customers leading edge products (because of the speed of getting products to market); swift, flexible service (because of the ability to fill customer orders quickly); and perhaps product customisation (because of the ability to finish or assemble orders to customer specification quickly). The 'right time' may therefore be a matter of supply chain responsiveness or agility: speed and flexibility of action.

Understanding supplier lead times

6.31   The expression 'lead time' has a number of different meanings, and it is important for users and procurement functions to understand the true or total length of the lead time to obtain goods, when operating demand management or stock replenishment systems.

- The **internal lead time** is the lead time for the processes carried out within the buying organisation: that is, the time between the identification of a need and the issue of a completed purchase order. This might therefore include the preparation of a specification; the identification and selection of suppliers; contract negotiation and so on.
- The **external lead time** is the lead time for the processes carried out within the supplying organisation: that is, the time between the supplier receiving the purchase order and fulfilling that order (by delivering the goods). It might therefore include manufacture, despatch and delivery time.
- The **total lead time** is therefore a combination of internal and external lead time: that is, the time between the identification of a need by the buyer to delivery of goods by the supplier. As the most comprehensive definition, this is the safest lead time to use in planning to obtain goods at the 'right time'.

6.32   Baily et al note that: 'Sometimes suppliers quote delivery dates which they cannot achieve. This may be an unscrupulous device to get the order, or the quote may be given in good faith but circumstances change and delivery dates are rescheduled. Sometimes the firms which fail to deliver on time may not be competent at production planning and control. Frequently, of course, purchasers are themselves the source of the delivery problem, through issuing inaccurate delivery schedules, continually amended, or by allowing insufficient time for delivery.' (*Purchasing Principles and Management*).

6.33   It may be important for a procurement planner to check whether supplier quoted lead times are realistic, based on available production capacity, delivery track record and so on).

Shortening lead times

6.34   It may also be necessary to reduce or shorten a lead time, in order to obtain an urgent delivery of supplies – or to make the supply chain generally more responsive (eg so that it can operate just in time supply or late customisation). There may be various options for shortening lead times, at various levels.

- Negotiating incentive prices for 'priority' or 'urgent' orders, for unusually swift turnaround and delivery by suppliers.
- Streamlining transaction and information-sharing processes (eg by integrating computer systems with regular supply partners)
- Working collaboratively with external and internal supply chain partners to reduce 'waste' time at all stages of the supply process: unnecessary waiting and idle time; unnecessary transport, handling or processing operations; and so on. Quality assurance by the supplier, for example, may shorten inspection time at goods inwards.
- Negotiating contracts with supply partners to pre-manufacture and hold stocks of work in progress (eg subassemblies), which can be more swiftly assembled and finished in response to demand: this is a key approach to late customisation, for example.

Securing on-time delivery

6.35   Achieving on-time delivery is one of the key objectives by which the performance of procurement or supply chain functions is measured. In order to ensure that suppliers deliver by the date specified in the purchase order or contract, buyers should:

- Ensure that users and procurement staff understand lead times, and check that lead times quoted by suppliers are realistic (given the demands of the job and the capability and track record of the supplier)
- Select suppliers with a good delivery track record and capability
- Ensure that suppliers understand the importance of on-time delivery: perhaps making it a key performance indicator for the evaluation of supplier performance, or including contract terms which state clearly that 'time is of the essence' (ie that the delivery deadline is a 'condition' or important term of the contract).
- Issue accurate and realistic delivery schedules to suppliers
- Give regular suppliers advance notice of ongoing or future requirements (where possible)
- Expedite (or 'chase') orders, if there are any concerns about delivery.

7   The right place

What is the 'right place'?

7.1   You might think the 'right place' is fairly obvious: as long as you've given your supplier the right address, how complicated could it be? The fact is that deliveries do go astray for various reasons, and buyers must take care to ensure that there is no misunderstanding about the delivery address. But there are many other issues involved in deciding 'the right place'.

- Do you ask the supplier to make deliveries directly to a number of different user sites (factories, branch offices or retail outlets, say), or to make a single delivery to a regional distribution centre, which will distribute them as required?
- What kind of transport will you ask the supplier to use, or arrange yourself, in order to ensure that the goods get to the right place (at the right time, safely and in good condition), with minimal cost and impact on the environment? How should the goods be packaged for this mode of transport?

7.2   Many of these decisions will already have been made. The organisation will either have a regional distribution centre, or use a third party logistics provider, or it won't. There may be company policies about the use of particular transport modes and packaging for different types of delivery. There will be existing procedures – and legal requirements – for preparing the relevant documentation. Nevertheless, buyers need to understand the basis on which these decisions are made.

7.3   Good practice dictates that the buyer will be concerned to achieve the greatest possible accuracy and efficiency of deliveries, with the lowest possible risk, at the best value for money – and (increasingly, these days) the lowest environmental impact.

7.4   However – as with all procurement operations – there is potential for things to go wrong.

- Goods may be delivered to the wrong address, incurring time delays and costs in retrieving them (and sorting out liability for the problem).
- Goods may be damaged in transit; or may deteriorate (if perishable) during delays in transit; or may be subject to losses through theft, pilferage or vandalism in transit.
- The costs of packaging, handling and transport may exceed the budgeted amount, or may erode the value secured by the buyer for the purchase price.

Key considerations in inbound delivery decisions

7.5   Key components in inbound delivery decisions therefore include:

- The correct *delivery point* (where the delivery should be sent to)
- The *timelines* of the delivery (when the delivery is needed and how it can be secured on time)
- The *exposure to risk* of goods in transit, the minimisation of such risk – and the minimisation of the buyer's liability for any loss or damage that does occur in transit
- The total *distribution cost* (including packaging, handling, transport and insurance)
- The *environmental impact* of transport (minimising the use of non-renewable fuel resources, pollution, traffic, noise/vibration and so on)
- The need to *monitor, track or 'expedite'* deliveries, so that their whereabouts and progress is known at all times – and so that potential problems can be identified and dealt with as early as possible.

7.6   Each of the following points should be covered in the purchase order, delivery specification or contract with a supplier.

- A full and accurate delivery address (with as much detail as possible to ensure that the driver can find the delivery point easily: eg if there is an unloading bay number)
- The contact person at the delivery address, who will have been informed of the incoming delivery and will be authorised to inspect and sign for it
- Packaging instructions (eg if goods require refrigeration or special handling for preservation, safety or security reasons; or if goods need to be packaged ready for handling or storage)
- Delivery instructions (eg if there is a defined schedule or 'window' of opportunity for deliveries, while a delivery bay is open, staffed and/or available; or if there are restrictions on the size of vehicle that can access the delivery point)
- Transport instructions, if the contract includes a particular type, speed or cost of transport (eg air, sea or rail freight)
- The point at which ownership/title in the goods (and therefore all risks and liabilities associated with them) 'pass' from the supplier to the buyer: this may be at any stage in the journey from supplier to buyer. Where the time in transit is lengthy and prone to risk, as in international deliveries, it is very important that the liability for risk (and insurance) is clearly established.

Goods inwards facilities

7.7 If the buying organisation receives a high volume of deliveries, and especially if they are large in bulk or weight, or require specialist handling, there is likely to be a dedicated delivery point, goods inwards area or receiving dock. (You don't want tonnes of raw materials delivered to the front reception desk of your offices!)

7.8 A dedicated *goods inwards facility* may feature:

- Special entry and access points: stopping, loading and unloading space for vehicles, where they do not interfere with general road traffic
- Materials handling equipment: forklift trucks, cranes, conveyor belts and other mechanical aids to loading, unloading and moving goods into storage
- Immediate proximity and accessibility to storage areas and facilities (to minimise the movement and handling of goods between unloading and storage)
- Space for the inspection of deliveries (to establish that goods have been delivered as ordered, in full and in good condition)
- Space (and/or equipment) for sorting, labelling and other required handling procedures
- Security (to protect vehicles and storage areas from theft or vandalism)
- A defined 'traffic flow' for entry and exit of vehicles, to avoid traffic snarl-ups.

7.9 You will cover a range of issues in warehousing, storage and materials handling – including the location and layout of facilities – in your CIPS studies.

Distribution centres

7.10 If the buying organisation has a number of sites (factories, branch offices or retail outlets, say) which require deliveries, it has two basic options for getting the goods to the 'right place'.

- It can arrange for the supplier to make *multiple direct deliveries*, to each of the sites, in quantities that meet their individual requirements.
- It can arrange for the supplier to make a *single bulk delivery* to a central warehouse or *distribution centre*. The buying organisation (or its logistics provider) will then take responsibility for splitting up the delivery into consignments (breaking bulk) and delivering them onward to each of its user sites. It may have one *central distribution centre*, or a network of *regional distribution centres (RDCs)* which act as 'hubs' for deliveries to user sites in each region – or both. International deliveries may be sent to the central distribution centre, for example, which breaks bulk and sends consignments to regional distribution centres, which in turn break bulk and send consignments to user sites.

7.11 Distribution centres thus fulfil two main purposes.

- *Breaking bulk*: a single large or bulk delivery can be ordered from the supplier (attracting bulk purchase and transport discounts). The distribution centre can then split the delivery up into smaller consignments for its separate sites/users. This is sometimes called a 'hub and spoke' arrangement.
- *Consolidating deliveries*: multiple items, delivered by different suppliers, can be combined in a single delivery to sites/users. This cuts down on the number of transport trips (saving on transport/fuel costs and reducing the environmental impacts of transport) and fills up the transport for each delivery (not wasting space and costs). Meanwhile, users receive only one (multi-item) delivery – rather than having to process multiple (single item) deliveries, reducing traffic at their receiving facilities. This is sometimes called a 'merge in transit' arrangement.

7.12 The distribution centre may even use *cross-docking*: having a staging area where inbound deliveries are sorted, consolidated and onward delivered with little or no storage time or space required. Such an arrangement may decrease storage costs, streamline inbound logistics, and increase the efficiency of transport planning.

7.13 We can depict the use of distribution centres as follows: Figure 2.7.

Figure 2.7 *Distribution centres*

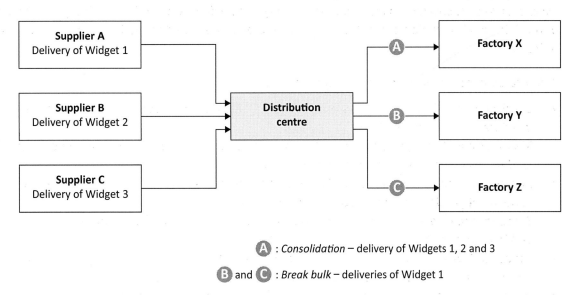

(A) : *Consolidation* – delivery of Widgets 1, 2 and 3

(B) and (C) : *Break bulk* – deliveries of Widget 1

7.14 Another option is for the buying organisation to outsource its inbound (and outbound) logistics handling to third party service providers, who manage transport and/or warehousing activities on its behalf.

Factors in the choice of transport

7.15 A number of different types or 'modes' of transport are available, including transport by road haulage; rail, air and sea freight; inland waterways (canals); express operators or couriers (such as DHL, Fedex or UPS); or pipeline (for specialist industries such as oil and gas).

7.16 How will a buyer decide which is the 'right' mode of transport for a given procurement – insofar as he has a choice in the matter? There are likely to be a number of factors in the choice or specification of transport, including the following.

- The points of departure and destination, for which limited transport options may be available. (The supplier may be in a land-locked country, for example, necessitating extra journeys and handling if it wants to use sea freight.)
- The length of the journey (in distance and time), raising issues of time, risk and cost
- The nature of the goods, which may dictate that they must be transported swiftly or in a special way: eg if they are perishable, dangerous or fragile
- The size or weight of the goods, which may rule out certain modes of transport (eg road haulage)
- Timescale and urgency of delivery, raising issues including: the frequency and flexibility of departures, and the journey speed, of a given mode of transport
- The environmental impact of different modes of transport: eg use of non-renewable fuels; pollution and emissions; noise; traffic congestion; environmental damage; and 'carbon footprint' (greenhouse gas emissions, thought to contribute to climate change).
- Availability of standardisation (eg of container sizes) for efficiency, especially if goods need to be transferred from one form of transport to another
- The buyer's goods inwards facility: whether it has space and equipment to receive and unload certain types of transport
- The security of goods in transit by various modes of transport
- The compatibility and relationship of a given haulier or logistics provider with the supplier and/or buyer (creating trust, the potential for collaborative efficiency improvements and so on)

- The costs of transport, handling and insurance associated with the mode of transport
- Company policy in regard to transport, or the use of a particular haulier.

Intermodal transport

7.17 The term *intermodal* (between modes) or *multimodal* (many modes) is given to a transport strategy which uses more than one mode of transport in a single movement from origin to destination (not including local pick-ups and deliveries by truck). A shipment by container from London to Nairobi might travel by road to an International Container Depot, by rail to the port, by sea to Mombasa, by rail to Nairobi, and by road to the buyer's premises – all without the need to handle the goods themselves when changing modes.

7.18 Specialist companies and shipping lines have taken the lead in developing these combined operations: the lead carrier, often the shipping line, acts as a combined transport operator. Intermodal transport has led to an increasing attempt to integrate transport modes, and to ensure that handling and storage methods are compatible, so that goods can 'cross' from one mode to another with minimal handling, minimal potential for damage, minimal space inefficiency – and associated costs. Examples include the design of standardised road or rail containers that can also be carried by air or barge/ship. Specialist documentation (allowing for multiple modes of transport) and handling equipment (allowing for the lifting and transfer of containers) have also been developed.

Logistics services

7.19 Many organisations regard storage and distribution as support functions, rather than as core activities of the organisation, and therefore use third party warehousing and distribution (or logistics) service providers. A buyer may therefore be dealing with a supplier's transport or logistics provider in organising for deliveries to the 'right place'. Indeed, the 'right place' itself may be a goods inward facility or distribution centre managed on the buyer's behalf by a third party logistics provider.

7.20 Outsourcing inbound logistics may thus give a buying organisation access to specialist expertise and resources that it might not be able to afford in-house. It may also allow it to spread risk in times of difficulty: saving it from being affected by in-house warehouse strikes or unusually high (or low) demand. Outsourcing also frees up resources (particularly financial capital and managerial time) which can be devoted to core activities of the business.

7.21 Despite these benefits, outsourcing any function is a difficult decision for a firm. It will need to select third party providers very carefully, and develop and manage contracts with a view to ensuring that the required levels of service are obtained – and maintained.

8   Other considerations

8.1 It is worth noting that while achieving the five rights may be *essential* for effective procurements from external suppliers, it may not be *sufficient*. There may be additional objectives to consider. Here are some examples.

- **Relationship development**: developing collaborative long-term relationships with suppliers, not just for the immediate supply contract, but for ongoing partnership and mutual advantage
- **Innovation and development**: not just 'right quality' now, but potential to come up with innovative products and processes, and make collaborative quality improvements over time
- **Ethics and corporate social responsibility**: ethical trading, social sustainability (eg using small local suppliers) and environmental protection (eg purchasing of environmentally friendly supplies) – which may not always be compatible with 'right price', for example.
- **Total costs of ownership** of procured items (especially large capital items such as machinery and equipment): not just 'right price' (purchase price), but the best total value package, including costs of installation, training, maintenance and repair, upgrading, insurance and so on.

8.2   We might, in fact, add a number of further 'rights' for external procurement.

- **The right procurement (or the right need)**
  The avoidance of waste is a key principle in adding value, so it is important that procurements:
  (a) Respond to a genuine and justifiable business need – in order to avoid the procurement of items that are unnecessary, unnecessarily varied (eg if other items already in stock would be just as good) or unnecessarily expensive (eg over-specified, with more features or higher quality than is actually required)
  (b) Are effectively described or specified – in order to ensure that the items procured accurately match the business need and fulfil their intended function to the required level.

- **The right supplier (or supply chain)**
  Selection of the right supplier will be crucial in achieving all the other procurement objectives. Arguably, the 'right supplier' is one who can deliver the right quantity and quality to the right place at the right time at the right price. However, there may be other considerations in the choice of supplier, such as the supplier's:
  (a) Financial stability and strength (ensuring its ability to keep trading)
  (b) Compatibility with the buying organisation (in terms of outlook and approach, as well as systems and technology)
  (c) Credibility, track record and reliability
  (d) Potential for innovation and development, and willingness to commit to continuous improvement and relationship development
  (e) Ethical, corporate social responsibility and environmental performance (labour conditions, environmental management systems and so on), in order to minimise the risk of reputational damage as a result of the relationship.

- **The right relationship**
  As we saw in Chapter 1, different types of procurement have different priorities – and therefore may benefit from different approaches. Where the priority is 'right price', a competitive or arm's length approach to suppliers may best leverage buyer power – but where the priority is supply security, quality or innovation, the preferred approach may be to establish closer, more collaborative long-term relationships with a few high-quality, compatible suppliers.

- **The right process**
  There is a wide range of approaches to the procurement process – and an even wider range of specific procedures which may be used for particular procurement categories and exercises – depending on factors such as the nature and value of the items to be procured, the systems and policies of the buying and supplying organisation, the structure and regulation of the supply market, and the relationship between buyer and supplier. The right process will generally be one that complies with the organisation's policies and external regulations (eg on sustainable procurement or the use of competition); is appropriate to the circumstances and context (eg in regard to supplier relationships or procurement category); reflects good practice and sound procurement disciplines and ethics; and is efficient, cost-effective and value-adding.

We will explore these considerations further as we work through best practice in a generic procurement process, in Chapter 5.

Value for money

8.3   Cost reduction is not the only or even the most important function of a procurement function – however much it may sometimes seem that way! As we have seen, there is a delicate balance between 'the right price' and the other four 'rights' of purchasing, which procurement professionals must be adept in managing. The overall objective can still be stated in terms of improving the profitability of the business, but 'profit' in this sense means any benefit, and particularly long-term benefits, accruing to the organisation – such as security and continuity of supply, innovation and quality improvements gained from developing partnerships with suppliers, and so on.

8.4   Value for money is an important strategic objective, particularly in the public and non-profit sector. It may be defined, at its most basic, as 'the optimum combination of whole life cost and the quality necessary to meet the customer's requirement'.

8.5   A number of procurement techniques can be used to obtain value for money.

- The use of value analysis to eliminate non-essential features: looking critically at all the elements that make up a product or service and investigating whether they are really necessary, and whether they could be done more efficiently or cheaply
- Challenging user-generated specifications, to minimise variety, stock proliferation and over-specification (specifying unnecessary features or quality)
- Proactive sourcing: challenging the complacency of usual or 'preferred' suppliers, to ensure competitive value. (Supply contracts may contain provision for year-on-year price reductions, for example, as an incentive to efficiency improvements.)
- Consolidating demand (eg by aggregating orders or forming a consortium with other buyers) to benefit from bulk discounts and higher bargaining power
- Adopting whole life costing methodologies, rather than focusing on price
- Eliminating or reducing inventory and other non-value adding 'wastes'
- Using IT systems to make procurement processes more efficient
- International sourcing (to take advantage of low-cost country production) – although this also brings with it a number of risks and additional costs.

8.6   Obtaining value for money means not paying too much for the total package of value (quality and service) you are getting. It also, perhaps more surprisingly, means not paying too little: a very low price may reflect a supplier's desire to win your business – but it may also result in corner cutting on quality somewhere along the line, because, as they say, 'if you pay peanuts, you get monkeys'!

Sustainability

8.7   Sustainability has become an extremely important aspect of procurement policy in both the public and private sectors in recent years. The term 'sustainability' is often used interchangeably with 'corporate social responsibility' and/or environmental responsibility. More specifically, however, it describes strategies designed to:

- Balance economic viability with considerations of environmental and social responsibility (Profit, Planet and People – sometimes referred to as the 'Triple Bottom Line')
- Avoid compromising the well-being of future generations

8.8   CIPS has adopted the definition of sustainable procurement used by the UK's Sustainable Procurement Task Force (SPTF) in its influential report, *Procuring the Future*.

'[Sustainable procurement is] a process whereby organisations meet their needs for goods, services, works and utilities in a way that achieves value for money on a whole-life basis in terms of generating benefits not only to the organisation, but also to society and the economy, whilst minimising damage to the environment.'

8.9   The phrase 'on a whole life basis' is explained as implying that: 'sustainable procurement should consider the environmental, social and economic consequences of design; non-renewable material use; manufacture and production methods; logistics; service delivery; use; operation; maintenance; re-use; recycling options; disposal; and suppliers' capabilities to address these consequences throughout the supply chain.' In other words, sustainable procurement takes into account the whole lifecycle of a purchase and purchased items – and the chain or network of supply relationships.

8.10   The 'Triple Bottom Line' concept argues that businesses should measure their performance not just by profitability, but by how well they protect or further the interests of wider stakeholders, on three dimensions.

- **Economic sustainability (Profit)**: profitability, sustainable economic performance – and its beneficial effects on society (such as employment, access to goods and services, payment of taxes, community investment and so on)
- **Environmental sustainability (Planet):** sustainable environmental practices, which either benefit the natural environment or minimise harmful impacts upon it. This may include the reduction of pollution, wastes and emissions; repairing environmental damage and degradation; using renewable or recyclable materials and designs; reducing the use of non-renewable resources and energy; educating and managing supply chains to support environmental practices; and investing in 'green' projects such as renewable energy.
- **Social sustainability (People):** fair and beneficial business practices towards labour and the society in which the business operates. This may include: ethical treatment of employees; support for small and/ or local suppliers; support for diversity and equal opportunity in employment and supply chains; the development of skills; promoting public health; and 'giving back' to communities.

8.11 There is a wide range of ways in which a procurement or supply chain function can develop and contribute to sustainability.

- Developing sustainable procurement (SP) objectives and policies, which can be communicated to stakeholders throughout the supply chain
- Working with internal customers and external suppliers to develop sustainable product designs and specifications, using fewer, recyclable, energy-saving, low-carbon-emission and other 'green' inputs
- Reducing product packaging or developing recyclable packaging, to minimise waste sent to landfill
- Considering whole lifecycle costs and implications of procurements (eg for recycling or disposal of assets at the end of their useful lives)
- Developing reverse logistics (product return) capabilities to support recycling or disposal of products
- Planning transport and logistics to minimise social and environmental impacts such as traffic congestion, noise, fuel use and emissions
- Selecting sustainable suppliers and developing sustainable supply chains: eg by setting sustainability criteria for evaluating suppliers; monitoring suppliers' ethical and environmental performance; or providing assistance with the development of sustainability policies and management systems
- Sourcing from local, small and/or diverse (women-owned, minority-owned) suppliers, where consistent with good value.

Innovation

8.12 Another way in which procurement can add value is by promoting innovation. Lysons and Farrington identify three main drivers of innovation.

- A need to meet the challenges of global and domestic competition
- The challenges of rapid and complicated technological advances
- Enhancement of the value of the enterprise derived from a reputation for innovation and new market development

8.13 To innovate means firstly recognising a need in the marketplace that is currently unsatisfied, and secondly being first to react in satisfying that need ahead of competitors. Working closely with suppliers is critical to both of these aspects, which means that the role of purchasing is again vital.

Market development

8.14 Finally, procurement can add value by developing markets. This means not just the traditional marketing strategy of identifying new market segments for existing products. It also means developing suppliers so as to transform the infrastructure of a market and increase the possible offerings to customers.

Chapter summary

- 'Added value' refers to the addition of greater value or worth to a product or service, as a result of all the processes that support its production and delivery to the customer.
- The five rights of procurement are a traditional formula expressing the basic objectives of procurement: the right quantity of goods of the right quality, delivered to the right place at the right time, at the right price. In practice, there are many trade-offs.
- Buyers will try to obtain a price that is affordable and offers competitive advantage, while permitting suppliers to cover their costs and earn a sustainable profit: this involves complex price and cost analysis. Modern thinking emphasises the total costs of ownership, or total lifecycle costs, of an asset, rather than just the basic purchase price.
- Procurement has a key role in achieving quality, through effective specification, the selection of quality suppliers, and ongoing programmes for supplier monitoring, motivation and development. There are two main approaches to quality management: quality control (defect detection) and quality assurance (defect prevention).
- Determining the 'right quantity at the right time' involves consideration of many factors, including estimated demand, inventory policy and required service levels. Holding stocks incurs costs, which must be balanced against production efficiency and customer service. In managing the timing of deliveries, it is important to consider realistic total lead times.
- 'Place' considerations include the organisation of goods inwards functions; the use of distribution centres; the choice of transport mode; and packaging for transport.
- Other considerations in procurements from external suppliers include: the right need, the right supplier, the right relationship and the right process.
- Value for money is defined as the optimum combination of whole life cost and the quality necessary to meet the customer's requirement'.
- Sustainable procurement is another key objective of procurement and supply chain functions, which sets economic value considerations alongside issues of environmental and social sustainability: Profit, Planet and People.

 ## Self-test questions

Numbers in brackets refer to the paragraphs where you can check your answers.

1   Suggest three ways in which procurement can contribute to added value (2.12)

2   Give examples of trade-offs between the 'five rights' of procurement. (3.3)

3   Explain what 'right price' means to a buyer (purchase price) and supplier (selling price). (4.5, 4.6)

4   List elements included in the total costs of ownership of a capital asset, other than basic purchase price (4.16)

5   Explain the term 'fitness for purpose' in relation to quality. (5.6)

6   Distinguish between quality control and quality assurance (5.18–5.21)

7   Distinguish between 'push' and 'pull' systems of inventory control (6.13, 6.25)

8   How can a buyer help to ensure that items are delivered on time? (6.34)

9   List the key issues in inbound delivery decisions. (7.5)

10 Define (a) value for money and (b) sustainability. (8.4, 8.8)

CHAPTER 3

Procurement and Supply Chain Management

Assessment criteria and indicative content

 Compare the concepts of procurement and supply chain management

- Definitions of procurement, supply chains, supply chain management and supply chain networks
- The length of a supply chain
- Definitions of logistics and materials management
- Comparisons of supply chain management with procurement

Section headings

1 Procurement, materials management and logistics
2 Supply chains and networks
3 Structuring supply chains
4 From procurement to supply chain management

Introduction

The syllabus has already referred to 'procurement and supply chain management', and we have largely glossed over the phrase 'supply chain management' in our coverage so far.

In this chapter we extend our exploration of the role of procurement – started in Chapter 1 – to reflect the increasing integration of management activities:

(a) Across a wider range of materials-related processes: a move from 'purchasing' to 'materials management' and 'logistics'

(b) Across a wider range of relationships, reflecting the fact that multiple organisations are often linked in the chain or system that provides a flow of value towards the customer: a move from 'procurement' to 'supply chain management'.

1 Procurement, materials management and logistics

1.1 As we saw in our definition of purchasing and supply and procurement in Chapter 1, the process of obtaining inputs is increasingly considered in relation to 'supply chains': as an issue of developing and managing flows of goods and value towards an end customer – not just as a series of one-to-one transactions or contractual relationships.

1.2 Procurement specialists now commonly take responsibility for many matters which go beyond the traditional activities of buying and contact administration. In particular, a more holistic view of the supply chain has emphasised the need to break down functional boundaries and barriers, so that materials-related activities can be *integrated* within a single management framework.

1.3 Dividing responsibility for inbound flows of materials between different functions, such as purchasing, transport, stores and production has historically led to difficulties in co-ordination, and also meant that no single manager took responsibility for total materials costs. This resulted in a lack of 'big picture' and 'joined up' thinking about how materials flows could be improved or streamlined to add value.

1.4   The attempt to achieve integration, cross-functional collaboration and joined-up thinking has formed a major trend in process organisation in recent decades. There has been progressive integration of materials activities, towards a 'total integration' picture which is often given the name 'logistics': Figure 3.1.

Figure 3.1 *Integration of supply chain activities*

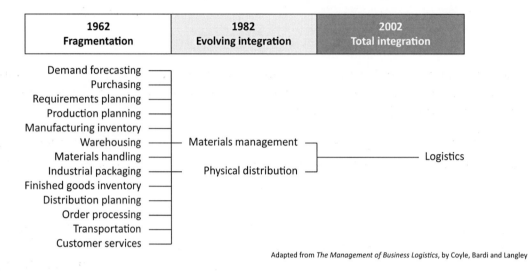

Adapted from *The Management of Business Logistics*, by Coyle, Bardi and Langley

Materials management

1.5   Materials management (MM) has been defined as 'the total of all those tasks, functions, activities and routines which concern the transfer of external materials and services into the organisation and the administration of the same until they are consumed or used in the process of production, operations or sales' (CIPS).

1.6   The CIPS definition emphasises that materials management involves activities in the *input phase* of the supply chain process: that is, the flow of goods into production, through sourcing and purchasing, inbound transport, storage of materials and delivery to their point of use.

1.7   Materials management may therefore include key activities (Zenz, *Purchasing and the Management of Materials)* such as the following.

- Materials and inventory planning: eg budgeting, product research and development, materials specifications and planning quantities to be purchased
- Procurement of the necessary materials, parts and supplies: processing requisitions; supply market research; sourcing; negotiation and contract award; the purchase to pay (P2P) cycle; contract and supplier management; and contracting for and supervising transport services for incoming items
- Storage and inventory management: stores or warehouse location and design; goods inwards (receiving and inspection) procedures; materials handling (unloading, moving, packaging and storing supplies); physical protection and control of stocks; issuing goods from stores to production; maintaining cost and inventory data; and disposing of surplus, obsolete or scrap items
- Production control: eg forward ordering of inputs; production scheduling; and quality management.

1.8   The advantages of co-ordinating materials-related activities in a single management framework can be summarised as follows.

- Costs relating to materials flows are isolated, enabling the materials manager to identify areas where costs are a concern and to take remedial action.
- Cost reductions may be achieved by eliminating wastes across the process.

- Cross-functional co-operation and co-ordination are improved by shared goals and management, emphasising a 'horizontal' flow of materials and information (rather than separate 'silos' of responsibility).
- Conflicting objectives can be reconciled, or trade-offs made, in the best interests of the process as a whole. (For example, purchasing's goal of achieving economies of scale might conflict with stores' goal of minimising inventory: a materials manager has the perspective to strive to achieve the best balance between both objectives.)
- World class manufacturing techniques – such as just in time supply or total quality management – can be introduced more easily, because of improved cross-functional integration.

Physical distribution

1.9 Physical distribution involves activities involved in the *output phase* of the supply chain process: that is, the flow of goods *from* production to the customer: storage and handling of finished outputs, and outbound transport to intermediaries, customers or consumers.

1.10 Physical distribution management (PDM) is therefore basically the method by which the outputs of production are moved from one location to another: typically, from a supplier to a customer. This involves the traditional combining of:

- Warehousing and storage
- Transport or distribution planning: optimising freight loads, transport routes and delivery schedules for cost-efficient (and environmentally sustainable) delivery
- Materials handling (eg moving, loading, packaging or containerising for outbound transport)
- Inventory management and control: keeping track of finished items in stock
- Transportation and delivery.

1.11 The basic objective of physical distribution is to deliver the right goods to the right place at the right time and at the right cost. (We discussed some of these aspects briefly in Chapter 2, as part of the 'place' element of the 'five rights'.)

1.12 Physical distribution can be local, national or international: even 'global' or worldwide – which presents particular challenges of transport planning and risk management.

Logistics

1.13 The concept of logistics management takes integration a step further, by integrating responsibilities for both the *input phase and the output phase:* the flow of materials inwards to the production process *and* the flow of finished goods outwards to the customer.

1.14 Logistics management has been defined as: 'the process of planning, implementing and controlling the efficient, effective flow and storage of raw materials, in-process inventory, finished goods, services, and related information from point of origin to point of consumption… for the purpose of conforming to customer requirements' (Council of Logistics Management Professionals, USA, cited by Coyle, Bardi and Langley, *The Management of Business Logistics*).

1.15 In other words, logistics potentially embraces the full range of supply chain activity, with an emphasis on the effective and efficient satisfaction of end-customer requirements.

Figure 3.2 *Logistics management = materials management + physical distribution management*

Procurement (purchasing or acquisition)	Materials management	LOGISTICS MANAGEMENT
Inbound transport and storage of materials, inventory management (flow of inputs to production)		
Production management and control: forward ordering of materials; preparing schedules; quality management, and so on		
Storage of finished goods, inventory management and outbound transport (flow of finished goods to the customer)	Physical distribution management	

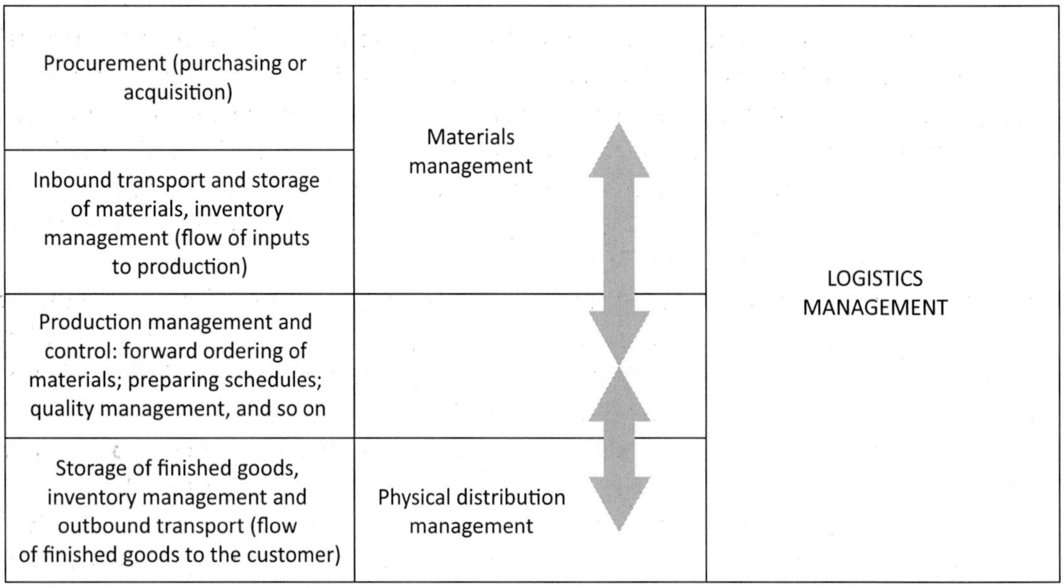

1.16 Some key advantages of integrating upstream and downstream materials handling activities into a logistics framework have been identified by Sharman (summarised by van Weele, *Purchasing Management: Analysis, Planning and Practice*).

- Shorter product lifecycles, with fast-changing consumer demand and technology. Companies seek to maintain their competitive advantage by constant product updating and innovation, putting pressure on efficient materials and information flows to support swift idea-to-market cycles *and* to avoid wasteful stocks of obsolete products.
- Globalisation: global sourcing, manufacturing and marketing, increasing the pressures on logistics to manage risk and overcome the challenges of distance.
- The development of information and communication technology (ICT), which supports integrated logistics planning and control capabilities.

1.17 A word of warning: Emmett *(Supply Chain in 90 Minutes)* notes that the terminology in this area can be loose and inconsistent. The term 'logistics', originally coined to encompass a range of activities across the whole supply chain, has come to be used simply as a new (more prestigious) name for 'transport', 'warehousing/stores' or 'distribution': freight transport companies (and their vehicles) are frequently rebadged as 'logistics', for example.

Increasing supply chain integration

1.18 Many writers have surveyed the development or evolution of the procurement function, and several of them have identified **supply chain integration** as the key dimension of change. For example, Syson *(Improving Purchase Performance)* charts 'the changing focus of purchasing as it evolves from a purely clerical routine activity to a commercial stage in which the emphasis is on cost savings and finally a proactive strategic function concerned with materials or logistics management'.

- **Clerical (transactional):** purchasing is perceived as a low-ranking routine function, characterised by a focus on internal performance and efficiency.
- **Commercial:** the focus shifts to price/cost savings, obtained mainly through the interface with suppliers. This stage is characterised by adversarial relationships with suppliers and the exploitation of short-term tactical advantages.
- **Strategic (proactive):** the focus is on effective contribution to competitive advantage. Strategies are introduced to improve the performance of external supply chains, through a more holistic approach to logistics or supply chain management.

1.19   Baily *et al* (among others) similarly chart increasing integration, specifically through information systems development.

- **Independence:** procurement operates within its own guidelines, with a focus on functional efficiencies and improvements. Standalone information systems are used for operational decision-making and data processing. A similar internal focus would apply in the production and distribution functions.
- **Dependence:** procurement dovetails with other functions via consultation and reporting, but still uses a standalone information system. Once the firm gets diminishing returns from functional efficiencies (or recognises the sub-optimality of such an approach) it is likely to take a more process-focused view of the 'end-to-end' materials flows within the organisation.
- **Business integration:** procurement systematically integrates with other functions in the internal supply chain. Integrated information systems are to support tactical decision-making, with a focus on efficient materials/information flows. This offers significant potential for improved internal co-ordination, supporting systems such as MRP or ERP.
- **Chain integration:** procurement has a key role in securing systematic co-operation and information sharing across the supply chain (an 'end-to-end' process now extending beyond organisational boundaries). Integrated information systems are used to support strategic decisions, with a focus on customer service and management information. This offers significant potential for improved internal *and* external co-ordination, supporting systems such as just in time supply and total quality management.

1.20   Integration can have significant benefits in terms of: cost reduction through eliminating waste at all stages of the process; more systematic planning, co-ordination and control; greater supply chain flexibility and responsiveness to customer demands (including fast, low-volume deliveries); the reconciling of conflicting sub-unit objectives; and support for world class manufacturing philosophies such as JIT and TQM.

1.21   The concept of supply chains – and closer 'links' between buyers and suppliers – is another important aspect of integration. As logistics management places a range of materials-handling activities within a single management framework, so the concept of 'supply chain management' sees all the 'players' in the flow of value towards the customer as an integrated value-adding and competitive system.

2   Supply chains and networks

What is a supply chain?

2.1   As we saw in Chapter 1, 'supply' may be defined simply as the act (or process) of providing something or making something available, often in response to buyers' or customers' requirements. It involves the transfer or flow of goods, services and information from one party to another.

2.2   The concept of the 'supply chain' can therefore be defined as follows.

- 'The supply chain encompasses all organisations and activities associated with the flow and transformation of goods from the raw materials stage, through to the end user, as well as the associated information flows. Material and information flows both up and down the supply chain.' (Handfield & Nichols, *Supply Chain Redesign*)
- 'The supply chain includes all those involved in organising and converting materials through the input stages (raw materials), conversion phase (work in progress) and outputs (finished products). The cycle is often repeated several times in the journey from the individual producer to the ultimate customer, as one organisation's finished good is another's input.' (Baily *et al*)
- A supply chain is 'that network of organisations that are involved, through upstream and downstream linkages, in the different processes and activities that produce value in the form of products and services in the hands of the ultimate customer.' (Christopher, *Logistics & Supply Chain Management*)

2.3   The two-way nature of the flows (highlighted by Handfield and Nichols) should be emphasised. Products, services or order fulfilments flow forward through the chain, while information (demand forecasts, order transmissions, delivery status reports, customer feedback) and payments flow back. Increasingly, there is also a flow of products from customers back to suppliers for refund, servicing, recycling and disposal: a process known as reverse logistics – or a 'closed loop' supply chain. *Baily et al* depict the principal flows (minus reverse logistics) in a very simple supply chain as follows: Figure 3.3.

Figure 3.3 *Principal flows in a simple supply chain*

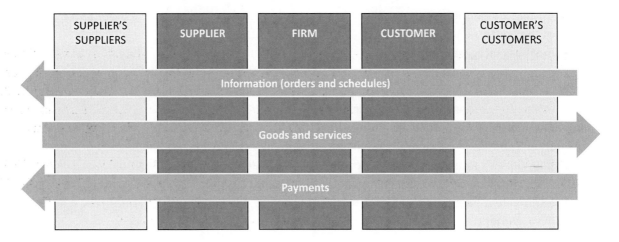

2.4   We can think of the basic 'stream' as flowing from a first supplier (perhaps a raw material extractor) to a final consumer, so in relation to the firm we are focusing on (the 'focal firm'):

- Suppliers (the firms from which it *buys* the *inputs* to its activities) are said to be **upstream**; and
- Customers (the firms or individuals to whom it *sells* the *outputs* of its activities) are said to be **downstream**.

2.5   A supply chain may be very short. As an example, you may have driven past a farm and noticed a sign advertising fresh eggs for sale: the farmer is producing the goods and selling direct to his customers with no intermediaries. In other cases, the supply chain may be very long. For example, if you purchase a washing machine from a department store there will clearly have been many organisations involved in the process (or flow of value) leading to your purchase: to analyse the supply chain you would have to go right back to the extraction of a metallic ore forming the main material of the washing machine.

Dyadic supply relationships

2.6   Commercial relationships – like interpersonal relationships – require at least two parties who are in contact with each other. If we focus on only two parties (for example, a single supplier and one of its customers, or a single buyer and one of its suppliers), the relationship will be a 'one to one' or 'two-party' (sometimes called 'dyadic') relationship: Figure 3.4.

Figure 3.4 *Dyadic supply relationships*

2.7   This used to be the main way in which supply chains were viewed, focusing on how the firm could secure and exploit the technical contribution of its immediate upstream suppliers, and what it could offer its immediate downstream customers.

2.8   The management of a firm's immediate upstream and downstream relationships is still important, as reflected in approaches such as supplier relationship management (SRM) and customer relationship management (CRM). Much of the effort of a procurement function or supply chain function is devoted to supplier selection, development, performance management and relationship management (particularly vital where services or operations have been outsourced); and the development of strategic relationships (such as partnerships and alliances) with selected suppliers.

2.9 Many of the procurement policies and practices discussed in this Course Book are relevant to dyadic supplier relationships: contacts and transactions with particular suppliers.

Inter-business supply chains

2.10 However, these kinds of focused buyer-supplier exchanges usually happen within the context of a lengthier supply process: an extractor or producer of raw materials supplies to a processing plant or producer of components, which supplies to a manufacturing or assembly organisation, which supplies to a distributor or retail outlet, which supplies to the consumer. It is this total configuration which is often called a chain, or channel. An **inter-business supply chain** is a linked sequence of contributors in different firms.

2.11 Part or all of an inter-business supply chain may in fact be brought within the control of a single holding company. Large oil companies, for example, typically have control over all the main stages of exploration, production, refining and retailing. In most cases, however, supply chains are controlled through supply contracts and collaborative relationships between separate, autonomous entities.

2.12 The chain metaphor highlights several useful characteristics of the supply process and relationships.

- It emphasises 'serial co-operation' (Jespersen & Skjott-Larsen) or 'working together in turn': each player contributes value at its stage of the sequence of activities.
- It emphasises mutual dependency and collaboration, because each link in a chain is essential to the completeness and strength of the whole: weak links and breakages (eg an underperforming or failing supplier or distributor) may disrupt the flow of supply.
- It emphasises the importance of 'linkages' or interfaces between members. This is a useful understanding when looking at the (internal) value chain and wider value system: we saw that, according to Porter, value is added not just by each element in the chain, but by the quality of the relationships between them.
- It is continuous (any given link in the chain can be regarded as the 'focal' firm for the purposes of analysis, with activities upstream and downstream of it) and non-directional (allowing conceptualisation of flows both 'forwards' and 'backwards' along the chain).

2.13 This has some clear implications for procurement roles and operations, because it emphasises the need to:

- Co-ordinate activities across the supply chain, in order to maximise the efficient flow of value towards the customer
- Develop appropriate relationships with suppliers, in order to ensure that linkages are maintained
- Structure supply chains effectively, in order to maintain control over their activities (to minimise the risk of supply disruption or reputational damage), while minimising the effort and cost of doing so (eg by dealing primarily with an immediate or 'first-tier' supplier with control over its own supply chain)
- Select, evaluate and develop suppliers in relation to the effectiveness of their *own* supply chain management
- Work collaboratively with supply chain members, to secure added value, cost and quality improvements throughout the supply chain as a whole – to the benefit of all its members.

Internal supply chains

2.14 It is also important for procurement professionals to realise that the supply chain concept can be applied *within* organisations – as well as *between* them.

2.15 The internal supply chain (or value chain) describes a similar flow of information and other resources *within* – into and through – a given organisation: from inbound activities (procuring and receiving inputs), to conversion activities (transforming inputs into outputs) to outbound activities (moving outputs onward to customers). Consider the sequential flow of materials, information and eventually finished goods from purchasing to goods inwards, inspection, storage, production, inspection (finished goods), storage (finished goods) and transport/ distribution. We might map the principal flows in an internal supply chain as follows: Figure 3.5.

Figure 3.5 *Principal flows in a (simplified) internal supply chain*

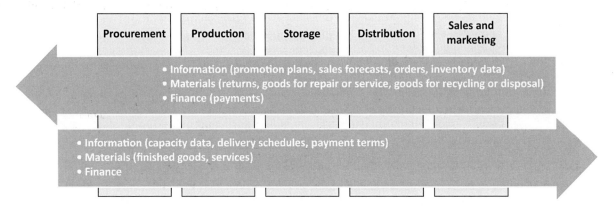

2.16 Seeing internal processes and relationships as a kind of supply chain therefore highlights the extent to which each function in an organisation acts as a link in the chain which delivers value to end customers. This is an important idea for the **internal customer concept**, which suggests that any unit of a firm whose task contributes to the task of other units can be regarded as a supplier of goods and services to those units. In order to fulfil its objectives, the supplying unit will need to anticipate and satisfy the requirements of these internal customers – just as a supplying firm will seek to do for its external customers.

2.17 For example, a road haulage company might have operational units for maintenance and servicing of vehicles, loading and driving. The procurement department is an internal supplier of tools, machine oil and overalls (among other things) to the mechanics, who are in turn suppliers of repair and maintenance services to the vehicle drivers – who are suppliers of the finished products to the company's external customers.

2.18 The procurement function is part of the internal supply chain: it is served by internal suppliers (for example, the finance function which provides budgetary reports and finance allocations, and the technical department which provides specifications and requisitions) and in turn serves internal customers (the various other functions on whose behalf it procures supplies, or to whom it gives advice).

2.19 Effective procurement will therefore make extensive use of cross-functional project teams, quality circles, and other mechanisms (such as integrated materials requirements planning and enterprise resource planning systems) which facilitate information sharing and collaboration with internal customers in other functions. Such a 'customer-focused' approach may have beneficial effects in:

- Integrating the objectives of units and functions throughout the value chain – and making each unit look at what added value it is able to offer.
- Encouraging procurement staff to be proactive in planning procurements (rather than responding reactively to requisitions from customer functions as they arise), enhancing the potential to add value
- Reducing resistance to procurement involvement in strategic issues and processes. Users are often alienated by the perception that procurement is solely concerned with cost cutting and low price, while ignoring other objectives legitimately pursued by user functions (such as quality and delivery).
- Enhancing procurement's role and status in the organisation, as it is able to demonstrate a strategic awareness of business processes and customer needs.

Supply chain networks

2.20   Even a tiered supply chain model (which we will examine in the next section of this chapter) offers a simplified picture. In reality, each organisation in the supply chain has multiple other relationships with its own customers, suppliers, industry contacts, partners and advisers – and even competitors (in trade associations or industry think tanks, say) – any and all of whom may also be connected with each other! Many writers (such as Cox & Lamming, and Christopher) now argue, therefore, that a more appropriate metaphor for the supply process is not a chain, but a network or web – which allows a more complex set of interrelated relationships and transactions to be depicted. Even the simplest set of relationships might look something like the following: Figure 3.6.

Figure 3.6 *A simple supply network!*

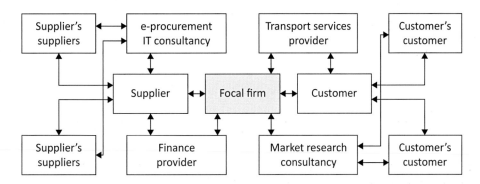

2.21   A typical retail supply chain – at its most simplified – is also more of a network, as can be seen from the following: Figure 3.7.

Figure 3.7 *A retail supply network*

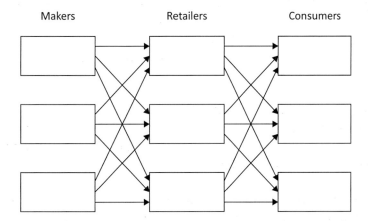

2.22   Seeing the supply chain as a network is helpful for a number of reasons.

- It is a more strategic model for mapping and analysing supply chain relationships, and therefore for seeking to exploit synergies and improve performance in innovative ways.
- It raises the possibility of a wider range of collaborations (eg supplier associations, buying consortia or strategic alliances) which may offer mutual advantages – and perhaps alter the balance of power in supply relationships.
- It recognises the potential of 'extended enterprises' and virtual organisations: extending the strategic capability of the firm through the collective resources and performance of network contributors.
- It recognises that extended enterprises may overlap (with particular suppliers or customers in common), creating complex patterns of relationship, competition and potential risk (eg to information and intellectual property).

3   Structuring supply chains

Tiered supply chain structures

3.1   Suppose that a manufacturer wishes to maximise its own part in the value adding process by taking in only a minimum contribution from outside suppliers. For example, the manufacturer buys in parts from a number of suppliers, and assembles them through a number of stages to produce a finished product. The structure of the supply chain in such a case is as illustrated in Figure 3.8.

Figure 3.8 *All manufacturing performed by top-level purchaser*

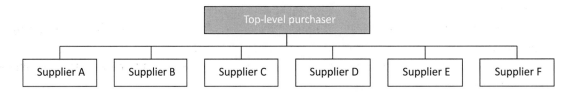

3.2   By contrast, suppose that the manufacturer sees strategic advantage in outsourcing all activities other than the final stages of production. In that case, its direct procurement relationship may be (in simplified terms) with a single supplier or tier of suppliers. Each supplier in the first tier would have an extensive role to fulfil in the manufacture of the final product, making use of 'second-tier' suppliers: Figure 3.9.

Figure 3.9 *Top-level purchaser outsources most manufacturing*

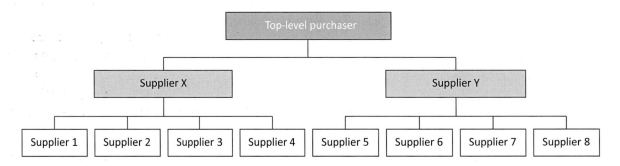

3.3   An organisation might adopt a deliberate policy of tiering its suppliers, so as to reduce the number of first-tier suppliers: the 'vendor/supplier base' with which it has to deal directly. This may be part of a process of supplier rationalisation or supply chain re-structuring, for example. The organisation deals directly only with its first-tier suppliers: second-tier suppliers deal with a first-tier supplier.

3.4   For example, in a manufacturing operation such as an automobile manufacturer, the top-level purchaser is the 'original equipment manufacturer' (OEM) or assembler. It might have 180 different suppliers with which it deals directly. In order to rationalise its commercial relationships, it might reduce its vendor base to, say, 20 first-tier suppliers (specialist manufacturers of subassemblies). These in turn will organise and manage a second tier of suppliers (component manufacturers, metal finishers and so on) from which they can source required items on the OEM's behalf.

3.5   The relationship between an organisation and its first-tier suppliers will obviously be critically important. First-tier suppliers are often expected to collaborate with the top-level purchaser to add value (making improvements and eliminating wastes) throughout the supply chain, and to pursue innovation in products and processes. With only a small number of first-tier supplier relationships, the top-level purchaser can focus on developing these as long-term, collaborative supply partnerships.

3.6 The impact of supply chain tiering on procurement roles and responsibilities in the top-level purchasing organisation or OEM may include the following.

- There are fewer commercial relationships to manage, so the function can direct its attention to managing, developing and improving these key relationships. Indeed, this is essential, since extensive responsibility has been delegated to the first-tier suppliers.
- In order to minimise business and reputational risk, procurement staff will still need to 'drill down' through the tiers in the supply chain, monitoring policies, systems and performance to ensure that the supply chain is being well managed.
- Procurement may be freed up to pursue a more strategic focus and contribution (such as sustainable procurement or supplier relationship development) with fewer operational tasks and transactions to handle.
- More and better supply chain improvements and innovations may be available from sharing information and collaborating with expert first-tier suppliers.
- First-tier suppliers may have the expertise, technology and resources to be able to co-ordinate supply chain activities more efficiently.

Closed loop supply chains (reverse logistics)

3.7 A number of EU directives have been introduced in the area of environmental responsibility, shifting the responsibility for disposal and recycling of end products to producers and importers. These developments have given rise to:

- The **closed-loop supply chain**, where the end-users effectively become suppliers of goods (once past their useful life) *back* to the manufacturer – making what was previously the 'end' of the supply chain part of a new cycle.
- Increased emphasis on **reverse logistics**: 'the process of planning, implementing and controlling the efficient, cost-effective flow of raw materials, in-process inventory, finished goods and related information from the point of consumption to the point of origin, for the purpose of recapturing value or proper disposal.' (Rogers and Tibben-Lembke, *Reverse Logistics Glossary*). Arrangements must be made for the gathering or return, recycling and 'cannibalising' (use of salvageable or reusable parts and materials) of goods.

3.8 Lysons and Farrington note that the two principal drivers of interest in reverse logistics have been the increased importance attached to the environmental aspects of waste disposal and a recognition of the potential returns that can be obtained from the reuse of products, or parts or the recycling of materials. In addition, there may be a reverse flow due to product recalls or returns, and the offering of repair and maintenance services.

3.9 Here are some management issues in closed-loop supply chains.

- Effective supply base management, integration and collaboration
- Effective supplier and customer relationships
- Supplier selection and contract award on the basis of recycling or ecologically friendly disposal capacity (among other green issues)
- Product and packaging design to facilitate return, recycling and safe disposal
- Visibility: the ability to access and view relevant logistics data, in order to manage the operation effectively
- Reverse logistical activities, including: collection of returnable items; inspection and sorting of returned items; and the implementation of options such as repair or reconditioning, upgrading, parts reclamation, recycling, disposal or on-sale.

Supplier base optimisation

3.10   The 'supplier base' is all the vendors that supply a given purchaser. Supplier bases are often described in terms of their size or range (broad, narrow, single-sourced); location (local, national, international or global); and characteristics (eg diversified or specialised).

3.11   One of the ways positive supplier relationships can be leveraged is by 'broadening supply'. The organisation can manage supply risk by having *more* potential suppliers of a given item or category of purchases, pre-qualified and approved as being able to meet its requirements. If there are supply shortages or disruptions (eg because of political unrest or bad weather in one supplier's area), or unforeseen peaks in demand (creating a need for extra supply), or a supplier failure, the organisation has established relationships with 'back-up' suppliers.

3.12   Another advantage of broadening the supply base is that as circumstances change – for both buyer and supplier – suppliers may become more or less compatible with the buying organisation, and more or less competitive in terms of their offering. Increasing the range of potential suppliers enables the buyer to be more opportunistic: taking advantage of the best available price, trading terms, quality, innovation and flexibility on offer.

3.13   More commonly, however, strong collaborative supplier relationships are used to 'narrow supply', enabling purchases to be concentrated on a smaller group of developed and trusted supply partners. *Supplier base rationalisation* (or optimisation) is concerned with determining roughly how many suppliers the buying firm wants to do business with. This enables the firm to:

- Control procurement costs: a large supplier base usually means more small orders and higher transaction and administration costs, while giving larger orders to fewer suppliers secures volume discounts and other savings (eg through systems integration with key suppliers)
- Exploit the added-value potential of concentrating on more collaborative relationships with fewer suppliers (eg continuous improvement, co-investment)
- Avoid waste, by eliminating suppliers who cannot (or can no longer) meet the firm's requirements, or are otherwise not often used
- Maintain the security of supply by ensuring that there are *enough* approved suppliers to cover supplier failure, shortages or other supply risks.

3.14   'The aim of supplier base optimisation is to leverage the buying power of an organisation with the smallest number of suppliers consistent with security of supplies and the need for high-quality goods and services at competitive prices.' (Lysons & Farrington)

3.15   In order to develop this opportunity, existing suppliers will be evaluated on performance, cost, service, quality, volume of business and potential/compatibility for closer relationship. An approved or preferred supplier list will usually be drawn up, weeding out unnecessary suppliers. For some purchases, a sole supplier may be selected for the development of closer partnership relations (with back-up suppliers, if required).

3.16   From our emphasis on security of supply, you might be able to infer the possible downside risk of reducing the supplier base. A very narrow supplier base opens the buyer to the risks of over-dependence on a single supplier, in the event of supplier failure (eg financial collapse or reputational damage); supply disruption (eg due to strikes, technology breakdown or natural disaster affecting the supplier or *its* suppliers) or the loss of the supplier's goodwill and co-operation. The buyer may also miss out on seeking or utilising new or more competitive suppliers in the wider supply market. There is also – as with any partnership – the risk that the established suppliers may grow complacent and cease to be competitive.

Value-adding supply chain strategies

3.17 Baily *et al* argue that 'It is desirable that developing good practices and concepts are implemented throughout the supply chain, by migrating these ideas both upstream and downstream. This will require inter-organisation co-operation, and may involve such factors as: cross-functional teams, recognition of the need to delight both internal and external customers; more flexible management structures; and effective partnerships. Such developments will reduce costs and add value *throughout the supply chain.'*

3.18 Here are some of the innovative value-adding strategies that have emerged as a result of supply-chain thinking.

- **Value engineering:** analysing the value (and added value potential) of products at the design and development stage, often using cross-functional teams and the early involvement of external suppliers
- **Lean supply:** collaborating closely with the supply chain to eliminate or minimise wastes (non-value-adding elements) in all activities and processes. Wastes include: waiting time; excess inventory; unnecessary operations and movements; unnecessary costs and so on.
- **Agile supply:** collaborating closely with the supply chain to increase its speed and flexibility of response to changing customer demands, with shorter idea-to-market cycles, delivery lead times and so on (if necessary, by holding some stock of work in progress, to support responsive processes such as late customisation or assembly-to-order)
- **Value-adding negotiations and relationships:** working collaboratively and constructively with suppliers to find ways of continuously improving and adding value, with mutual benefit to all parties. (This forms a contrast to traditional adversarial or 'competitive' approaches, in which each party sought to maximise its own share of value from a transaction or relationship – eg by 'winning' on price negotiation – at the expense of the other.)

4 From procurement to supply chain management

Supplier management

4.1 Lysons and Farrington define supplier management as follows.

'That aspect of purchasing or procurement which is concerned with rationalising the supplier base and selecting, co-ordinating, appraising the performance of and developing the potential of suppliers, and where appropriate, building long-term collaborative relationships'.

4.2 They argue that this is a more strategic and cross-functional activity than 'purchasing', which is focused on transactional and commercial activities: Table 3.1. Purchasing and supplier management are both activities within the umbrella function of 'procurement': obtaining required supplies or services by any means.

Table 3.1 *Purchasing and supplier management*

PROCUREMENT	
Purchasing activity	**Supplier management activity**
Focus on non-critical (low profit, low risk) items	Focus on critical/strategic items
Ordering or calling off purchases	Sourcing and appraising suppliers
Order expediting	Rationalising the supplier base
Maintaining inventory	Developing supplier potential
Receipt and storage of supplies	Early supplier involvement
Arranging payment	Negotiation
	Supplier relationships
	Monitoring supplier performance
	Ethical and environmental issues

4.3   The focus on the firm's suppliers and supplier relationships also distinguishes 'supplier management' from related concepts such as:

- **Supply management**, which focuses on management of the operational aspects of the supply process and purchasing cycle: ensuring that supplies flow efficiently into and through the organisation, and fulfilling the 'five rights of purchasing' (getting the right supplies of the right quality to the right place at the right time and at the right price)
- **Contract management**, which focuses on management of supplier performance through securing compliance with agreed contract terms. (This is one aspect of supplier management, and will be discussed in Chapter 5.)
- **Supply chain management**, which focuses on processes and relationships across the whole supply chain, from first supplier to ultimate consumer.

4.4   Van Weele & Rozemeijer *(Revolution in Purchasing)* identify a key trend in the development of supplier management towards supply chain management: 'involving supply partners in different business processes, instead of simply buying goods and services from them as efficiently and effectively as possible'.

What is supply chain management?

4.5   In the procurement literature, the term 'supply chain management' is often used both:

- In a specific and technical sense, to refer to a particular, modern strategic approach to supply network relationships and management (supply chain management or SCM)
- In a more loose and general sense, to refer to the role of a procurement function in managing not just transactions, but suppliers and supply chain activity. (This is the sense in which it may be given the name 'supply chain function' instead of 'procurement function'.)

4.6   In the technical sense, the term supply chain management (or SCM) has been given to a particular strategic approach which recognises the interdependent nature of supply issues, and what Saunders *(Strategic Purchasing and Supply Chain Management)* calls 'the systemic nature of supply activities, as captured by such phrases as "supply chains", "value systems", "networks" and "extended enterprises".'

4.7   Supply chain management has been defined in various ways.

- 'The management of upstream and downstream relationships with suppliers and customers to deliver superior customer value at less cost to the supply chain as a whole' (Christopher)
- 'The integration and management of supply chain organisations and activities through co-operative organisational relationships, effective business processes, and high levels of information sharing to create high-performing value systems that provide member organisations a sustainable competitive advantage' (Handfield & Nichols)
- 'The management of relations and integrated business processes across the supply chain... Use of the SCM concept entails that the links in the supply chain plan and co-ordinate their processes and relationships by weighing the overall efficiency and competitive power of the supply chain'. (Jespersen & Skjøtt-Larsen, *Supply Chain Management in Theory & Practice*)

4.8   In other words, where supplier management looks mainly at the relationship between the buying firm and its own immediate suppliers, and procurement focuses on the processes required to obtain goods and services from an immediate supplier, supply chain management looks at all the interactions and linkages between all the organisations that make up the supply chain.

4.9   SCM consists primarily of building collaborative relationships across the supply chain, so that the whole chain works together to add value for the end customer in a profitable way. Christopher *(Logistics and Supply Chain Management)* argues that, these days:

'The real competitive struggle is not between individual companies, but between their supply chains or networks... What makes a supply chain or network unique is the way the *relationships and interfaces in the chain or network are managed.* In this sense, a major source of differentiation comes from *the quality of relationships that one business enjoys, compared to its competitors.'*

4.10 'Business processes' is another key focus of SCM. It implies the planning and management of whole sequences of activity (what Emmett calls 'buying, making, moving and selling') that provide products, services and information from original suppliers to end users: examples include order processing, customer service, supply, distribution and product development. Processes are essentially horizontal, cutting across functional and organisational boundaries.

4.11 The third key feature is therefore 'integration': co-ordination across functional lines and organisational boundaries. Jespersen and Skjøtt-Larsen note that co-ordination may be organisational (eg cross-organisational teams and interfaces); systems related (eg integrated information systems); or planning related (eg exchange of data on inventory status, sales forecasts or production plans).

Drivers for supply chain management

4.12 Andrea Reynolds *(Strategic Supply Chain Management)* suggests a number of other pressures in the modern business environment, which act as 'drivers' for SCM.

- Cost pressures (the need to reduce inventory and other wastes)
- Time pressures (the need for faster, more customised deliveries)
- Reliability pressures (the need to ensure that quality/delivery commitments to increasingly demanding customers can be met)
- Response pressures (the need to provide real-time information to increasingly demanding customers)
- Transparency pressures (the need to make the status of orders visible, to support planning)
- Globalisation pressure (the need to co-ordinate multiple, complex global supply networks)

Potential benefits of an SCM approach

4.13 The benefits of an SCM approach include the following.

- Reduced costs, by eliminating waste activities and implementing cost reduction programmes throughout the supply chain. ('Often there are many activities that do not create value involved in trade between two companies. Jointly locating and eliminating these activities, as well as developing co-operative goals and guidelines for the future, can focus resources on real improvements and development possibilities': Jespersen & Skjøtt-Larsen)
- Improved responsiveness to customers' requirements (by emphasising the continuous flow of value towards the customer) – hopefully resulting in greater customer loyalty and sales revenue
- Access to complementary resources and capabilities (eg joint investment in research and development, technology-sharing, ideas-sharing and so on)
- Enhanced product and service quality (eg through collaborative quality management, continuous improvement programmes and enhanced supplier motivation and commitment)
- Improving supply chain communication (through increased information sharing and integration of systems), which in turn offers benefits for more efficient planning and co-ordination, reduced inventory, and potential for innovation and flexibility.
- Sharing demand forecasting and planning information enables suppliers to produce only what is required, when it is required, reducing inventory – an approach which you may recognise as just in time supply.
- Faster lead times for product development and delivery also mean that new and modified products can be offered in response to changing customer demand – an approach which is sometimes named 'agile' supply.
- Better communication allows greater transparency. Information on costings, performance, and the status of individual orders and stock movements is available quickly or in real time: building trust, and enabling all parties to plan ahead and to manage contingencies as they emerge.

4.14 However, it is important (in exams, as in real life) to be realistic about the benefits claimed for SCM – and to analyse whether a radical, strategic SCM approach is relevant, possible or beneficial for a particular organisation. It is not for everyone!

- It requires considerable investment, internal support and supplier/client willingness – any or all of which may be absent.
- It also involves focusing on closer relationships with a smaller number of suppliers and clients, and this may be risky: if the relationships don't work out, for example – or if the firm becomes dependent on a supplier which later has problems, or becomes complacent, or no longer produces what the firm needs.
- Network information-sharing may expose the firm to loss of control over commercial, informational, intellectual assets and distinctive competencies, opening it to imitation and competition (perhaps even from within the extended network).
- There may be problems in fairly distributing the gains and risks of co-operation among supply chain partners.

4.15 Jespersen and Skjøtt-Larsen suggest that a company needs careful internal analysis and discussion of what it is seeking to achieve, clarifying its motivation in focusing on supply chain efficiency. If a firm has not first co-ordinated its own internal processes, and made them efficient, it will generally not be prepared to co-operate more closely with other supply chain participants, nor to define clear areas for improvement – and the potential advantages of SCM will not accrue.

4.16 Please note, however, that whether or not a firm pursues a radical strategic SCM approach, *supplier management* and *management of the supply chain* (in a more general sense) will still be required!

Developing supply chain management

4.17 SCM consists primarily of collaborative, integrative relationships across the supply chain, which may take the form of:

- Product/process information exchange (eg joint demand forecasting or the sharing of costing information)
- Operational linkages (eg e-procurement links and just in time arrangements)
- Co-operative definition of norms and expectations (eg through trust-building and collaborative strategic planning exercises); and
- Relationship-specific adaptations (eg joint projects and investments).

Comparing procurement and supply chain management

4.18 The essence of the distinction between 'supply chain management' (or SCM) and 'procurement' is that SCM is based on prioritising the recognition that an organisation is just one link in a chain of suppliers and customers. Along the whole chain the objective is to increase value and reduce waste, but this will not be done most effectively if buyers concentrate only on the organisation they happen to work for, or on the dyadic (one-to-one) relationship between the buyer and a first-tier supplier: they need to adopt a wider perspective.

4.19 Emmett *(Supply Chain in 90 Minutes)* summarises the difference between the 'traditional ways' (which may be equated with traditional purchasing and procurement disciplines) and the 'new ways' (which embody supply chain management thinking): see Table 3.2.

Table 3.2 *Traditional vs new views of SCM*

TRADITIONAL WAYS	NEW WAYS
Key feature: Independence	Key feature: Integration
Independent of next link	Dependency
Links are protective	End-to-end visibility
Uncertainty	More certainty
Unresponsive to change	Quicker response
High cost, low service	High service, lower cost
Fragmented internally	'Joined up' structures
'Blame' (adversarial) culture	'Gain' (collaborative value-adding) culture
Competing companies	Competing supply chains

4.20   This does not imply any sacrifice of the procurement function's objectives. Rather, it recognises that the best way of achieving procurement objectives may be to co-operate strategically with other organisations, both upstream and downstream. This way of thinking has led some commentators to coin the phrase 'extended enterprise', meaning that buyers look beyond the boundaries of their own organisation to achieve mutual benefit and collaborative competitive advantage.

4.21   One major implication of supply chain management is that the procurement (or supply chain) function must establish effective relationships with suppliers. As we saw in Chapter 1, the nature of an effective supplier relationship will vary with circumstances, and on the relative importance to the buying organisation of the supplier's product or service. However, where procurement may be 'transactional' (focused on securing value from procurements on a case by case basis), supply chain management is by definition 'relational' (focused on securing value from supply chain relationships and collaboration over time).

Chapter summary

- In recent decades, procurement specialists have taken responsibility for a widening spectrum of activities, including many aspects of materials management and physical distribution. Increasing supply chain integration has caused procurement to become a more strategic, less clerical, function.
- The concept of a supply chain means that a buyer's responsibility extends the boundaries of his own organisation. (Though it is also valuable to understand the concept of an internal supply chain.)
- In many cases, an organisation may reduce the number of suppliers it deals with directly by 'tiering' its supply chain.
- The supply chain management concept implies that purchasers are concerned with all the linkages between all the organisations in the supply chain.

Self-test questions

Numbers in brackets refer to the paragraphs where you can check your answers.

1   List advantages of co-ordinating materials-related activities. (1.8)

2   List the stages of supply chain integration identified by (a) Syson and (b) Baily *et al.* (1.18, 1.19)

3   Give a definition of 'supply chain'. (2.2)

4   What are the implications of the supply chain concept for procurement roles and operations? (2.13)

5   Why is it helpful to view the supply chain as a network? (2.22)

6   Sketch a tiered supply chain structure for a manufacturer who wishes to outsource as much as possible. (Figure 3.9)

7   In relation to the procurement staff within an OEM, what are the implications of supply chain tiering? (3.6)

8   What is meant by 'supplier base optimisation'? (3.13)

9   Give a definition of 'supply chain management'. (4.7)

10   List potential benefits of a supply chain management approach. (4.13)

CHAPTER 4

Stakeholders of a Procurement or Supply Chain Function

Assessment criteria and indicative content

1.4 Differentiate the stakeholders that a procurement or supply chain function may have

- Defining stakeholders
- Examples of stakeholders for a procurement or supply chain function
- Mapping stakeholders for a procurement or supply chain function

Section headings

1. Introduction to stakeholders
2. Stakeholders of a procurement or supply chain function
3. Corporate social responsibility (CSR)
4. Stakeholder management

Introduction

In Chapter 3, we noted that there are internal *and* external supply, or value, chains and networks – and we recognised that a procurement and supply chain function forms important relationships with internal customers as well as external suppliers.

In this chapter we explore in more depth the roles, requirements and influence of a range of participants or 'stakeholders' in supply chain processes.

Stakeholders are, simply, groups which have an interest or 'stake' in something. Stakeholders are important to organisations – and supply chains – for a number of reasons. They may have direct or indirect influence on decisions, or the implementation of plans – whether as participants, or resource providers, or influential voices. They are an integral part of the environment within which the organisation – and procurement function – must operate, and with which they must 'get along'.

We start by defining and categorising the stakeholders of a procurement or supply chain function, and explore what kind of 'stake' they have in – and what influence they might bring to bear on – its operations.

Next, we examine the concept of corporate social responsibility, which embodies how an organisation sees its relationship with its external stakeholders. This is an extremely important concept within the procurement profession.

Finally, we look at how stakeholders can be managed, including some helpful tools for classifying and prioritising stakeholders, and determining management approaches.

1   Introduction to stakeholders

What are 'stakeholders'?

1.1   'Stakeholders are those individuals or groups who depend on the organisation to fulfil their own goals and on whom, in turn, the organisation depends.' (Johnson & Scholes)

'A stakeholder of a company is an individual or group that either is harmed by, or benefits from, the company *or* whose rights can be violated, or have to be respected, by the company.' (Jobber)

1.2   From these definitions, you might note that the members (managers and employees) of an organisation are stakeholders in its activity and success. So are its supply chain partners (suppliers, intermediaries and customers) and others in direct business relationship with it (such as its owners/shareholders, the banks that lend it money and so on). An organisation therefore has both *internal* and *external* stakeholders.

1.3   The group of external stakeholders is, however, wider than you might think. It includes a number of parties who are not directly connected to the organisation, but who contribute to its activities, or are impacted on *by* its activities, in some way. They include the government, pressure groups and interest groups (including professional bodies and trade unions), the news media, the local community and wider society.

1.4   An organisation negotiates legal (and psychological) contracts with its employees, financiers and supply chain partners – but why should it enter into any kind of relationship with these more peripheral groups? Stakeholder theory recognises that an organisation affects its environment and is affected by its environment. Each of the secondary stakeholder groups mentioned may contribute something to the organisation, or exert some kind of influence over it; and each may be affected (positively or negatively) by its plans and activities. The concept of corporate social responsibility argues that organisations should, as Jobber's definition suggests, respect the rights of such groups where possible.

1.5   For the purposes of this module, we will focus on the stakeholders of a particular function (such as procurement or supply management) or of a particular project, plan or decision (eg stakeholders in a project to implement e-procurement or a decision to outsource a service). From this point of view, the key internal stakeholders of procurement would be those functions and groups within the organisation who impact on, or are impacted by, procurement decisions and activity. Its key external stakeholders would be shareholders, suppliers, financiers, service providers and so on.

1.6   Indeed, a procurement or supply function is likely to have an important role in an organisation's stakeholder management, because – as we saw in Chapter 3 – it occupies a key role at the interface between the internal and external supply chains: connecting internal stakeholders (eg in cross-functional project teams) and connecting the organisation to the external supply chain.

Why are stakeholders important?

1.7   Stakeholders form an important part of the procurement context for the following reasons.

- They may seek to influence the organisation, if they perceive that their interests are threatened. Staff and/or suppliers may negotiate for better terms, for example, or activists may threaten a boycott if the organisation uses environmentally-damaging or labour-exploiting suppliers.
- There is strong public and regulatory pressure for business organisations to be 'socially responsible': taking into account the wider social and environmental impacts of their activities on a range of stakeholders.
- Organisations themselves increasingly follow (and publicise) ethical and corporate responsibility frameworks, acknowledging their responsibility not to trample on stakeholders' interests – whether or not they have an influential 'voice' in the matter.

Categories of stakeholders

1.8   The stakeholders of an organisation include internal, connected and external groups.

- **Internal stakeholders** are members of the organisation: the directors, managers and employees who operate within the organisation's boundaries. Key internal stakeholders in procurement plans and activities include: senior management (who need the procurement or supply chain function to do its job in order for overall corporate strategies to be fulfilled); procurement managers (who are responsible for the function's performance); and the managers and staff of other functions or units of the organisation whose work and goals intersect with those of the procurement or supply chain function – as discussed in Chapter 3.
- **Connected stakeholders** have direct legal, contractual or commercial dealings with the organisation. They include: shareholders (the owners of the firm) and other financiers, such as banks; customers/ consumers; suppliers; and distributors.
- **External or secondary stakeholders** do not have direct contractual or commercial dealings with the organisation, but have an interest in, or are affected by, its activities. They include: the government and regulatory bodies (which seek to control business activity); professional bodies and trade unions (which represent the interests of their members within the organisation); various interest and pressure groups (which promote and protect the interests of their members, or a particular cause); and the local community (within which the organisation operates).

1.9   Stakeholders are *affected by* the organisation's activities in different ways and to different degrees. Any given stakeholder group will have a bundle of needs, wants, expectations and concerns in regard to the organisation: 'interests' which the group will seek to protect or promote in their relationship with the organisation. So, for example, suppliers will have an interest in efficient information flows, payment as agreed, fair treatment of tenders, and mutually-beneficial ongoing business. Customers will have an interest in safe and satisfying products and services, value for money, ethical business dealings and so on.

1.10   Stakeholders also have power to *affect* the organisation's activities in different ways and to different degrees. Financiers have the power to withhold resources if their needs are not met. Customers can similarly withhold their custom and support. Suppliers influence the quality, cost and timely availability of products and services, and therefore the organisation's competitive advantage. And so on.

1.11   Let's briefly survey the interests and influence of some of the main stakeholders in procurement activities and performance.

2   Stakeholders of a procurement or supply chain function

Internal stakeholders of procurement

2.1   Internal stakeholders include general groups such as managers and employees (and/or volunteer workers or other types of members, in not-for-profit organisations). For example, the procurement function may have to market itself to senior management or management teams, or may have to communicate changes in procurement policy and procedures to all staff. More specifically, as we saw in Chapter 2, the internal supply chain and cross-functional activity in the organisation mean that other functional departments are key internal stakeholders in procurement activity and performance.

2.2   Internal stakeholders for a given procurement decision or exercise may therefore include:

- The owner or sponsor of a project or activity, who puts authority and resources behind it, initiates it, and sets its objectives
- Customers and users of the activity or its outputs: departments who receive procurement advice or assistance, or end users of the procured resources and services
- Participating staff, who may be drawn from the procurement team or from other functions, whether

through cross-functional working and information flow, or in dedicated cross-functional project teams (depending on the activity and its organisation).

2.3 The interests and influence of some key internal stakeholder groups are summarised in Table 4.1.

Table 4.1 *Internal stakeholders*

STAKEHOLDER	INTERESTS/NEEDS/DRIVERS	INFLUENCE/CONTRIBUTION
Directors/managers	• The organisation's profitability, survival and growt • Fulfilment of objectives and projects for which they are responsible (requiring purchasing inputs and/or support)	• Formal authority over planning • Shape the commitment and motivation of staff • Influence through politics, networking and influencing skills
Staff/team members or other organisation members	• The organisation's profitability and survival, for continued employment • Support, information and inputs to fulfil task goals and earn rewards • Healthy and safe working environment • Fair and ethical treatment	• Scarce resource: competitive edge in times or areas of skill shortage • Threat of withdrawn labour • Potential to add value through skilled, motivated performance, flexibility etc (especially in services)
Technical/design function	• Accurate fulfilment of specifications • Timely, relevant, expert advice on price and availability issues • Connection to suppliers who might contribute innovation and expertise	• Determine specifications and materials which the buyer will have to translate into purchase orders
Manufacture/ production/ operations function	• Right inputs at right price and right quality, delivered to right place at right time to maintain efficient flow of production • Supplier management and SCM to support flexibility, JIT supply, innovation etc. • Sourcing and procurement services (eg for capital equipment) or consultancy	• Key internal customer: purchasing performance measured by fulfilment of 'five rights' • Provision of feedback on quality of inputs to aid supplier and contract management
Sales and marketing function	• Quality, customisation and delivery levels that will satisfy customers • Fulfilment of promises made to customers; responsiveness to feedback and demands • Information on products and delivery schedules for promotions • Sourcing and procurement services (eg printing services, office supplies, sales force cars) or consultancy (eg for own media space buying or agency selection)	• Provision of market research and customer feedback information to influence product specifications and quality management • Promises made to customers via marketing communications, which purchasing must contribute to delivering
Finance/admin function	• Adherence to financial procedures (eg budgetary control, invoicing arrangements) • Notification of terms negotiated with suppliers (eg discounts, payment terms) • Support for cost control and/or reduction • Provision of info for budgetary control, costing, credit control etc • Sourcing and procurement services (eg for IT systems and stationery) or consultancy	• Control or influence budget allocations • Action payment of suppliers • May impact on supplier relationships (eg if payment for supplies is late or withheld) • May be leaders or champions of cost control and reduction initiatives
Storage and distribution (or logistics) – if not part of purchasing and supply function	• Timely info about incoming and outgoing orders, for transport and storage planning • Policies for 'green' transport planning, safe goods handling etc. • Sourcing and procurement services (eg for equipment) or consultancy	• Control or influence timely flow of incoming and outgoing deliveries • Influence on wastage, damage and obsolescence of supplies (eg through safe, secure, efficient transport and storage)

Connected stakeholders

2.4 Connected stakeholders often have a significant stake in organisational activity, by virtue of their contractual or commercial relationships with the organisation. Some of the interests and influence of these groups are summarised in Table 4.2.

Table 4.2 *Connected stakeholders*

STAKEHOLDER	INTERESTS/NEEDS/DRIVERS	INFLUENCE/CONTRIBUTION
Shareholders	• Return on investment, dividends • Corporate governance: transparency, accountability, directors protecting their interests	• Owners and financiers of firms • Voting power at company meetings • Power to sell shares (influencing share price, perceptions of financial markets)
End customers	• Satisfaction of a complex bundle of expectations and motives for purchase (eg value for money, quality, service experience) – NB different for consumer and business or industrial buyers.	• Focus of all business activity • Source of sales revenue and profits • Source of feedback information (via surveys, complaints etc) • Power to switch or withdraw custom
Intermediary customers (eg agents, distributors, retail outlets)	• Ethical, efficient trading practices and systems • Sales support: product info, reliable supply, promotional support, sales force training • Earnings and profits (eg through discount margins, fees or commissions) • Mutually beneficial ongoing relationship	• Help to promote and distribute products • Part of total customer 'value delivery system' for competitive advantage • Potential for collaborative promotion • Source of feedback info on sales, customers etc • Power to withhold distribution or promotion, or to aid competitors (eg with exclusive distribution deals)
Suppliers	• Clear specifications (fewer disputes) • Efficient transaction and relationship handling • Fair procedures for awarding contracts • Timely payment of debts • Opportunities for reasonable profit taking • Opportunities for development through regular trading, alliance or partnership • Feedback info to support service	• Provision of potentially key inputs (at required quality, price, time) • Power to withhold or restrict supply • Expertise (eg for product development and specification) • Potential for added value (eg via JIT, lean supply, collaborative waste reduction, continuous improvement)
Financial institutions/ lenders	• Financial strength and stability of the company (for security of the loan) • Return on investment (eg via interest) • Mutually beneficial ongoing relationship	• Short-term and long-term loan finance to maintain and develop operations • Added value services (eg insurance, currency management) • Power to restrict or withdraw credit facilities

The supplier as stakeholder

2.5 The main external focus of procurement's stakeholder management activity is likely to be:

- External suppliers, who have a key stake in any procurement exercise, and are the subject of purchasers' key social responsibilities *(*Lysons & Farrington*)*
- External collaborators, such as outsourced-service providers (project management, logistics etc), research consultants, legal advisers and so on.

2.6 Large or strategic suppliers – and, arguably, the supply chain as a whole – are potentially key stakeholders in any organisation. The activities and performance of suppliers are directly affected by their dealings with buyers, and the buyer-supplier relationship. The buying organisation has contractual responsibilities in regard to suppliers (eg to pay for goods supplied) and also ethical responsibilities (eg to allow adequate profits for survival, to pay on time, and to manage sourcing exercises fairly) – especially if the balance of power is in the buyer's favour, or if the supplier is highly dependent on the buyer for its survival.

2.7 On the 'power' side of the equation, suppliers have the ability to influence supply reliability, quality, costs and pricing decisions, the efficient flow-to-market of goods, potential for innovation – and therefore the buying organisation's competitive advantage. They may also have power through the control of strategic resources (supplies which are critical to the buying organisation), needed expertise (eg in the case of subcontractors and consultants) – and perhaps interpersonal influence with managers (eg if trust has been built up between buyer and supplier).

2.8 High-quality, motivated and committed suppliers have the potential to contribute significant added value in areas such as the following.

- New product development and process innovation: contributing ideas based on their expertise in the materials, components and technologies involved. (The term 'early supplier involvement', or ESI, is used for this early-stage collaboration on product development.)
- Availability/delivery: offering swift, flexible delivery of materials and components, so that the organisation can hold less inventory (and benefit from lower inventory costs) while still being able to fulfil orders
- Quality: ensuring the quality of the materials, components and services delivered; collaborating with procurement and operations to improve quality management processes; and committing to continuous improvement programmes
- Value for money: keeping materials, supply and inventory costs low, or collaborating with procurement on cost reduction programmes
- Service, advice and information: eg in the case of advertising agencies, management consultancies, third party logistics providers and so on.

External stakeholders of procurement

2.9 Traditionally, the interests of secondary stakeholders have been peripheral to business organisations, whose primary responsibility is to their shareholders. However, the view of what constitutes a legitimate stakeholder has broadened from a focus on groups involved directly with the organisation, function or project to a wider range of groups who are less directly affected by its activities and their results.

2.10 The emerging concept of corporate social responsibility, in particular, has emphasised that secondary or 'indirect' stakeholders have a legitimate interest which should be protected as far as possible. Businesses have, in particular, become increasingly aware of the need to maintain a positive reputation in the marketplace, and this may require a more inclusive approach to stakeholder management.

2.11 External stakeholders are likely to have quite diverse objectives and degrees of influence. Some of these are summarised in Table 4.3.

2.12 Secondary stakeholders impacted by procurement or supply chain exercises may include: the communities from which supplier labour is drawn; those affected by the environmental and economic impacts of the project; or interest groups concerned with the environment, trading practices, consumer rights and so on.

Table 4.3 *External stakeholders*

STAKEHOLDER	INTERESTS/NEEDS/DRIVERS	INFLUENCE/CONTRIBUTION
Government and regulatory bodies	• Corporate tax revenue • Healthy level of economic activity • Compliance with legislation and regulation • Reports and returns • Support for community development and employment	• Power to enforce requirements through legislation, regulation, penalties • Control over tax levels and public funding (eg via grants) • Bargaining power as a large customer or supplier of goods or services • Support and guidance for business
Pressure groups (eg Greenpeace) and interest groups (eg consumer associations, trade unions)	• Promotion and increased awareness of a cause or issue (eg fair trade, environment) • Protection of rights and interests of members • Access to information and accountability • Sponsorship or donation funding	• May shape policy (eg via lobbying) • Inform and mobilise public and consumer opinion for or against the organisation • Source of info re issues and impacts • May collaborate to enhance ethical credentials of the firm or brand • Power to mobilise protests or boycotts
Community and society at large	• Access to products and services, employment • Product safety • Affordability of essential goods and services • Socially responsible business and environmental practices: harm minimisation	• Pool of current and potential customers, suppliers and employees • Power to mobilise government policy and consumer opinion

3   Corporate social responsibility (CSR)

What is corporate social responsibility?

3.1   Business activity can have a negative effect on local communities, for example through environmental damage, traffic congestion, the squeezing out of small businesses, unemployment as a result of downsizing and so on. These impacts also impose financial costs on society, which the business itself does not account or pay for (and which are therefore sometimes called 'externalities'). It has therefore been argued that business has a responsibility to minimise these impacts and to 'give something back' to the communities that support them – and provide them with resources, staff and customers.

3.2   The concept of corporate social responsibility (CSR) emphasises the need for corporations to take into account the interests of secondary stakeholder groups. There are important issues which face an organisation as it formulates policies about how it can interact with its various stakeholders in an ethical, responsible and sustainable way.

3.3   One CIPS examiner has summed up CSR as follows.

'CSR means the commitment to systematic consideration of the environmental, social and cultural aspects of an organisation's operations. This includes the key issues of sustainability, human rights, labour and community relations, and supplier and customer relations beyond legal obligations. The objective [is] to create long-term business value and contribute to improving the social conditions of the people affected by our operations.'

3.4   Although corporate (and procurement) objectives may primarily be financial, particularly in the private business sector, many firms now also set social responsibility objectives, in relation to matters such as the following.

- **Sustainability issues**: conserving the world's limited natural resources (eg by minimising the use of non-renewable resources, minimising fuel use in transporting goods, or using recycled materials); supporting small and local suppliers; and supporting local communities through investment and employment

- **Environmental issues**: specifying 'green' materials; controlling pollution; managing wastes; avoiding environmental disfigurement and loss of wildlife habitats; supporting recycling; minimising carbon emissions; and so on – and ensuring that the supply chain does the same
- **Ethical trading, business relationships and development**: ensuring product safety and quality to protect consumers; improving working (and social) conditions for employees (and suppliers' employees, particularly in developing nations); avoiding the abuse of buyer power to squeeze supplier prices (fair trading); upholding ethical employment practices (such as health and safety, equal opportunity and employment protection); and supporting supply chain diversity.

3.5 Some of these matters will be covered by legislative and regulatory requirements, and/or professional codes of practice.

- Legislative requirements include, for example, an employer's duty to provide a safe and healthy workplace (eg the Health and Safety at Work Act in the UK) and the various legal protections afforded to employees by successive Employment Acts.
- Regulatory requirements include, for example, those laid down by specific industry regulators such as, in the UK, Ofcom for the communications industry, the Competition and Markets Authority (regulating merger and acquisition activity), and the the Advertising Standards Authority (regulating media advertising).
- Professional codes of practice include, for example, the ethical codes published by such bodies as the Chartered Institute of Procurement and Supply and the Institute of Chartered Accountants in England and Wales. Members of these bodies are obliged to comply with the rules they lay down.

3.6 Some organisations may have a 'compliance based' approach to ethics which strives merely to uphold these minimal requirements. However, the term 'corporate social responsibility' (CSR) covers policies which the organisation adopts for the good and wellbeing of stakeholders, taking a more proactive 'integrity based' approach.

3.7 The procurement or supply chain function can make a significant contribution to these objectives. Examples include: using small, local and diverse suppliers; allowing sustainable profit-taking by suppliers; supporting the development and specification of environmentally-friendly, safe and healthy products; organising reverse logistics for the recovery and recycling of materials and waste products; organising the safe disposal of non-recyclable wastes; selecting suppliers that conform to environmental and ethical standards; ensuring the safe and ethical testing of products and materials; and planning transport to minimise energy use and pollution.

3.8 A buying organisation can also encourage (or even insist on) ethical employment and/or environmental practices in its suppliers: non-use of child labour or forced labour, the paying of reasonable wages, the provision of adequate working conditions, health and safety, and the protection of workers' rights. Supplier conduct can be monitored by site visits and audits – but where this is difficult (eg with international or subcontracted suppliers), the buyer may use references, approved supplier or stockist lists and, where available, third party monitoring and certification services. The importance of such measures was illustrated in a recent high-profile case concerning the global charity, Oxfam. It suffered severe embarrassment when it emerged that its overseas suppliers of 'Make Poverty History' wristbands were themselves exploiting their workers.

Environmental responsibility

3.9 Areas of environmental concern in which procurement staff have a role to play are summarised by Saunders (*Strategic Purchasing & Supply Chain Management*) as follows.

- Recycling and re-using of materials and waste products (which may require new reverse logistics processes to recover products from consumers)
- Safe disposal of waste products that cannot be recycled

- Supplier selection policies (and tender criteria) to support firms that conform to environmental standards (eg with regard to air, water and noise pollution)
- Supplier and product selection policies that reflect concern for conservation and renewal of resources
- Safe and animal-friendly testing of products and materials
- Concern for noise, spray, dirt, vibration and congestion in the planning and operation of transportation

3.10 We might also add the following.

- Acting as the interface between suppliers and product development and design departments, to encourage knowledge sharing, research and innovation for 'greener' product specifications and collaborative processes
- Monitoring, managing and perhaps supporting the environmental performance of suppliers on an ongoing basis, to ensure their compliance with the buyer's environmental standards (in order to minimise the reputational risk of being associated with an environmental disaster)
- Sourcing materials and services for environmental protection and reclamation (eg re-planting trees or cleaning up polluted areas).

3.11 A commitment to avoiding materials that are harmful to the environment, if alternative products are available at a similar price and quality, shouldn't be controversial. However, *cost* has been a significant obstacle in the past: 'green' products have typically been more expensive than their 'non-green' equivalents. The last few years have seen radical changes in this situation, and in many cases actual savings are to be made in choosing a green or sustainable alternative. (Energy efficient light-bulbs, for example, may cost more upfront but the savings will come further down the line in reduced energy use.)

3.12 If no cost-effective or value-adding green alternatives are available, the buyer may need to work with suppliers to reduce the damaging environmental impact of a product – or with production colleagues to see if the product can be replaced.

3.13 In 2007, the UK retailer Marks & Spencer launched a CSR programme called 'Plan A' (so called because 'There is no Plan B'), built on five 'pillars', three of which are environmental.

- *Climate change*: 'We'll aim to make all our UK & Irish operations carbon neutral by 2012. We'll maximise our use of renewable energy and only use offsetting as a last resort. And we'll be helping our customers and suppliers to cut their carbon emissions too.'
- *Waste*: 'We'll significantly reduce the amount of packaging and carrier bags that we use, and find new ways to recycle materials. By 2012, we aim to ensure that none of our clothing or packaging needs to end up as landfill.'
- *Sustainable raw materials*: 'From fish to forests, our goal is to make sure our key raw materials come from the most sustainable sources available to us, protecting the environment and the world's natural resources for future generations.'

3.14 This is regarded as a cutting edge example of an eco and ethics plan. If you want to know more, the outline of the plan (and progress reports) makes accessible reading: check out http://plana.marksandspencer.com.

Private and public sector stakeholders

3.15 It is worth noting that in the private sector, priority is given to a relatively small and well defined group of stakeholders: internal and connected stakeholders – mainly, shareholders. Public sector organisations have a wider and more complex range of stakeholders, because in theory they are managed on behalf of society as a whole.

3.16 While private sector businesses often have profit maximisation as their primary objective, public sector and not-for-profit organisations have a range of non-economic and social goals, many of which reflect the interests of wider stakeholders: participants, supporters, donors, beneficiaries, interest groups, communities, the public interest and so on. In practice, this means that public and third-sector organisations are more likely to take a range of stakeholder views into account when making major decisions: often consulting with stakeholder groups, taking their feedback into account and carefully communicating decisions and outcomes to them.

3.17 However, it should also be noted that public sector stakeholders often have less direct influence (in the form of market power) to protect their interests. In the private sector, dissatisfied shareholders can threaten to withdraw their finance, employees their labour and customers their business, in order to make their voices heard. In the public sector, taxpayers and ratepayers have no equivalent market sanctions or resource power to influence a state enterprise or agency: they rely heavily on the government, audit authorities and other regulators to represent their interests.

4 Stakeholder management

4.1 Because stakeholders may have an interest in influencing organisational (or procurement) decisions – and may have the power to do so – it is important to:

- Take their interests and likely responses into account
- Communicate effectively with them on matters that affect them
- Engage the interest, support and commitment of influential (and potentially helpful) groups
- Manage potential issues and problem areas that might arouse resistance or opposition from influential groups.

4.2 However, the interests and expectations of stakeholder groups will often be different – and even conflicting. Shareholders, for example, will want to maximise profits (to increase the value of their shares), while suppliers will want to protect their own profit margins; interest groups may resist profit-taking at the expense of the environment; and employees may want to maximise their pay and conditions. Similarly, in the case of procurement stakeholders, the marketing function may want to maximise customisation and delivery-on-demand, while the operations function wants to be able to plan ahead and reduce variances, and the finance function wants to cut costs. You can't please all of the stakeholders all of the time!

4.3 Boddy (*Management: An Introduction*) concludes: 'The overall message is that it is important to the long-run success of organisations to embrace stakeholder expectations, but that the degree of priority they give to each is unequal and changing (over time).' The most common method of prioritising stakeholder relationships is stakeholder mapping.

Mapping stakeholders

4.4 Mendelow's power/interest matrix is a useful tool for mapping stakeholders according to two key factors.

- Their power to influence organisational (or procurement) activity
- The likelihood that they will use that power: that is, the strength of their motivation to do so, based on the strength of their interest in a given issue or decision.

4.5 The purpose of the Mendelow matrix is to prioritise stakeholders according to their importance. This enables the procurement or supply chain function to:

- Identify stakeholders whose needs and expectations will define value and shape the function's priorities and policies (eg senior management or key suppliers)
- Identify stakeholders whose interests will be most affected by a decision or action, and towards whom the organisation may therefore recognise some moral or legal obligations (eg communities impacted by logistics operations)
- Identify stakeholders who will need to be informed, consulted or involved in the design or implementation of procurement exercises and policies (eg internal and external supply chain partners)
- Prioritise stakeholder interests, so that resources are utilised efficiently or leveraged for maximum advantage.

4.6   To use the Mendelow model, you simply draw up a blank two-by-two matrix and, for any given situation, allocate each relevant stakeholder group to the quadrant which best describes its power/interest level. Each quadrant comes with a recommended relationship management strategy, which we have inserted into the matrix: Figure 4.1.

Figure 4.1 *Mendelow's power/interest matrix*

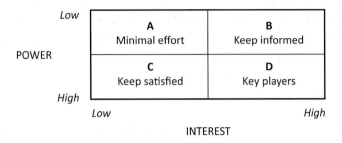

4.7   Working through each of the segments in turn:

- Stakeholders with neither power nor interest (A) are a low-priority group: resources will not be wasted taking their goals or potential response into account. Small investors, or large suppliers with whom the organisation only does a small volume of business, may be in this category. So too may the local community or other organisational functions, in relation to particular decisions with low immediate impacts on them.

- Stakeholders in Segment B are important because of their high interest: they may have low direct influence, but unless they are kept 'in the loop' and understand the need for decisions, they may seek additional power by lobbying or banding together to protect their interest. Community, small supplier and employee groups may be in this category, in relation to decisions which impact significantly on their interests. The recommended strategy is to keep them informed of plans and outcomes, through stakeholder marketing, communication and education programmes (discussed later in the chapter).

- Stakeholders in Segment C are important because of their high influence: they currently have low interest, but if dissatisfied or concerned, their interest may be aroused. A large institutional shareholder, or large supplier, may be in this category, as may government agencies and regulatory bodies (if the organisation is broadly compliant). Senior managers in departments not directly affected by a procurement decision may also fall into this category. The recommended strategy is to keep these stakeholders satisfied, so that they do not need to exert their influence.

- Stakeholders in Segment D are known as 'key players': they have influence and are motivated to use it in their own interests. Major customers, key suppliers and intermediaries, senior procurement managers and strategic allies/partners may be in this category. The recommended strategy is one of early involvement and participation, so that the stakeholder's goals can be integrated with organisational goals as far as possible – securing support, rather than resistance.

Stakeholder position analysis

4.8   It may also be helpful to map internal and external stakeholders according to their support for or opposition to procurement proposals. In another well known model, used in change management, Egan (*Working the Shadow Side*) divides stakeholders in a change or proposal into nine distinct groups, in relation to the leader or agent of change.

- *Partners*: those who support the change agent
- *Allies*: those who will support him or her, given encouragement
- *Fellow travellers*: passive supporters, who are committed to the agenda, but not to the change agent personally
- *Bedfellows*: people who support the agenda, but do not know or trust the change agent
- *Fence sitters*: those whose allegiances are not yet clear

- *Loose cannons:* people who may vote either way on agendas in which they have no direct stake
- *Opponents:* people who oppose the agenda, but not the change agent personally
- *Adversaries:* people who oppose the change agent and the agenda
- *The voiceless:* 'silent' stakeholders who are affected by the agenda, but lack advocates or power to influence decisions (eg future generations, disenfranchised people/workers, and flora and fauna).

4.9 Like Mendelow, Egan argues that different groups should be managed differently.

- Supporters (in various groups) must be encouraged and kept 'on side'. Partners may not require much interaction, but the organisation cannot afford to lose their interest or support. Allies require some encouragement, but infrequent contact (a 'light touch') is usually sufficient. Passive supporters (fellow travellers and bedfellows) require more intensive rapport- and relationship-building contacts to mobilise their commitment.
- Fence sitters may or may not have the potential to become valuable supporters or harmful opponents. The potential value of their allegiance, or potential cost of their resistance, will determine how much is invested in communication.
- Opponents need to be 'converted' by persuading them of the merits of the change and addressing their reasons for resistance: this is often done via formal, structured communication (eg meetings for negotiation and conflict resolution). Adversaries, on the other hand, may be too difficult and costly to 'win over', and may have to be marginalised or otherwise neutralised, so they cannot mobilise further opposition.
- The view of corporate ethics and social responsibility is that the needs of the voiceless should also receive attention, despite their relative powerlessness. Again, low-frequency contact should be all that is necessary to monitor the response of these stakeholders or their advocates and allow them to feel heard.

Stakeholder management

4.10 Stakeholder management recognises the need to take stakeholders into account when formulating and communicating plans. This may be helpful to a procurement or supply chain function in several ways. It enables it to gain expert input from stakeholders at the planning stage of a project. Stakeholders are more likely to 'buy into' or support plans to which they have had input: this will make ongoing collaboration easier. Gaining the engagement (interest and commitment) and support of powerful stakeholders may, in turn, help to mobilise power and resources within the organisation in support of procurement plans. At the very least, sources of resistance (from stakeholders whose goals are incompatible) can be anticipated and planned for.

4.11 Once key stakeholders have been identified, it is possible to plan a management strategy for each. You might use a standard process such as the following.

- **Goal analysis.** What motivates these stakeholders? What are their goals or desired outcomes from your plans? What fears or issues might your plans raise for them? Where might they support you – and where might they oppose you?
- **Desired outcomes.** What do you want or need from these stakeholders? What levels of support do you want from them? What role(s) would you want them to play in your project or plan?
- **Stakeholder marketing and communication programmes.** What messages will you need to convey to these stakeholders? How can you increase your credibility with them? How can you 'sell' them the benefits of what you are proposing or doing, to secure their support or 'buy in'?
- **Relationship management.** How will you manage communication to, and input from, each of these stakeholders? How will you keep your key supporters motivated? How will you win over or neutralise resistance? How will you engage the interest of potential supporters?
- **Issues management.** How will you raise potential issues and problems, where stakeholders' goals may differ from yours? How will you gain stakeholders' early involvement, and collaborate with them in minimising or managing the impacts?

4.12 A systematic approach to managing stakeholders is therefore as follows: Figure 4.2.

Figure 4.2 *Stakeholder management*

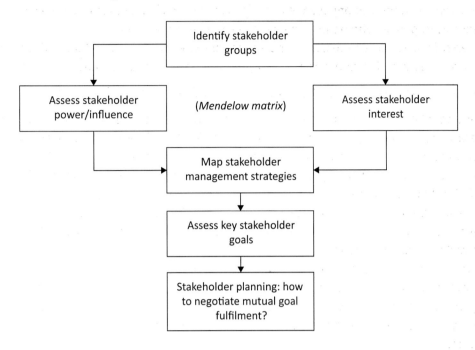

4.13   Stakeholder relationship management therefore involves processes such as:

- Gathering information about groups and their interests
- Prioritising groups which have most potential impact
- Establishing what each group may gain and lose from the procurement decision or plan – and using this information to (a) strengthen support and (b) mitigate losses and risks where possible
- Ensuring consistent and coherent communication with key stakeholder groups, in order to secure their 'buy in' to plans and proposals
- Establishing opportunities for co-operation and synergy (where available)
- Continuously monitoring, evaluating and adjusting the relationship over time.

Stakeholder communication

4.14   In addition to routine stakeholder communication (such as upward reporting to your manager on a regular basis), there may be a need for a planned series of information flows or communication initiatives on a particular subject, in order to inform stakeholders, engage their interest and support (or 'buy in'), and shape their response to the information. Such a planned series of information flows is called a 'communication programme'.

4.15   Communication programmes are often planned in situations involving the management of change. Examples might include the introduction of new technology; a change of key supplier or distributor; corporate restructuring, redundancies or changes in work methods; the adoption of new procurement policies (eg environmental or ethical standards); the launch of a new or modified product or service; or response to a potential public relations crisis (eg a product recall, environmental disaster or allegations of unethical behaviour).

4.16   A stakeholder communication plan might include the following elements.

- A list of all stakeholders and their information requirements
- Communication mechanisms to be used (advertisements, written reports, newsletter, emails, briefing and consultation meetings, workshops, conferences, general meetings, media releases and communiqués, the website, intranets and extranets and so on) – taking into account the need for feedback and dialogue where appropriate

- Key elements of information to be distributed by the different mechanisms, and the level and frequency of communication required
- Roles and responsibilities of key individuals in ensuring that communication is adequate, appropriate and timely
- Identification of how unexpected information from other parties (eg media reports or internet discussion) will be handled within the scope of the activity.

Internal stakeholder communication

4.17   Internal stakeholder communication is particularly important.

- Organisations depend on their employees (the human resources of the business) to implement plans and deliver services. Employee awareness of, engagement in and commitment to organisational goals is essential to support external customer satisfaction and business success.
- People need to work together across functional boundaries, as we saw in Chapter 3. There therefore needs to be both systematic communication between functions, and 'internal marketing' so that different functions understand each other's needs and contributions. (We discuss 'procurement marketing' in Chapter 7, for example.)
- Good employee communication enhances job satisfaction, and may help to create positive 'employer brand': that is, a reputation as a good employer, which may help to attract and retain quality staff.
- Employee communication, consultation and involvement is, in many countries, provided for by law (eg in the EU, in regard to consultation about redundancies, and the use of works councils to discuss matters of concern to employees).
- Communication is a cornerstone of positive employee relations, building stable and co-operative relationships between management and employees, and minimising conflict.

4.18   Some of the methods used for employee and cross-functional communication include: office manuals and in-house newsletters; a corporate intranet (staff-only web pages); team meetings, briefings, presentations and conferences; bulletins and announcements on noticeboards (and their website equivalents); personalised email, letters and memoranda; day-to-day information passed on by managers to individuals and teams; and so on.

4.19   Tools which may more specifically encourage feedback or upward communication include: formal negotiating and consultative meetings (eg with employee representatives); suggestion schemes; performance appraisal interviews (where opportunities are given to discuss problems, issues and suggestions for improvement); quality circles and other consultation/discussion groups; employee attitude surveys; management participation in informal networks; and so on.

Chapter summary

- Stakeholders are people or groups with a legitimate interest in the organisation. It is important to take their views into account so as to derive benefits and avoid negative consequences.
- Organisational stakeholders are often classified as internal, connected and external. Internal: directors and employees etc; connected: business contacts such as customers and suppliers etc; external: government, pressure groups, the general public etc.
- Corporate social responsibility is the concept that organisations have a duty to behave as good citizens, taking account of their own impact on environmental, social and cultural issues.
- An important tool in stakeholder analysis is Mendelow's matrix, which classifies stakeholders according to their power and their interest. An alternative model is Egan's nine stakeholder groups.
- The purpose of analysing stakeholders is so that an appropriate management strategy may be selected for each group.
- It is important to keep stakeholders informed, particularly when new information emerges, or there have been changes to ideas previously agreed upon.
- Stakeholder communication techniques include focus groups, consultation forums, briefings, seminars and conferences.

Self-test questions

Numbers in brackets refer to the paragraphs where you can check your answers.

1   Distinguish between internal and external stakeholders. (1.8)

2   Give examples of internal, connected and external stakeholders. (1.8, Tables 4.1, 4.2 and 4.3)

3   How does an organisation benefit from paying attention to sustainability and environmental issues? (3.4)

4   Sketch Mendelow's power/interest matrix. How should we manage the stakeholders in each quadrant? (Figure 4.1)

5   List the nine stakeholder groups identified by Egan. (4.8)

6   What activities are involved in stakeholder relationship management? (Figure 4.2)

7   List reasons why internal stakeholder communication is important. (4.17)

CHAPTER 5

The Procurement Process

Assessment criteria and indicative content

2.1 Explain the main aspects of sourcing processes

- Defining the stages of a generic sourcing process from identification of needs to contract and supplier management
- Analysis and planning, tender management and contract management
- Differentiating between pre contract award and post contract award stages

2.2 Analyse the main stages of a sourcing process

- Stages of the sourcing process that relate to defining needs, creation of contract terms, supplier selection, contract award and contract or supplier management
- The purpose and added value that is created by each of the stages of the sourcing process

2.4 Analyse the relationship between achieving compliance with processes and the achievement of outcomes

- Organisational needs for structured sourcing processes
- The relationship between process compliance and the achievement of added value outcomes

Section headings

1. Overview of the procurement process
2. The need for structured processes
3. Identifying and defining needs
4. Developing contract terms
5. Supplier selection
6. Contract award
7. Contract or supplier management

Introduction

Procurement procedures and policies will naturally vary widely from one organisation to another – and even within organisations, according to different types of purchases (as we will see in Chapter 7). However, there are certain stages which almost any procurement exercise will involve – from identification of a need to post-contract management – and these stages can be described as a 'generic procurement process'.

It may seem a bit odd to have placed coverage of this 'overview' topic so late in the learning objectives: many aspects have already been touched on in connection with earlier topics. However, we have broadly moved from 'principles' (such as the five rights and stakeholder management) to 'procedures': putting the principles into practice in chronological order!

In this chapter, we will look at the various stages of the procurement process, and at what happens during each stage. Our descriptions accord with general best practice – but of course we cannot incorporate all of the variations that will be experienced in your professional work, or in exam case studies. You will need to follow the policies and procedures of your own organisation in your day-to-day work – and will need to pay careful attention to the context of any case study presented in the exam.

1 Overview of the procurement process

1.1 A generic procurement process comprises all of the procurement activities that typically take place from the initial identification of a need to the final satisfaction of that need, in a simplified chronological sequence.

1.2 A 'process' is an essentially linear model of what may take place in the course of a typical procurement exercise, from 'identification of need' to 'performance' (satisfaction of the need): you might depict it as a linear flow chart. However, it is also possible to view procurement activity as a 'cycle' or continuous loop, because further needs will constantly emerge, requiring ongoing repetition of the procurement process.

1.3 The main stages of a procurement process – depicted as a cycle – are shown in Figure 5.1. The process starts with the identification of the need. All the unshaded boxes are part of the pre-contract-award sourcing process. The shaded box is the post-contract-award purchase performance process.

Figure 5.1 *A generic procurement cycle*

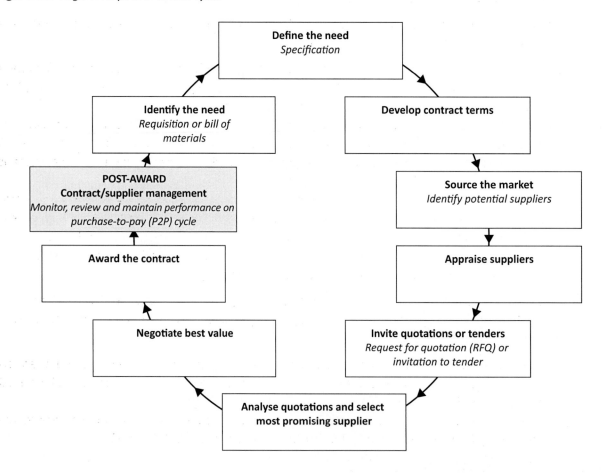

1.4 Before we go on to demonstrate the key stages of this process in detail, it is worth making a few general points.

Different procurement situations

1.5 Not every procurement will follow every stage of this generic process.

- If a procurement is a **straight re-buy** of items already sourced from a supplier, for example, it will not be necessary to establish a specification, survey and source the market, invite quotations and select a supplier: the buyer may already have a preferred supplier (and perhaps a standing purchase agreement or 'call off contract' with them).
- If it is a **modified re-buy**, in that some of the requirement has changed, it may be necessary to re-

specify the need or re-negotiate the contract, but the same supplier may be used (or *vice versa*: the specification may stay the same, but a new supplier will be sought).

- **New buys** are more likely to conform to the full procurement process.

Pre-contract-award and post-contract-award stages

1.6 A procurement process (such as the acquisition process depicted in the CIPS Purchasing and Supply Management Model) incorporates both:

- **Pre-contract-award** stages, which together make up the sourcing process, including identification and definition of need, sourcing planning, consideration of sourcing and tendering options, development of the contract, market survey and engagement, appraisal and selection of suppliers, receipt and evaluation of offers, and contract award *and*
- **Post-contract-award** stages, including activities such as expediting, payment, contract or supplier management, supplier development, ongoing asset management, and post-contract 'lesson learning'. This stage in the procurement cycle forms the 'purchase-to-pay' (P2P) cycle, to which we will return in Section 7 of this chapter.

1.7 This may seem obvious from our cycle diagram, but it is helpful to differentiate between pre-contract (sourcing) and post-contract stages for several reasons.

- It emphasises the continuing role of procurement and supply chain staff in managing fulfilment of the contract after a 'purchase' has been sourced: seeing the procurement through to completion (including learning lessons for future procurement exercises).
- It emphasises the importance of post-award contract and supplier management in the successful completion of procurements. Just having a contract is not, in itself, sufficient to guarantee fulfilment: follow-through by the procurement or supply chain function is essential to support performance – and future performance improvement and development.
- It helps to distinguish between processes such as the auditing and appraisal of suppliers, which happen *both* before and after contract award. So, for example, it is important to differentiate between supplier appraisal (evaluating the capability of *potential* suppliers, in the pre-contract sourcing stage) and supplier *performance* appraisal (or 'vendor rating': evaluating the performance of actual suppliers, or vendors, in the post-contract performance stage).

1.8 It also helps to distinguish between terms such as 'sourcing' and 'purchasing', which are often differentiated in the design of e-procurement systems (eg as 'e-sourcing' and 'e-purchasing' or P2P systems).

- *Sourcing* is the part of the process concerned with 'how and where services or products are obtained' (CIPS): ie pre-contract award stages such as requirements definition, tendering, supplier selection and contract award.
- *Purchasing* generally refers to post-contract transactional aspects such as ordering, receipting and payment. (This is sometimes called the purchase-to-pay cycle or P2P cycle.)

Beyond contract award: supplier relationship

1.9 We might call 'the right supplier' the sixth right of purchasing – and 'the right relationship' the seventh. Supplier relationships are beyond the scope of this syllabus – and will be covered in detail in the *Managing Contracts and Relationships* module. However, it is worth emphasising that some reliable suppliers will be used again and again for ongoing requirements: the buyer may decide not to go through the sourcing stages of the procurement process for each contract, but instead may choose to develop a relationship with a preferred – or even a sole – supplier for certain types of procurement.

1.10 There is a broad 'spectrum' of relationships or sourcing options that a buyer may seek with its suppliers, from one-off transactions (placed on a purely competitive arm's length basis) to close partnership relations with a trusted supplier of strategically important items or services (for which competitive bidding will no longer be relevant or appropriate). On the scale from distant to close, these approaches may cover:

- *Spot buying*: making one-off procurements to meet requirements as they arise, taking advantage of best available terms at the time
- *Regular trading*: giving repeat business to a group of preferred (known, trusted) suppliers
- *Fixed or call-off contracts*, framework agreements or blanket ordering: establishing agreed terms of supply with suppliers for a defined period
- *Single sourcing*: giving exclusivity to one preferred supplier – implying a high degree of trust and commitment
- *Strategic alliance*: agreement to work together with a supplier for long-term mutual advantage in a particular area (eg systems integration or joint new product development)
- *Partnership*: agreement to work closely together long-term, and on a range of issues, for collaborative problem-solving and development.

1.11 Which relationship is the 'right' one? Again, you will cover this in detail elsewhere in your studies, but essentially the decision depends on:

- The *nature and importance of the items being procured*: low-value, routine or one-off procurements are unlikely to justify heavy investment in long-term collaboration – whereas complex, customised, high-value procurements in unstable supply markets may well justify such investment, in order to secure control over the supply specification, quality and availability
- The *competence, capability, co-operation and performance* of the supplier (and reciprocal conduct of the buyer), and therefore the degree of trust developed between them: trust being a necessary foundation for closer relationship
- *Geographical distance*: close relationships may be more difficult to establish and maintain with overseas suppliers, especially if there is little communication infrastructure
- The *compatibility* of the supply partners: if their strategic aims, values and systems are incompatible, it may be too costly to attempt to bridge the distance or overcome the barriers (as long as more compatible alternatives are available)
- The organisation's and procurement function's *objectives and priorities*: best available price (suggesting a competitive, opportunistic or transactional approach) or security and quality of supply, whole life value for money and long-term added value through improvement or innovation (suggesting a more collaborative, long-term approach)
- *Supply market conditions*: if supply is subject to risk (eg due to weather or economic conditions), the buyer may wish to multi-source; if prices are fluctuating, it may wish to use opportunistic spot-buying; if the market is fast-changing and innovative, it may want to avoid being locked into long-term supply agreements; if there are only a few high quality suppliers, it may wish to enter partnership with them – and so on.

2 The need for structured processes

Why have structured procurement processes?

2.1 In any organisation, goods and services are purchased or procured by someone. In a very small business with a simple business model, this may be a relatively *ad hoc* – or more or less planned – activity, carried out reactively in response to notified or emerging requirements (eg for office supplies). Increasingly, however, organisations have chosen to formalise procurement processes and procedures.

- **Processes** are the sequence of actions or steps – or a flow of information and resources – by which a team or organisation performs its functions and pursues desired outcomes or goals. A 'business process' can be defined as a sequence of activities, often crossing functional and organisational boundaries, involved in (for example) transforming inputs into outputs, delivering value to the customer or developing new products. The overall picture of inter-connected process flows can be presented in the form of a 'process map' or flow chart.

- **Procedures** are formal, structured processes developed and laid down as 'good practice' for performing functions competently: how things should be done in order to achieve target outcomes efficiently and effectively. Procedures often take the form of standardised sequences of tasks – plus the guidelines, instructions, rules and tools which will support people in performing them.

2.2 A formal, systematic approach to structuring processes and procedures (in procurement and a range of other functions) has several advantages for an organisation.

- It ensures that all tasks have been performed that *need* to be performed, without 'gaps' (things which are forgotten, or the importance of which is underestimated by the person performing the task, or which one participant in a process assumes will have been done by another)
- It ensures adequate co-ordination of effort between parties collaborating in a process: no gaps, no wasteful duplication of effort, no divergent or conflicting efforts undermining each other. (This may be particularly important where a process or procedure is cross-functional.)
- It helps to maintain consistency in processes and outcomes, as opposed to the uncertainty and risk of doing things *ad hoc*.
- It prevents conflict and sub-optimal behaviour, where different participants pursue their own interests and objectives, at the expense of the outcomes of the process as a whole: the structured process or procedure should balance competing goals to arrive at the best solution for the organisation or customer.
- It fosters efficiency, by mandating the most efficient method or procedure (rather than inefficient alternatives, or people 'reinventing the wheel' every time a decision has to be made).
- It supports good governance and managerial control, by ensuring that adequate checks and controls are in place in critical areas (such as fraud prevention or quality management).
- It supports compliance with relevant standards, law and regulation.
- It enables the documentation and sharing of good practice, to support ongoing continuous improvement and development.
- It enables meaningful process analysis, problem-solving and improvement.
- It supports the systematic development of procurement staff, systems, technology and other resources, to match well-defined competence requirements and outcomes.
- It supports the devolution of some procurement tasks to non-procurement staff (such as users and budget holders), as it ensures that good procurement practice will be followed, regardless of knowledge or expertise.

2.3 In general, compliance with soundly-designed, structured processes support good practice procurement and ensure that added value outcomes (discussed in Chapter 2) are achieved. 'Good practice' is simply:

- A technique, method, process or procedure that is believed to be effective and efficient at delivering desired outcomes
- An effective and efficient way of achieving a task, based on learnable and repeatable procedures that have proven themselves in practice, over time and in a range of contexts.

2.4 By using 'the right methods' (process compliance) you are likely to achieve objectives with fewer problems, unforeseen complications, risks and wastes. You don't have to 're-invent the wheel' or solve common problems afresh each time. You can be confident you are doing 'the right things' in 'the right ways'.

2.5 Good practice in procurement therefore includes a range of activities, decision rules, processes and procedures that are designed to help procurement officers to achieve the optimum mix of the five rights, and other procurement or supply chain management objectives.

Best practice

2.6 Standards schemes, codes of practice and procurement procedures often reflect 'good practice', setting a higher benchmark for quality, safety and environmental protection. However, there is a growing emphasis on aspiring to 'best practice': that is, ensuring that your organisation's policies and practices reflect the highest standards in use in your industry.

2.7 There are various approaches to attaining best practice.

- *Best practice sharing* eg in industry forums, knowledge banks and continuing professional education (in the case of purchasing professionals, say)
- *Applying for quality awards* such as the Deming Prize, the EFQM Quality Award (based on the Excellence model), the UK Business Excellence Award and regional Excellence Awards. This is a highly effective (if costly) way of comparing your performance against best practice and other organisations.
- *Benchmarking*: comparing your processes and practices to those of other 'leaders' in the field, and striving to emulate their successful behaviours. There are various types of benchmarking, including internal benchmarking (comparison with high-performing units in the same organisation); functional benchmarking (comparison with a best-practice external example of your function eg procurement); competitor benchmarking (comparison with a high-performing competitor); and generic benchmarking (comparison of business processes with 'excellent' companies or an excellence framework, regardless of industry).

Distinguishing between process and outcomes

2.8 The syllabus requires you to 'analyse the relationship between achieving compliance with processes and the achievement of outcomes'. This should be common sense.

- **Outcomes** are what an organisation or procurement function is *aiming to achieve* – and/or what it *actually* achieves. So, as we saw in Chapter 2, the intended or desired outcomes of an effective procurement process are the 'five rights', and 'added value' outcomes such as cost reduction, improved profitability, collaborative supplier relationships, supply chain innovation, value for money procurement or sustainable procurement.
- **Processes** are the *means* or steps by which desired outcomes are pursued, or which an organisation or procurement function follows in order to secure good practice.

2.9 In practice, however, there are several pitfalls in confusing outcomes and processes – or in getting the balance between them wrong.

2.10 Stannack and Jones *(The Death of Purchasing Procedures)* argue that procurement is narrowly outcome- (or product-) focused at an early or immature stage of its development: concerned with the 'five rights', which focus exclusively on a narrow range of target outcome dimensions by which the purchase of tangible products can be defined. Once procurement develops greater maturity, it moves beyond a concern with basic purchase-related outcomes and becomes 'process-focused': measuring and managing the processes by which the outcomes are delivered. The highest level of maturity is 'performance-centred' procurement, which uses an integrated approach to managing both processes and outcomes, in collaboration with suppliers.

2.11 Organisations may become overly focused on target outcomes such as cost reduction or maximised profits – at the expense of good practice and innovative, value-adding processes. So, for example, a short-term focus on best price (outcome) may foster adversarial approaches to negotiation and supplier relationships and development (processes) – which may, in the long run, miss out on the value-adding potential for supply chain (process) improvement, sustainable procurement, collaborative whole life cost reduction, agile or flexible supply and so on.

2.12 Organisations may, on the other hand, become overly focused on 'correct' processes and procedures – and become rigid, inflexible, inwardly focused (without thinking about the best flow of value to the customer), resistant to change, and incapable of adapting to the challenges of changing competitive initiatives and customer demands.

2.13 Excessive value given to 'doing things the right way' (as opposed to 'doing the right things') can create the kinds of cultural problems commonly associated with large bureaucratic organisations. People don't seek to add value through initiative, discretion or innovation: they merely follow the procedure (which may, or may not, be a well developed, up-to-date approach to a business or customer need).

2.14 An emphasis on compliance (rather than commitment, creativity or the customer) may stifle the flexibility required for added value outcomes in dynamic environments. However, as we noted at the beginning of this section, process compliance is important in ensuring the consistent achievement of best practice and added value outcomes. It may be particularly necessary in highly controlled environments – eg in order to maintain health and safety, reduce risk, assure quality, or achieve standards accreditation. The key lesson is to ensure process compliance – while ensuring that processes are reviewed and adapted on a regular basis, to avoid inflexibility, and to take advantage of emerging new sources of added value.

2.15 Having said all that, let's now explore each of the key stages of the procurement process in more detail.

3 Identifying and defining needs

Identifying needs: requisition

3.1 Before any procurement exercise or transaction can begin, someone must notice that something is needed which is not currently available, and this need must be notified to the procurement function (or other staff responsible for procurements).

3.2 The need may be identified by a user department: for example, a designer may recognise the need for new software. Or the driver for procurement may come from a stores department or warehouse: a check of inventory levels (as discussed in Chapter 2) may reveal the need to replenish stocks of materials or components.

3.3 In either case, the normal procedure would be for the department concerned to issue a **requisition**. This form (or its electronic equivalent) describes the item needed and instigates action by the procurement function. In a paper-based system, the originator of the requisition would keep a copy of the form, while the other copy is forwarded as appropriate.

- If the originator is the stores department, the copy is forwarded to the procurement function.
- If the originator is a user department, the copy may be forwarded to stores. Stores will meet the need if the item is in stock: if not, the requisition will be passed on to procurement.

3.4 A requisition form (whether printed or electronic) will typically include the following details.

- A description of the product or service required: identified by brand name or model number (if known), or accompanied by the specification (if already available)
- The quantity required
- The delivery or provision date
- The internal department code, or budgetary code, to which the expenditure is to be charged
- The name and signature of the originator of the requisition, and its date. This may act as an official authorisation of the need, giving procurement authority to act upon it, so the signature should be that of an individual with appropriate authority.

3.5 If the organisation operates a materials requirements planning (MRP) system, the identification of the need may instead by signalled by a 'bill of materials' (BOM). Briefly, the approach is to forecast the manufacturing schedule for finished products, and to translate this into details of the materials and parts needed for production: the bill of materials. This can then be compared with stock files, where relevant, to establish which materials and parts will have to be procured.

Challenging needs

3.6 Requisition and bill of materials forms will contain details of the required item(s) in a standardised form. However, in some cases the procurement function will not simply act on this description without enquiry. It may be appropriate to refer the requisition back to the originator:

- For clarification
- To challenge over-specification or unnecessary variation, or
- To suggest alternatives that will offer better quality or lower price than the item requisitioned.

3.7 This is a key potential source of added value in the procurement process, since it is designed to minimise waste in the form of unnecessary variation, features, quality or service levels – and associated unnecessary costs.

Defining needs

3.8 The process so far relates to the identification and description of the need *within* the buying organisation. The next step will be to establish a detailed description of the requirement which can be communicated to potential suppliers. Detailed descriptions may already exist (if the purchase is a re-buy, for example), but for new procurements, they may have to be drawn up, in the form of:

- Specifications (of various types)
- Service level agreements (added to the specification of services)
- Contract terms which set out the obligations of buyer and seller in relation to the fulfilment of the specification.

Specification

3.9 A specification can be simply defined as a statement of the requirements to be satisfied in the supply of a product or service.

3.10 As part of the procurement cycle, the purpose and value addition of an effective specification is to:

- *Define the requirement* – encouraging all relevant stakeholders (including the procurers and users of the supplied items) to consider what they really need, and whether this is the only, most cost-effective or most value-adding solution
- *Communicate the requirement* clearly to suppliers, so that they can plan to conform – and perhaps also use their expertise to come up with innovative or lower-cost solutions to the requirement
- *Minimise risk and cost* associated with doubt, ambiguity, misunderstanding or dispute as to requirement, and what constitutes satisfactory quality and fitness for purpose
- *Provide a means of evaluating the quality or conformance* of the goods or services supplied, for acceptance (if conforming to specification) or rejection (if non-conforming), to ensure that 'right quality' is achieved, and to minimise failure costs
- *Support standardisation and consistency,* where items are procured from more than one source.

3.11 The main potential downsides of using specifications are as follows.

- Detailed specification is an expensive and time consuming process, and almost certainly uneconomic for small-value purchases.
- The costs of inspection and quality control are greater than if a simpler form of need definition (eg by brand name) is used.
- Specifications can become too firmly embedded: they need to be regularly reviewed, to ensure that the latest design decisions, and the latest developments in the supply market, are being taken into account.
- Specifications can create a temptation to over-specify, increasing cost (without necessarily adding value).

3.12   There are two main types of specification: conformance specification and performance (or functional) specification. With a **conformance specification**, the buyer details exactly what the required product, part or material must *consist of*. The supplier may not know in detail, or even at all, what function the product will play in the buyer's manufacturing. It is its task simply to *conform to the description* provided by the buyer.

3.13   A conformance specification may take the form of:

- An *engineering drawing, design or blueprint* (technical or design specification): commonly used in engineering and construction or architecture environments, which require a high degree of technical accuracy and very low tolerances (because of the complexity of assembly and machine function)
- A *chemical formula or 'recipe' of ingredients and materials* (composition specification): commonly used where particular physical properties (eg strength, flexibility or durability) are important for safety or performance (eg the metal used in car manufacture) or where materials are restricted by law, regulation or codes of practice, for health, safety or environmental reasons (eg the use of lead in paint)
- The specification of a *brand name and model name or number,* if a marketed product meets the buyer's criteria. Branded products tend to be of good quality and easy to source, if available. Purchasing by brand may be essential if a particular part or material is patented or prestigious (eg Intel microprocessors for computers).
- A *sample* of the product, with a requirement for the supplier simply to duplicate the features and performance of the sample. This is a quick and easy method of specifying requirement without having to describe it, and offers some assurance (eg the ability to test the sample for suitability, prior to procurement)
- The specification of *compliance with a recognised standard* (eg British Standards, market grades, or International Standards): offering certified quality assurance and uniformity (standardisation).

3.14   A **performance (or functional) specification** is a relatively brief document (compared to a conformance specification), in which the buyer describes what it expects a part or material to be able to *achieve*, in terms of the functions it will perform, the level of performance it should reach, and any relevant input parameters and operating conditions. It is up to the supplier to furnish a product which will *satisfy these requirements*. The specification defines the functionality or performance to be achieved – but does *not* (unlike a conformance specification) prescribe *how* they are to be achieved (in terms of materials, designs or processes).

3.15   A typical performance specification might include the following details.

- The functionality, performance or capabilities to be achieved, within specified tolerances
- Key process inputs which will contribute to performance, including available utilities (electricity, solar power and so on)
- The operating environment and conditions in which the performance is to be achieved (and extreme or unusual conditions in which it is not expected)
- How the product is required to interface with other elements of the process
- Required quality levels (including relevant standards)
- Required safety levels and controls (including relevant standards)
- Required environmental performance levels and controls (including relevant standards)
- Criteria and methods to be used to measure whether the desired function has been achieved.

3.16   There are a number of advantages to performance specification over conformance specifications, which have made them increasingly popular.

- Performance specifications are easier and cheaper to draft, compared to a more detailed, prescriptive (conformance) approach.
- The efficacy of the specification does not depend on the technical knowledge of the buyer (unlike

conformance specifications). Suppliers may well know better than the buyer what is required, and how it can best be manufactured.

- Suppliers can use their full expertise, technologies and innovative capacity to develop optimum, lowest-cost solutions (whereas conformance specifications are prescriptive and inflexible).

- A greater share of specification risk is borne by the supplier: if the part supplied does not perform its function, the buyer is entitled to redress (whereas, with a conformance specification, the specifier bears responsibility for the functionality of the finished result).

- The potential supply base is wider than with a conformance specification. If the task is to supply something – anything – that will perform a particular function, the expertise of different suppliers could potentially provide a wide range of solutions.

3.17   It is particularly appropriate to use performance specifications in the following circumstances.

- Suppliers have greater relevant technical and manufacturing expertise than the buyer – so that the best knowledge is being used and leveraged. It should also be noted that the buyer will be highly reliant on the supplier's expertise: this puts pressure on effective supplier selection and evaluation.

- Technology is changing rapidly in the supplying industry – so that the buyer is not in a position of specifying yesterday's methodologies, but gets the best out of suppliers' innovation capacity and technological development.

- There are clear criteria for evaluating alternative solutions put forward by suppliers competing for the contract. These should be clearly communicated to potential suppliers, who may invest considerable time and resources in coming up with proposals, and will want to be assured that the selection process is fair.

- The buyer has sufficient time and expertise to assess the potential functionality of suppliers' proposals and competing alternatives (particularly if the supplier is using technology with which the buyer is unfamiliar). The complexity of the evaluation process is the major disadvantage of the performance specification approach.

Specifying services

3.18   We noted in Chapter 1 that services (and service elements) present buyers with problems additional to those that arise in purchasing materials or manufactured goods, when it comes to specifying requirements.

- Services are intangible and lack 'inspectability': specifying service levels – and subsequently checking whether or how far they have been achieved – is therefore fraught with difficulty. As Steve Kirby notes: 'How clean is clean? How long should it take to repair a computer? What is the definition of a well-cooked meal?'

- Services are variable: every separate instance of service provision is unique, because the personnel and circumstances are different. It is hard to standardise requirements.

- Services are provided in 'real time': transport, accommodation and catering services, for example, are only relevant when they are needed. Specifications therefore need to include the time of provision, so that the supplier can schedule provision accordingly.

- Many services can only be performed in particular locations (eg accommodation provided at a hotel premises, cleaning provided at the buyer's offices). Specifications may need to include explicit understandings about where the service is to be provided, the access required and related issues (such as confidentiality, if suppliers are working on the buyers' premises).

- A service may be procured for a long contract period, during which requirements may change from the original specification, requiring review, flexibility and change controls.

3.19   The more work that can be done at the pre-contract stage, the better. This means agreeing service levels, schedules and the basis for charges in as much detail as possible before the contract is signed: disputes often stem from differing expectations on the part of buyer and supplier!

Roles in specification development

3.20 In most cases, the lead role in specification development is taken by users of the product (often designers or engineers) or service. After all, they may be most familiar with the requirement, and most technically 'savvy' about what is required. However, procurement specialists may also take a lead role where they are technically expert in the product or category specified (eg knowledgeable about brands, grades and standards). The term 'early buyer involvement' (EBI) is sometimes given to the involvement of procurement specialists in product design, development and specification.

3.21 In less straightforward cases, the development of a specification may require *cross-functional input*, in order to balance:

- Design considerations of function (the priority of the engineering function)
- Marketing considerations of consumer acceptance and satisfaction (the priority of the marketing function)
- Manufacturing considerations of economical production (the priority of the operations function)
- Commercial and procurement considerations (the priority of the procurement function).

3.22 The procurement function is in a good position to add value through contributing:

- *Supply market awareness*: the availability of standard or generic items (for variety reduction), the availability of capable suppliers, the possibility of alternative suppliers and solutions (especially if expensive branded products are requisitioned), market prices, supply market risk factors, and availability issues
- *Supplier contacts*, to discuss potential solutions in advance of specification, or to introduce pre-qualified suppliers to the design team (early supplier involvement), which may in turn improve technical specification
- Awareness of *commercial aspects* of procurements, eg the need to include requirements for just in time (low inventory) supply, response times, maintenance cover, spares availability, warranty periods and user training in the specification
- Awareness of *legal aspects* of procurements, eg the need to comply with standards and regulations on health and safety, environmental protection and (in the public sector) procurement methods
- Procurement *disciplines*, for variety reduction, value analysis, cost reduction and so on. The buyer should be ready to discuss the real needs of the user, and to question desired performance levels or tolerances, to pursue gains in these areas. The greatest scope for cost reduction is at the design and specification stage.

3.23 Whatever approach is used in preparing the specification, it is advisable to ensure controlled *signing off* procedures. Before a specification is released to a supplier, it must have the formal approval of the procurement officer and ideally the prior certification of the supplier. This reduces the common risk of changes being made in order to solve problems not envisaged at the time the specification was finalised. This precaution should then be followed up by ensuring that any changes which are deemed necessary are subjected to appropriate approval procedures and documented in writing.

Early supplier involvement

3.24 The principle of early supplier involvement (ESI) is that organisations should involve suppliers at an early stage in the product or service development process. This contrasts with the traditional approach, whereby the supplier merely provides feedback on a completed product design specification. In service contracting, it is common for a potential service provider to collaboratively develop and negotiate service specifications and service level agreements, as part of a cross-functional team with users and purchasers.

3.25 The main purpose of ESI is to enable a pre-qualified supplier (with proven supply and technical abilities) to contribute technical expertise which the buying organisation may lack, by making proactive suggestions to improve product or service design, or to reduce the costs of production. For example, a supplier may provide constructive criticism of designs, and suggest alternative materials or manufacturing methods at a time when engineering changes are still possible.

3.26 The benefits to be gained from ESI have mainly focused on relatively short-term organisational gains via more accurate and achievable technical specifications, improved product quality, reduction in development time, and reduction in development and product costs. However, there may also be some long-term benefits. ESI can, for example, be a catalyst for long-term, partnership relationships with excellent suppliers. It can also improve the buyer's understanding about technological developments in the supply market, with potential for further exploitation.

3.27 As with most approaches, practitioners also need to be aware of potential drawbacks. The product or service may be designed around the supplier's capabilities, which (a) may be limiting, and (b) may lock the buyer into a supply relationship. This may become a problem if the supplier becomes complacent and ceases to deliver the quality or innovation it once did – or if market developments present better alternatives. In addition, ESI may pose confidentiality and security issues (eg the risk of leakage of product plans to competitors).

4 Developing contract terms

4.1 The role of a contract is to set out the roles, rights and obligations of both parties in a transaction or relationship. A contract implies an intention to 'enter into legal relations': that is, both parties agree to be legally bound by the specified roles and responsibilities. It may take the form of a verbal agreement or 'understanding' (eg based on a regular trading relationship that has developed over time), but more complex contracts are usually formalised in writing.

4.2 Contract law is a highly complex area, beyond the scope of this syllabus. However, you should be aware of the nature of a procurement contract, as a statement of:

- Exactly what two or more parties have agreed to do or exchange (incorporating specifications, prices, delivery and payment dates and so on)
- Conditions and contingencies which may alter the arrangement (eg circumstances under which it would not be reasonable to enforce certain terms, or agreement that if party A does x, then party B may do y)
- The rights of each party if the other fails to do what it has agreed to do ('remedies' for 'breach of contract')
- How responsibility or 'liability' will be apportioned in the event of problems (eg who pays for damage or loss of goods)
- How any disputes will be resolved (eg by a third-party arbitration process, in preference to litigation or pursuit of a dispute through the courts of law).

Contract terms

4.3 Contract terms are statements by the parties to the contract as to what they understand their rights and obligations to be under the contract. They define the content of the 'offer' (or counter-offer) which becomes binding once accepted by the other party.

4.4 Contract terms define both parties' rights and obligations, and it is important that there should be genuine and specific agreement on what these are, from the outset. After the contract has been made, it is too late for either party to alter its terms unilaterally: such a variation is effective only if it is made by mutual agreement (ie by another contract).

4.5 Terms can be expressly or explicitly inserted into a contract by either or both of the parties (*express terms*) or can be implied or assumed to be included in the contract (*implied terms*) because they are a recognised part of common or statute law.

- **Express terms** are clearly stated and recognised in the contract between the parties. The most common examples of express terms would be where the parties specify price, delivery dates, how carriage and insurance costs will be shared, and so on. Another example is an exclusion or exemption clause, which states that one party will not be liable (or will have only limited liability) for some specific breach of contract, or a *force majeure* clause which specifies special circumstances in which a party will not be liable for failure to fulfil its contract obligations.
- **Implied terms** are terms which are assumed to exist by virtue of common law (accepted legal principles, such as *caveat emptor* or 'buyer beware') and statute (legislation) and therefore form part of the contract – whether or not they are mentioned within it. For example in the UK, the Sale of Goods Act 1979 implies certain terms – such as the buyer's right to expect goods supplied to be of satisfactory quality and fit for purpose – into all contracts for the sale of goods. The printed terms and conditions of a contract cannot be viewed in isolation: buyers and suppliers must bear in mind that they may have responsibilities or rights not specifically dealt with in the terms of the contract.

4.6   Usually, each term of a contract can be classified as either a 'condition' or a 'warranty'.

- A **condition** is a vital term of the contract, breach of which may be treated by the innocent party as a substantial failure to perform a basic element of the agreement. In such a case, the innocent party has the option of treating the contract as ended (releasing it from any further obligations) and claiming damages for any loss suffered.
- A **warranty** is a less important term which is incidental to the main purpose of the contract. Breach of a warranty does not constitute a substantial failure of performance, so the whole agreement need not collapse: the innocent party may claim damages for the breach, but cannot 'repudiate' (reject) the contract.

4.7   The contract may expressly declare that some term is to be a condition: one important example is when the *time of performance* is declared to be 'of the essence of the contract' (so that late delivery would be considered a breach of condition, rather than a breach of warranty).

Standard and model form contracts

4.8   Most commercial concerns do not go to the trouble of drawing up a special contract every time they procure or sell goods or services. For most routine transactions, they rely on **standard terms**. Each firm will draw up its own 'standard terms of business', and will seek to ensure that these terms are accepted by other firms with whom they deal.

4.9   One of the advantages of negotiating contracts with suppliers, agreeing specific terms and conditions – which may include some of the buyer's standard terms and some of the seller's – is that it avoids any ambiguity or conflict about whose terms apply in a given situation. (Buyer and seller have conflicting interests in many areas: is the price fixed or is price escalation permitted? Who bears the risk of accidental loss or damage to goods? Who bears the costs of carriage or insurance? Can the buyer reject the goods or not?)

4.10   However, it would be extremely time-consuming and expensive to negotiate and formulate contract terms and clauses afresh for every new contract. In many situations, it would also be a case of 'reinventing the wheel', since the terms would be substantially similar for most business dealings of a similar type. Buyers and sellers may therefore agree to use a *standard or 'model' form of contract*: a contract 'template' based on generally accepted practice in an organisation or industry.

4.11   Where an organisation has recurring dealings with a supplier, or recurring requirements for a product or service, it may develop its own *standard contract* for use in particular types of dealings. For example, a publisher might have a standard contract for authors, another for printers, another covering sale to book distributors and another for sale to bookshops. Each standard contract would incorporate standard terms and conditions which have proved acceptable and workable in each type of contractual relationship in the past. A supplier or buyer could accept the contract as it stands, or negotiate to vary specific terms.

4.12 *Model form contracts* are published by third party experts (such as trade associations and professional bodies), incorporating standard practice in contracting for specific purposes within specific industries, and ensuring a fair balance of contractual rights and responsibilities for buyer and seller. For example, CIPS has published a range of model form contracts and contract clauses, which members are licensed to use in support of their employment. The Joint Contracts Tribunal (JCT) publishes a Standard Form of Building Contract (including a model form for framework or call-off contracts) for construction.

Service level agreements

4.13 Service level agreements (SLAs) are formal statements of performance requirements, specifying the exact nature and level of service to be provided by a service supplier.

4.14 The main purpose of a service level agreement is to define the customer's service level needs and secure the commitment of the supplier to meeting those needs: this can then be used as a yardstick against which to measure the supplier's subsequent performance, conformance (meeting standards) and compliance (fulfilling agreed terms). SLAs are therefore, potentially, a useful tool for client-supplier communication and relationship management; expectations and conflict management; cost management; and performance monitoring, review and evaluation.

4.15 The basic contents of a generic SLA are as follows – although of course they will be adapted to the specific nature and context of the particular service being supplied.

- What services are included (and not included, or included only on request and at additional cost)
- Standards or levels of service (such as response times, speed and attributes of quality service)
- The allocation of responsibility for activities, risks and costs
- How services and service levels will be monitored and reviewed, what measures of evaluation will be used, and how problems (if any) will be addressed
- How complaints and disputes will be managed
- When and how the agreement will be reviewed and revised. (Service specifications may need to change as requirements or circumstances change.)

4.16 The key value-adding benefits of effective SLAs, as summarised by Lysons & Farrington, are as follows.

- The clear identification of customers and providers, in relation to specific services
- The focusing of attention on what services actually involve and achieve
- Identification of the real service requirements of the customer, and potential for costs to be reduced by cutting services or levels of service that (a) are unnecessary and (b) do not add value
- Better customer awareness of what services they receive, what they are entitled to expect, and what additional services or levels of service a provider can offer
- Better customer awareness of what a service or level of service costs, for realistic cost-benefit evaluation
- Support for the ongoing monitoring and periodic review of services and service levels
- Support for problem solving and improvement planning, by facilitating customers in reporting failure to meet service levels
- The fostering of better understanding and trust between providers and customers

4.17 Note our emphasis on ascertaining what services and levels of service are *actually* required, and on examining what they actually achieve and whether they add value. It is important not to *over-specify* requirements – for services as for goods. Specifying unnecessarily high standards or frequency of service, tight response times or grade of staff adds cost without necessarily adding value. (This is a point worth making in a time of global recession – and worth looking out for in exam case studies, where procurement functions may well be under cost pressures.)

5 Supplier selection

5.1 Where the item required is a standard or routine one, the sourcing stage of the procurement cycle (identifying and selecting potential suppliers) may be by-passed. Preferred or approved suppliers will already be identified, and perhaps contracted on a standing basis (eg using framework agreements or call-off contracts, whereby the buyer contracts to source its requirements from the supplier, and procurement officers or users can simply 'call off' orders on the agreed terms, as needs arise).

5.2 There may, however, be the need to source a new or non-standard product or service – or the buyer may simply wish to stay aware of potential alternative providers in the supply market, if requirements (or existing suppliers' performance) change, or if opportunities arise to investigate better-value or more innovative solutions. In such cases, it will be important to locate, investigate and appraise potential suppliers.

5.3 The extent of this investigation must be proportionate to the importance and value of the item. It would not be worth the time and cost of detailed supplier appraisal for light bulbs or toilet paper, say. Systematic sourcing processes will be essential, however, for strategic or non-standard items; for major high-value procurements (eg capital equipment); for potential long-term partnership relations with a supplier; and for international sourcing and outsourcing exercises (because of the risks involved).

Surveying and engaging the market

5.4 'Surveying the market' means identifying or locating suppliers that may potentially be able to supply the requirement. Buyers will constantly be monitoring the supply market(s) relevant to their organisation's requirements, as well as the performance of the existing supplier base. They may also carry out formal supply market research for a given requirement.

5.5 Here are some possible sources of information about potential suppliers.

- Procurement database records and lists of preferred, approved or authorised suppliers (indicating which suppliers have already been pre-qualified for use)
- Supplier catalogues, sales force presentations and websites
- Printed and web-based listings of suppliers and stockists; trade registers and directories (such as Dun & Bradstreet); searchable databases; and specialist resources (such as the Purchasing Research Service)
- Online market exchanges, auction and review sites and supplier/buyer forums – which may also allow the posting of requests for quotation and other exchanges
- Trade or industry press (magazines, journals and bulletins) and specialist procurement journals (such as *Supply Management* or *Procurement Professional)*
- Trade fairs, exhibitions and conferences, which may provide opportunities for visitors to view competing products and prototypes, meet supplier representatives, discuss requirements, and gather relevant literature
- Networking with other procurement professionals (who may be willing to give recommendations and referrals to suppliers with whom they have been satisfied).

5.6 Suppliers may be short-listed according to a variety of criteria: size or capacity, price, reputation, recommendation – and perhaps the buyer's sustainability policies (eg using small or local suppliers where possible).

5.7 Potentially interesting suppliers may be contacted by telephone or email to request a brochure or catalogue, a visit to the buyer by the supplier's sales representative, or a visit by the buyer to the supplier (sometimes called a 'site visit'). A formal, systematic approach to information gathering about the supplier may be required. This is variously known as 'supplier appraisal', 'supplier evaluation', 'supplier quality assessment' or 'supplier pre-qualification'.

Appraising or pre-qualifying suppliers

5.8 The purpose of supplier appraisal or pre-qualification is to ensure that a potential supplier will be able to perform any contract or tender that it is awarded, to the required standard. Such a process adds value by avoiding the wasted cost, time, effort and embarrassment of awarding a contract (on the basis of lowest price) to a tenderer who *subsequently* turns out to lack capacity or technical capability to handle the work, or turns out to have systems and values that are incompatible with the buying organisation, or turns out to be financially unstable and unable to complete the work because of cashflow problems or business failure!

5.9 In addition, having a list of pre-qualified suppliers reduces the investigations needed for individual tenders and purchases: the buyer already knows that any supplier on the approved list has been assessed as capable of fulfilling requirements. This may be particularly helpful where routine purchasing activity is devolved to user department buyers, who may not have the expertise to evaluate or select new suppliers for themselves: instead, they can choose from a list of suppliers pre-assessed and qualified by purchasing specialists.

5.10 Remember that supplier appraisal is not the same as appraisal of the *performance* of contracted suppliers, in order to ensure that the contract is being fulfilled. To distinguish between the two, pre-contract evaluation is usually called 'supplier appraisal' or 'pre-qualification' while post-contract evaluation is usually called 'supplier performance appraisal' or 'vendor rating'.

5.11 A supplier appraisal may cover a wide and complex variety of factors that a buyer may consider essential or desirable in its suppliers. Pre-qualification criteria should be related to the requirements of the particular buying organisation and procurement type, but one model frequently referred to in the procurement literature is the '**10 Cs**', which we have adapted (from Ray Carter's original framework) as follows.

- *Competence* (or *capability)* of the supplier to fulfil the contract: whether it can produce the kinds of items, or deliver the kinds of services, required; what management, innovation, design or other relevant capabilities it has
- *Capacity* of the supplier to meet the buying organisation's current and future needs: eg how much volume the supplier will be able to handle (its production capacity); and how effectively managed its own supply chain is
- *Commitment* of the supplier to key values such as quality, service or cost management – and to a longer-term relationship with the buying organisation (if desired)
- *Control* systems in place for monitoring and managing resources and risks; eg willingness to comply with procedures, rules or systems required by the buyer; quality or environmental management systems; financial controls; risk management systems and so on
- *Cash* resources to ensure the financial status and stability of the supplier: its profitability, cashflow position (whether it has working funds to pay its bills, buy materials and pay workers), the assets it owns, the debts it owes, how its costs are structured and allocated, and so its overall financial 'health'. These factors will reflect on the ability of the supplier to fulfil its contract with the buyer. They may raise the risk of delivery or quality problems – and more drastic disruption to supply (and complex legal issues) if the supplier's business fails and it becomes insolvent. They will also impact on the prices the supplier will be able to charge.
- *Consistency* in delivering and improving levels of quality and service: eg a 'track record' of reliability, or 'process capability' (robust processes, quality assurance and controls)

- *Cost*: price, whole life costs and value for money offered by the supplier
- *Compatibility* of the supplier with the buying organisation: both cultural (in terms of values, ethics, work approach, management style and so on) and technological (in terms of processes, organisation and IT systems)
- *Compliance* with environmental, corporate social responsibility or sustainability standards, legislation and regulation
- *Communication* efficiency (and supporting technology) to support collaboration and co-ordination in the supply chain.

Gathering and verifying pre-qualification information

5.12   Information about suppliers may initially be acquired by various means.

- Self-appraisal questionnaires completed by suppliers – although the buyer will need to verify the truth and accuracy of supplier-compiled information
- Financial appraisal: analysis of the supplier's financial statements, reports and accounts – or analyses published by credit rating companies (such as Dun & Bradstreet) – providing information on the supplier's financial status and stability; sources of financial risk (such as an excessive debt burden or ineffective debtor/creditor management); efficiency; cost structure and profitability; and so on
- Checking the supplier's certifications, accreditations, quality awards and policy statements, in order to assess the robustness of its management systems in areas such as quality, environmental management and corporate social responsibility
- References from existing customers, to assess the levels of reliability and customer satisfaction attained by the supplier
- Work sampling: checking output samples, prototypes or portfolios of work. This may be done by requesting product samples; randomly sampling production outputs as part of a site visit; making small trial orders; or sampling services with small test contracts or trial periods.

5.13   Once a short-list of potential suppliers has been identified, the buyer may use a more resource-intensive method such as a **supplier audit** or **site visit** or **capability survey**. These methods require visits to the supplier's premises by a cross-functional appraisal team (comprising experts on procurement, quality assurance and engineering, say) which shares responsibility for the decision to approve or reject the supplier on the basis of their observations. A supplier visit can be used for various purposes.

- To confirm information provided by the supplier in an appraisal questionnaire
- To observe and discuss, in greater detail, the supplier's premises, personnel, equipment, processes (particularly quality management) and outputs
- To enable the buyer to make personal contact with supplier-side account managers and other individuals whose co-operation will be relied on if delivery or other problems occur.

Supplier approval

5.14   Following the appraisal process, one or more suppliers may be officially recognised as being able to meet the standards and requirements of the particular buyer, and therefore eligible for invitations to quote or tender for contracts: this is known as supplier approval. The approval may be for a one-off tender, or may mean that the supplier is put on a list of approved suppliers from which user-department purchasers can source products as required.

6 Contract award

Different approaches to contract award

6.1 A requirement can be signalled to pre-qualified or approved suppliers in various ways, depending on the type of procurement and company policies in this area (as discussed in Chapter 7).

6.2 The organisation may already have negotiated a **framework agreement** or 'standing contract' with a supplier, to meet a requirement of a certain type. In such a case, the requirement will simply be notified by a purchase or call-off order, on the pre-agreed terms.

6.3 There may be only one available supplier, or the organisation may have negotiated a **preferred supplier or sole supplier agreement** with a dependable supply partner. In such a case, the buyer may simply negotiate a contract for the particular requirement with the available, preferred or designated supplier.

6.4 The organisation may send an 'enquiry' or **request for quotation** to one or more short-listed suppliers. The RFQ will set out the details of the requirement: the contact details of the purchaser; the date and requisition reference; the quantity and description of goods or services required; the required place and date of delivery; and the buyer's terms and conditions of business. It will then invite the supplier(s) to submit a proposal and price (a 'quotation') for the contract. Quotations may be evaluated:

- On a competitive basis: eg the best value bid or quotation 'wins' the contract (as in competitive bidding or tendering)
- As a basis for negotiation with a preferred supplier. (Note, however, that it is not ethical practice to solicit quotations from more than one supplier if you have already decided where the contract will be awarded – eg just to 'motivate' a preferred supplier. The preparation of quotations costs unsuccessful suppliers time and resources.)

6.5 An organisation may have different procedures in place for orders of different volume or value.

- For order values under $100, say, there may be no formal requirement for supplier selection.
- For orders between $100 and $5,000, there may be a negotiation process, or a minimum of three suppliers may be requested to provide quotations, to ensure competitive pricing and value for money.
- For orders over $5,000 in value, a full competitive bidding or tendering process may be required.

Competitive bidding or tendering

6.6 The organisation may prefer to use a *competitive bidding* or tendering procedure, in which pre-qualified suppliers are issued with an invitation to tender (ITT), or an invitation to bid for a contract, with the buyer intending to choose the supplier submitting the best proposal or the lowest price.

6.7 When should a procurement function use competitive bidding rather than a negotiation? Dobler and Burt (*Purchasing & Supply Management*) give the following guidelines for making the decision: Table 5.1.

Table 5.1 *The use of competitive bidding*

FIVE CRITERIA FOR THE USE OF COMPETITIVE BIDDING	FOUR SITUATIONS IN WHICH COMPETITIVE BIDDING SHOULD NOT BE USED
The value of the procurement should be high enough to justify the expense of the process	It is impossible to estimate production costs accurately
The specifications must be clear and the potential suppliers must have a clear idea of the costs involved in fulfilling the contract	Price is not the only or most important criterion in the award of the contract
There must be an adequate number of potential suppliers in the market	Changes to specification are likely as the contract progresses
The potential suppliers must be both technically qualified and keen to win the business	Special tooling or set-up costs are major factors in the requirement
There must be sufficient time available for the procedure to be carried out	

6.8 We might add that competitive bidding should be used where it is *required* by organisational policy (eg for particular procurement categories or contracts of a certain value) or by external regulation. Competitive tendering is compulsory in the UK public sector, for example, for procurements by public bodies over a certain financial threshold, under the EU Public Procurement Directives (enacted in UK law by the Public Contracts Regulations 2015). We will discuss the particular requirements of the regulations in Chapter 10, in the context of public sector procurement.

6.9 There are several value-adding advantages to competitive bidding or tendering. It ensures fairness and genuine competition between suppliers. It ensures that procurement decisions are soundly based on cost and value for money. It also engages a wide choice of suppliers (particularly if open tendering, or open advertisement of the tender, is used) – which may encourage innovative solutions to requirements.

6.10 However, there are also drawbacks, particularly to open tendering processes.

- Wide competition may discourage some potentially suitable bidders.
- There may be inadequate pre-qualification of bidders, creating the risk of capability or capacity problems emerging late in the process.
- Competition based primarily on the lowest price may put insufficient focus on important criteria such as quality and sustainability: the lowest-price bid may not represent the best long-term value.
- Tendering places a potentially large administrative burden on buyers.
- Contract award may be a one-off, not leading suppliers to expect further business. In other words, competitive tenders do not result in deepening buyer-supplier relationships. This may lead to a widening of the supplier base – whereas the trend is to develop closer value-adding collaborative relationships with fewer suppliers. There may also be little incentive for suppliers to perform to the highest standard (as a committed, loyal supply chain partner might do), over and above compliance with the minimum standards set by the contract specification.

Tender management

6.11 Tendering is simply the process by which suppliers are invited to put themselves forward (or 'bid') for a contract. There are two main approaches to this.

- **Selective tendering**, in which potential suppliers are pre-qualified and 3–10 suppliers are short-listed for invitation to tender – as discussed above
- **Open tendering**, in which the invitation to tender is widely advertised and open to any potential bidder.

6.12   In the public sector, open competitive tendering is *compulsory* for contracts above a certain value threshold, in order to stimulate fair and open competition. However, where the buyer has a choice, *selective* tendering will often be used for the following reasons.

- It is less time-consuming and costly for both buyer and suppliers
- It is less likely to present later problems with technical capability or capacity
- It is less frustrating for non-pre-qualified suppliers who may incur the trouble and expense of tendering without having a realistic chance of succeeding.

6.13   A best-practice tender procedure would have the following steps.

- Preparation of detailed specifications and draft contract documents
- Decision on whether to use open or selective tendering (where not already determined by regulation or company policy)
- Determination of a realistic timetable for the tender process, allowing reasonable time for responses at each stage
- Issue of invitations to tender, accompanied by specifications, and the selection criteria to be applied. In selective tendering, this would be by means of an invitation to bid or RFQ sent to short-listed suppliers. In open tendering, it would be by means of a public advertisement, with invitations to bid issued to suppliers who respond within the stated time frame.
- Submission of completed tenders or bids by potential suppliers, within the deadline specified
- Opening of tenders on the appointed date. Tenders received after this date should be returned un-opened. The tenders received should be logged, with the main details of each listed on an analysis sheet for ease of comparison.
- Analysis of each tender, according to the stated selection criteria, with a view to selecting the 'best offer'. This will usually be on a lowest-price or best value basis, but other selection criteria (such as environmental compliance or innovation) may be taken into account, as long as they have been clearly notified in the invitation to tender.
- Award of the contract, and advertisement or notification of the award
- 'De-briefing': the giving of feedback, on request, to unsuccessful tenderers, to enable them to improve the competitiveness of future bids.

Analysing quotations and tenders

6.14   The general principle is that the successful tender will be the one with the lowest price or the 'most economically advantageous tender' (on whatever value selection criteria have been specified). However, there is more to it than this.

- The selection criteria issued when inviting tenders must be applied.
- The evaluation team may need to analyse whether and how effectively each bid meets the requirements of a performance or functional specification.
- There may be considerable variety in the total solution 'package' being offered by bids: one may be more attractive (innovative, environmentally friendly, risk-reducing, value-adding) than another – even if price tells against it.

6.15   It will be important, therefore, for any invitation to tender to state clearly that the buyer will *not* be bound to accept the lowest price quoted, and that *post-tender negotiation* may be entered into, if necessary to qualify or clarify tenders, or to discuss potential improvements or adjustments to suppliers' offers.

6.16   The following guidelines summarise the main points to take account of in analysing tenders: Table 5.2.

Table 5.2 *A checklist for analysing tenders*

1.	Establish a routine for receiving and opening tenders, ensuring security
2.	Set out clearly the responsibilities of the departments involved
3.	Establish objective award criteria, as set out in the selection criteria in the initial invitation to tender
4.	Establish a cross-functional team for the appraisal of each tender
5.	Establish a standardised format for logging and reporting on tenders
6.	Check that the tenders received comply with the award criteria. Non-price criteria will need to be carefully reviewed (and more details sought, if required).
7.	Check the arithmetical accuracy of each tender!
8.	Eliminate suppliers whose total quoted price is above the lowest two or three quotes by a specified percentage (say 20%).
9.	Evaluate the tenders in accordance with predetermined checklists for technical, contractual and financial details.
10.	Prepare a report on each tender for submission to the project or procurement manager (and as a basis for feedback to unsuccessful bidders, where relevant).

Contract negotiation

6.17 Negotiation may be the main approach by which contract terms are arrived at, or may be used in support of tendering (eg to improve aspects of the preferred tender, or to ensure that all aspects of the requirement, bid and contract are understood).

6.18 Negotiation is a massive area of study in its own right, and you will cover it as part of your studies for *Negotiating and Contracting*. Basically, negotiation is defined by Dobler *et al*, in the purchasing context, as: 'A process of planning, reviewing and analysing used by a buyer and a seller to reach acceptable agreements or compromises [which] include all aspects of the business transaction, not just price'.

6.19 The process is summed up by Gennard and Judge *(Employee Relations)* as one of:

- *Purposeful persuasion*: each party tries to persuade the other to accept its case or see its viewpoint and
- *Constructive compromise*: both parties accept the need to move closer to each other's position, identifying the areas of common ground where there is room for concessions to be made.

6.20 In a contract negotiation, the buyers' main objectives may be (*Dobler et al*): to obtain a fair and reasonable price for the quality specified; to get the supplier to perform the contract on time; to exert some control over the manner in which the contract is performed; to persuade the supplier to give maximum co-operation to the buyer's company; and/or to develop a sound and continuing relationship with competent suppliers. Where a relationship is ongoing, one particular issue may have come to the fore, but more often there are multiple objectives, especially in negotiations with a new supplier or potential supplier.

6.21 Objectives should be ranked as high priority, medium priority or low priority. Most negotiations depend on concessions from both sides, and this ranking procedure will help negotiators to determine where they can best afford to give ground or make concessions (low priority objectives) and which areas are non-negotiable (high priority objectives). If one side's low priority (easy to concede) objectives coincide with the other's medium or high priority (valuable to gain) objectives, there is significant potential for constructive bargaining.

Awarding the contract

6.22 The contract should now be formally recognised by issuing the relevant contract documentation. Typically, the components for the actual contract will be the specification and/or invitation to tender, the supplier's written proposal, plus any terms or modifications which may have been agreed in negotiation. The contract should be issued in duplicate and signed by both parties, with each party retaining an original copy.

6.23 Where practical, all contract papers should be bound together in date order, and a duplicate copy issued for the supplier's retention, so that both parties can be satisfied as to the completeness of contract documentation. Any subsequent contract variations should be attached to all the copies as and when they are issued.

7   Contract or supplier management

The purchase-to-pay (P2P) cycle

7.1 Once the contract has been awarded, a new 'cycle' of activity is required to follow it through to completion. This is often called the purchase-to-pay or P2P cycle, but it can be depicted as a two-way flow of transactions as follows: Figure 5.2.

Figure 5.2 *Purchase-to-pay activities*

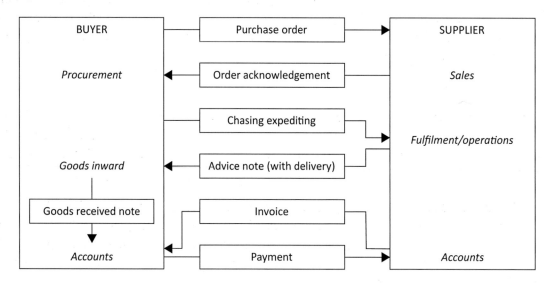

Purchase order and acknowledgement

7.2 For simple procurements, which do not require a negotiated contract, the buyer may make out a *purchase order*: in most cases, a standard form (printed or electronic). The effect of the form will, however, be to create a legally binding contract, so it usually contains the firm's standard legal terms and conditions of purchase. In some cases, an order may be placed by phone: usually, where some kind of blanket or 'call off' order system is in place. If not, phone orders should be confirmed in writing, to include the relevant terms and conditions of purchase.

7.3 A number of copies of the purchase order are prepared, so that appropriate departments can be informed. One copy goes to the supplier (often with a second copy, which can be signed and returned as acknowledgement of the order and acceptance of the legal terms contained on it). One copy will be retained by the procurement function. Other copies may be sent to the stores department, accounts department and user departments, notifying them to await delivery.

Expediting the order

7.4 There will often be a need to follow-up, chase or 'expedite' an order. The buyer may chase the supplier to return the acknowledgement copy of the purchase order, for example, or check that the delivery will be on schedule, or 'track' the progress of the order and its delivery (eg using online 'track and trace' systems, in which each step in the fulfilment of an order, and its transport, is logged for monitoring).

7.5 Usually, these routines are triggered by review of outstanding orders. Most often, purchase orders are logged on a computer system which will automatically flag when follow-up routines are needed: this will be discussed further in Chapter 6.

Goods inwards

7.6 When an order of goods is ready for delivery, a number of routines usually follow in a defined procedure.

- The supplier sends an *advice note* or *delivery note* to the buyer with (or in advance of) delivery of the goods, to notify the buyer of the content and time of the delivery.
- The Goods Inwards department of the buying organisation receives and inspects the goods, to check that the supplier has delivered the correct goods in the correct quantity, without obvious quality defects. The goods must correspond to what was ordered (ie the advice note should correspond to the purchase order).
- The Goods Inwards department sends a *goods received note* (GRN) to the procurement and accounts functions, to indicate that the goods have arrived. This will also note any discrepancies or defects in the order, which the procurement function will need to raise and resolve with the supplier, prior to authorisation of payment.

Invoicing and payment

7.7 The supplier will in due course send an invoice or request for payment to the buyer. The buyer should check that it corresponds to the order or contract (in regard to the agreed price) and to the GRN (in regard to items actually received), and then *either* query discrepancies with the supplier *or* authorise the invoice for payment and pass it to the accounts department for payment.

7.8 Invoices should be paid within the period stated in the agreed terms of trade: often 30, 60 or 90 days. Credit periods are an issue for cashflow, for both the buyer and the supplier. The buyer may want to pay as late as possible, in order to retain cash (or earn interest on banked funds), but the supplier will want to be paid as early as possible, to obtain those same benefits – especially since it has already incurred the cost of supplying the product or service.

7.9 It is part of ethical trading to pay supplier invoices *on time, as agreed*. It also impacts on the buyer's standing as an attractive (or unattractive) customer for suppliers, and on the ongoing relationship with suppliers. An unjustly unpaid invoice may result in stoppage of supply until the matter is settled, and/or the threat of legal action by the supplier. Repeated late payment or disputed payment of invoices can significantly damage the buyer's credibility, the supplier's loyalty and commitment (and therefore future reliability and quality), and in the worst case, the buyer's ability to find suppliers willing to do business.

7.10 Commercial payments are often made by *electronic credit transfer*, through the banking system, which is safe and swift. (One disadvantage, however, is that payments tend to be handled on regular days of the month, on a payment cycle, which may represent a late payment for a supplier, or prevent the buyer from receiving an early payment discount.)

7.11 Another possibility is payment by *corporate credit card* or *purchasing card*, which allows the delegation of routine purchases to user-department staff, and is efficient in terms of invoicing and other transaction costs. However, this may also allow 'maverick' spending by non-purchasing specialists, unless safeguards are in place: eg spending limits on the use of cards, authorised supplier lists and so on.

Contract management

7.12 Contracts for the supply of goods or services may be much more complex, and longer in duration, than a simple purchase order. Once contracts are signed, therefore, it is not as simple as saying: 'The supplier will now do *that*'. There will be obligations to be followed up on either side. If contingencies arise, the contract may (or may not) lay down what happens next. If the supplier's performance falls short in any way, there will be a variety of options for pursuing the matter. Circumstances and requirements may change, and contract terms may have to be adjusted accordingly. This is an ongoing process through the life of the contract – which is where contract management comes in.

7.13 Contract management is the process designed to ensure that both parties meet their obligations, and that the intended outcomes of a contract are delivered. It also involves building and maintaining a good working relationship between the buyer and supplier, continuing through the life of a contract.

7.14 For smaller contracts, a single individual may be able to carry out all contract management responsibilities, but for larger contracts, a team may be required, especially in the early stages, which are often more demanding in terms of management time. Buyer- and supplier-side contract managers should be appointed before the contract is awarded, so that they can be involved in contract development and implementation.

7.15 The key processes and activities involved in contract management include the following.

- **Contract development:** the formulation of contracts. Contract negotiation should support ongoing contract management by clearly identifying both parties' rights and obligations, and working methods. A copy of the contract document should be given to those involved with managing it on a day-to-day basis. A register should be kept of each copy issued, and these should be version-controlled to ensure that amendments and updates are properly incorporated in all copies.
- **Contract administration:** implementing buyer- and supplier-side procedures to ensure that contract obligations are fulfilled. This may include procedures for:
  - Contract maintenance, updating and change control: ensuring that changes to the contract are agreed, authorised, accurately documented and implemented by both parties, and ensuring that all versions and related documents (such as budgets and service level agreements) are consistent
  - Contracts database management
  - Budgeting and costs/charges monitoring
  - Purchase-to-pay procedures
  - Management reporting
  - Dispute resolution (including escalation to higher levels if required)
- **Managing contract performance.** Service level agreements (SLAs) and performance measures (such as key performance indicators or KPIs) may be developed to express the desired outputs from the contract: these documents will form an operational tool with which the respective contract managers can monitor performance on a day-to-day basis. Such documentation will usually be more flexible than the contract document itself.
- **Contract review.** Contract managers from both buyer and supplier organisations should meet periodically to review progress, performance, compliance and delivery of contract outputs. There may be regular issues to discuss (eg customer feedback or a complaints log), while other agenda issues will relate to issues arising during the review period.
- **Supplier relationship management:** developing the working relationship between the buyer and supplier, through regular contacts, communication and information sharing; developing and applying supplier incentives (to motivate suppliers); managing and resolving conflicts; and developing approaches to collaboration and mutual support (including supplier assistance or development).
- **Contract renewal or termination:** reviewing the success of the contract and relationship and the status of the supply need, towards the end of the contract period. If an ongoing need remains,

and the contract has been satisfactorily fulfilled, it may be renewed. If the need has been met, or performance has been unsatisfactory, it may be terminated.

7.16   Many of the value additions (cost savings and improvements) available from procurement are achieved by how buyer and supplier work together *after* the contract has been awarded. If contracts are not well managed by the buying organisation the following adverse outcomes may occur.

- The supplier may be obliged to take control of contract performance and problem-solving, resulting in unbalanced decisions that do not serve the buying organisation's interests.
- Decisions may not be taken at the right time (or at all).
- Buyer and supplier may fail to understand – and fulfil – their obligations and responsibilities.
- There may be misunderstandings and disagreements, and too many issues may be escalated inappropriately, damaging the relationship.
- Progress may be slow, or there may be an inability to move forward.
- The intended benefits and value from the contract may not be realised.
- Opportunities to improve value for money and performance may be missed.

7.17   On the other hand, there are value-adding benefits of positive contract management.

- Improved risk management in developing and managing contracts
- Improved compliance and commitment by the supplier
- Incentives and momentum for ongoing relationship development and performance improvement
- Better value for money (arising from efficient contract administration and performance)

Supplier management

7.18   Buyers have often given high priority to identifying and evaluating potential suppliers, while paying less attention to the management of supplier relations once contracts have been awarded. Partly, this arose from a climate in which large stockholdings were accepted as an indispensible safety mechanism: if a supplier let you down, it need not be a disaster. But this is no longer the case, as we saw in Chapter 2. Organisations have been pressured to reduce wastes, costs and inventory – and therefore to manage supplier relationships more carefully in order to ensure that they *aren't* let down.

7.19   'Supplier management' is an umbrella term for many aspects of sourcing, contract management and supplier relationship management. Lysons and Farrington define it as:

'That aspect of purchasing or procurement which is concerned with rationalising the supplier base and selecting, co-ordinating, appraising the performance of and developing the potential of suppliers, and where appropriate, building long-term collaborative relationships'.

7.20   There are significant value-adding benefits to the positive and proactive management of supplier relationships, including the following.

- The company incurs fewer costs of identifying, appraising and training new vendors, and fewer transaction and contracting costs of multiple sourcing and competitive bidding, by developing a small core group of trusted suppliers.
- Quality and other problems can be ironed out progressively, and continuous improvements made, over a period of feedback, problem-solving and co-operation.
- Goodwill developed with positive relationships may earn preferential treatment or flexibility from suppliers in the event of emergencies (such as materials shortages or underestimated demand leading to urgent orders).
- Suppliers may be more motivated (especially by the promise of long-term, stable business) to give their best performance – and to add value through innovation, flexibility, commitment to continuous improvement and so on.
- Motivated suppliers may be willing to co-invest (eg in research and development, systems integration or staff training).

- There is less risk of supplier failure or poor performance, if performance standards are regularly agreed, monitored and managed.

7.21 After the sourcing, selecting and contracting of suppliers, therefore, it remains the buyer's responsibility:

- To *maintain regular contact* with the supplier, to check on progress and ensure that any issues or problems are discussed
- To *monitor the supplier's performance* against the agreed terms and standards, to ensure that they are being fulfilled: the process of contract management (discussed above).
- To *motivate the supplier*. Of course, the supplier should in any case be motivated by the thought of not gaining repeat business if performance is poor, but this is a somewhat negative incentive. More positively, buyers may introduce systems of recognition for suppliers who achieve consistently high performance.
- To work with the supplier to solve any *performance problems*. Buyers should be ready to accept that their own firm's success depends on the supplier's ability to perform: the process of supporting suppliers in performing well (by sharing information, offering training and so on) is referred to as 'supplier development'.
- To work with the supplier to resolve any *relationship problems* or disputes – ideally, without the costs and damaged relationships arising from taking matters to court (litigation). Constructive and proactive conflict management is essential within long-term partnerships – and to preserve important sources of supply.

Supplier performance appraisal or vendor rating

7.22 The effective evaluation of supplier performance potentially adds value in several ways. According to Lysons & Farrington, supplier performance appraisal can:

- Help identify the highest-quality and best-performing suppliers: assisting decision-making regarding: (a) which suppliers should get specific orders (or be invited to tender for a contract); (b) when a supplier should be retained or removed from a preferred or approved list; and (c) which suppliers show potential for closer partnership relationships.
- Suggest how relationships with suppliers can (or need to be) enhanced to improve their performance (eg to evaluate the effectiveness of purchasing's supplier selection and contract management processes)
- Help ensure that suppliers live up to what was promised in their contracts
- Provide suppliers with an incentive to maintain and/or continuously improve performance levels
- Significantly improve supplier performance, by identifying problems which can be tracked and fixed, or areas in which support and development is needed.

7.23 Again, remember that *supplier appraisal* (pre-contract, for the purposes of supplier selection) is a somewhat different process from *supplier performance appraisal* (post-contract, for the purposes of management control). The former assesses a potential supplier's capability to fulfil the buyer's requirements; the latter assesses a current supplier's performance in fulfilling them. In order to distinguish the two more clearly, the post-contract process is sometimes referred to as **vendor rating**: a vendor being a person or organisation that currently sells you something, and rating being a way of evaluating or 'scoring' performance.

7.24 Vendor rating is the measurement of supplier performance using agreed criteria, usually including:

- *Price*: eg measured by value for money, market price or under, lowest or competitive pricing, good cost management and reasonable profit margins
- *Quality*: eg measured by key performance indicators (KPIs) such as the number or proportion of defects, quality assurance procedures
- *Delivery*: eg measured by KPIs such as the proportion of on-time in-full (OTIF) deliveries, or increases or decreases in lead times for delivery

Other measurable factors might include: after-sales service, efficiency and accuracy of contract management and administration, willingness to commit to continuous improvement, quality of contacts and communication, contribution to innovation, flexibility and responsiveness to urgent or unusual requests – and so on.

7.25 There are two basic approaches to vendor rating. One common approach is based on the use of a *supplier performance evaluation form*: a checklist of key performance factors, against which supplier managers assess the supplier's performance as good, satisfactory or unsatisfactory: Figure 5.3. A *weighting* is applied to each factor, so that the supplier's performance in key performance areas, and overall, can be summarised as good, satisfactory or unsatisfactory. This is comparatively easy to implement, once meaningful checklists have been developed, but it is fairly broad and subjective.

Figure 5.3 *Excerpt from a supplier evaluation form (adapted from Dobler & Burt)*

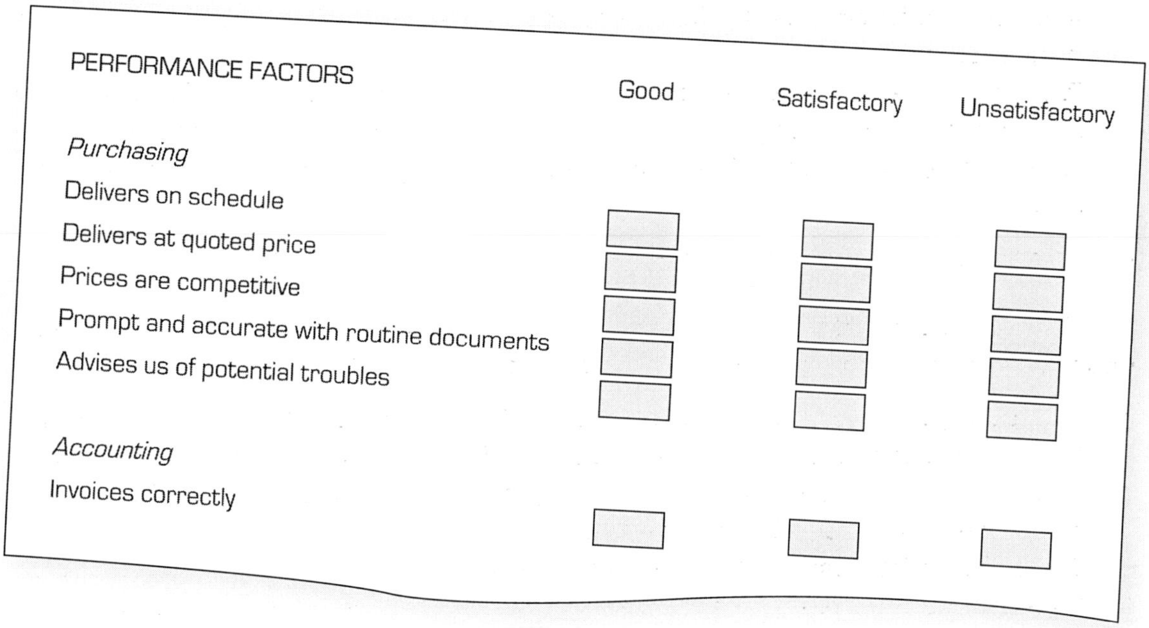

PERFORMANCE FACTORS	Good	Satisfactory	Unsatisfactory
Purchasing			
Delivers on schedule	☐	☐	☐
Delivers at quoted price	☐	☐	☐
Prices are competitive	☐	☐	☐
Prompt and accurate with routine documents	☐	☐	☐
Advises us of potential troubles	☐	☐	☐
Accounting			
Invoices correctly	☐	☐	☐

7.26 Another approach is the *factor rating method*, which gives a numerical score for each key assessment factor. For example, the measure of quality performance might be '100% minus percentage of rejects in total deliveries': a supplier whose deliveries contained 3% rejects would score 97% or 0.97 on this measure. Each of the major factors is also given a weighting, according to its importance within overall performance, and this is applied to each score, to end up with an overall score or rating. This can be used to compare and rank suppliers. It may also be used year on year, to provide a measure of whether a supplier's performance is improving or declining.

7.27 Of course, neither approach diagnoses the *causes* of any performance shortfalls identified, nor what needs to be done to address them. A vendor rating should therefore be seen within the whole process of supplier performance management.

Supplier development

7.28 Supplier development may be defined as: 'Any activity that a buyer undertakes to improve a supplier's performance and/or capabilities to meet the buyer's short- or long-term supply needs'.

7.29 Hartley & Choi identify two overall objectives for organisations engaging in supply development programmes.

- Raising supplier competence to a specified level (eg in terms of reduced costs, or improved quality or delivery performance). *Results-oriented* development programmes therefore focus on solving specific performance issues: the buyer supports the supplier in making step-by-step technical changes, to achieve pre-determined improvements.
- Supporting suppliers in self-sustaining required performance standards, through a process of continuous improvement. *Process-oriented* development programmes therefore focus on increasing the supplier's ability to make their *own* process and performance improvements, without ongoing direct intervention by the buyer.

7.30 A wide variety of approaches may be used to bridge perceived performance or relationship gaps. Here are some examples.

- Enhancing working relationships (eg by improved communication systems and routines)
- Clarifying or increasing performance goals and measures (eg KPIs for improvements in waste reduction or delivery lead times), and associated incentives and penalties to motivate improvements
- Seconding the buying organisation's staff to the supplier (or *vice versa*) for training, coaching, consultancy, support or liaison
- Providing capital (eg to help finance a new development project or the acquisition of new plant and equipment)
- Providing progress payments during the development of a project or product, to support the supplier's cashflow
- Loaning machinery, equipment or IT hardware. (CIPS guidance cites some practical examples including: a buyer providing electronic terminals to suppliers, so that buyers can use purchasing cards; a buyer paying for a supplier's manufacturing processes to be updated, in return for discounted supplies in future; and a buyer giving an outsource supplier the machinery previously used to perform the activity in-house.)
- Granting access to IT and ICT systems and information (eg extranets and databases, inventory systems, computer aided design capability and so on)
- Using the buying organisation's bargaining power to obtain materials or equipment for the supplier at a discount
- Offering training for the supplier's staff in relevant areas (eg technical aspects of the requirement, or best practice)
- Providing help or consultancy on value analysis (waste reduction) programmes, whole life costing or other areas of expertise.

7.31 Bearing in mind the expense and effort that may be involved in supplier development, buyers will expect to make significant value gains from: sharing in the specialist knowledge of the supplier; taking advantage of the supplier's capabilities to support the outsourcing of non-core activities; or improving supplier and supply chain performance to achieve better quality, delivery or cost. Like other forms of collaborative relationship, however, the aim is for benefits to accrue to both sides.

Chapter summary

- It is useful to view a procurement process as a series of stages beginning with identifying a need and continuing through to management of the supplier and contract. Not all procurements will go through all the stages of the cycle.
- There is a spectrum of buyer-supplier relationships. A buyer may adopt different relationships with different suppliers.
- It is useful for an organisation to have a formal, systematic approach to procurement processes and procedures.
- Users may identify a need by submitting a requisition. This may be translated into a specification (either a conformance specification or a performance specification).
- Contract terms may be express or implied. Many contracts are drawn up in standard form, sometimes based on model form contracts.
- There are numerous sources of information on possible suppliers. A buyer will usually appraise and pre-qualify a potential supplier before contract award.
- Approaches to contract award include framework agreements, requests for quotation from shortlisted suppliers, or competitive bidding (tendering).
- The procurement process does not end once the contract has been awarded. The buyer must still manage supplier performance to ensure a successful outcome.

Self-test questions

Numbers in brackets refer to the paragraphs where you can check your answers.

1   List the stages in a typical procurement process. (1.3, Figure 5.1)

2   List possible types of buyer-supplier relationship. (1.10)

3   List benefits of a systematic approach to structuring procurement processes. (2.2)

4   Suggest approaches to attaining best practice in procurement. (2.7)

5   What details are usually included on a requisition form? (3.4)

6   Distinguish between a conformance specification and a performance specification. (3.12, 3.14)

7   In what ways may a term be implied into a contract? (4.5)

8   What is a service level agreement? (4.13)

9   List possible sources of information about potential suppliers. (5.5)

10   List Carter's 10Cs of supplier appraisal. (5.11)

11   Describe four situations in which competitive bidding should not be used. (Table 5.1)

12   List steps in a best-practice tender procedure. (6.13)

13   What is meant by 'expediting' an order? (7.4)

14   List benefits of positive contract management. (7.17)

CHAPTER 6

E-procurement

Assessment criteria and indicative content

2.3 Explain how electronic systems can be used at different stages of the sourcing process

- E-requisitioning, e-catalogues, e-ordering, e-sourcing and e-payment technologies
- The impact of electronic purchase to pay (P2P) systems on the procurement process

Section headings

1 Electronic systems in the procurement process
2 E-requisitioning
3 E-sourcing
4 E-ordering
5 E-P2P
6 E-payment

Introduction

In our discussion of a generic procurement process in Chapter 5, we frequently noted that there were 'electronic equivalents' to many of the actions and documentation involved. In this chapter, we look in more detail at some of the electronic systems that can be applied to various stages of the procurement process, and at their impact on procurement operations and efficiency.

There are several other major applications of information and communications technology (ICT) to procurement tasks – such as inventory management, demand management, project management and supply chain communications. These are the focus of a separate syllabus topic, as part of the organisational infrastructure within which procurement operates: we will discuss them in Chapter 9.

1 Electronic systems in the procurement process

The impact of information and communications technology (ICT)

1.1 Broadly speaking, developments in ICT have radically changed the way people do business in the following ways.

- Dramatically increasing the speed of communication and information processing. This also supports more genuine interactivity in information gathering and transaction processing. Real-time answers to enquiries, updating of information, processing of transactions and conversations can be conducted via a computer network or the internet.
- Offering wider access to knowledge and information, especially from global sources. The internet offers unrestricted, constant access to formal information resources via websites, databases, libraries, expert agencies etc. In addition, the internet allows access to many informal information sources in the form of network contacts forums etc.
- Facilitating 24-hour, 7-day, global business. The internet and email allow companies to offer service and maintain communication across office hours, international time zones and geographical distances.
- Supporting paperless communications (eg electronic mail messages), business transactions (eg

electronic ordering and payment) and service delivery (eg web-based information and education services).

- Creating 'virtual' relationships, teams and organisations, by making location irrelevant to the process of data-sharing, communication and collaboration. This is particularly important when developing and supporting global buyer-supplier relationships and supply chains.

The internet and e-commerce

1.2 The internet is a worldwide computer network allowing computers to communicate via telecommunications links. The network can also be accessed from laptop computers and personal hand-held devices such as tablets and smartphones.

1.3 The term 'e-commerce' (short for electronic commerce) refers to business transactions carried out online via ICT – usually the internet. E-commerce has facilitated direct marketing, linking customers directly with suppliers across the whole value chain. It is a means of automating business transactions and workflows – and also streamlining and improving them.

1.4 Some websites exist only to provide information about products, services or other matters. They might provide contact details for would-be customers to make direct enquiries or orders, or to find a local retail outlet or distributor. A transaction-supporting website, however, can be a 'virtual' retail outlet, warehouse, supermarket, auction room or market exchange – enabling buyers to investigate suppliers, post requirements, receive offers, and conduct a range of P2P functions (from ordering to track-and-trace to payment).

1.5 Perhaps the most obvious way in which the internet has supported the growth of e-commerce and specifically e-procurement (see below) is in providing information in an accessible, up-to-date and voluminous form. By accessing a portal for, say, buying plumbing supplies, the purchaser can view an entire information centre on all types of product from all suppliers who have access to the portal, with prices, specifications, stock levels and delivery times.

1.6 More sophisticated users of e-commerce can engage in electronic value chain trading, which means that information on their entire value chain from customers via partners to suppliers is opened up for collaboration and co-operation on finding new and better ways of doing things.

1.7 For a procurement function, the internet has also provided other benefits.

- Wider choice of suppliers, including global and small suppliers, via the internet. (Procurement professionals still have to make strategic and tactical choices: ICT merely provides better quality information for doing this.)
- Savings in procurement costs, through electronic communication, greater accuracy and electronic transaction processing. (In a research project in 1997, management consultants McKinsey noted that the biggest effect of the internet for business overall is the huge saving in transaction and interaction costs – the costs of 'the searching, coordinating and monitoring that people and companies do when they exchange goods, services or ideas'.)
- Support for low inventory and efficient stock turnover (as in just in time systems), due to the speed or responsiveness of the system
- Improved supply chain relationships and coordination, arising from data-sharing. These in turn facilitate collaboration and improved customer service (by streamlining and integrating supply chain processes).

E-procurement

1.8 CIPS defines e-procurement as 'the combined use of information and communication technology through electronic means to enhance external and internal procurement and supply management processes.'

1.9   The term 'e-purchasing' is often used in this context. In CIPS terminology, however, e-purchasing specifically addresses the 'purchase-to-pay' stage of the procurement cycle: the stage from when a purchase has been approved to the receipt of the product, and then (often, but not always) the payment for the product.

1.10   The term 'e-sourcing' refers to the earlier stages in the cycle, when a need is identified and requisitioned, the market is surveyed, suppliers are appraised and pre-qualified, and relationships with suppliers are set up (eg through e-tendering or e-auction and contract award): Figure 6.1

Figure 6.1 *The e-procurement cycle*

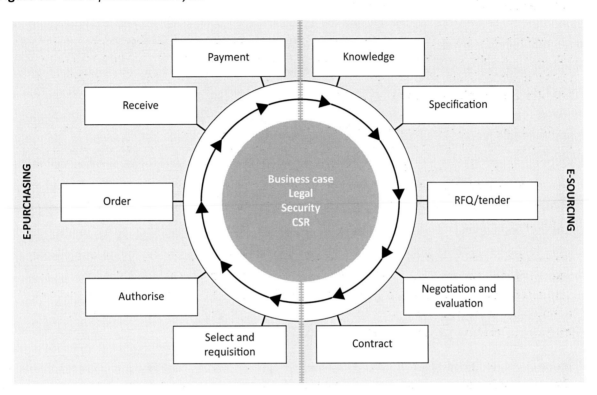

1.11   In some versions of the above diagram, the cycle as a whole is called the e-commerce cycle and the two distinct phases are called e-sourcing and e-procurement. Naming the cycle 'the e-procurement cycle' and the second phase 'e-purchasing', as above, is arguably a clearer approach which is consistent with terminology used when the process is not electronic.

1.12   A broad ranging e-procurement cycle allows procurement staff to perform the following tasks (some of which we will go on to explore in more detail in later sections of this Chapter): Table 6.1.

Table 6.1 *E-procurement tools*

STAGE OF THE PROCUREMENT CYCLE	E-FUNCTIONS AND TOOLS
Identifying and defining needs	• Check real time inventory, and issue requisitions as required • Access spend analysis, trend analysis and investment analysis tools to support procurement decisions • Create e-specifications and e-contracts
Sourcing the market	• Access to supply market intelligence tools • Access to catalogue, supplier and supplier performance data • Locate, appraise and pre-qualify suppliers and verify price information • Issue invitations to tender or requests for quotation, and receive and evaluate tender submissions • Participate in auctions or run reverse auctions • Issue call off orders from partners (under framework or systems contracts) or allow partners to control stock and deliveries (vendor managed inventory) for low-value purchases • Access negotiation planning data • Generate and transmit purchase orders or contracts (with automatic updating of the contract management database)
Purchase to Pay (P2P) and contract management	• Track and trace of deliveries • Expediting by exception • Automated receipt and inspection (eg by barcode or RFID), verifying delivery to trigger payment authorisation or automatic payment – and update inventory records • Capturing of supplier performance data, budgetary control/spend data • Use of dedicated email facility, extranet or intranet for supply chain communication • Receipt of invoices: using self-billing, automated invoice matching and electronic invoice generation • Generation of paper payments (eg cheques) and e-payments (eg by funds transfer)

Benefits of automating procurement and supply chain processes

1.13 Intense competition in the private sector – and pressures for cost efficiency and value for money in the public sector – are forcing organisations to look at developing innovative business process solutions. This often means performing activities faster, better and more cheaply than before – and procurement and supply chain processes are a major area for consideration.

1.14 Procurement and supply chain processes are often a combination of automated and manual elements. Automated business processes are supported by electronic ICT systems. Manual processes may still be necessary for some business requirements (eg the preparation of goods receiving paperwork) where technology is not available – although there is an increasing range of electronic solutions for many tasks (eg with hand-held devices, electronic scanners and electronic forms for data input and sharing).

1.15 There is a significant potential cost saving (for both buyers and suppliers) in the effective automation of procurement, through streamlining and speeding up processes: minimising inefficient (and potentially inaccurate) manual data and document handling tasks such as data input and transfer, verification, calculation, formatting, disseminating; and so on. Survey results indicate a 10:1 cost ratio when comparing manual to automated processing costs.

1.16 However, the benefits are not limited to cost reductions. Other potential benefits are listed below.

- Improved communication and 'transparency' of information throughout the internal and external supply chain, to support co-ordination and decision-making (eg enabling procurements – and suppliers' production plans – to be more closely aligned to customer demand or usage rates)
- Higher accuracy of data input, manipulation (eg calculations or modelling) and transfer. Greater data accuracy can support decision-making (eg in regard to inventory levels), as well as minimising the risks

of errors (such as incorrect order quantities or delivery requirements conveyed to suppliers)

- Reduced cycle and lead times (through the streamlining of procurement processes, and more accurate data for demand forecasting). Automated processes are generally more responsive: so, for example, suppliers may also benefit from reduced cycle times for the payment of their invoices, using e-invoicing and e-payment systems.
- Improved supplier relations (eg through improved speed and clarity of communication and data sharing, and the potential for 'virtual' collaboration and supplier management using ICT communication links)
- Real-time information (eg on inventory levels or delivery progress) to support planning, decision-making and expediting
- Reduced risk of fraud (falsified records, intentional miscalculations, theft) through fewer cash transactions, less human intervention in transactions, controlled access to data systems, and the automatic identification of discrepant (non-matching) data
- Improved management information, decision support and feedback.

Risks and costs of electronic procurement processes

1.17 Organisations can get very enthusiastic about the possibilities of new technology. However, they must recognise that a given technology may not be the most effective, or cost-effective, solution to every business or procurement challenge. Here are some drawbacks of technology.

- High capital investment and set-up costs (design and development, hardware and software costs) – which may put more sophisticated applications (such as electronic data interchange or EDI) beyond the reach of small firms.
- High initial learning curve costs: training of users, cost of initial errors while users learn the system, potential confusion of running the system in parallel with old methods during the initial period
- Reliability issues, especially at an early stage of development, with the risk of 'bugs' in the software and initial teething troubles. Reliability may continue to be a problem, however, with the risks of network breakdown, power failure or viruses contaminating the system – and this can often cause chaos if the firm has become dependent on the technology (eg to communicate with suppliers or access information), with no backup systems in place.
- Compatibility issues, if the system is required to work together with the different systems of suppliers, say – or if key suppliers (eg in countries with less developed infrastructure) do not have access to the technology.
- Ethical issues, such as forcing smaller suppliers to invest in collaborative technologies, automating processes previously carried out by people (implying redundancies), and the need for stakeholder management.
- Data security risks, arising from unauthorised or malicious access to data, corruption or loss of data, computer viruses or other 'malware'.

1.18 Table 6.2 summarises some of the measures that organisations can take to protect themselves from breaches of data security and fraud in the use of electronic procurement systems.

Table 6.2 *Minimising data security and fraud risks of e-procurement processes*

Physical security	• Physical business protection related to hardware theft • Disposal routines for old computers should consider the deletion of sensitive information prior to resale
Data backup routines	• Backing up data to removable media (eg an external hard drive or 'cloud' server) on a daily basis • Running data verification routines after backup routines
Passwords	• Develop robust password systems
System upgrades	• Minimise vulnerability by keeping systems as up to date as possible
Firewall systems	• Hardware or software security that inspects, allows, and/or blocks traffic along information networks
Malicious software (malware) protection	• Malware is the general term that refers to any type of malicious software, including viruses, worms, Trojans, adware and spyware. • Most threats can be removed by dedicated software protection and removal tools
Authorisation procedures	• Data integration to enable matching of records (eg invoices with orders and goods received notes) and identification of discrepant data • Automatic routing of e-requisitions, procurement orders and invoices to appropriate budget holders for managerial sign-off or authorisation.

2   E-requisitioning

Electronic requisition

2.1   Electronic requisitioning is designed to simplify the process whereby the procurement function captures requisitions from users, and provides information about both the requisitioner and the requirement.

2.2   The database contains records of all materials and parts, code numbers, descriptions, usage records and current balance – as well as prices of recent acquisitions and supplier details. Stock levels are automatically updated as items are received into, or issued from, inventory, and re-orders are generated automatically when a pre-determined level is reached, or when a master production schedule (or bill of materials) dictates. Where the economic order quantity (EOQ) model is used, the system can compute and requisition the appropriate re-order quantity.

Requirement planning and specification systems

2.3   Here are some examples of requirement planning and specification tools.

- Integrated systems for resource planning, such as materials requirements planning (MRP), manufacturing resources planning (MRP II) or enterprise resource planning (ERP) systems. These will be discussed in Chapter 9.
- Design and development systems (eg computer aided design and manufacture – CAD/CAM)

2.4   In each case, detailed 'bills of materials' (lists of requirements) are created automatically from production plans, project work breakdown structures (WBS) or design specifications.

Electronic point of sale (EPOS) systems

2.5   Point of sale devices involve the use of barcoding and radio frequency identification (RFID) tagging to record sales at point-of-sale terminals, which are linked to IT systems. Electronic point of sale (EPOS) systems can be connected to inventory management systems, to trigger automatic stock requisition and replenishment.

2.6   In such a system, data on the cost structure and current stock status of each product is stored on a centralised database. When a product sale is processed at the point of sale (using EPOS), the transactional adjustment is made to the product stock status. This enables a real time update of all stock status or inventory records, which can be used to trigger electronic requisitions. When stocks fall to a pre-determined re-order point, the EPOS system generates a replenishment report. In the case of a supermarket branch store, for example, this information would be transmitted to the central distribution centre to arrange delivery of the relevant products.

2.7 EPOS can also be used to track product sales, stock availability and location, and the location of deliveries (using global positioning systems or GPS technology). It can be connected to point-of-sale payment systems (via electronic funds transfer) and management information systems (for sales analysis, demand forecasting and inventory). In marketing contexts, it also supports the use of loyalty cards, as a way of incentivising customer loyalty and gathering customer data.

2.8 The main benefits of an EPOS system are as follows.

- Efficient and accurate processing of customer transactions, reducing queuing time
- Stock management: the real time nature of the EPOS database enables automatic creation of replenishment orders
- Rapid communication of supply and demand information throughout the supply chain, to support demand forecasting, production planning and responsive replenishment (particularly useful for retailers of fast moving consumer goods, where product shelf-life is a key business factor)
- Access to data on wastage, profit margins, sales trends, consumer purchasing patterns and so on, to support procurement and operations decision making.

3 E-sourcing

3.1 E-sourcing is defined as 'using the internet to make decisions and form strategies regarding how and where services or products are obtained' (*CIPS*): in other words, using electronic tools for the pre-contract or 'sourcing' part of the procurement cycle.

3.2 A range of e-sourcing tools may be available to the procurement function.

- **E-catalogues:** suppliers exhibit their products in electronic catalogues, which can be viewed online or downloaded by potential purchasers.
- **Supplier portals and market exchanges**: sites where multiple buyers/sellers share information about requirements and offerings
- **E-tendering**, using e-RFQs (electronic requests for quotation) and specifications posted online or emailed to potential suppliers. Bids can also be received and evaluated electronically against pre-set criteria.
- **E-auctions**, conducted online using the buyer's or seller's website, or third party auction sites. In an auction, suppliers offer goods online, and potential buyers bid competitively. All bids are 'open' (visible to all participants, minus the names of the suppliers), so buyers may raise their offers competitively during the auction. At the end of the specified bidding period, the highest bid (as evaluated by the auction software) wins. You may be familiar with this system from eBay, for example.

  In a *reverse auction,* the *buyer* specifies its requirements, and *suppliers* submit competitive quotes. Again, all bids are open, so suppliers may lower their prices competitively during the auction. At the end of the bidding period, the lowest bid compliant with the specification (as evaluated by the software and/or according to agreed 'auction rules' eg whether the lowest bid must be accepted) wins.
- **Online supplier evaluation data**: third party reports, customer feedback, registers and directories of approved or accredited suppliers, benchmarking reports, market intelligence tools and so on.

Supply market data

3.3   The internet is the most-used source of information on supply markets. The advantages and disadvantages of using it to identify potential suppliers can be summarised as follows: Table 6.3.

Table 6.3 *Using the internet to identify potential suppliers*

ADVANTAGES	DISADVANTAGES
Global, 24/7 available source of data	Excess volume of information
Low-cost, fast, convenient info search	Information may be unreliable/outdated
Information generally frequently updated	Difficulty verifying data, source credibility
Access to small, niche, global suppliers	Limited ability to 'sample' product/service
Access to customer feedback, reports, ratings, certification data etc.	Supports global sourcing – creating logistical challenges, risks etc.
Some ability to 'sample' product/service (eg virtual tours, digital samples)	May discriminate against developing country suppliers
Facilities for direct contact (eg via email)	

E-auctions

3.4   The increasingly common practice of using online reverse auctions has attracted much comment in the procurement literature. Many benefits are claimed for online auctions (particularly by software firms marketing online auction systems!)

- Efficient administration and reduction in acquisition lead time, through eliminating time-consuming manual processes of supplier engagement, quotation requests and comparisons, negotiations and so on
- Savings for buyers, over and above those obtained from negotiation, as a result of competition
- Improved value for buyers, by giving a 'wake up' call to existing suppliers on the need to reconsider their cost base and pricing in order to remain competitive
- Access for buyers to a wider range of potential suppliers and sources of market information, including a global supply base
- Less time 'wasted' on interpersonal interaction eg meeting supplier representatives (although, of course, this may be a *drawback* where a buyer wishes to develop closer, more collaborative relationships with its supply chain)
- Opportunities for suppliers to enter previously closed markets or accounts (especially valuable for smaller suppliers)
- Opportunities for suppliers to gather competitor and market pricing data (and a clear indication of what is required in order to win business) in order to develop and maintain their own competitiveness.

3.5   Online auctions have also come in for criticism, on the following grounds.

- Online auctions are based on a zero-sum, adversarial or 'win-lose' approach: profit for either party is at the other's expense. This may get in the way of collaborative supply chain relationships, and the value gains available from collaboration.
- Suppliers are vulnerable to coercion (being forced to participate on threat of lost business) and manipulation (eg 'fake' bids by a buyer to force down prices; or forcing prices lower by 'apparent' competition, while always intending to use a pre-selected supplier). Suppliers may feel exploited, leading to loss of trust and goodwill in the buyer-supplier relationship.
- There may be long-term adverse effects on the economic performance of the supplier: forced to competitive price reductions which are unsustainable.
- There may be long-term adverse effects on the economic performance of the buyer: eg if supplier failure (and/or loss of goodwill) reduces the future supply base and incurs further costs (eg quality

problems).

- Promised savings may not materialise, due to factors such as: the costs of switching suppliers, or retaliatory pricing by alienated suppliers (especially when buyers have urgent requirements).
- Suppliers get the message that price is the most important factor in winning business, and may therefore downgrade the quality, innovation or sustainability of their offerings, in order to compete on cost.
- The process leaves little scope to take adequate account of non-price criteria (eg quality, customer service or sustainability) and stakeholder input.

3.6   Lysons & Farrington argue that: 'Lowest-price reverse auction processes should be used only where there is little concern about production specifications or the suppliers selected. They are not appropriate for complex products or projects requiring collaboration or considerable negotiation.'

E-tendering

3.7   The use of e-tendering replaces traditional manual paper-based processes for competitive tendering (discussed in Chapter 5) with electronically facilitated processes based on best tendering practices.

- The invitation to tender (ITT) is published on the buyer's e-tender web portal, for potential suppliers to view. Bid-related documents are posted for interested suppliers to download.
- Suppliers respond to the ITT by sending their bids using secure email to the e-tendering system's 'electronic vault', and are registered as bidders.
- Buyers can observe and manage the tendering process through a 'front end' web function, enabling them to answer queries for clarification and so on.
- In-built security features prohibit access to any of the tender responses until a specified time. Once the tender deadline has been reached, the tender evaluation team can 'open' (view) the tenders and collaborate online to evaluate the submitted bids.
- The system may include automatic scoring and evaluation capability. Alternatively, data can be cut and pasted from e-tender documents to a spreadsheet for ease of comparison.
- Successful and unsuccessful bidders can be automatically notified of the award.

3.8   In addition to these core functions, most e-tendering systems provide additional support such as archiving, document management, early warning of opportunities to suppliers, and maintenance of approved and/or potential supplier lists. If such a system is integrated with the organisation's contract management system, the complete lifecycle of the contract can be managed, and re-tendering (when the contact comes up for renewal) co-ordinated.

3.9   Many business benefits are claimed for e-tendering.

- Embedding tender best practice, and enabling the devolution of tendering tasks to non-procurement specialists
- Process efficiencies: reducing tender cycle times; reducing labour-intensive tasks and paperwork; and enabling procurement specialists to focus on more strategic value-adding activities
- Giving non-discriminatory access to the tender process for small suppliers and worldwide suppliers (which may offer cost or innovation benefits to the buyer)
- Facilitating cross-functional communication and data sharing about procurement projects
- Facilitating fast and accurate screening of bids against pre-qualification data, enabling the automatic rejection of suppliers that fail to meet the tender specification
- Enabling faster response to questions and points of clarification during the tender period (eg using dedicated email facilities)
- Improving the transparency and fairness of the tendering process: all suppliers getting the same information, operating to the same time-scales, being evaluated on the same criteria, able to track the progress of the tender – and so on.
- Improving the audit trail (the recorded history of events and decisions leading up to contract award):

enabling managers to evaluate procurement decisions and learn lessons; providing data for the de-briefing of unsuccessful bidders; and providing evidence of best practice in the event of a legal challenge to the contract award decision.

3.10 Drawbacks to e-tendering include: limited access for suppliers lacking the technical know-how or equipment to bid electronically; issues around the security of commercial information and intellectual property shared in the course of the tender exercise; and significant investment costs associated with specialist equipment, software, staff training and so on.

Potential benefits of e-sourcing

3.11 The potential benefits of developing e-sourcing in general are as follows.

- Reduced costs through increased purchasing process efficiencies, reduced sourcing costs, improvements in contract performance management etc.
- Best practice development: consistent, transparent use of controlled procedures, enabling non-procurement staff to participate in sourcing without compromise of good practice or sound procurement disciplines.
- Enhanced quality and capability, because the total sourcing and management process is transparent. Without e-sourcing it is often difficult for buyers to evaluate fragmented information about potential suppliers and to compare one with another in order to make a final decision.
- Reduced sourcing cycle times
- Improved training and efficiency: e-sourcing applications can be used as offline training tools to give employees hands-on experience with the application without jeopardising the company's actual data.

3.12 The website of the UK's Office of Government Commerce (OGC) claimed a number of benefits for e-sourcing in the public sector: Table 6.4.

Table 6.4 *Advantages of e-sourcing in the public sector*

BENEFIT	EXPLANATION
Process efficiencies	Reducing time and effort spent on tendering and contract management; reduced paperwork; fewer human errors
Compliance	With regulations, eg with the provisions of the Efficiency Review and the National Procurement Strategy for Local Government in the UK
Cost savings	Reducing the direct costs of tendering (for both buyer and suppliers); more efficient comparison, supporting savings through competition
Collaboration	Making it easier for purchasers to work together on common sourcing projects across different departments and regions: creating 'virtual buying organisations' to increase bargaining power
Strategic focus	Allowing purchasing professionals to focus on value-added and strategic procurement activity (such as supplier screening, supply base development and relationship management), rather than administration

3.13 To gain maximum benefits, e-sourcing must be part of an overall procurement strategy. Whilst e-sourcing software has the potential to achieve many business benefits it should not be perceived as replacing proven best practice. E-sourcing enhances these practices to allow buyers both the time and the visibility to make more effective and efficient decisions.

4   E-ordering

E-catalogues

4.1   An online catalogue is the web-based equivalent of a supplier's printed catalogue, providing product specifications and cost information. However, an interactive e-catalogue also includes integrated stock database interrogation, ordering and payment facilities – allowing for efficient and cost-effective procurement of proprietary goods and services.

4.2   One potential downside to the use of e-catalogues is the lack of human contact, which might be necessary for clarification or negotiation of terms or special delivery instructions. Most online catalogues have integrated help-line facilities to assist the buying process when needed.

Desk-top procurement systems

4.3   Once an e-requisition has been confirmed, the buyer may specify the selected supplier (where relevant) and the system generates documentation for purchase, accounts, acknowledgement, receiving and inspection. Desk-top procurement systems generally also allow users to place electronic orders with approved suppliers, within the framework of a supply contract already set up by the procurement function: for example, a framework agreement or a systems or call-off contract.

Automatic ordering

4.4   Orders or re-orders (stock replenishment) may be automatically generated, without human intervention, in the case of requisitions triggered by MRP, ERP, EPOS or electronic inventory management systems, where framework or systems contracts have already been placed with approved suppliers. Nissan UK, for example, operates a just in time system whereby a centralised system produces daily manufacturing schedules, which are transmitted to computers on the production lines – which in turn transmit orders direct to component manufacturers as components are required.

E-contracting

4.5   Electronic contracts can be created and transmitted to suppliers (and other relevant stakeholders). This has particular value-adding benefits.

- Enabling the 'cutting and pasting' of standard contract terms, and the variation of draft terms, in an efficient and flexible way
- Enabling strong controls over confidentiality (eg by password-protected access to contract drafts and details)
- Enabling strong contract variation, change and version control (eg with clearly flagged variations and versions; 'read only' versions, which cannot be amended by non-authorised users; and the ability to make amendments confined to authorised individuals)
- Integration with a contract management database, enabling contract managers to access contract details, manage versions, capture supplier performance data and so on

5 E-P2P

5.1 The term 'e-procurement' is sometimes used to refer to the stage which follows e-sourcing: the application of information and communication technology specifically to the purchase-to-pay part of the purchasing cycle. All stages of the P2P cycle can be computerised, with tools such as the following.

- **Electronic data interchange:** the exchange of transaction documents in a standardised electronic form, directly from a computer application in one organisation to an application in another. We will discuss this in the context of supply chain communication systems, in Chapter 9.
- **Online track and trace:** the ability to trace the location and progress of deliveries, using barcodes or RFID tagging integrated with global positioning systems (GPS). Such systems are commonly used by logistics companies such as Fedex and DHL, for example, enabling shipments to be located through key transit points at which their arrival has been logged. The advantages of such systems include: easy location of consignments; electronic proof of delivery and acceptance of goods; enhanced customer service and empowerment; and the effective 'outsourcing' of expediting to the customer.
- **Expediting by exception:** the ability to track the progress of transactions, contracts and deliveries, where the system 'flags' activities that have not happened how or when they should have. These 'exceptions' can then be expedited (or 'chased') as appropriate: meanwhile, buyers are free to ignore the large majority of activities that are progressing smoothly. Systems generally allow procurement staff to access the 'open orders' file at any time, or according to a pre-programmed reporting schedule. The system may also generate follow-up messages to suppliers after defined intervals have elapsed.
- **Receipt and inspection**: the ability to scan goods received (using barcode readers or RFID), automatically logging and disseminating receipt data.
  - Inventory records can be updated to reflect received stock
  - Defects, returns or short-falls can be flagged for problem-solving
  - The status of the order can be changed in procurement and tracking systems (eg from 'on order from supplier' to 'received from supplier')
  - Supplier performance data (in terms of delivery and quality) can be captured for future reference
  - Internal customer systems can be updated automatically, informing stores and user departments when orders have been fulfilled
  - Automatic payment can be triggered by verification of receipt and acceptance of the goods in satisfactory condition.
- **Electronic payment:** automated generation of invoices for orders verified as satisfactorily received (self-billing); matching of supplier invoices with orders and goods received data; payment by electronic funds transfer; or the use of credit-card style purchasing cards.
- **Contract management systems:** creation of electronic contracts; reporting of any performance discrepancies (expediting by exception); contract updating and variation/version control; and so on
- **Database information:** centrally stored and managed data concerning supply markets, customers, supplier performance or other areas, which can be updated and interrogated in real time.

5.2 This technology makes it possible for users who are *not* procurement specialists to manage the buying process according to systematic procurement disciplines – so it is often used to devolve buying to user departments.

Benefits of electronic P2P systems

5.3 The consequences of computerising purchasing systems can be dramatic. The UK government's booklet *Supplying the Challenge*, for example, described the process at confectionery company Mars. 'Buyers have replaced paper and files with electronic information and links to company operational data: now the company is reaping the rewards through more co-ordinated – increasingly pan-European – buying, better scheduled deliveries, and more information available more quickly to [internal] customers throughout the organisation. Everyone creating a requisition does so on a computer screen. Buying authorisations are registered on-screen and buyers create priced orders from the information brought together by the system. This alone saves huge amounts of time and money. Perhaps more important, the system helps Mars plan further ahead and control its purchasing better.'

5.4 Typical benefits to be gained from the use of electronic P2P systems are as follows.

- Streamlining and improving the flow of work through the system potentially both reduces costs and enhances the cashflow cycle. It may also increase business responsiveness in general.
- The interface between the organisation and its suppliers is improved by accurate, swift transaction processing and information, potentially improving supplier relations (and making the buying organisation a more 'attractive' customer to suppliers).
- Error rates, associated with data input, transfer and processing, are reduced.
- Procurement and finance personnel are freed from purely administrative burdens, to focus on managing crucial areas of their roles.
- The system provides for procedural consistency, compliance and control, enabling P2P tasks to be devolved to non-specialists with less risk of 'maverick' behaviour or lapses in good practice.

6 E-payment

6.1 As mentioned above, several invoicing and payment functions in the P2P process can be effectively automated, or electronically assisted.

Electronic consolidated invoicing

6.2 An electronic consolidated invoice (sent to a buyer by a supplier) is an electronic file containing all the information required to enable the finance department to effect payment. This saves the finance department from having to re-input the information already generated by suppliers.

Automatic invoice matching

6.3 An electronic invoice (or details from a paper invoice) entered on the system is automatically matched with the referenced purchase order and goods received data, so that it can be immediately passed for payment.

Evaluated receipt settlement (self-billing)

6.4 Evaluated receipt settlement – also called 'self billing' or 'payment on receipt' – removes the need for a supplier to submit a hard copy invoice. Acceptance of the goods, or confirmed delivery of the service – following verification that they have been delivered to the required quality standard – is logged in the buyer's system. This triggers the generation of receipt documentation and payment of the agreed amount for the goods or service received (drawn from the order database) to the supplier.

Electronic funds transfer

6.5 Electronic funds transfer (EFT) is the process of transferring monies between bank accounts using electronic means. This can cover a wide range of applications (such as salary payments and cash withdrawals from ATM facilities), but is also used for direct payments to suppliers. In the UK, EFT is generally conducted via BACS (the Bankers' Automated Clearing System) or CHAPS (Clearing House Automated Payment System). International transfers can be made using the SWIFT system (Society for Worldwide Interbank Financial Telecommunications).

6.6 EFT presents significant advantages for P2P transactions, including savings in administrative costs, and improved security (compared to the use of cheques). It also shortens the cash cycle within the supply chain (from placing order to making payment): this is of particular importance to smaller organisations, where cashflow is usually critical to business survival.

Purchasing cards

6.7 Many companies use purchasing cards or corporate charge cards, which are issued to staff who regularly make discretionary, *ad hoc* or low-value procurements. This presents an efficient alternative to manual 'petty cash' systems, or the processing of multiple small-transaction invoices. The card issuer (a bank or credit card company) charges a fee for the service (a flat amount per transaction, or a monthly management fee, or a percentage of the value of transactions) – but this is commonly outweighed by cost savings from the aggregation of purchases into a single statement.

6.8 Each employee would have a code, and possibly subsidiary job codes, for which there would be a pre-set limit on spending. When the card is offered in payment, authority is sought via the ICT system for the amount of credit, according to job and/or employee code. Instead of a purchase order being raised by the procurement department, authorised by a manager and processed through the purchase ledger, the process is simplified to an electronic check and a statement at each period-end. The credit card company pays each supplier separately – and the company pays off the card balance each month, in a single payment.

6.9 Monthly reports follow a 'line item detail' approach, in which each cardholder's transactions with each supplier are listed line by line. Although this can lead to quite a voluminous report, it allows the buying organisation to monitor and control external expenditure using the cards. Reports may also group purchases by supplier, enabling buyers to see easily how much is being spent with each supplier (spend analysis) – which may be useful information if bulk discounts are available.

6.10 Purchasing cards are often limited to use with certain preferred suppliers, enabling the company to benefit from negotiated bulk contracts with suppliers, as well as from reduced administration costs.

Chapter summary

- Developments in ICT have radically changed the way that people do business.
- E-purchasing is the combined use of ICT through electronic means to enhance external and internal purchasing and supply management processes.
- EPOS systems use barcoding and RFID tagging to update stock records and to provide sales reports.
- It is increasingly common for buyers to use electronic reverse auctions. However, this practice has attracted much criticism.
- E-ordering, based on the use of electronic catalogues, is a common technique for modern buyers.
- All stages of the purchase-to-pay cycle can be performed with electronic tools.
- Payment procedures can also be computerised, eg by use of electronic funds transfer.

Self-test questions

Numbers in brackets refer to the paragraphs where you can check your answers.

1   In what ways have ICT developments transformed the way that people do business? (1.1)

2   List benefits of automating procurement processes. (1.13–1.16)

3   What are the drawbacks of automating procurement processes? (1.17)

4   List benefits of EPOS systems. (2.8)

5   List a range of e-sourcing tools. (3.2)

6   What criticisms have been made of online auctions? (3.5)

7   What are the benefits of developing contracts electronically? (4.5)

8   What are the benefits of electronic P2P systems? (5.4)

9   Explain the use of purchasing cards in procurement. (6.7)

CHAPTER 7

The Organisational Context

Assessment criteria and indicative content

3.1 Explain the main aspects of corporate governance of a procurement or supply chain function

- Conflicts of interest
- The need for documented policies and procedures for procurement
- Organisational accountability and reporting for procurement roles and functions
- The status of procurement and supply chain management within organisations
- Codes of ethics in procurement
- The CIPS Code of Ethics

3.2 Analyse the impact of organisational policies and procedures on procurement

- Aspects that can be included in procedures for procurement and supply, such as responsibilities for procurement, regulations relating to competition, levels of delegated authority, responsibilities for the stages of the sourcing process, invoice clearance and payment
- The use of procurement policies, procurement strategies and procurement manuals
- The involvement of internal functions and personnel in the procurement process
- Responsible purchasing and the International Labour Organisation core conventions

Section headings

1. Corporate governance of procurement
2. Procurement ethics and responsible procurement
3. Organisational accountability and reporting
4. The status of procurement in the organisation
5. Corporate policy and procedures
6. Involvement in the procurement process

Introduction

In this chapter we begin to look at the broader organisational context or 'infrastructure' within which procurement and supply chain functions operate – and which shape their scope and operations.

We start by explaining the concept of 'corporate governance' as it applies to procurement processes. Governance is basically concerned with sound managerial control: ensuring that business processes and relationships are ethical, responsible and not excessively vulnerable to the risk of mismanagement, fraud or misuse of funds. We therefore explore issues such as the use of ethical codes in procurement; structures of accountability and reporting; and internal controls to prevent fraud and mismanagement.

Another key framework for procurement activity is provided by corporate policies and procedures. While these are likely to vary from organisation to organisation, we explore a range of policy considerations, and matters that are typically included in procurement and supply procedures.

Finally, we look at the organisational context of procurement by considering the function's role in the value chain, and how it relates to other functions.

1 Corporate governance of procurement

What is 'corporate governance'?

1.1 The term 'corporate governance' refers broadly to the rules, policies, processes and organisational structures by which organisations are operated, controlled and regulated, to ensure that they adhere to accepted ethical standards, good practices, law and regulation. The UK's Cadbury Report defined it as 'the system by which organisations are directed and controlled' in the light of business ethics and responsibility to stakeholders.

1.2 Governance principles, structures and processes may be defined by the shareholders or constitution of the organisation (as, for example, in the Articles of Association by which a business is incorporated) or by the managers of the organisation (as, for example, in the policies, procedures and codes of conduct developed for various aspects of activity).

1.3 They may also be defined by external forces such as government policy, law and regulation; professional bodies (such as CIPS) which develop ethical codes and best practice frameworks; national or international standard-setting bodies (such as the International Standards Organisation); or membership of voluntary associations and initiatives (such as the Ethical Trading Initiative or International Labour Organisation).

1.4 In a more specific sense, 'corporate governance' refers to the system by which private sector organisations are directed and controlled in order to protect the interests of shareholders. Corporate governance issues first came to public attention in the 1970s and 1980s, with high profile corporate scandals and collapses. In particular, concerns were expressed by investors about the power of directors, and the transparency and truthfulness of financial reporting.

Why is procurement governance important?

1.5 Governance mechanisms such as internal controls, checks and balances, audit reviews and defined accountabilities are important in any situation of stewardship and trust. However, it may be argued that procurement staff are more exposed to temptation than most professionals.

- They potentially control large sums of organisational funds.
- They are faced by many opportunities to commit financial fraud or to misuse systems or information for personal gain.
- Their decisions typically benefit some suppliers over others – creating an incentive for suppliers to try and influence those decisions. Meanwhile, it can be difficult to determine wholly objective criteria for deciding between rival suppliers, allowing bias or unfairness to enter the process.

Such factors place great responsibility on buyers to maintain personal ethical standards – as well as to comply with all corporate policies and regulations.

1.6 It may also be argued that it is particularly *important* to maintain governance standards in procurement, for several reasons.

- Procurement professionals are in a position of trust within a business, with control over potentially strategic decisions and expenditures which could impact on the interests of the organisation and its shareholders. There is a 'duty of care' to protect those interests, which may be jeopardised by unethical conduct.
- Procurement professionals are in a 'stewardship' role, responsible for the custodianship of finance and assets which are owned by other people. Unethical conduct may represent the theft, loss or damage of assets belonging to the shareholders (or other funders/owners) of the business.
- The standing, credibility and trust of the profession (and the employing organisation) may be damaged by fraud and other forms of unethical conduct – and enhanced by ethical conduct. Ethical

standards are an important element in managing reputational risk.

- Supply chain relationships may be damaged by unethical conduct, to the detriment of the buying organisation – and enhanced by ethical conduct. Ethical procurement practices are an important element in a buyer's maintaining 'good customer' status with suppliers, and supplier commitment and loyalty.

1.7 Typical obstacles to achieving good procurement governance, however, may include factors such as the following.

- Lack of executive support
- Lack of co-operation from stakeholders in the internal or external supply chain
- Poor ICT systems and systems integration
- Lack of clarity in the governance model, codes of conduct, rules and procedures
- Lack of resources (including time) to incorporate governance requirements
- Lack of coherence and co-ordination of procurement responsibilities

A governance framework for procurement

1.8 Here are some key elements of a comprehensive governance framework for procurement.

- **Regulatory mechanisms**: criminal law (in areas such as fraud, corruption and money-laundering); public procurement law and regulations; financial regulations (eg on financial reporting); standing orders, codes of practice and ethical codes
- **Checks and balances**: internal and external audits; support for whistle-blowers; financial disclosure requirements; freedom of information and reports in the public domain (to support transparency); the right for suppliers to challenge contract award decisions; external oversight (eg by regulatory bodies); and professional diligence
- **Prevention**: professional independence (eg of auditors); professionalism (eg CIPS Code of Conduct); and anti-fraud measures
- **Correction**: compliance with law and regulation; resolution of challenges and disputes; organisational learning and continuous improvement; and self-regulation.

Typical governance mechanisms for procurement

1.9 Mechanisms supportive of good governance in procurement therefore include the following.

- A strong internal control environment designed to support business objectives and manage identified areas of risk: robust internal policies, checks and control mechanisms
- The development and application of codes of ethical conduct in procurement activities
- The development of fair, ethical, transparent and consistently applied procedures
- The effective budgeting, control and monitoring of procurement spend across the organisation
- Clearly defined roles, responsibilities, accountabilities and reporting structures for procurement
- Controls over the authority levels of individual buyers
- Clear requirements for approvals and authorisations of requisitions, procurements and payments
- The requirement of clear audit trails or 'paper trails' to enable the tracking of procurement decisions
- The segregation of procurement duties (so that, for example, the same person is *not* responsible for authorising and making payments, which might enable falsification of transactions)
- Rotation of project buyers, to avoid any particular buyer becoming too 'cosy' with any particular supplier
- Controls over preferred supplier lists and single-sourcing deals, to ensure that they are in the best interest of the organisation
- The use of e-procurement tools to minimise cash transactions; to minimise human potentially fraudulent intervention in procedures; and to automatically highlight discrepant (non-matching) data
- The use of physical security measures (such as safes, password protection and controlled access to facilities) to protect assets, cash and data

- The effective vetting, selection, supervision and development of staff in positions of responsibility
- The use of standard terms and conditions of contract
- Internal audit of procurement processes, decisions and controls, including accounting checks and reconciliations, and periodic procurement audits.
- Encouraging suppliers and employees to report ethical breaches ('whistleblowing') without fear of reprisal
- Establishing an ethics forum or committee to discuss conflicts of interest and ethical issues arising in the course of work: open communication is the cornerstone of an 'integrity based' approach to ethics management

2 Procurement ethics and responsible procurement

What are 'ethics'?

2.1 'Ethics' are simply a set of moral principles or values about what constitutes 'right' and 'wrong' behaviour. For individuals, these often reflect the assumptions and beliefs of the families, cultures and educational environment in which their ideas developed. Ethics are also shaped more deliberately by public and professional bodies, in the form of agreed principles and guidelines which are designed to protect society's best interests.

2.2 Ethical issues may affect businesses and public sector organisations at three levels.

- At the **macro** level, there are the issues of the role of business and capitalism in society: the debate about the impacts of globalisation, the exploitation of labour, the impacts of industrialisation on the environment and so on. This is the sphere addressed by the Ethical Trading Initiative, for example: an alliance of companies, non-governmental organisations and trade unions committed to working together to promote internationally agreed principles of ethical trade and employment.
- At the **corporate** level, there are the issues which face an individual organisation as it formulates strategies and policies about how it interacts with its various stakeholders. Some of these matters will be covered by legislative and regulatory requirements, and an organisation may have a 'compliance based' approach to ethics which strives merely to uphold these minimal requirements. The sphere generally referred to as 'corporate social responsibility' covers policies which the organisation adopts for the good and wellbeing of stakeholders, taking a more proactive 'integrity based' approach. As we saw in Chapter 4, this includes issues such as environmental protection and sustainability, fair trading and employment, impact minimisation and community investment.
- At the **individual** level, there are the issues which face individuals as they act and interact within the organisation and supply chain: refusing to be party to fraud, say; not discriminating in the award of tenders; or deciding whether to accept gifts or hospitality which might be perceived as an attempt to influence a buying decision. This is the sphere which is often covered in a corporate or professional code of conduct, such as that operated by CIPS.

2.3 Before we look at the use of ethical codes in procurement, let's briefly focus on some of the potential ethical 'issues' in the field.

Use of information

2.4 One of the key principles of business ethics is the provision of fair, truthful and accurate (not false or misleading) information. This makes unethical, for example, the practice of deliberately inflating estimates of order sizes in order to obtain a price that would not be offered if the true usage patterns were admitted.

2.5 Another key ethical principle is protecting the confidentiality of information, where appropriate. Confidential information obtained in the course of business should not be disclosed without proper and specific authority, or unless there is a legal duty to disclose it: for example, if there is suspicion of money laundering or terrorist activity.

Fair dealing

2.6   Another key principle is what might be called 'fair dealing'. A temptation may be offered, for example, where a supplier or potential supplier makes an error in a quotation or invoice; where there is potential to pay late; where quotations or tender bids are sought from suppliers where there is no intention to purchase (eg if the contract has already been awarded); or where some vendors are favoured over others in a tender situation (eg providing them with more information, or allowing post-tender negotiation). Deception or unfairness in such situations may be perceived as unethical and potentially damaging to ongoing trading relationships.

Conflicts of interest

2.7   Another key principle of business ethics is not offering or accepting gifts or inducements which may – or may be *perceived* to – influence the recipient's decision-making. A related principle is that individuals should not make decisions (or divulge confidential information) for personal gain. Such situations create a 'conflict of interest', because the best interests of the firm or internal client (eg contract award on the basis of best value) conflicts with the personal interests of the individual (eg personal gain). Another such situation would be if the buyer stood to gain from promoting a particular supplier because (s)he had a financial or personal interest in the supplying firm: as a shareholder, perhaps, or as someone with a close relationship to the supplier's management.

2.8   The giving of gifts and offers of hospitality are among the common courtesies of business dealings. The problem for procurement professionals is to decide when such practices amount to an attempt to induce a favourable sourcing or contract award decision, information disclosure or other favourable treatment. There are obvious cases where buyer and seller collude to ensure that the seller wins a contract, the buyer in return receiving a reward: this is defined as bribery – and it is illegal in the UK under the Bribery Act 2010 (with strict legislation covering public bodies, in particular).

2.9   The more problematic cases are those where no explicit link is made between the gift and the award of business. A major difficulty may be the difference in perceptions between buyer and seller. To the seller, a gift may be merely a token of appreciation, of a kind that his organisation virtually expects him to bestow on most or all customers. To the buyer, however, the gift may become a material inducement to favour that supplier. (In international business dealings, this difference in perception may also be a cultural issue.)

2.10   Most organisations have clear rules on the receiving of gifts and hospitality, where this is perceived as an ethical issue. This is also the subject of codes of ethics in the procurement profession. As a general principle, any potential interest or conflict of interest should be *disclosed,* so that proceedings are transparent and open to control.

Fraud

2.11   Procurement officers need to be aware of the range of activities that may be considered fraudulent – and there should be clearly articulated organisational policies, rules and expectations in this regard. 'Many companies have to put up with missing stationery, personal telephone calls and even the theft of mobile phones or computers. Larger scale fraud is often carried out by employees working in collusion with suppliers. Such frauds can be as simple as accepting kickbacks or they can be more complex affairs where an employee deliberately rejects goods already paid for as defective, returning them to the supplier who then resells them as new.' (*The Times,* 20/09/05)

Ethical codes and standards

2.12   National and international bodies representing procurement professionals have published ethical codes setting out (usually in fairly broad terms) what moral principles or values are used to steer conduct, and what activities are considered unethical.

2.13   The **CIPS Code of Conduct** is the ethical standard and disciplinary framework (the basis of best conduct) for procurement professionals in the area of procurement ethics. The code makes it clear that seeking membership of the Institute is in itself an undertaking to abide by ethical standards, and failure to do so may be dealt with according to a defined disciplinary process.

2.14   The code emphasises the principle that members should not use a position of authority for personal gain. Equally, members have a responsibility to enhance and protect the standing (dignity and reputation) of the procurement profession and the Institute, by their conduct both inside and outside their employing organisations.

2.15   Specific guidance is also offered in the following areas.

- Members must disclose any personal interest which might impinge on their impartiality in decision-making, or which might appear to do so in the eyes of others.
- Members must respect the confidentiality of information and must not use information received for personal gain. The information they provide should be true and fair.
- Members should avoid any arrangements which might prevent fair competition.
- Except for small-value items sanctioned by the employer, business gifts should not be accepted.
- Only modest hospitality should be accepted. Members should not accept hospitality which might influence a business decision, or which might appear to do so.

(You should download the CIPS Code of Conduct from the CIPS website, if you have not already done so as part of your studies or work.)

Responsible procurement

2.16   As we noted earlier, at the corporate level, business ethics generally addresses a range of issues under the heading of 'corporate social responsibility' – or, in a procurement context, 'responsible procurement'. Corporate social responsibility was discussed in detail in Chapter 4, in the context of the responsibilities of a corporation towards its wider stakeholders: refresh your memory of this material, if you need to.

2.17   Here, we will simply mention briefly some major governance frameworks in the area of social sustainability, human/labour rights and ethics, which may impact on procurement: the International Labour Organisation conventions and the Ethical Trading Initiative. (There are equivalent charters and standards in the area of environmentally sustainable procurement, but these appear to be beyond the scope of this syllabus.)

International Labour Organisation (ILO) conventions

2.18   The ILO is the UN's specialised agency promoting human, civil and labour rights. It develops consensus documents (Conventions), and less formal codes of conduct, resolutions and declarations (Recommendations). These have included the *Declaration of Principles Concerning Multinational Enterprises and Social Policy* ('The MNE Declaration'), on the contribution of multinational enterprises to economic and social progress, and how to minimise and resolve problems arising from their actions.

2.19   The general aims of the ILO include the following seven core principles: Table 7.1.

Table 7.1 *Objectives of the ILO*

Decent work for all	Decent work considers the aspirations of people in their working lives, such as their aspirations for opportunity and income; rights, voice and recognition; and fairness and gender equality
Employment creation	The ILO identifies policies that help create and maintain decent work and income, formulated in a Global Employment Agenda
Fair globalisation	Globalisation enables global economic growth – but may also exploit some of the poorest in society. The ILO seeks ways of ensuring that the benefits of globalisation reach more people
Rights at work	The ILO identifies four fundamental principles relating to workers' rights: freedom of association; elimination of forced labour; elimination of discrimination; and elimination of child labour
Social dialogue	The ILO supports negotiation, consultation and exchange of information between, or among, representatives of governments, employers and workers on issues of common interest
Social protection	Access to an adequate level of social protection (medical cover, social security payments etc) is recognised as a basic right of all individuals. It is also indispensable for social peace and thus improved economic growth and performance
Working out of poverty	People should have the ability to improve their situation not only in terms of income but also in terms of respect, dignity and communication. Improvements in these areas will lead to economic, social and political empowerment.

2.20 The MNE Declaration makes recommendations for:

- General sustainable development and compliance policies
- Employment (increasing employment opportunities and standards, building links with local supply chains, and promoting equal opportunity, employment security and fair treatment)
- Training (encouraging skill development)
- Work/life conditions (providing equitable and competitive remuneration, benefits and conditions, recognising the need for work/life balance, respecting minimum employment ages, and maintaining high standards of health and safety)
- Industrial relations (respecting freedom of association, collective bargaining and representation, and allowing for consultation and fair grievance and dispute procedures).

The Ethical Trading Initiative (ETI)

2.21 The ETI is an alliance of companies, non-governmental organisations (NGOs) and trade union organisations committed to working together to identify and promote internationally agreed principles of ethical trade and employment, and to monitor and independently verify the observance of ethics code provisions, as standards for ethical sourcing.

2.22 The ETI publishes a code of labour practice (the ETI Base Code) giving guidance on fundamental principles of ethical labour practices, based on international standards.

1 Employment is freely chosen.
2 Freedom of association and the right to collective bargaining are respected.
3 Working conditions are safe and hygienic.
4 Child labour shall not be used.
5 Living wages are paid.
6 Working hours are not excessive.
7 No discrimination is practised.
8 Regular employment is provided.
9 No harsh or inhumane treatment is allowed.

Fair Trade

2.23   Similar principles are advocated by the International Fair Trade Association's Fair Trade standards, including:

- Creating opportunities for economically disadvantaged producers
- Integrity (transparency and accountability in dealings with trading partners)
- Capability building (developing producers' independence by providing continuity, during which producers can improve their skills and access new markets)
- Fair payment (paying a fair price which covers not only the cost of production but enables production that is just and sound, and takes into account the principle of equal pay for equal work by men and women)
- Working conditions (provision of a safe and healthy working environment for producers)
- Gender equity and children's rights
- The environment (encouraging better environmental practices and the application of responsible methods of production).

3   Organisational accountability and reporting

Accountability

3.1   'Accountability' is the liability of each person who is given (or delegated) authority to give an account of their use of that authority (ie their performance, or their stewardship of resources) to the person who delegated it to them.

3.2   Procurement staff need to take responsibility – and recognise that they are liable to be called to account – for their plans, decisions and use of resources. Otherwise, they may behave irresponsibly: carelessly, or (as we have seen) in their own interests. At the organisational level, it is helpful to assign clear accountabilities for key tasks and results, so that problems can be located and dealt with in a targeted manner.

3.3   Some key differences between public sector and private sector procurement arise from the question of accountability. As we noted in Chapter 4, the stakeholders in a public service are more diverse than those of a private firm. Buyers in the public sector may be required to account for their actions to a wide constituency, and one effect of this is an insistence on detailed procedures and record keeping: it may be difficult later to justify a course of action which breaches defined procedures or which is poorly documented.

Procurement reporting structures

3.4   If there is no dedicated procurement function in the organisation, staff involved in procurement activities usually report through another functional head. There are generally three possibilities.

- **Production/operations**. The focus of attention for any procurement activity will be on production-related logistical difficulties. Procurement will be unlikely to make a valuable contribution to wider issues such as design, marketing and competitiveness, given that it will not secure the involvement of suppliers in proactive processes such as value analysis, early supplier involvement in design and development, or supply chain development.
- **Finance**. Reporting through the finance department can suppress procurement's potential for proactive, innovative process improvements. Responsibility for external expenditure and the management of supplier credit may be used as crude short-term cost reduction mechanisms, which may stifle the development of supply chain partnerships and longer-term value-adding aspirations.
- **Commercial**. A commercial director who also acts as procurement manager should have responsibility for the final decision on proposals and quotations. There should be a formal set of procedures to examine the appropriateness of any bid to overall corporate strategy.

Procurement monitoring and reporting

3.5 Monitoring, ongoing progress measurement (for adjustment of plans or activities) and review (looking back at performance over a planning period, in order to evaluate the process) may be carried out in various ways.

- Continuous monitoring may be possible in some procurement processes: close supervision and/ or electronic monitoring tools, for example, allow variance or exception reports to be produced whenever results (eg quality standards, delivery times or stock levels) deviate from plan, within defined parameters or tolerances.
- Periodic audits and reviews are often used: examining results against defined measures or targets at regular/fixed intervals. The purpose of such reviews is generally 'formative': supplying feedback information while it is still relevant for the adjustment of performance or plans.
- Annual audits and reviews may also be used to evaluate specific plans and processes and/or the general performance of individuals, teams and functions. The purpose of such reviews is often seen as 'summative' (retrospectively evaluating performance), but they should always be used as an opportunity for feedback and identification of learning for further planning and improvement.

Project monitoring and control

3.6 Project management uses a range of control and reporting methodologies, in order to keep the complex and interrelated elements of the project 'on track'.

- End stage assessments are carried out at completion of each stage of a project, using reports from the project manager and representatives of sponsor and user groups. Plans for the following stage are reviewed and approved, and any management issues can be raised if necessary.
- Highlight reports are submitted regularly by the project manager to the steering committee or project board. These are the principal mechanism of regular feedback control: they are often submitted monthly (or at intervals agreed at project initiation). They are basically progress reports, with brief summaries of the status of the project in regard to schedule, budget and deliverables.
- Checkpoints are used for feedback and control by the project team: they involve progress review meetings, often held weekly (more frequently than highlight reports) for continuous monitoring by team members and leaders.
- Project plans often include milestones (key stage targets) and gates (measurement points where each stage of work 'passes' or 'fails' against acceptance criteria).

3.7 Techniques such as project budgets, Gantt charts and network analysis (critical path analysis, CPA) can be used to monitor progress against specific quality, cost and schedule targets. Complex project management software (such as Microsoft Project) may be used to co-ordinate planning, progress tracking and reporting data.

3.8 There are further opportunities for feedback gathering and reporting at the end of each project. The project manager should produce a completion report, summarising the project objectives and outcomes achieved; budget and schedule variances; and any ongoing issues or unfinished business (and how these will be followed up).

3.9 A 'post-completion audit' is often used as a formal review of a programme or project, in order to assess its impact and ensure that any lessons arising from it are acknowledged and learned. Such an audit may be carried out using a survey questionnaire of all project team members and key stakeholders, or meetings to discuss what went well and what didn't.

Procurement audits

3.10   An 'audit' may be defined simply as a 'check' or examination. A 'procurement management audit' is 'a comprehensive, systematic, independent and periodic examination of a company's purchasing environment, objectives and tactics, to identify problems and opportunities and facilitate the development of appropriate action plans' *(Scheuing, Purchasing Management)*.

3.11   The purposes of procurement audits (Evans & Dale) are broadly as follows.

- To monitor and enforce compliance with the procurement policies laid down by senior management (preventing 'maverick' buying and risk)
- To ensure that the organisation is using good or best practice procedures, working methods, tools and techniques (compared to benchmark standards, or the benchmarked performance of best practice organisations, centres of excellence or competitors)
- To monitor and measure the extent to which organisational resources are being used effectively, efficiently and with an eye to best value
- To support the prevention and detection of fraud, error, mismanagement of funds, inadequately managed risks and other governance problems.

Procurement policies, procurement strategies and procurement manuals

3.12   A detailed **purchasing policy manual** will address the regulations and roles relating to the procurement process of an organisation. The manual will add detail in regard to operational processes. The manual is categorised under a number of headings, which we will summarise below. The manual serves to detail the role of purchasing within an organisation and the operating practices consistent with company or government policies.

3.13   **Introduction and scope**. The manual provides guidance on the rules that apply to staff involved in the procurement activity. Adherence to the policies set out in the manual is mandatory.

3.14   **Definition**. Procurement is the process of buying goods, services and works from external suppliers. The procurement process begins when a need to buy something is identified and will generally end after the contract has been awarded. Contract management will be carried out throughout the duration of the contract.

3.15   **Procurement roles, responsibilities and compliance**. The purchasing profession has a whole range of different job titles depending on the elements required for each post. Most companies will have a 'model' that works best for them, but here are some of the job titles that you may come across.

- Procurement officer
- Buyer
- Supply chain manager
- Supplier relationship manager
- Contract manager
- Category buyer
- Purchasing manager
- E-procurement manager
- Assistant buyer

3.16   These job titles will have defined roles and responsibilities within a reporting hierarchy. However, the business goals and strategies will be dictated by the sector they are in, whether public, private, or not-for-profit. The manual may require details of the roles and responsibilities of these positions together with the title given to each job in the company or organisation. A job description will refine the duties and responsibilities further.

3.17   **Delegated purchasing authority**. Delegated purchasing authority (DPA) is the authority to enter into a contract for goods, services and works and to oversee the process leading up to and including the award of a contract and any subsequent contract changes.

3.18   DPA is granted to permanent staff only and will be in writing based on the business need and the training and experience of staff concerned. It will specify the value of contracts that the individual will be authorised to award. DPA is intended to allow business units the opportunity to manage requirements within the business area.

3.19   DPA is personal to an individual only whilst occupying their current position. DPA does not automatically transfer to their successor should they leave their current position, nor does it transfer with them to another position. If DPA is to be withdrawn by the Director for any reason this will be confirmed in writing.

3.20   **Commitment to a contract**. A contract is a legally binding agreement between the organisation and one or more suppliers for the supply of specified goods, services and works. The contract sets out the details of what the organisation is buying from whom and the rights and obligations of the parties.

3.21   **Separation of duties**. Organisation policy may well require that there are at least two defined roles in the procurement process.

- The budget holder or customer who perceives the need and makes out the business case to obtain any necessary approval to spend
- The Delegated Purchasing Officer (DPO) who is responsible for ensuring that the procurement process fully complies with procurement policy

3.22   **Ethical standards**. Organisation policy may well require that staff must preserve the highest standards of honesty, integrity, impartiality and objectivity in all dealings with suppliers and potential suppliers.

4   The status of procurement in the organisation

4.1   In recent years, the role performed by the procurement function has generally become less administrative or clerical, and taken on a more strategic aspect.

- As we saw in Chapter 1, the cost base of most manufacturing companies has changed dramatically in recent decades. Procurement responsibility now extends to a larger proportion of the organisation's spending – and procurement decisions can make a significant impact on the bottom line, in the crucial area of external expenditure.
- World class manufacturing approaches – including just in time techniques, total quality management and lean production (the elimination of wastes from the supply chain) – have enhanced the role of procurement and supply chain functions. It is now widely recognised that they have a strategic part to play, through their value-adding roles in quality management, waste reduction, and supply chain innovation and development.
- The need to secure proactive, consistent, high-quality performance from supply chains has driven a shift towards strategic supplier relationships and supply chain management development.

4.2   In general, the level at which a procurement and supply chain function operates in the organisation – and its perceived status, credibility and influence – will increase as its strategic importance is more widely recognised.

4.3   Lysons identifies three hierarchical levels at which procurement may now operate.

- At the first level, 'purchasing' is a routine clerical function. This may well be the case in a small business, or perhaps in a group situation where centralised policies and procedures leave little scope for initiative at the local or devolved level.
- As procurement develops, it may become a middle management function: the head of procurement

may report to a production director, if purchasing is seen primarily as a support service for production, or to a finance director. This situation may also apply if procurement is seen primarily as one element in a materials or logistics management structure.

- At the highest level of development, procurement may find representation on the senior management team, perhaps on the main board of directors.

4.4 Progression through these stages may be driven by growing recognition of procurement's potential to add value and impact positively on profitability.

Influences on procurement status

4.5 Lysons & Farrington argue that, within any given organisation, the status of the procurement and supply management function will depend on four main factors: leverage, focus, structural factors and professionalism.

- **Leverage** can be defined as the perceived power of procurement to make a measurable value contribution, notably by enhancing profitability. 'The greatest scope for making savings lies in the areas of greatest expenditure, and for most organisations... this lies in the area of bought-out items. When purchases form a high proportion of total costs, a modest saving on bought-out items will result in a similar contribution to profit as would a substantial increase in sales.' Procurement may gain leverage by demonstrating a meaningful contribution to other core competencies and critical success factors of an organisation, such as product development or sustainable supply.
- **Focus** refers to the perception of procurement as having a transactional (clerical/administrative/ purchasing) focus, a commercial focus (supporting business results) or a strategic focus (focusing on added value and sustainable competitive advantage through the supply chain). The more procurement becomes involved in commercial and strategic areas – and shifts its focus from 'efficiency' (doing things right) to 'effectiveness' (doing the right things) – the greater will be its perceived relevance and contribution to corporate objectives.
- **Structural factors** reflect the position and visibility of the procurement function in the organisation: for example, the job title of the executive responsible for procurement, and at what level he reports; the total spend for which procurement is responsible; the financial thresholds beyond which procurement staff must refer decisions to higher authority; the committees and projects on which procurement staff are represented; and so on.
- **Professionalism** in a general sense implies a businesslike attitude; technical competence, often based on systematic training and education; and adherence to a code of professional ethics. In a more technical sense, it means the increasing qualification of procurement staff, as members of a professional body such as the Chartered Institute of Procurement and Supply, which acts as a 'guarantee' of technical and ethical standards, best practice sharing and ongoing professional development. The status of procurement in an organisation will be enhanced to the extent that its members inspire confidence, trust and respect, and professionalism is one way of achieving this.

Procurement marketing

4.6 Procurement marketing is, simply, the way the procurement function 'markets' itself in the organisation, to protect or enhance its status and standing. In the same way as the organisation (through its marketing function) promotes itself and its brands, products and services to potential customers in the external market, so the procurement or supply chain function needs to promote itself and its services to its internal customers. This is particularly important if those internal customers have the option of obtaining services elsewhere (eg from a procurement consultancy or outsourced service provider, or by carrying out purchasing activity themselves).

5   Corporate policy and procedures

The impact of policy and procedure on procurement

5.1   As we saw in Chapter 5, the promotion of consistent 'good practice' (or best practice) in procurement typically involves the development and application of a range of decision rules, processes and procedures that are designed to help procurement staff to achieve the optimum mix of the five rights, and other procurement or supply chain management objectives.

5.2   Organisations may need to develop effective policies in regard to procurement and supply chain issues such as the following.

- An intention to comply with all relevant laws, regulations, standards, codes of practice and best practice benchmarks
- Responsibilities for procurement at different stages of the procurement process; or in cross-functional procurement teams (eg whether the organisation favours early buyer and supplier involvement in product development and specification)
- Levels of delegated authority for procurement: in other words, what levels or grades of staff have the authority to take different types of procurement decisions; when decisions need to be 'escalated' or referred; and what checks, authorisations and sign-offs are required for various tasks (such as the passing of invoices for payment)
- The use of defined procurement procedures, decision rules or guidelines to support consistent good practice (eg in areas such as the administration of tenders or e-auctions; supplier appraisal and vendor rating; the use of approved supplier lists; or the use of call-off contracts, e-ordering systems and purchasing cards)
- Sourcing decisions (eg in regard to sustainable sourcing, single or multiple sourcing; supplier segmentation and relationship development; international or global sourcing; or the use of competitive tendering or e-auctions)
- Ethical and sustainable procurement (with objectives and commitments for local sourcing and supplier diversity; fair trade; supply chain labour standards; or 'green' specification and sourcing).

5.3   Procurement managers may have responsibility for developing some of these policies and procedures to enable strategic procurement objectives to be met. Many procurement-related policies will affect the operations of other departments and links in the supply chain, however. Procurement managers may not have the authority to impose systems, procedures, standards or controls, but may have the *influence* (by virtue of their specialist expertise) to recommend them, and advise on their design and implementation.

5.4   The impact of corporate policy and procedure on procurement decision-making depends in part on the nature of the decision in each case.

- **Routine decisions:** repetitive, programmed (often low-level) decisions, depending heavily on the use of pre-established *procedures or rules*, which reflect corporate policy and good practice. Examples include replenishing stock items at pre-determined order points and quantities; issuing call-off orders, or ordering from approved suppliers; and administering tender procedures. There are likely to be detailed guidelines for the steps to be followed, the parameters within which judgement can be used, the requirement for sign-offs and authorisations, and so on.
- **Adaptive decisions:** higher-level decisions which require human judgement – but can be supported by relatively simple decision tools (such as supplier appraisal or cost-benefit analysis). Examples include capital procurement decisions and sourcing decisions for non-standard procurements. At this level, there may still be *corporate or functional policies* about the level at which such decisions can be taken or authorised; guidelines for how such decisions should be made and what kind of 'audit trail' is required; budgetary constraints and the requirement for a business case or cost-benefit analysis; and the need to comply with relevant policy frameworks (such as sourcing policies or sustainable procurement policies).

- **Innovative decisions:** unique, first-time decisions for which there is no existing model or procedure. These are generally strategic decisions, such as whether to develop global sourcing, e-procurement, or partnership relations with a supplier. They are often made by professionals or top managers, on a team basis, and while they may need to be compliant with relevant corporate policies (eg on ethics or CSR) – policies may also have to be developed or amended to take account of new strategic directions.

5.5   We will look briefly at some of the aspects that can be included in procedures for procurement supply, focusing on the examples mentioned in the syllabus.

Compliance

5.6   Law and regulation places certain requirements on products and services which may need to be taken into account in procurement decision-making and controls. Here are some examples.

- Quality standards and tolerances required to be *accredited* by various international quality standards, or to receive the European Community (CE) quality mark
- Quality standards and tolerances required for *product safety*, under health and safety and consumer protection legislation and industry codes of practice (eg the strength, flexibility or weight-bearing capacity of construction materials; the chemical composition of materials to avoid health hazards; the restriction of ingredients such as additives in food products)
- Controls on the use, storage and transport of *substances and materials* which may be dangerous to health (eg chemicals, poisons, lead paint, asbestos, flammable or explosive materials, corrosive materials such as acids). Examples from the UK include the COSHH (Control of Substances Hazardous to Health) and CHIPS (Chemicals: Hazard Information and Packaging for Supply) Regulations
- *Environmental protection* law and regulation, dealing with issues such as the safe disposal or recyclability of waste and end-of-life products (including electrical and electronic waste and batteries)

5.7   Suppliers should be expected to be knowledgeable about, and compliant with, legislation relevant to their industry and products. However, the buyer is still liable in law if he incorporates outlawed materials or components in his products. One high-profile case study is the problems encountered by global toy company Mattel, which was forced to recall millions of toys, manufactured under licence in China, because the contractors had purchased paint contaminated with US/EU-banned levels of lead, from unauthorised suppliers.

5.8   Procurement professionals should therefore take proactive steps to:

- Draw specification teams' attention to known legal requirements
- Draw suppliers' attention to known legal requirements – especially if the law in the suppliers' country of operation is different from that of the buyer's
- Implement their own compliance checks (audits, monitoring and inspection) on suppliers and supplies
- Use suppliers which are certified under quality and environmental standards, or encourage favoured suppliers to become so certified.

Procurement roles and responsibilities

5.9   The organisation structure and corporate policy framework will dictate the way in which specialist procurement roles and responsibilities are grouped and allocated. Guidance issued by CIPS indicates that certain roles are broadly 'typical': Table 7.2.

Table 7.2 *Typical procurement roles*

ROLE	RESPONSIBILITIES
Head (or Director) of Procurement (or Supply Chain Management)	Generally takes overall responsibility for the work of the procurement or supply chain function, providing direction and strategic leadership in areas such as policy development. He is also responsible for representing the function in its dealings with other departments. This calls for strong leadership and communication skills – especially in the need to convey to senior management the value-adding potential of procurement. In practice, it is unlikely that an HoP will be able to exercise control over every aspect of procurement: even in a strongly centralised environment, there is likely to be a role for user departments (eg in purchasing routine, low-value items).
Senior Procurement Manager (SPM)	Typically leader of a team of Procurement Managers, co-ordinating their activities. The SPM will work within the strategy and policy framework developed by the HoP: within these guidelines, he will be responsible for broad decisions on market evaluation, sourcing, the appraisal and selection of suppliers, negotiation and award of contracts, and supply chain management. Depending on the organisational structure, the SPM may be responsible for just a single category of purchase (eg IT, raw materials or commodities) or for external spend in general. A relatively common structure in large organisations would involve an SPM in charge of one large category of expenditure, with a number of Procurement Managers taking responsibility for sub-categories or tasks.
Procurement Manager(s)	Similar responsibilities to the SPM, but at a lower level. Depending on the size of the function, the PM will not generally become involved in day-to-day contract administration and management: the role typically ends with contract award.
Contracts Manager(s)	Responsible for contract and supplier management of large, complex contracts: monitoring supplier performance, expediting payments, checking and approving contract variations and so on – in other words, ensuring that both parties fulfil their obligations under a particular contract. This is usually a closely defined role: general supplier relations may be the responsibility of a separate Supplier Manager or Supply Chain Manager.
Supplier Manager(s)	Responsible for supplier performance monitoring and evaluation (eg operating 'balanced scorecard' measures or vendor rating); follow-up of collaborative continuous improvement agreements; supplier development programmes; relationship management and dispute resolution; and so on.
Expediters	Following up on placed orders, to ensure timely delivery
Procurement Analyst or Research Manager	Responsible for investigating the supply market, gathering data and organising it into information that can be used by other members of the procurement and supply chain team. This is essentially a support role for the procurement function as a whole.

The role of the 'part-time' purchaser

5.10   In most organisations, a number of procurement activities will be undertaken by people who are not members of the procurement function or profession, and whose main activities are nothing to do with procurement.

- Part-time purchasing predates the introduction of a dedicated procurement function in many organisations, and user departments may have developed their own supplier contacts and 'ways of doing things'.
- User or budget-holder departments may believe themselves best qualified to make procurement decisions that affect their operations – particularly where items are very technical in nature, and users do not trust the procurement function to have sufficient specialist knowledge.
- Users may deliberately keep spending decisions away from the procurement department: a phenomenon sometimes known as 'maverick buying'. They may wish to control their own external expenditure, or may have a conflicting agenda (especially if procurement's priority is perceived to be cost or variety reduction, say).

5.11 There are some obvious disadvantages associated with part-time purchasing – as the phrase 'maverick buying' may suggest!

- Procurement decisions may be made unwisely, or processes carried out inefficiently, without the use of procurement expertise, disciplines and systems.
- User buyers may be too preoccupied with their main role to give sufficient attention to procurement procedures and decisions.
- It may be difficult to budget and control external spend if responsibilities for procurement are dispersed throughout the organisation.
- Uncoordinated specifications and procurements by users, according to their own needs, typically lead to inefficiencies such as stock proliferation and over-specification (where procurement might challenge specifications, recommend generic or stocked items, and pursue standardisation or variety reduction).

5.12 However, there are also potential advantages to the devolution of procurement activities to part-time purchasers.

- Delegating responsibility for routine, low-value purchases frees up time for procurement specialists to devote to more complex and strategic tasks.
- Users may have technical skills and knowledge that need to be harnessed (eg for the development of effective specifications and service level agreements).
- The procurement function should be concerned to communicate good practice procurement disciplines as far as possible throughout the organisation – and devolved procurement may be a positive means to this end (if maverick buying can be controlled eg through framework agreements, approved supplier lists, checks and approvals).

5.13 We will look at these issues in more detail when we explore the structuring of the procurement or supply chain function, in Chapter 8.

Delegated authority for procurement

5.14 Defined levels and limits to delegated authority are vital to the governance of procurement, especially where procurement activities are devolved. In the public sector, in particular, best practice requires a clear 'Scheme of Delegation' for procurement activity, setting out the minimum level of authorisation for each category of procurement in different value ranges. A typical example is given in Table 7.3.

Table 7.3 *Scheme of delegation for a procurement organisation*

TRANSACTION TYPE	VALUE	CATEGORY	PROCEDURE	AUTHORISER
Low value	<€1k	Goods/Services/Works	Single verbal/written quotation	Local officer
	<€5k	Goods/Services	Single written quotation	Local officer
	<€10k	Works	Single written quotation	Local officer
Intermediate value	€5k–€50k	Goods/Services	Three written quotations	Section manager
	€10k–€50k	Works	Three written quotations	Section manager
High value	€50k – EU threshold	Goods/Services/Works	Sealed tender	Department head
	Over EU threshold	Goods/Services/Works	EU tender exercise	Procurement Unit

5.15 The most common sources of information on levels of approval for procurement, and means of obtaining the authority to proceed, are to be found in 'Standing Orders', 'Finance Manuals' or 'Procurement Manuals'. In addition to general delegation levels for procurement, such documents will also typically include rules and instructions for standard best practice procedures (eg the opening of tenders and key stages of contract approval).

Authorisations and sign-offs

5.16   Buyers spend huge sums of money, often a very large proportion of the total earned by the organisations that employ them. It is vital to ensure that the organisation receives full value for the sums spent – and that funds are not mismanaged, misused or misappropriated. To a large extent this is achieved by reliance on the ethical and technical standards of procurement professionals, but the principles of sound governance also require a defined system of checks and controls.

5.17   Authorisations or sign-offs may be required at a number of stages of the procurement process.

- When a **requisition** is originated in a user department, it must be signed by an authorised individual before being passed to procurement. This gives procurement the assurance they need that the requisition is for an item that is genuinely needed, and that the expenditure has been approved by the budget-holder.
- Before a **specification** is released to a supplier, it must have the formal approval of the procurement officer and ideally the prior certification of the supplier. This reduces the common risk of changes being made in order to solve problems not envisaged at the time the specification was finalised. This precaution should then be followed up by ensuring that any changes which are deemed necessary are subjected to appropriate approval procedures and documented in writing.
- When the **purchase order** is completed, it must be signed by an authorised person within the procurement department. The person signing it will usually do so with sight of the requisition and any other relevant documentation – and in the light of sourcing policies such as the use of preferred or approved suppliers lists, or the use of call-off or systems contracts where available.
- When the supplier's **invoice** is received, it should not be passed for payment to the accounts department until procurement staff have carried out verification checks on goods inwards records, the purchase order or contract and so on. (We discuss this in more detail a bit later.)
- **Contract changes** must be authorised by the relevant contract manager, in order to ensure that uncontrolled variations do not spring up, resulting in multiple versions, uncertainties and subsequent disputes.

Competition

5.18   One area in which an organisation may have policy and procedure frameworks is the question of when, or in what circumstances, procurements must be subject to competition. For examples, there may be strict policies for:

- How many quotations must be obtained, from different suppliers, for orders or contracts of different values
- When, or at what value threshold, procurements must be put up for competitive tender, or subjected to a competitive bidding process.

5.19   An organisation may have different procedures in place for orders of different volume or value.

- For order values under $100, say, there may be no formal requirement for supplier selection (although the policy might require the use of purchase cards or e-procurement systems, or referral of the requirement to the procurement function for consolidation, in order to minimise unnecessary transaction costs).
- For orders between $100 and $5,000, there may be a negotiation process (perhaps with preference given to approved or preferred suppliers), or a minimum of three suppliers may be requested to provide quotations, to ensure competitive pricing and value for money.
- For orders over $5,000 in value, a full competitive bidding or tendering process may be required.

5.20   Standing Orders or Procurement Procedures Manuals may also provide for the authorisation of exceptional cases where it has not been possible to follow 'usual policy' (eg to obtain three written quotations for a procurement). They should nominate a manager of suitable rank, who may authorise exceptions to the rule, if there are reasonable grounds for them. The reason should be formally documented and recorded on file with the appropriate authorisations. This is important to create an 'audit trail', where decisions may be subject to internal and/or external scrutiny at a later date – as is particularly the case in the public sector.

5.21 Competition is a key value in public sector procurement, in order to obtain best value and give a wide range of suppliers fair access to contracts. There are defined value thresholds above which contracts for goods, works and services *must* be awarded by competitive tender. The EU Public Procurement Directive (enacted in UK law in the Public Contracts Regulations 2015) set out detailed policies and procedures for public procurements, and the promotion of competition.

Invoice clearance and payment

5.22 When an invoice or request for payment is received from a supplier, the buyer should check that it corresponds to the order or contract (in regard to the agreed price and payment terms) and to the GRN (in regard to items actually received), and then *either* query discrepancies with the supplier *or* authorise the invoice for payment and pass it to the accounts department for payment.

5.23 Invoices should be paid within the period stated in the agreed terms of trade: often 30, 60 or 90 days. There may be defined policies (in addition to general ethical principles) about paying supplier invoices on time, as agreed.

6 Involvement in the procurement process

Internal functions and personnel involved in the procurement process

6.1 The main functions involved in the procurement process, and internal supply chain, include design and engineering, production, accounting and finance, and marketing. Some of the main areas of interaction are summarised in Table 7.4

Table 7.4 *Procurement's links with other functions*

INTERNAL CUSTOMER	INVOLVEMENT IN THE PROCUREMENT PROCESS
Design and engineering	• Value engineering and value analysis • Quality assurance • Evaluation of availability and price of materials • Preparation of specifications
Production/operations	• Make or buy decisions • Preparation of delivery schedules • Control of inventory and scrap • Co-operation in implementing world class manufacturing and supply techniques (eg lean supply, total quality management, JIT) • Demand/inventory planning to minimise disruption to operations
Accounting and finance	• Budget preparation, and monitoring of actual input costs against budget • Administration of procurement, eg in processing of invoices and progress payments • Stock valuation, stocktaking and insurance of stock
Marketing	• Communication with key downstream stakeholders: key messages eg re reverse logistics • Market, customer and competitor research, providing data for product development and need identification: impacting on objectives of procurement re product features, quality and price • Customer expectations re delivery deadlines, impacting on management of cycle times

6.2 Functional organisation can be a problem because business processes – such as the flow of products through the internal supply chain – are in fact 'horizontal': work and information must flow freely across functional boundaries, without the vertical barriers created by specialisation, departmental job demarcations and communication channels. Think about the experience of customers: they need to speak to different functions (sales, delivery, accounts, after-sales service) as they proceed through the purchase process: they don't want to know that each stage of their experience is the domain of a different department – much less that the departments don't talk to each other! Similarly, product development, quality management and supply are all essentially horizontal activities, requiring co-operation and information exchange across functional boundaries.

6.3   This is particularly the case with procurement, which serves a diverse customer base, consisting of different value activities and functions. Lysons and Farrington note that, while in many organisations procurement is a separate department responsible solely for the procurement of supplies, there is an increasing trend towards more integrated structures which take in the wider process of logistics or supply chain management: the whole sequence of activities from the adoption of suppliers to the delivery of finished products to end-user customers. 'Such structures emphasise the importance of cross-functional decision-making', because business processes are *horizontal,* cutting across departments and disciplines: Figure 7.1.

Figure 7.1 *Business process flows across an organisation*

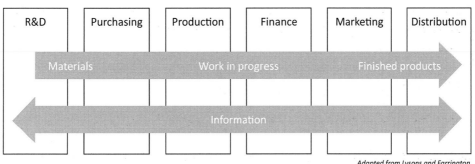

Adapted from Lysons and Farrington

6.4   As we saw in Chapter 3, procurement is an important link in the internal supply chain: purchasing professionals are the interface between other links in the chain, such as the specifiers of business needs, the users of the inputs obtained, and the financers of the procurement – any or all of whom may be from different functional departments. For any given procurement exercise or project, members of different functions will therefore have to work together, share information, communicate and co-ordinate their activities. Increasingly, this collaboration is structured using cross-functional teams (which will be discussed in Chapter 8).

6.5   Poor relationships between procurement and other departments will lead to inadequate understanding by procurement of requirements elsewhere in the organisation – and inefficiency in translating these requirements into the necessary materials and supply chain support actions.

6.6   The other side of the coin is that procurement's own activities will be hampered through inadequate information, and in extreme cases by actual obstruction caused by inter-departmental frictions.

Divergent perspectives of different functions

6.7   There is particular potential for conflict between technical specialists (in engineering or production functions) and buyers.

- A specialist may specify a particular material, component or brand because it is high-quality, or known to the specialist from previous experience. From the commercial point of view of procurement, however, there may be opportunities for variety reduction (using items already in stock, or generic items) or value analysis (challenging over-specification), or the sourcing of more sustainable inputs.

- A specialist may insist on a particular supplier – again because of quality or familiarity. From the wider perspective of procurement, however, there may be an opportunity to introduce new suppliers (for more innovative solutions), competitive sourcing (for a better deal) or local, small or diverse suppliers (to promote sustainability).

6.8 In the public sector the buyer's position is strong. In most cases, competitive tendering is a legal obligation, and it is not open to the specialist to (in effect) award the contract to a favoured source. In the private sector there is no such obligation, and the situation must be resolved by appropriate discussion and negotiation between specialist and buyer.

6.9 Designers and engineers have the primary responsibility for the nature and content of a company's products and the processes of their manufacture. But the discussion above has emphasised the element of choice that runs through many design and engineering processes. There is no single right way to design and manufacture a product, and once the question is of choosing between alternatives, procurement staff have a vital role to play.

6.10 Zenz (*Purchasing and the Management of Materials*) argues that: 'Engineering must not be so exacting that its demands override price and market considerations, and purchasing must not stress price to the point where it interferes with sound engineering requirements. Engineering has the responsibility for setting specifications and has the final say. Purchasing can ask for and suggest changes but cannot make changes.'

6.11 In other words, there is a spectrum of choice in the inputs that can be used, and procurement staff are in a strong position to advise on the cost effects of different choices. Further, where engineering choices are in question – eg the degree of tolerance to be specified – procurement again has a role to play, in challenging tolerances and service levels to maximise value and minimise waste.

6.12 As we noted above, another area of possible conflict is the issue of standardisation. Procurement specialists typically favour the use of a relatively small number of more or less standardised parts, while designers and engineers tend to see good cause for ordering 'specials': items of a non-standard type. Procurement staff have an overview of the materials and components available and in stock, and can spot when requisitions are made for 'special' items which are practically identical to generic or stocked items. They must be able to balance quality and cost issues sensitively, and to discuss these factors in language that makes sense to designers.

6.13 In some organisations, procurement's value-adding role in standardisation and variety reduction is formalised in the development by procurement of an approved list of standard parts. All departments are encouraged to specify as far as possible on the basis of the approved list, and departures from this principle will be scrutinised and challenged if necessary.

The impact of organisational structure

6.14 Organisation structure may be defined as 'the pattern of relationships among positions in the organisation and among members of the organisation. Structure makes possible the application of the process of management and creates a framework of order and command through which the activities of the organisation can be planned, organised, directed and controlled' (Mullins, *Management and Organisational Behaviour)*. This highlights a key point about the importance of structure for governance: the organisation structure embodies the system through which procurement (and other organisational processes) are controlled.

6.15 An effective organisation structure will have features such as the following.

- Clear paths of reporting and accountability
- Effective mechanisms for multi-directional information flows and co-ordination

- Effectively short chains of decision-making
- Minimal duplication of effort (ie co-ordination and efficiency)
- Soft 'vertical' barriers between functions, to support the smooth flow of value 'horizontally' towards the customer (eg via internal supply chains)
- In-built flexibility (in order to remain responsive to changing business environments and customer demands)

6.16 A key issue in organisational structure is the division of labour between different functions. In a very small company, people can simply share the tasks between them according to their skills. Once an organisation grows beyond a certain size, however, systematic specialisation is required, and this typically involves the grouping together and allocation of specific aspects of the work to different departments: a process called 'departmentation'. This is typically done on the basis of criteria such as:

- Functional specialisation
- Geographical area or territory
- Product, brand or customer.

6.17 In a *functional* structure (Figure 7.2), tasks are grouped together according to the common nature or focus of the task, and the specialised skills, resources or technology required.

Figure 7.2 *Functional organisation*

6.18 In a *geographical* structure (Figure 7.3), tasks are grouped together according to the region in which the activity takes place, or within which target markets or market segments are located. Multi-site organisations (eg a procurement function organised by plant) and sales departments (with allocated 'territories') are often organised this way.

Figure 7.3 *Geographical organisation*

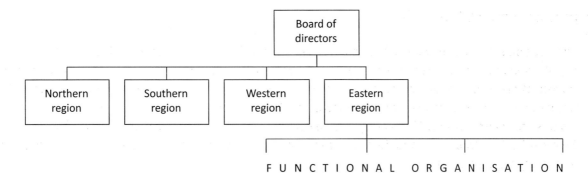

6.19 In a *product, brand or customer* structure, tasks are grouped together according to the product, product line, customer, or procurement category they relate to. Companies with families of distinct brands (such as Kraft or Unilever) often organise in this way, so that there is specialisation of brand marketing and identity – and separate brand accountabilities. Similarly, companies with key customer types, such as publishers (for example trade, educational institutions, libraries, online) may group together tasks in this way. In procurement, the equivalent may be organisation by category of items procured (eg raw materials, commodities, IT and services): Figure 7.4.

Figure 7.4 *Product (or category) organisation of a procurement function*

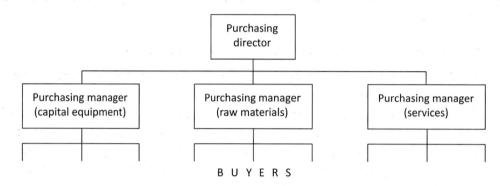

6.20 The advantages and disadvantages of the various forms of organisation are summarised in Table 7.5.

Table 7.5 *Different structural forms*

ORGANISATION	ADVANTAGES	DISADVANTAGES
Functional	• Pools and focuses specialised skills and knowledge • Share specialised technology and equipment for efficiency • Facilitates the recruitment, training and management of specialist staff • Avoids duplicating functions within area/product departments: enables economies of scale	• Focuses on inputs/processes rather than outputs/customers (necessary for customer satisfaction) • Creates vertical barriers to cross-disciplinary communication (necessary to flexibility and coordination)
Geographical	• Decision-making at the interface between organisation and local stakeholders (with distinctive needs) • Cost-effective (because shorter) lines of supply and communication to local markets or plants	• Duplication of functional activities • Loss of standardisation, due to local differences
Product/brand/customer	• Clearer accountability for the profitability of different products/brands/customer groups • Specialisation of production and marketing expertise • Coordination of different functions by product managers	• Increased managerial complexity and overhead costs • Possible fragmentation of objectives and markets

Matrix structures

6.21 The 'matrix' structure emerged at American aerospace company Lockheed in the 1950s, when its customer (the US government) became frustrated at dealing separately with a number of functional specialists when negotiating defence contracts. The concept of the 'project co-ordinator' or 'customer account manager' was born.

6.22 The essence of matrix structure is dual authority: staff in different functions or regions are responsible both:

- To their departmental managers, in regard to the activities of the department, and
- To a product, project or account manager, in regard to the activities of the department related to the given product, project or account.

So, for example, a procurement specialist may report to the procurement manager in regard to general procurement activities – but may also report for a period to the project or programme manager for a given project requiring procurement input (say a construction or IT systems development project). This may also work at a divisional level, with project/area-based divisions 'buying' in human resources from a centralised procurement unit.

6.23 The advantages of a matrix structure can be summarised as follows.

- Combines the resource efficiency of functional organisation with the accountability of project or product organisation
- Fosters interdisciplinary and cross-functional co-operation in pursuit of project goals
- Involves all functions more closely in achieving the flow of value to the customer
- Encourages cross-functional communication for flexibility and organisational learning
- Brings any ambiguities or conflicts of role and accountability into the open, highlighting potential governance problems which may need to be solved.

6.24 Some of the disadvantages of a matrix structure include:

- Potential inefficiency (with ambiguous priorities and constant switching between tasks)
- Potential stress on staff 'caught' between competing or conflicting demands
- Conflict between managers competing for staff and resources – or blaming one another for problems
- More complex (potentially slower) decision-making processes
- Costs of an added management layer, meetings and so on.

6.25 However, it is worth noting that an organisation need not have a formal or complete matrix structure to take advantage of the benefits: matrix (or 'horizontal') elements can be incorporated through project or cross-functional teamworking – and even provision for regular cross-functional communication (eg in quality circles or briefing meetings).

6.26 We will look at various methods by which a procurement or supply chain function can be structured in Chapter 8.

7

Chapter summary

- There are particular reasons why good governance is important in the procurement function.
- Ethical issues affect organisations at the macro level, the corporate level and the individual level. Buyers must be sensitive to ethical issues, including conflicts of interest.
- Buyers should comply with ethical standards created by (for example) the ILO, the ETI, and CIPS.
- All buyers must accept accountability for their actions, but in the public sector this is particularly important.
- Modern thinking has emphasised the increasingly strategic role of procurement. Nowadays, procurement tends to operate at a higher level in the organisation structure.
- Corporate policy and procedure have an important influence on procurement governance.
- There are some advantages in the practice of 'part-time purchasing', but this must be done within appropriate procedures laid down by the procurement function.
- Organisational functions that may be involved in procurement processes include design and engineering, production, accounting, and marketing.
- Possible organisational structures include functional specialisation, organisation by geographical area or territory, or organisation by product, brand or customer. In a matrix structure, some of these elements may be combined.

Self-test questions

Numbers in brackets refer to the paragraphs where you can check your answers.

1   Why may procurement staff be more exposed than others to a risk of poor governance? (1.5)

2   List mechanisms that may support good procurement governance. (1.9)

3   Explain how conflicts of interest may arise for a purchasing professional. (2.7)

4   What specific guidance is offered by the CIPS Code of Conduct? (2.15)

5   What are the general aims of the ILO? (2.19, Table 7.1)

6   List methods of ongoing progress measurement for a procurement function. (3.5)

7   What are the purposes of a procurement audit? (3.11)

8   What four factors are identified by Lysons & Farrington as determining the status of the procurement function? (4.5)

9   List areas in which organisations may need to develop effective policies in regard to procurement. (5.2)

10   What are the advantages and disadvantages of 'part-time purchasers'? (5.11, 5.12)

11   Explain the potential conflict between a procurement function and an engineering or production function. (6.7)

12   List features of an effective organisational structure. (6.15)

CHAPTER 8

The Procurement Function in the Organisation

Assessment criteria and indicative content

3.3 Compare the different structures of a procurement or supply chain function

- The use of centralised and devolved structures
- Hybrid structures of a procurement or supply chain function (such as consortium structures, shared services, lead buyer structure and outsourced)
- Interacting with other people and building rapport
- The need for customer service and value-for-money outcomes

Section headings

1. The procurement or supply chain function
2. Structuring procurement operations
3. Cross-functional team and project working
4. Outsourcing procurement operations
5. Consortium procurement

Introduction

In this chapter we draw conclusions from some of the aspects discussed in Chapter 7 – corporate governance, strategic policy and organisational structure – for the resourcing and structuring of a procurement or supply chain function.

We start by looking again at the role of the function in relation to other units and functions (including the need for internal customer service) and then consider various ways in which it can be structured in practice. There are three basic alternative models: centralised, devolved (or decentralised) and mixed (or hybrid) structures. We survey the characteristics and advantages of each.

Finally, we explore some key related issues, including the use of cross-functional teams in procurement projects and processes; the potential to outsource procurement operations to external service providers; and the potential to share procurement with other buying organisations (consortium procurement).

1 The procurement or supply chain function

Procurement as a support or service function

1.1 One way of gaining an insight into procurement's role in the internal and external supply chain, is the concept of the **value chain** (introduced in Chapter 1: refresh your memory by referring back to Figure 1.3 if you need to).

1.2 At its simplest, Porter's value chain model illustrates procurement as a support or service provider to a range of primary activities.

- It may have direct responsibility for inbound and/or outbound logistics, or may manage the outsourcing of those functions (eg through third-party storage and logistics providers).
- It serves operational and service activities by fulfilling the 'five rights of purchasing': ensuring that the right goods, of the right quality, are delivered to the right place at the right time, and at the right price.
- It supports marketing and sales by providing product and delivery information, sourcing marketing services (eg advertising agency or printing services), or advising marketing staff on how to source requirements for themselves.

1.3   Another key point of the model, for our current purpose, is that activities within the value chain are inter-dependent: each element can affect the costs or effectiveness of another in the value chain. So, for example, improvement of the quality of materials and other inputs procured may reduce the need for after-sales service. On-time delivery requires the integration of procurement, operations, outbound logistics and service activities. These 'linkages' require co-ordination in order to optimise the flow of value – which is why internal supply chain relationships are so important.

1.4   It is also important to note that 'each activity within a value chain provides inputs which, after processing, constitute added value to the output received by the ultimate customer in the form of a product or service' (Lysons & Farrington). Procurement can therefore be seen as an integral part of the flow of value to the end customer, not just as an internal administrative support function. In recent decades this has been increasingly recognised, giving procurement a more integrated and strategic role in organisational management, with input into strategic decisions such as: make/do or buy/outsource decisions; new product development; supply chain development; process re-engineering and so on.

Procurement as an internal consultancy or business partner

1.5   'Consulting' is a process in which one person or team (the consultant) helps another individual, group or organisation (the client) to mobilise internal and external resources so as to deal with problems. The outcomes of consulting are typically the issuing of analysis and recommendations to the client, and possibly the development and implementation of an action plan in collaboration with the client.

1.6   External consultants provide expertise and insight from outside the system they are attempting to help, with the benefit of an outsider's perspective. Organisations often employ management, market research, logistics and other consultancy firms or agencies for this reason. Internal consultants operate as part of the system they are attempting to help or improve.

1.7   Internal consultancy is a complex role, requiring careful relationship management. The consultant will often have no direct authority over the client's decisions, and will have to use its expertise and influence to gain the client's agreement to implement recommendations and/or the support of executive management to enforce them. On the other hand, both consultant and client share the same overall goals (the increased effectiveness of their organisation), which should support collaboration.

1.8   Internal consultants are often called in to solve a particular problem or fulfil a need that cannot be efficiently or effectively satisfied with the internal resources and expertise of the client unit. The procurement function may adopt an internal consultancy role in an organisation, where:

- Procurement activity is undertaken by 'part-time' buyers or non-procurement staff in user or budget-holder departments. Since these staff may lack the specialist skills, disciplines and contacts for effective and cost-efficient procurements, the advice and guidance of procurement professionals may be required.
- Procurement is required for a multi-functional project (such as construction or IT development). The procurement function is ideally placed to research and recommend procurement solutions.
- Specific disciplines, skills or information are required by other functions, project teams or managers,

which procurement is in a position to contribute. Procurement may be asked to provide advice or training for sales personnel in negotiation techniques, say; or may be asked to act as introducers and facilitators, putting the product development team in touch with potential supply partners (for early supplier involvement in designs and specifications); or may be asked to carry out a benchmarking exercise on competitors' logistics or quality management processes, to support competitive strategy development.

- Procurement lacks the formal organisational authority (mandate) to impose procurement disciplines, procedures or decisions on other departments – and must therefore exercise influence by promoting its value-adding expertise.

1.9   Internal consultancy may be structured as a discrete consultancy engagement or project: the procurement specialist works with the client to articulate specific desired outcomes from an intervention; gathers data on the problem or issue; feeds back findings to the client; and makes recommendations or works with the client to develop solutions (depending on the terms of the agreement between them). Such a consultancy project approach may be suitable for specific interventions such as the engagement or appraisal of an advertising agency on behalf of the marketing department; or a feasibility study for the introduction of a new computer system; the evaluation of make/do or buy decisions; or implementation of a sustainable procurement approach.

1.10   Internal consultancy – in the sense of offering other departments the benefit of procurement's specialist expertise – may also operate via a variety of operational mechanisms.

- Established procurement policies and procedures – acting as guidelines for buyers in other departments, to help them source and purchase inputs more cost-effectively and with less risk
- Preferred and approved supplier lists, framework agreements and call-off contracts – ensuring that buyers in other departments use suppliers pre-selected (and agreements negotiated) using purchasing expertise
- Purchasing research and information (eg supply market or category updates) – providing planners and buyers with relevant data to support their decisions, based on procurement's in-depth knowledge and contacts
- Standard terms and conditions in supply contracts – managing risk by providing sound contract terms and minimising the risk of legal problems
- Negotiation services and skills – conducting negotiations on behalf of other departments, or advising/ training them in negotiation skills, as a way of maximising the organisation's share of value from transactions and relationships
- Management of supplier and supplier relationships – creating and developing sources of collaboration and information which may benefit other organisational activities.

1.11   The departments using procurement's consultancy services may or may not have to pay for them in a direct way, as with the fees paid to external consultants. Some internal charge may be made, however. This can enhance the perceived value of the service – since you tend to pay more attention to information you have paid for! – but it may also make internal clients more demanding in terms of schedules, results and value for money.

1.12   Procurement may need to prove the value of its service (or present a 'business case' for its service) by collecting and presenting data on performance measures such as: fulfilment of specific agreed consultancy/performance objectives and service levels; cost reductions and/or quality improvements achieved; client compliance (eg with procurement policies and procedures) and satisfaction; and so on.

1.13   Internal consultancy can be a successful model for ensuring that procurement disciplines are pursued throughout the organisation. It can also help the procurement function to raise its status, credibility and influence in the organisation: encouraging it to develop a list of services to its internal customers, and to market its services on the basis of customer benefits, value for money and business case. It may also help to minimise potential political problems in the organisation, since procurement is seen as advising, consulting and serving user departments – rather than 'interfering' in their activity or 'imposing' procurement-focused solutions.

1.14   However, effective internal consultancy is not always easy to develop or apply.

- The structure, senior management and culture of the organisation must support the cross-functional sharing of information and expertise, and the acceptance of the value of specialist knowledge (rather than functions resenting 'interference' by others).
- Procurement, as an internal consultant, must develop skills, expertise, contacts and knowledge which are valued by other functions, and the business as a whole – and must 'market' these effectively to potential internal clients, presenting a clear business case for its services.
- There must be clear, effective mechanisms in place for gathering and sharing information; for monitoring, measuring and feeding back performance data; and (where relevant) for costing, valuing and charging for internal consultancy services.

The need for customer service and value for money outcomes

1.15   As we saw in Chapter 3, the concept of the internal supply chain has increasingly focused attention on the provision of service to 'internal customers'. So, for example, procurement may regard project or production managers as a customer or client, because their needs, wants and expectations define the key operational objectives of procurement.

1.16   Like all functions in an organisation, however, procurement must be sensitive to the needs of external customers. With its increasing strategic role in all stages of the value chain from product design to delivery (and perhaps reverse logistics), it may be argued that the procurement or supply chain function should see itself as part of the flow of value towards the end customer or consumer.

1.17   Procurement may have a direct impact on external customer satisfaction. One obvious example is the case of buyers in retail environments, whose job is to buy goods that customers will want to buy. Procurement staff also procure services that are directly passed on or delivered to customers: in the private sector, this might include product warranties or call centres; in the public sector, it may include a wide range of public services commissioned by a local authority.

1.18   More generally, procurement will have an indirect impact on external customer satisfaction, as part of the value chain.

- As we have seen, the five 'rights' of procurement are designed to ensure timely, high-quality, cost-effective inputs, which are essential for the timely delivery of high-quality outputs to customers at a price they can afford – and for the maintenance of market competition, which benefits customers through choice and value.
- Procurement has an important role in the development of new products, which benefits external markets by meeting their changing needs and expectations and extending their choice.
- Procurement may also source peripheral goods and services that add to the overall 'package of benefits' offered to customers: for example, IT systems for customer service, product packaging, delivery or recycling capability.

1.19   This shift is reflected in a variety of models of the historical development of the procurement function. Reck & Long, for example, have classified the development of procurement into four stages.

- *Passive:* procurement has no strategic direction, and mainly reacts to the requests of other functions. Its function is mainly clerical.
- *Independent:* procurement adopts the latest procurement techniques and processes, and its own functional strategies. The focus is mainly on functional efficiency, with contribution measured in terms of cost reduction and supplier performance.

- *Supportive:* procurement supports the firm's competitive strategy by adopting techniques (such as just in time or lean supply) and products which strengthen its position. Its role is now that of a strategic facilitator, measured by contribution to competitive objectives.
- *Integrative:* procurement's strategy (along with those of other functions) is fully integrated into the firm's overall strategy. Its role is that of a strategic contributor, and is measured by strategic contribution. The emphasis is on cross-functional information-exchange and understanding.

1.20 Let's now look at the implications of all these roles and relationships for the structuring of procurement operations.

2 Structuring procurement operations

Factors in structuring procurement

2.1 A number of key factors may influence the design of a procurement or supply chain function.

(a) The **size, nature and role** of the procurement task in the organisation.
- As we saw in Chapter 7, for example, it may be transactional, commercial or strategic in orientation (reflected by its expenditure and level of reporting in the organisation).
- It may cover a range of activities, dictating a degree of specialisation: as size and specialisation grows, additional attention may need to be given to mechanisms for control and communication.
- It may be a dedicated function, reporting at the highest level of the organisation – or it may (increasingly rarely, in large organisations) be a subsidiary function reporting through production, finance or commerce.

(b) **Alignment with corporate structure and strategy.** Procurement accountabilities may be subdivided by: category of procured items (eg MRO, commodities, vehicles); the product category for which supplies are to be used; the stage of manufacture (eg raw materials, components, finished assemblies); plant location; supplier group; or internal customer group (eg different departments in a local authority).

(c) The **structure and environment** within which procurement operates (as we saw in Chapter 7):
- The internal organisation structure: what functions procurement reports to (and at what level); what mechanisms there are to co-ordinate procurement activities with those of other functions; who the internal customers of procurement are; the nature of procurement's role in relation to them (direct service provider, advisor, regulator); how procurement competence and contribution is perceived and measured in the organisation; the impact of corporate policy on procurement roles and responsibilities; and so on.
- The external supply market and the organisation's supply base: its size, geographical spread, structure, degree of specialisation, and critical success factors.

(d) The **strategic objectives** of the procurement function. If cost reduction is the priority, procurement may be centralised to enable economies of scale, for example. If customer service is a priority, it may be devolved (or decentralised) to allow responsive 'local' decision-making, or organised by customer group. If supply performance is a priority, the function may be organised by commodity (for specialisation) or supplier group (for better relationship management). And so on.

2.2 *Lysons and Farrington* highlight two further key structural issues for purchasing and supply.

- Increasing focus on business processes and supply chains, leading to the increasing integration of supply activities and the creation of 'horizontal' (cross-functional and inter-organisational) structures, to support logistics and supply chain management and logistics (as discussed in Chapter 3).
- The existence of diversified and/or geographically dispersed multi-divisional organisations, raising the issue of whether to centralise or devolve procurement functions.

Centralised and devolved structures

2.3   An important organisational issue is the extent to which procurement responsibilities should be centralised or departmentalised (ie placed in the hands of a single department reporting to a single executive) or devolved or decentralised (ie devolved to procurement officers in different strategic business units or user departments). In service firms, in particular, it is common to find that procurement is carried out by users or budget-holders, rather than by procurement or supply chain specialists.

2.4   The question is further highlighted in the case of multi-site operations. An organisation that operates through a number of branches or divisions, perhaps separated by considerable distances, may consider a single procurement function at head office (centralisation) or separate functions at each division (devolution or decentralisation). The choice is rarely clear-cut.

2.5   Most commentators suggest that responsibilities for supply management activities at a higher level (policy development, supplier selection and relationship management, major contract negotiations and so on) should be centralised – ie they should lie as far as possible with procurement specialists, in order to leverage core procurement and supply chain competencies.

2.6   However it may not always be feasible to centralise procurement operations.

- If various divisions (or strategic business units) use and procure different materials from different external supply markets. In such cases, there may be a need for specialist expertise, relationships, systems and procedures to 'fit' the distinctive markets and requirements of the division, and to be 'close to' clients and customers in order to respond to their changing needs.
- If strategic business units or operational sites are widely dispersed geographically (especially in areas where transport and communication infrastructures are less developed). In such cases, there may be a need for a 'local' procurement presence, to support local procurement and supply: minimising difficulties, risks and costs of long transport and communication lines.

Advantages of centralised procurement

2.7   The key advantages of centralised procurement are as follows.

- Specialisation of procurement staff. Buyers can focus on a particular area (particular skills, such as contract negotiation, or particular materials and markets, such as machinery or chemicals) and develop their knowledge to greater depth, with potential to improve quality and lower costs. (If 10 procurement staff are located in 10 divisions, each of them will have general responsibility for a wide range of activities and requirements, fostering generalist knowledge and skills. If 10 procurement staff are based in a single, centralised unit, there is the opportunity for each buyer to develop knowledge in more specialised techniques, procedures or categories of procurement.)
- Potential for the consolidation of requirements: that is, putting multiple requisitions from different units together into single, larger orders or contracts. This reduces the frequency of small orders for commonly purchased items; reduces transaction and transport costs; and enables buyers to obtain better prices (with economies of scale, bulk discounts, etc) and higher levels of service (as potentially more significant customers of suppliers). The number of suppliers is likely to be smaller, too, and administration of orders and contracts may be more streamlined.
- Greater co-ordination of procurement activities. Uniform procurement policies, procedures and good practice can be introduced and applied, facilitating standardisation, variety reduction, better value for money and improved compliance – and minimising 'maverick', *ad hoc* procurements. Staff training and development can also be undertaken more systematically.
- Greater standardisation of specifications, which may enhance quality and efficiency in a number of ways: facilitating the consolidation of orders; reducing inventory and handling costs (less variety and greater utilisation); focusing the supplier base (fewer 'specialist' requirements); improved quality management (ease of inspection); and simpler and more accurate communication about requirements.

- More effective control of procurement activity. Procurement performance can be monitored and compared with defined KPIs; budgetary control may be applied to the function (and total external expenditures); and the unit may be viewed as a separate cost or profit centre for closer accountability.
- Avoidance of conflict between business divisions, which may otherwise arise due to competition for scarce materials, unequal budgetary allocations of procurement expenditure, or differences in price or value obtained in procurements.
- Access to specialist skills, contacts and resources (such as procurement research), which may not be available at divisional level.

Advantages of devolved procurement

2.8 There are also significant advantages in devolving procurement to a decentralised, 'local' level. (You should be able to read, from these, the corresponding *disadvantages* of *centralised* procurement, in case you are asked to discuss these in an exam.)

- Better communication and coordination between procurement and operating departments, benefiting from user expertise and minimising 'maverick' buying by users. (In centralised procurement functions, ICT mechanisms may have to be highly developed to facilitate regular contact and data-sharing with internal customers: we discuss this further in Chapter 9.)
- Customer focus. Buyers are 'closer' to internal and external customers, so they can develop a better understanding of user needs and problems, and a 'big picture' business focus, rather than a parochial identification with their own functional objectives. This may also help to keep procurement outward-focused, creating a culture open to learning and change.
- Quicker response to operational and user needs and environmental changes and problems by local buyers who are close to the scene of operations.
- Knowledge of, and relationships with, locally based suppliers. There are advantages in sourcing from short distances – such as reduced transport cost and environmental impacts; reduced transport risk and delivery times; the ability to personally appraise and monitor suppliers; and the ability to negotiate and resolve disputes face-to-face. (The corresponding disadvantages of international sourcing should not be overstated, however, given the increasing globalisation of business, the potential for cost savings in low-cost-labour countries, and the support of ICT for supplier communication.)
- Smaller purchase quantities: sacrificing economies of scale, but reducing costs and risks of holding inventory (tied up capital, risk of deterioration or obsolescence etc), and possibly supporting social sustainability policies and innovation (by enabling small, local suppliers to bid for contracts).
- Accountability: divisional managers can be held accountable for performance only if they have genuine control over operations (which is not the case if procurement has been taken out of their hands).
- Freeing central procurement units to focus on higher-level, value-adding tasks.

2.9 As the last point highlights, even if procurement is carried out at a local level, it is likely that there will still be a need for a centralised procurement function to carry out specialised activities, such as supply market research or the procurement of specialised and capital items. Often long-term 'framework' contracts may be negotiated by the central procurement office, with divisional buyers or users calling off requirements against the contracts.

Centralised procurement: a shared services approach

2.10 Shared services are those support functions that are used by many different departments within a large organisation (eg finance, IT, human resources or procurement). A shared service unit (SSU) is a dedicated provider of such services to internal users. Individual strategic business units (such as regional divisions) retain their autonomy but in effect 'outsource' their need for specialist services. The difference compared with conventional outsourcing is that the outsource provider is not an external company, but an internal function.

2.11   The SSU is responsible for managing the costs, quality and timeliness of its services. It employs its own dedicated resources, and usually has contractual agreements with internal customers based on service level agreements.

2.12   Advantages claimed for this approach include cost savings (cost of back-office processes is usually reduced when they are taken out of individual business units), common standards across the organisation, and a strengthening of corporate value. The approach works best when there is a good measure of uniformity among the business units within the organisation; it is less effective if business units are very diverse in their nature and activities.

2.13   However, there are also criticisms of the SSU approach.

- It may encourage a centralised approach that stifles innovation and initiative.
- The value and performance levels of SSUs are not easily measured.
- An SSU may sacrifice effectiveness in favour of efficiency in order to achieve predetermined service levels.
- Staff in SSUs may be remote from end users.

The structure of a centralised procurement or supply chain team

2.14   The way in which procurement and supply chain tasks are divided among members of staff in a dedicated unit (or department) obviously depends mainly on size. In a very small procurement unit there may be just a single buyer with perhaps an assistant and a small number of support staff. The organisation structure for the department might be something like Figure 8.1.

Figure 8.1 *Organisation of a small procurement department*

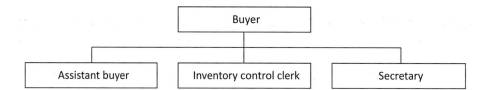

Clearly this structure leaves little scope for specialisation. Most buying policies and decisions will be initiated by the buyer, with routine matters delegated as far as possible to the assistant buyer.

2.15   In larger organisations, the procurement function is likely to be more developed, with more staff and greater specialisation: Figure 8.2.

Figure 8.2 *Organisation of a medium-sized procurement department*

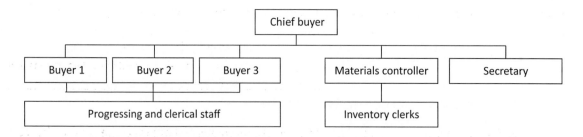

2.16   In this kind of organisation, the chief buyer will be responsible for procurement policy, as well as for managing the smooth running of the department, but many (perhaps most) of the day-to-day decisions will be taken by the buyers, who have the opportunity to specialise.

- One possibility is that each buyer deals with a particular range of items, or 'category' of procurements (such as IT, commodities or MRO supplies).
- Another possibility relevant to project-based organisations (eg construction companies) is to allocate responsibility for each project's procurement to a particular buyer.

2.17 In a large department (Figure 8.3), the problems of communication and control are likely to be much greater, and must be addressed carefully if optimum performance is to be obtained.

Figure 8.3 *Organisation of a large procurement department*

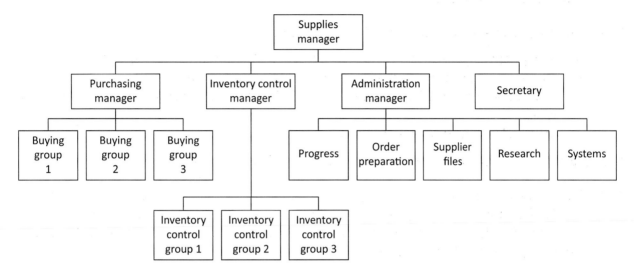

Hybrid structures

2.18 Lysons suggests that a mix of centralised and devolved procurement is common in practice, with both central and 'local' (devolved) procurement functions dividing tasks between them: Table 8.1.

Table 8.1 *Typical division of roles between local and central procurement functions*

LOCAL PROCUREMENT FUNCTION	CENTRALISED PROCUREMENT FUNCTION
Small order items	Determination of major procurement and supply chain policies
Items used only by the local division	Preparation of standard specifications
Emergency procurements (to avoid disruption to production)	Negotiation of bulk contracts for a number of divisions
Items sourced from local suppliers	Stationery and office equipment (generic, shared supplies, which can be bought most economically in buik)
Local procurement undertaken for social sustainability reasons	Procurement research
	Procurement of capital assets
	Procurement capability development eg training and development

2.19 Lysons and Farrington further elaborate on this model, by showing that procurement may be 'centralised' across a spectrum from highly centralised to highly devolved.

- *Centralised procurement*: procurement strategy, policy, systems and standards are controlled centrally and all procurement activities are also carried out centrally. (This may be suitable where the items required by each strategic business unit or plant are largely the same.)

- *Co-ordinated devolved procurement*: procurement strategy, policy, systems and standards are controlled centrally; procurement of items common to more than one strategic business unit are usually centralised; but other operational procurement activities are carried out within the SBUs. (This may be suitable where SBUs or plants produce widely dissimilar products.)
- *Consultative centralised procurement*: procurement activities – both strategic and operational – are devolved to strategic business units, which merely take guidance and advice from a centralised procurement function.

2.20 A number of specific hybrid models and approaches have been developed, of which the most popular are CLAN, SCAN, lead buyer and business partner.

2.21 The **CLAN** (centre-led action network) approach is a relatively devolved model.

- Procurement staff are mainly located in different business units. They report primarily to the local management of their business unit, with secondary responsibility to a small procurement centre (generally located at corporate head office).
- The role of the procurement centre is to lead and co-ordinate the network of local buyers, by formulating policy, setting standards and encouraging best practice.
- Elements of centralisation, devolution and matrix structure are therefore used to achieve co-ordinated devolution.
- CLAN offers some key advantages: procurement is identified closely with local needs and can react swiftly to business needs. But there is a potential loss of leverage (as in all devolved models), and constant energy is required from the centre to drive co-operative activity.

2.22 The **SCAN** (strategically-controlled action network) approach is a relatively centralised model.

- Structurally, it is similar to a CLAN, except that local procurement staff (business purchasing teams) report primarily to the head-office central procurement unit.
- The central unit is responsible for strategy, policy, training and performance management. It also includes centralised category managers, who are responsible for particular categories of goods and services procured across the organisation.
- SCAN has overtaken CLAN in many large organisations which want to leverage procurement expertise – although it shares the corresponding disadvantages of centralised procurement.

2.23 The **lead buyer** approach is one way in which responsibilities can be devolved in a CLAN. Defined procurement responsibilities are delegated to designated members of user departments, as 'lead buyers' for a particular category of procurements.

- The key benefit of such a structure is that user departments are closely involved in procurement decisions, where this is important for agility and local advantages.
- Lead buyers are not procurement professionals, and may require support from policies, procedures and guidance from a centralised procurement team. However, where implemented effectively, this can serve to improve communication and relationships between procurement and user departments, and to spread procurement best practice more widely in the organisation.

2.24 A **business partnering** approach is one way in which procurement guidance can be exercised in a SCAN. A member of the procurement team works within a user department (typically, one in which there is large or complex external spend). He represents the procurement function, liaises with the user function, and identifies situations where procurement or supply chain expertise can add value.

3   Cross-functional team and project working

Cross-functional teams in procurement

3.1   Multi-disciplinary or cross-functional teams bring together individuals with different skills and specialisms, so that their competencies and resources can be pooled or exchanged, and/or so that their (potentially divergent) goals and interests can be represented and integrated. An example might be a multi-functional procurement strategy team, or even a multi-organisational supply management team (involving representatives of all the stakeholders in the supply chain).

3.2   Ongoing cross-functional working is often organised as a matrix structure (discussed in Chapter 7). *Project* teams, on the other hand, are typically cross-functional teams set up to handle specific strategic developments (such as the introduction of a just in time approach), tasks relating to particular processes (such as the computerisation of inventory control), tasks relating to particular 'cases' or accounts (such as co-ordination of traffic with a particular supplier) or special audit and investigation of procedures or improvement opportunities (such as a review of order parameters or supplier ethical codes).

3.3   Dobler *et al* (*Purchasing & Materials Management*) identify four key roles for a procurement or supply management professional on a cross-functional team: providing process knowledge and expertise (eg in supply base research or negotiation); providing content knowledge (eg of a specific market or commodity area); liaising with supply staff to ensure project needs get attention and priority; and putting forward the supply management point of view (eg re trade-offs, priority-setting and policy decisions).

3.4   The trend towards cross-functional teamworking in procurement and supply chain management can be attributed (Lysons and Farrington) to factors such as:

- The increasing involvement of procurement staff in strategic decisions
- The increasing adoption of a supply chain philosophy, creating the need to deal with value flows in a more integrated way
- Its ability to make best use of developments in ICT
- The adoption of advanced world class systems (such as MRP and TQM) which require co-ordinated cross-functional implementation
- The increasing complexity and dynamism of global markets and technologies, creating the need for a range of expert input and support
- The need to leverage human resource capability: teams outperform individuals for certain tasks.

3.5   Cross-functional procurement teams are particularly valuable in increasing team members' awareness of the big picture of their tasks and decisions – and therefore dovetailing functional objectives and agendas with the overall objectives of the organisation or project.

3.6   They enable a wider pooling of viewpoints, expertise and resources, and represent a wider range of stakeholder interests (users, suppliers, procurement specialists and so on). This can help to generate innovative and integrative solutions to problems, and suggestions for collaborative performance or process improvements .

3.7   Cross-functional procurement teams and projects are a key tool for co-ordinating work flow and communication across vertical organisational boundaries. This is important so that the flow of added value towards customers is not impeded by vertical barriers. It can also reduce the time it takes to get things done! Cross-functional teams support innovation and learning through the pooling of different expertise and knowledge, and they enable swift decision-making by avoiding lengthy vertical channels of communication and authorisation.

3.8   However, there are difficulties to cross-functional team or project working.

8

- While representing different viewpoints and interests can enhance decisions (and their acceptability), it also adds potential for time-consuming complexity, conflict and consensus-seeking.
- Matrix-style structures and cross-functional relationships may lack clear lines of authority: members may need to exert informal influence through persuasion, politics, negotiation or personal leadership in order to have their functional perspective heard.
- All teams take time to develop before they perform effectively: to overcome conflict, build trust, allocate roles and determine a shared working style.
- There may be difficulties of dual authority structures and conflicting demands, if cross-functional team members also report to their individual functional managers.
- There may be practical difficulties of organising meetings and information flows, given different functional work patterns, locations and so on. (ICT links may be used to support 'virtual' teamworking, meetings, data-sharing and so on.)

Interacting with other people

3.9 It is worth remembering that business people are people. This may seem obvious, but it is all too possible to approach dealings with key stakeholders as if they were 'resources' or 'elements in the value chain' or 'problems' – without remembering that they are also human beings.

3.10 The core leadership quality of emotional intelligence includes being aware of, or sensitive to, the needs and emotions of other people – and being able to respond flexibly to those needs and emotions in such a way as to build relationships and get the best out of people.

Rapport

3.11 Rapport may be defined, most simply, as the sense of relationship or connection we have when we relate to another person.

3.12 We have 'positive rapport' with people we find warm, attentive and easy to talk to: we are inclined to feel comfortable and relaxed with them, or attracted to them. We all know from experience that some people are easier to relate to than others. Some individuals seem distant or uninterested in us, or we feel less comfortable around them: we would call this low or negative rapport.

3.13 Rapport is a core skill for influencing, in simple terms, because: 'influencing is easier if the other person feels comfortable with you; if they feel they trust you; if they feel you understand them' (*Gillen*). In more detail, rapport:

(a) Helps to establish trust and a belief in the common ground between you and the other person: your viewpoint is then more likely to be received openly, rather than defensively.

(b) Is the basis of the positive influencing approach, sometimes called **pacing and leading**. First you 'pace' the other party (listening to, empathising with and reflecting back their views, feelings and needs). This earns trust and rapport from which you can 'lead' (influence) the other person (eg by reframing the problem or changing the emotional tone of the discussion).

(c) Creates a reason for people to agree with you, or do what you want them to do, because they like you! (A powerful motivator, even in business contexts…)

(d) Overcomes some of the barriers created by power imbalances and differences or conflicts of interest, reducing the tendency towards adversarial or defensive attitudes.

3.14 Key **rapport-building techniques** are based on the idea that it is easier to relate to someone who is (or appears to be) *like* us in some way; with whom we share some beliefs, values, interests or characteristics; and who treats us as a valued and interesting person. Some useful techniques therefore include:

- Subtly matching or 'mirroring' the other person's posture, body language and/or volume, speed and tone of voice. (This also reflects their mood and helps them to feel understood.)

- Picking up on the other person's use of technical words, colloquialisms and metaphors – and using them too (if you can do so with understanding and integrity) or incorporating them in comments and discussion summaries.
- Picking up on the other person's dominant way of experiencing and expressing things, which tend to be based on sight, sound or feeling ('I see what you mean', 'I hear what you're saying', 'That just hit me') and using similar modes of expression ('Do you see?', 'How does that sound to you?', 'What's your feeling about that?')
- Listening attentively and actively to what the other person is saying; demonstrating this with encouraging gestures, eye contact (where culturally appropriate) and so on; and asking supportive questions or summarising, in order to show that you are interested and want to understand. (This is the first-order skill of **empathy**.)
- Finding topics of common interest, and emphasising areas of agreement or common ground where possible
- Remembering and using people's names.

4 Outsourcing procurement operations

What and when to outsource

4.1 Like any other activity, procurement and supply chain management can be considered as candidates for outsourcing. More and more firms are following a strategy of focusing on their core competencies, while outsourcing more peripheral functions.

4.2 Lysons and Farrington identify a number of situations in which outsourcing of the procurement function should be considered: see Table 8.2.

Table 8.2 *When procurement should be outsourced*

CIRCUMSTANCES	WHAT ACTIVITIES TO OUTSOURCE
Procurement (or 'purchasing') is a peripheral rather than a core activity (low or generalised skill requirements, internally focused responsibilities, well-defined or limited tasks, jobs that are easily separated from other tasks)	• Purchase orders • Locally and nationally procured needs • Low-value acquisitions • Brand name requirements • Call-offs against framework agreements • Administration and paperwork associated with purchasing needs
The supply base is small and based on proven cooperation, and there are no supply restrictions	• Well-defined or limited tasks • Jobs that are easily separated from other tasks • Jobs that have no supply restrictions
The supplier base is small, providing non-strategic, non-critical, low-risk items	• Outsource purchasing to specialist purchasing and supplier organisations, or to buying consortia

Benefits and challenges of outsourcing procurement

4.3 There has been much debate in the professional media about the benefits and costs of procurement outsourcing: that is, the transfer of some, or all, of an organisation's procurement activity to a third party. Here are some of the benefits of outsourcing procurement.

- The freeing up of resources (eg management time, office space and equipment) which may be deployed for greater added value elsewhere
- The ability to draw on procurement (or particular category) knowledge, experience, expertise, contacts, systems and technology (eg e-auction software) which may not be available in the in-house procurement function, and may be costly to develop. This may enable the implementation of best-practice purchasing processes and practices.

- The potential for third party purchasers to aggregate demand and consolidate orders for different clients, resulting in cost savings through economies of scale, bulk discounts and so on. Conversely, third party purchasers may be able to break bulk for clients, getting around the constraints of minimum order quantities.
- The re-focusing of remaining internal procurement staff on strategic issues such as input to make-buy decisions, sustainable procurement policy, setting of KPIs for the outsourced service, and so on.
- Greater flexibility to adjust to peaks and troughs of demand for procurement activity. The contracting organisation no longer has to cope with excess payroll in slack periods or overtime in peak periods.

4.4 As with any outsource strategy, however, there are also risks and costs associated with outsourcing procurement functions.

- The organisation loses a critical commercial skill and knowledge base.
- The organisation may lose control over vital data and intellectual property (as a result of sharing plans and specifications with a third party).
- An additional management layer is needed to manage the outsource provider.

5 Consortium procurement

5.1 A buying consortium is a group of separate organisations that combine together for the purpose of procuring goods or services.

5.2 A buying consortium might be created when a group of organisations see mutual benefit in aggregating their requirements: creating larger contracts, for economies of scale and increased bargaining power to secure advantageous terms. This might be especially beneficial if one organisation's requirements, on their own, are insufficient to attract attention – or discounts – from high-quality suppliers.

5.3 The consortium is represented in discussions with suppliers by a centralised or shared procurement unit, which may be the procurement function of one of the members, or a third party procurement service. The cost is shared by the consortium members.

5.4 With a buying consortium, the relationship with a supplier is more likely to be transactional, because it could be difficult for a supplier to develop long-term partnership relationships with a group of different organisations. This is particularly the case when the members of the consortium change over time, with some new members joining and existing members leaving the group.

5.5 Buying consortia can be found in both the public and the private sectors, but are particularly encouraged in the public sector, in order to maximise value for money. In the UK, several local government authorities might form a consortium with a centralised buying unit. Similarly, there are buying consortia in parts of the automotive industry.

Benefits and drawbacks of consortium procurement

5.6 The benefits of consortium procurement may be summarised as follows.

- By means of enhanced bargaining power, the consortium can obtain discounts that would not be available to individual members – although there may be difficulties in allocating such discounts fairly among them.
- A consortium can establish framework agreements, simplifying purchase administration for members. This can lead to significant reductions in transaction and contracting costs, especially in the case of low-value items where the administrative cost is disproportionate to the purchase price of the items.
- Consortium members can pool expertise, knowledge and contacts, where these would be beneficial for particular procurement categories or exercises.

5.7   However – as always – it is not all good news. There are some costs and disadvantages associated with consortium purchasing.

- There are costs and effort associated with communication and coordination, staff development and policy development.
- There is an issue of transparency between consortium members. Buyers need full information about plans, processes, designs and costs in order to make informed procurement decisions: this may expose some members of a consortium to commercial or intellectual property risk.
- Consortia may suffer from lengthy negotiation and decision processes, which are inefficient – and may deter some suppliers from dealing with the consortium.
- Aggregated demand may create very large contracts, which might disadvantage small or medium sized enterprises (including local and minority-run businesses) from accessing the business: this may be contrary to social sustainability or corporate social responsibility policies – and may also suppress supply market innovation (since SMEs are often more entrepreneurial and innovative).
- Members are not obliged to purchase to the agreed specification.
- Very large consortia may fall foul of laws and regulations designed to prevent dominant market players from abusing their dominant market position (eg by dictating pricing).

Chapter summary

- Procurement is a support or service provider to a range of primary activities.
- Procurement often acts in a role of internal consultancy or business partner.
- There are various ways of structuring procurement activities, eg by centralising or devolving the function or by the use of hybrid models such as CLAN or SCAN.
- Increasingly, procurement specialists work as part of cross-functional teams.
- Like any other activity, procurement can be considered as a candidate for outsourcing.
- There are advantages for organisations who combine their procurement operations by means of consortium buying.

Self-test questions

Numbers in brackets refer to the paragraphs where you can check your answers.

1   Which primary activities may procurement provide support to? (1.2)

2   In what circumstances may procurement function as an internal consultancy? (1.8)

3   How does the procurement function impact on the satisfaction of external customers? (1.18)

4   List advantages of (a) centralised and (b) devolved procurement. (2.7, 2.8)

5   Suggest a division of roles between local and centralised procurement functions. (2.18, Table 8.1)

6   What factors have led to the increasing use of cross-functional teamworking for procurement? (3.4)

7   What are the drawbacks of cross-functional teamworking? (3.8)

8   In what circumstances should outsourcing of the procurement function be considered? (4.2, Table 8.2)

9   What are the drawbacks of outsourcing the procurement function? (4.4)

10   List (a) benefits and (b) drawbacks of consortium procurement. (5.6, 5.7)

CHAPTER 9

ICT Systems

Assessment criteria and indicative content

3.4 Explain the common IT systems that can be used by a procurement or supply chain function.

- P2P systems
- Systems for inventory management
- Enterprise Resource Planning (ERP) technologies
- Communication systems for internal and external use

Section headings

1. The broader impact of ICT on procurement and supply chain management
2. Inventory management systems
3. Enterprise resource planning (ERP)
4. Communication systems

Introduction

This chapter addresses another key aspect of organisational context or infrastructure which may support or constrain procurement and supply chain operations: technology, systems and information flows.

Although the syllabus refers to 'IT' (information technology) systems, we have preferred to use the more comprehensive term 'ICT' (information and communication technology), which recognises the extent to which 'computing' is nowadays inextricably linked to telecommunications and communication networks.

This chapter should be viewed alongside Chapter 6, which looked at the impact of ICT on the procurement process, and the tools available for electronic sourcing and procurement. In the context of the e-procurement process, we also covered electronic P2P or 'purchase to pay' systems (often associated with e-procurement). Although P2P systems re-appear in the syllabus at this point, we will not repeat or re-cap the material again: please simply refresh your memory of Chapter 6 if you need to.

1 The broader impact of ICT on procurement and

duct markets through the potential for product innovation: think of the relatively new markets for digital cameras, MP3 players, music and book downloads, plasma TVs and so on. These new markets impact on purchasing by creating new sourcing requirements.

1.1 Technological developments have a range of impacts on business and purchasing activity.

1.2 Automation and computerisation *raise productivity* by allowing faster, more accurate, more consistent work than human beings can achieve alone. A supplier with access to advanced design, manufacturing, goods handling and transport technology should be able to fulfil orders faster, more cheaply and with more consistent (though not necessarily higher) quality.

1.3 Technology opens up new *product* markets through the potential for product innovation: think of the relatively new markets for tablets and smartphones, music and book downloads, plasma TVs and so on. These new markets impact on purchasing by creating new sourcing requirements.

1.4 Technology also opens up new *supply* markets, eg by giving purchasers access to information on international suppliers via the internet, and facilitating communication and transaction processing. Technology may also be a differentiating or cost-saving factor, lowering barriers to entry and allowing small new producers or service providers access to established markets.

1.5 Technology changes business processes. It may be used to perform operational functions more safely (eg automated production and materials handling) or easily (eg recording and tracking stock movements using barcoding or RFID). In recent decades, it has changed both production processes and supply and distribution processes.

- Production processes, with an emphasis on labour-saving equipment and machinery – impacting purchasing through the need for investment appraisal and capital purchases. Examples include the increasing use of automated (or robotic) production, computer-aided design and manufacture, computerised monitoring of quality and process, and so on.
- Supply and distribution processes. Examples include: access to new global supply and product markets through e-commerce and faster transport; electronic sourcing and procurement systems (which we discussed in Chapter 6); and new methods of service delivery (such as ATM machines, online entertainment ticketing and online banking).

1.6 Technology changes the amount of labour and types of skills required by businesses (eg through the use of labour-saving automation) and how they can be organised and managed (eg the use of information and communication technology to facilitate off-site and mobile working, and 'virtual' teamworking). This may in turn support the use of outsourcing and subcontracting, which may be driven and managed by the procurement function. It may also create a changing skill profile for procurement staff (eg use of e-procurement tools).

The impact of information and communication technology (ICT)

1.7 As we saw in Chapter 6, information and communication technology (computers and telecommunications) has had a particular impact on procurement.

- Dramatically increasing the speed of communication and information processing. Real-time answers to enquiries, updating of information and processing of transactions can be conducted via a computer network or the internet.
- Offering wider access to environmental and supply market information (especially from global sources). The internet offers constant access to formal information resources (in the form of websites, databases, libraries, expert agencies and so on) and informal resources in the form of network contacts. This has had the effect of opening up new supply markets, by giving purchasers access to information about suppliers and supply markets worldwide.
- Facilitating 24-hour, 7-day, global business. The internet and email allow companies to offer service and maintain communication across office hours, international time zones and geographical distances.
- Supporting paperless communications (eg electronic mail messages), business transactions (eg online ordering and payment) and service delivery (eg online ticket reservations, information and education services, and so on). Information storage and retrieval is less wasteful of physical space and resources – and of administrative time.
- Offering opportunities for cost savings, through a wider supply base, streamlined processes and lower prices (eg via e-auctions)
- Freeing up buyers' time – previously taken up by routine and repetitive clerical tasks – for creative, strategic and relational aspects of their roles
- Enhancing management information (eg via databases and systems which record, store and analyse a wide range of transaction, business and environmental data).
- Creating 'virtual' supplier relationships, teams and organisations, by making location irrelevant to the process of collaboration.

1.8 ICT can also be used to develop supply chain relationships, for example by:

- Providing real-time information for transaction processing, delivery tracking and other value-adding services
- Streamlining procurement and delivery processes for higher levels of customer service
- Supporting the customisation of products and services and the personalisation of contacts for supplier or customer relationship management
- Creating knowledge communities – eg sharing information via extranets
- Facilitating the coordination of collaborative activities.

1.9 We looked at the application of ICT to sourcing, procurement and P2P processes in Chapter 6. Here, we will look at a number of other applications in the wider context of the organisation and its information systems.

2 Inventory management systems

2.1 Inventory management covers a variety of activities.

- *Demand management*: ensuring that supplies are available in the right quantities at the right time for the needs of internal (and external) customers
- *Forecasting demand* (and therefore supply requirements) in order to avoid over-stocking
- *Controlling stock levels* (in terms of quantity and value held), and monitoring and maintaining target minimum and maximum stock levels – to avoid over-stocking and production 'bottlenecks' due to stockouts
- Ensuring that supplies are *replenished* in accordance with procurement policies
- Developing cost-effective *systems and procedures* for ordering and procurement of supplies
- *Controlling* the receipt, inspection, storage and issuing of supplies to users
- Ensuring that stocks are *safe and secure* from deterioration, damage, theft or obsolescence

2.2 Electronic systems can support a number of these activities.

Data capture for stock tracking

2.3 As we saw in Chapter 6, electronic point of sale (EPOS) systems are commonly used in retailing to capture sales data (using barcodes) and to update inventory records automatically. Similarly, online track and trace systems and inventory management systems use barcodes and radio frequency identification (RFID) to capture data on delivery and stock movements, locations, numbers and so on. Data is input direct to an information system and linked to related database records and applications. This allows accurate counting and recording of materials and finished items moving into and out of stock, or in transit.

2.4 **Barcodes** are, in effect, code numbers, represented in the form of optical bars, printed on a data carrier (such as a label, tag or card). The coded information (eg product identification) is read using a scanner, which inputs the data to an IT system and links it to related database records (eg the price, supplier, classification and stock levels of the item). Barcoding has a number of inventory management applications. Goods received may be barcoded either by the supplier (in an integrated system) or by the buying organisation. Receiving staff scan the barcode in order to transmit updating information to the inventory system. If incoming materials are packaged or containerised in standard quantities, the process can be streamlined even further.

2.5 Barcodes may also be scanned for:

- Tracking deliveries in transit, at key points of contact (eg loading bays, delivery offices, international delivery points or customs check-points)
- Recording issues of items from stock, linked to requisitions and picking lists, updating stock levels
- Recording outgoing deliveries (or sales, in an EPOS system) to customers.

2.6   **Radio frequency identification (RFID)** is one of the 'hottest' technologies in automatic data capture. An RFID tag (transponder) is attached to or placed inside items, and its micro-electronic circuits store data for transmission to a remote RFID reader. This offers significant advantages, compared to the conventional optical scanning of barcodes.

- The tag doesn't have to be scanned or 'seen' by the reader: it can be used for updating inventory of moving and 'hidden' items in complex storage and transport environments. The costs of manual scanning can be saved – and dust and other problems for barcode reading do not apply.
- Data can be flexibly interrogated and updated for stock control, re-order triggering and so on. Multiple tags can be read and written at the same time.
- A *CIPS Practice Guide* argues that RFID can offer improved product availability; improved utilisation of resources; lower total operating costs; and enhanced safety, security and quality control.

Inventory management systems

2.7   Inventory control and information systems perform a range of integrated tasks, including:

- Capturing goods inwards information accurately (delivery, receipt, inspection and acceptance), and integrating this information with stock balance, contract management and payment systems
- Recording stock movements (receipts, issues, transfers) and locations
- Translating issue requisitions into stock 'picking and packing' tasks (for warehouse and stores staff to select and prepare items for issue)
- Maintaining stock balances (for verification during physical stocktakes) and stock valuations (for use in financial reporting and insurance decisions)
- Triggering automatic replenishment requisitions or orders at pre-established order points, calculating economic order quantities where appropriate
- Monitoring productivity and utilisation, to derive usage rates for feeding into demand management calculations
- Maintaining stock integrity, by recording and identifying damage, deterioration and losses of stock, and ensuring that stock rotation and specific storage needs (eg careful handling, refrigeration or safe storage) are being met
- Producing evidence of stock movements for invoice verification and audit trails
- Producing management reports using any or all of the above data

Warehouse management systems (WMS)

2.8   More fully integrated warehousing and distribution management systems might have additional functions, including the following.

- Modelling proposed changes to warehouse location, design and layout, to support decision-making to maximise efficiency (eg accessibility of fast-moving stocks, full utilisation of the cubic capacity of space, maintenance of health and safety etc)
- Modelling or mapping operational processes, to support the prioritising of materials flows, the discarding of flows and activities that do not add value (wastes) and the streamlining or automating of flows where possible.
- Controlling automated goods vehicles (AGVs) for storing, retrieving and moving items within the facility
- Vehicle tracking, to support delivery expediting and health and safety compliance (eg in regard to driver hours)
- Transport planning (eg optimising vehicle loads, route planning and scheduling)
- Direct input of consignment information and documentation to HM Customs & Excise systems, for imports and exports. Accredited exporters and importers using simplified clearance procedure (SCP) or period entry can upload Customs entries on a regular basis in a predetermined format.

2.9　　In the warehousing and distribution environment – as in e-procurement – systems need to integrate in such a way as to produce real-time information in both a planned and 'by exception' way. Regular reports, particularly on stock levels and value, and supplier delivery performance, are of particular interest. The facility to call on reports or information by exception also permits an increased responsiveness, particularly in internal customer service.

3　　Enterprise resource planning (ERP)

Management information systems (MIS)

3.1　　Management information is data collected (often from the transaction processing systems of the organisation), processed and formatted in such a way as to be useful to managers to aid them in planning, control and decision-making. Management information tools include the following.

- **Databases and database management systems**: capturing and storing data (eg on customers, products and inventory, suppliers or transactions in progress) in a structured way, so that they can be shared by different users, and interrogated flexibly for a variety of applications.
- **Decision support systems**: eg spreadsheets and computer models, used to examine the effect of different inputs and scenarios on the outcomes of a plan or decision. Examples in procurement include trend and spend analysis tools, and tender evaluation tools.
- **Management information systems**: integrated systems for recording, storing and analysing a wide range of sales, purchase, point-of-sale, inventory, maintenance, HR, financial and business intelligence data, to support management decision-making.

3.2　　A key problem in many organisations is that management information is fragmented within the business: separate functional IT systems may have evolved over many years, resulting in 'islands of information', so that information is available to one function but not visible or accessible to other internal (or external) stakeholders. Below we look at modern systems that attempt to overcome this problem.

Materials requirements planning (MRP)

3.3　　Materials requirements planning (MRP) is a set of logically related procedures, decision rules and records for managing dependent demand items. It is designed to develop a master production schedule (MPS), from which can be derived a bill of materials (a breakdown of all the materials and components required for production) into time-phased 'net-requirements' (taking into account existing stock levels) which trigger requisitions and procurements of appropriate quantities at appropriate times.

- The MPS is derived from the company's sales forecast, actual sales data, current customer orders and relevant production policies and schedules.
- The MRP software 'explodes' the MPS into a bill of materials (BOM): calculating how many of each component is required in order to manufacture the finished products specified in the MPS, based on materials specifications.
- The inventory status file supplies data on which of the required items are already in stock, and in what quantities, in order to arrive at a 'net requirement' for each material and component (to be procured from suppliers).
- The system takes into account estimates of supplier lead times for the items required (based on historical data or contract terms where available), to arrive at a time-phased procurement schedule for items.

3.4　　The process is depicted in Figure 9.1.

Figure 9.1 *The MRP process*

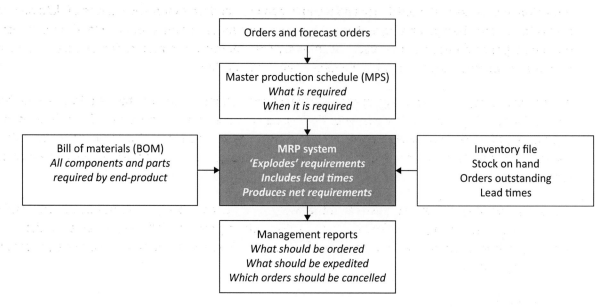

The figure shows the MRP process flow with boxes:
- Orders and forecast orders (top)
- Master production schedule (MPS): What is required / When it is required
- MRP system: 'Explodes' requirements / Includes lead times / Produces net requirements
- Bill of materials (BOM): All components and parts required by end-product (left)
- Inventory file: Stock on hand / Orders outstanding / Lead times (right)
- Management reports: What should be ordered / What should be expedited / Which orders should be cancelled

3.5 It should be obvious that this requires the integration of several information systems (demand forecasting, production planning, inventory and procurement) – and that it is therefore ripe for automation. MRP systems are integrated computer systems, offering planning tools used in production or manufacturing to determine: what input materials are required, in what quantities, and when. MRP systems are one of the parts of an enterprise resource planning (ERP) system, discussed further below.

3.6 There are certain pre-requisites for using MRP effectively. There must be comprehensive, accurate materials specifications for the product; all of the quantity relationships to end products must be known (eg how many wheels to a truck; how many wheel nuts to a wheel); inventory items must be identified and in the system; the inventory status of all items must be up-to-date; lead times for all items must be known, realistic and updated on an ongoing basis; and there must be reliable, flexible suppliers who are committed to supplying against MRP schedules and who will make the system work.

Automatic planning and scheduling (APS)

3.7 APS is often a module within MRP (and ERP) systems. Its purpose is to gather and analyse data on sales, procurements, production and inventory, to ensure that the right quantities of materials required for production are procured and issued at the right time.

Enterprise resource planning (ERP)

3.8 Enterprise resource planning (ERP) is a development of MRP in the direction of further integration. ERP systems (such as SAP) consolidate materials, manufacturing, logistics, supply chain, sales and marketing, finance and HR planning information into a single integrated management system: a single database able to offer 'real time' information for solving a range of business problems.

3.9 CIPS defines ERP as: 'Computer-based systems designed to process an organisation's transactions and facilitate integrated and real-time planning, production and customer response.'

3.10 ERP systems are cross-functional and enterprise-wide: all functions involved in operations are integrated in one system – including manufacturing, warehousing and distribution, accounting, HR, marketing, strategic management and procurement. ERP systems align closely with the concept of supply chain management, and ERP II software extends the system to include links with suppliers and other supply chain stakeholders.

3.11 The benefits claimed for ERP include: integration and automation of many business processes; a general reduction in process costs; efficiency and flexibility gains; standardisation and sharing of data and practices across the enterprise; generating and accessing decision support information on a 'real-time' basis; quicker response times and improved customer service; improved communication and data-sharing; and potentially improved supply chain management and relationships.

3.12 An ERP system represents a very large IT investment and commitment: one that requires careful thought and evaluation. Implementation is frequently phased in over a period of anywhere from three months to two years. Software packages offered by the leading suppliers – such as SAP and Oracle – offer this facility, allowing for the adaptation of existing, 'legacy' systems (designed to meet the particular needs of different functions).

3.13 Many large companies have successfully integrated ERP systems. Others have not been so successful: Hershey Foods, for example, suffered disruptive distribution problems following a flawed initial implementation. Further development may be required before ERP technology is genuinely accessible to smaller organisations.

4 Communication systems

Electronic data interchange (EDI)

4.1 Information sharing is obviously crucial to the co-ordination of both internal and external supply chains. We will look at some of the technologies supporting supply chain communication and data sharing.

4.2 One of the most important developments in IT from a procurement viewpoint was the introduction and widespread adoption of electronic data interchange (EDI). EDI is defined as 'the exchange of structured data between computer applications without manual intervention': in other words, the automated integration of buyer- and supplier-side procurement and supply processes. The word 'structured' in the definition is important: the data transferred between buyer and seller must be in a mutually agreed standard format, according to specially designed protocols – often requiring the services of a specialist thirdparty provider.

4.3 Large purchasing organisations such as Marks & Spencer in the UK were early adopters of the EDI system, and often put pressure on suppliers to adopt EDI technology, often supporting them with investment and training assistance.

4.4 The development of the internet has enabled businesses to develop the potential of EDI more widely, cheaply and flexibly. Instead of dedicated networked computer systems with bespoke data-sharing protocols (necessitating significant investment), buyer- and supplier-side information systems can now be linked via standard telecommunication networks and protocols, using the world wide web. Such linkages are referred to as 'extranets' – which will be discussed further below.

Intranets

4.5 The internet and the world wide web are an accepted framework for implementing and delivering information system applications. The internet is a global collection of telecommunications-linked computer networks, which has revolutionised global communication and commerce through tools such as email, and interactive, transaction-enabled websites. However, the same network protocols can be used more locally as a tool for internal and external supply chain communication.

4.6 An **intranet** is a set of networked and/or internet-linked computers. This private network is usually only accessible to registered users, within the same organisation or work group. Access is restricted by passwords and user group accounts, for example.

4.7   Intranets are used in internal supply chain and employee communication: only authorised internal users are able to access relevant web pages and dedicated email facilities (as well as having access to the wider internet).

4.8   Intranets offer significant advantages for integrating internal supply chain communications. They support multi-directional communication and data-sharing; link remote sites and workers in 'virtual' teams; allow authorised access to shared database and e-procurement platforms; give employees wider access to corporate information; encourage more frequent use of reference sources (such as procurement manuals, standing orders and policies) and updating of information; and save on the costs of producing and distributing the equivalent printed documents and messages.

Extranets

4.9   An extranet is an intranet that has been extended to give selected external partners (such as suppliers) authorised access to particular areas or levels of the organisation's website or information network, for exchanging data and applications, and sharing information. Examples you might be familiar with include the registered-user-only pages of corporate websites, and the member-only pages of professional bodies' websites (like the CIPS website's student and member areas).

4.10 Supplier access to a buyer's extranet system is generally protected, requiring defined verification of identity (eg via a user ID), supplier codes and passwords.

4.11 Extranets are particularly useful tools for relationship management, inter-organisational partnerships and direct e-procurement transactions (which might have previously been carried out by EDI protocols). An extranet may be used to publish news updates and technical briefings which may be of use to supply chain partners; publish requirements and/or conduct e-tenders or e-auctions (via a market exchange portal); exchange transaction data for electronic P2P processes (orders, payments, delivery tracking and so on); share training and development resources (eg as part of collaborative quality or sustainability management); and so on.

4.12 Procurement-focused extranets usually provide suppliers with:

- Real-time access to inventory and demand information, enabling them to proactively manage the buyer's needs, rather than merely reacting to spot orders
- Authorised report information eg their vendor rating analysis – enabling them to be proactive in managing and improving their performance and competitiveness.

4.13 Extranet systems provide potential for removing process costs and increasing supply chain communication, real-time information-sharing, co-ordination and responsiveness (eg for improved demand management and just in time supply). They support the automation of routine procurement tasks (as seen in Chapter 6), and therefore support the increasing focus of procurement professionals on strategic value-adding roles rather than transactional and communication tasks. Suppliers can similarly become more focused on developing innovative, competitive and continuously improving supply solutions.

4.14 Business Link listed the following potential benefits that can be gained from using extranet systems.

- Assists in achieving improved supply chain integration via the use of online ordering, order tracking and inventory management
- Reduces operational costs, for example by making manuals and technical documentation available online. This reduces cost and increases the speed of inter-business communication.
- Improved collaboration and relationship potential by enabling involved parties to work online using common documentation; again this accelerates the business process as well as saving cost by reducing the need to hold expensive meetings.
- Suppliers can directly access authorised business information which often enables them to resolve their own queries.

- Provides a single user interface between business partners.
- Improved security of communications since exchanges take place under a controlled and secure environment.

4.15 However, integrating supply chain processes via extranets still creates challenges and risks. In recent years, the corporate landscape has become littered with extranet initiatives that failed to deliver tangible value. Research indicates that common reasons for failure can be identified as: inadequate planning and preparation; unrealistic expectations; and lack of a clear business case for how the extranet will support organisational objectives. It is easy for extranets to become nothing more than glorified chat groups. It is therefore important that the extranets provide tangible benefits. For best value, such benefits should be aligned to support and achieve overall business and supply chain objectives.

4.16 Extranet security is another critical design consideration. Hackers increasingly probe connected computers for weaknesses in their security, and data corruption, loss or theft – eg through the use of 'malware' (as discussed in Chapter 6) – is a key issue for risk management.

Virtual team-working and supply chain relationships

4.17 'Virtual' teams and organisations are interconnected groups of people who may not be present in the same office, site or organisation (and may even be in different areas of the world), but who:

- Share information and tasks (eg technical support provided by a supplier)
- Make joint decisions (eg on quality assurance, demand forecasts or production and delivery schedules)
- Fulfil collaborative functions: ie working together.

4.18 Information and communications technology has facilitated this kind of collaboration, simulating the dynamics of teamworking via tools such as teleconferencing, video-conferencing, web-conferencing, and internet linkages.

4.19 Partners in the supply chain, for example, can use such technology to access and share up-to-date product, customer, stock and delivery information (eg using web-based databases and data tracking systems).

4.20 Electronic meeting management systems allow virtual meeting participants to see and talk to each other using web-conferencing facilities, while sharing data and using electronic 'whiteboards': all on their PC, laptop, tablet or internet-enabled mobile phone. This supports enhanced supplier relationships and the management of outsourcing, particularly international outsourcing (or 'offshoring'): you don't need to be within reach of people to monitor their performance, stay in touch – or even have meetings.

Mobile telecommunications

4.21 Mobile telecommunications have exploded onto the social and business scene in recent years, particularly as digital networks have supported more reliable connection and data transmission. Mobile phones allow off-site employees (particularly field sales and transport and delivery personnel) to send and receive telephone messages, text messages (SMS) and email – as well as internet-based data sharing and access to intranets and extranets.

4.22 Using the latest web-enabled mobile telecommunications provides numerous benefits.

- A wide range of business activities can be undertaken outside the office or on the move. (This may be particularly helpful for suppliers' field sales staff or account managers visiting buyers. It is also used for tracking deliveries in transit, and notifying delivery delays from the road.)
- Buyers and suppliers have continuous access to key contacts, for improved customer service, without having to leave messages and experience call-back delays.
- Mobile e-commerce, via the internet, enables users to download data and access websites both to

facilitate conventional procurement (eg locating stockists or interrogating supplier databases prior to meetings) and for e-procurement.

4.23 You should be able to draw on your own personal experience of other 'newish' (and constantly developing) communications tools and systems, including email and the use of 'apps' (applications) on tablets and smartphones.

The internet and e-commerce

4.24 The internet is a worldwide computer network allowing computers to communicate via telecommunications links. The network can also be accessed from tablets and smartphones. The internet has exploded in the last decade as a business tool, for:

- Marketing: supporting advertising, direct marketing, social media, customer communication, public relations and market research (eg using online surveys and browsing or transaction histories).
- Direct distribution: of products (through online product ordering, or the downloading of electronic products such as music, video or educational content) and services (eg information, ticketing, consultancy and e-learning).
- Customer service and technical support: through email enquiries, FAQs (frequently asked questions), access to database information etc.
- Partnership development: through better information-sharing and communication with suppliers and business networks.

4.25 The term 'e-commerce' (short for electronic commerce) refers to business transactions carried out online via ICT – usually the internet. E-commerce has facilitated direct marketing, linking customers direct with suppliers. It is a means of automating business transactions and workflows, and usually a means of streamlining and improving them. (However, it must be remembered that at some point, goods may have to be physically transported from the producer to the purchaser – and at this point, the speed of transaction-processing may not be matched by the speed of delivery.)

4.26 For the procurement function, the internet has provided particular benefits.

- Wider choice of suppliers, including global and small suppliers. (Purchasing professionals still have to make strategic and tactical choices: ICT merely provides better-quality information for doing this.)
- Savings in procurement costs, through electronic communication, greater accuracy and electronic transaction processing. In a research project in 1997, management consultants McKinsey noted that the biggest effect of the internet for business overall is the huge saving in transaction and interaction costs – the costs of 'the searching, coordinating and monitoring that people and companies do when they exchange goods, services or ideas'.
- Support for low inventory and efficient stock turnover (eg just in time supply).
- Improved supply chain relationships and coordination, arising from better data-sharing.

Chapter summary

- Developments in ICT have had a radical effect on procurement activities and the development of supply chain relationshsips.
- Inventory management systems are increasingly automated and frequently rely on barcoding and/or RFID tagging.
- Organisations increasingly attempt to integrate their management information systems. The use of ERP systems is an advanced stage in this process.
- Communication along the supply chain has been greatly enhanced by the use of EDI, intranets and extranets, the internet, and mobile telecommunications.

Self-test questions

Numbers in brackets refer to the paragraphs where you can check your answers.

1   List some of the impacts that technological developments have had on business and purchasing activity. (1.2–1.6)

2   In what ways can ICT be used to develop supply chain relationships? (1.8)

3   What activities are typically included in the process of inventory management? (2.1)

4   What are the advantages of RFID technology compared with barcoding? (2.6)

5   List typical features of a warehouse management system. (2.8)

6   Explain the workings of an MRP system. (3.3)

7   Define 'enterprise resource planning'. (3.9)

8   Explain how EDI works. (4.2)

9   What is an extranet and how is it used? (4.9)

10   What benefits does a procurement specialist derive from use of the internet? (4.26)

9

CHAPTER 10

The Sector and Industry Context

Assessment criteria and indicative content

4.1 Identify different economic and industrial sectors.

- Economic classifications including public and private sectors, charities, not for profit and third sector
- Industrial classifications and sectors such as manufacturing, retail, construction, financial, agriculture and service

4.2 Analyse the impact of the public sector on procurement or supply chain roles

- Objectives of public sector organisations such as improving services, communities and corporate social responsibility
- Regulations that impact on procurement and supply chain operations
- Need for competition, public accountability and value for money

Section headings

1 Classifying economic sectors
2 The impact of economic sector on procurement
3 Classifying industry sectors
4 Primary industries
5 Secondary industries
6 The services sector
7 The retail sector

Introduction

In this chapter we begin to look at the wider context in which procurement and supply chain management occurs: the economic and industry sectors within which organisations operate.

Sectors are simply ways of grouping or classifying organisations.

- **Economic sectors** are grouped by ownership (public or private) and primary objective (profit-making or not-for-profit)
- **Industry sectors** may be grouped by industry type (resource extraction, production or service provision), area of activity (eg retail, manufacturing, construction, finance) or size (eg the small business sector).

In this chapter we explore the nature of the public, private and third sectors, and a range of different industry sectors, and the different procurement and supply chain objectives and challenges of each.

In Chapters 11 and 12 we will go on focus in more detail on the particular requirements imposed by each of the public, private and third sectors.

1 Classifying economic sectors

Different ways of classifying organisations

1.1 There are various ways of classifying organisations involved in procuring goods and services.

- By *structure and ownership,* including issues of incorporation (the legal structure of the organisation), ownership, control and funding. On this basis, the economy is often divided into the private sector (eg business companies), the public sector (eg government, health authorities, police and defence forces), and the third sector: sometimes subdivided into the voluntary sector (eg churches and charities) and subscription-paid sector (eg clubs, societies and associations).
- By *primary objective.* Profit-oriented organisations (common in the private sector) aim to generate profits for their owners, or return on investment. Not-for-profit organisations (common in the public and third sectors) aim to provide public, social or charitable services, protect stakeholder interests or fulfil the purposes of their members – without aiming to make a profit from doing so. Any 'surplus' of funds is reinvested in the organisation's activity.
- By *activity:* extraction of raw materials, generation of energy, manufacturing, retail, health care, information technology, media and so on. Organisations performing different activities are likely to have different objectives, technologies and practices, in order to meet the particular challenges of their task and environment.
- By *size:* special categories are often given, for example, to small and medium enterprises (SMEs) at one end of the scale and multinational corporations (MNCs) at the other.

1.2 We will look briefly at some of these distinctions and their impact on procurement and supply chain operations in this chapter.

The private and public sectors

1.3 As most readers will be aware, a private sector organisation is one that is owned by private individuals, either few in number (such as a small family business) or very numerous (as with a large company owned by millions of private shareholders). Public sector organisations on the other hand are 'owned' by the public in general: the UK National Health Service, for example, is headed by a Government minister whose responsibility is to run the service efficiently and effectively on behalf of the State.

1.4 We will look at both sectors in detail in the following chapters, but some key differences between them can be summarised as follows.

1.5 In the *private sector*:

- Organisations are owned by their investors (owner/proprietors or shareholders), and controlled by directors or managers on their behalf
- Activity is funded by a combination of investment, revenue (from the sale of goods or services) and debt
- The primary purpose is the achievement of commercial objectives: generally, maximising profits for their owners, or for reinvestment in the business. Managerial decisions are assessed on the extent to which they contribute to organisational profit or shareholder wealth.
- Competition is a key factor. Several, or many, firms may offer goods or services of a particular type, with consumers free to choose between their offerings: consumer choice ensures that quality and efficiency are maintained at an acceptable level.
- The core 'constituency' served by firms is shareholders, customers and employees, all of whom are involved with the firm by choice. Firms can and must, therefore, focus their activity on meeting the needs of these few key stakeholders.

1.6   In the *public sector:*

- Organisations are owned by the government on behalf of the State, which represents the public.
- Activity is financed by the state, mainly via taxation – as well as any revenue the organisation's activities may generate.
- The primary purpose is achieving defined service levels: providing efficient and effective services to the public, often within defined budgetary constraints and sustainability strategies.
- There has traditionally been little or no competition, although in the UK, since the 1980s, successive governments have sought to introduce some market disciplines (eg competitive tendering). In the absence of consumer choice, quality and efficiency are imposed by mechanisms such as regulation, watchdogs, customer charters, performance targets and competition for funding allocations.
- The 'constituency' of concerned stakeholders is wider and more diverse, including government, taxpayers, funding bodies, those who consume services – and society as a whole. There is a far greater need for accountability and stakeholder consultation in managing the organisation.

Why have a private and public sector?

1.7   Looking at the big picture, economic activity can't produce *everything* that might conceivably be wanted or needed by consumers, because the resources to do so (the 'factors of production': land, natural resources, labour, capital and knowledge) are limited. Some mechanism is required to decide how these resources should be used, and what goods and services should be produced.

1.8   A **market economy** operates on the basis of supply and demand: people will purchase goods and services to satisfy their wants and needs, at a price they are able and willing to pay. Commercial organisations have to offer goods and services which are in demand, at prices which maintain that demand, in order to compete with others in the market. In other words, consumer choice decides which goods and services are produced, and at what price they can be sold. This has been the basis of the private sector, ever since commerce began with barter and trade in ancient rural economies.

1.9   However, some goods and services are perceived as essential for the wellbeing of individuals and society – such as health, education, utilities and security services – even if commercial organisations don't want to produce them, because consumers are unwilling or unable to pay the market price. In such circumstances (ie when the market mechanism of supply and demand 'fails') government must step in to control production, funded via taxation and public borrowing, so that basic goods and services are available to everyone on a free or subsidised basis. This is the basis of the public sector. In its extreme form (a *centrally planned economy),* the government would control all factors of production: all business would be publically owned or 'nationalised'.

1.10   A **mixed economy** is one in which there is neither complete capitalist control nor complete government control of resources. Instead, the state controls essential public services and basic industries which cannot raise adequate capital investment from private sources, while at the same time supporting private enterprise and the open market in other fields.

1.11   The functions of the public sector in a mixed economy are therefore as follows.

- To provide essential goods and services which might not be provided by the private sector, owing to 'market failure'
- To redistribute wealth, via taxation, in order to provide financial support for non-wage earners such as the sick, pensioners and the unemployed
- To regulate private sector activity in the public interest, eg in the case of bodies such as, in the UK, the Competition and Markets Authority or the Health and Safety Executive
- To 'bail out' private enterprises, where necessary in the public interest. There were several high profile examples in the recent global financial crisis: eg UK regulators were forced to vouch for the viability of Britain's biggest home loan provider, HBOS, among fears it was facing collapse – on the same day that

the US central bank had to agree to pump $US85 billion into American International Group (AIG) to prevent the failure of the world's biggest insurance company.

1.12 The balance of a mixed economy – and therefore the relative size of the public or private sector – will depend partly on political factors. Communist or socialist governments (as in Cuba, China, Sweden or Norway) are more likely to support a large public sector, with government expenditure representing a higher proportion of the GDP. Capitalist societies with conservative governments are more likely to reduce the public sector (eg by privatisation of public services and industries). In highly committed 'free enterprise' economies, such as Japan and the USA, few services are provided by the state.

The third sector

1.13 As we noted earlier, the primary objective of most public sector organisations is the delivery of services, rather than the generation of profits. A number of organisations in the private sector are also operated on a not-for-profit (NFP) basis, including: charities, churches, private schools and hospitals, political parties, museums, clubs and associations, interest/pressure groups, trade unions and professional bodies such as CIPS. These are often identified separately as the 'third' sector of the economy.

1.14 Organisations in this sector have typically been set up to achieve a defined objective (eg for a charitable purpose or to represent the interests of a group of people) rather than to maximise profit. They usually derive their income from donations, legacies (money left to the organisation in someone's will), sponsorships and government grants and subsidies, although they may also have a trading arm to generate revenue (as in the case of 'charity shops', say). They may be owned by their members (as in a club or association) or by a trust (as in a charity), and managed by a board of trustees or directors.

1.15 We will look at the third sector separately in Chapter 12.

2   The impact of economic sector on procurement

2.1 Although the private sector is the focus of most procurement and supply chain literature – and arguably represents best practice in some areas of procurement and supply – the public sector is an important context for procurement operations. The spending power of public sector enterprises is enormous, and despite widespread programmes of privatisation in most developed economies, the sheer range of public sector service provision is vast: including roads, law and order, education, health and leisure services, emergency services, defence and much more.

2.2 Public and private sector organisations and environments are different in some key respects, as we noted above. The key implications for procurement have been summarised by Gary J Zenz (*Purchasing and the Management of Materials*), whose analysis forms the basis of Table 10.1, with our own points added.

2.3 The differences between public and private sector purchasing should not be overemphasised, however. Differences in objectives, organisational constraints and so on may not necessarily lead to differences in operational *procedure*.

- Public sector buyers may not be seeking to maximise profit, for example, but they will still be concerned to achieve value for money.
- Public sector buyers may not seek competitive advantage, but they will still aim to ensure the quality of inputs in order to support the quality of outputs (to fulfil the terms of a customer charter, say).
- Meanwhile, private sector buyers may not have non-economic goals as their primary objective, but they are increasingly being challenged to consider the interests of wider stakeholders in society (through pressure for corporate social responsibility).

Table 10.1 *Differences between public and private sector procurement*

AREA OF DIFFERENCE	PRIVATE SECTOR PROCUREMENT	PUBLIC SECTOR PROCUREMENT
Objectives	Usually, to increase profit	Usually, to achieve defined service levels
Responsibility	Buyers are responsible to directors, who in turn are responsible to shareholders	Buyers are responsible ultimately to the general public
Stakeholders	Purchasing has a defined group of stakeholders to take into account.	Purchasing has to provide value to a wider range of primary and secondary stakeholders.
Activity/process	Organisational capabilities and resources used to produce goods/services	Add value through supply of outsourced or purchased products/services. (Tend not to purchase for manufacture.)
Legal restrictions	Activities are regulated by company law, employment law, product liability law etc	Most of this applies equally to public sector, but additional regulations are present too (eg EU procurement directives)
Competition	There is usually strong competition between many different firms	There is usually no competition
Value for money	Maintain lowest cost for competitive strategy, customer value and profit maximisation.	Maintain or improve service levels within value/cost parameters.
Diversity of items	Specialised stock list for defined product/ service portfolio.	Wide diversity of items/resources required to provide diverse services (eg local government authority).
Publicity	Confidentiality applies in dealings between suppliers and buyers	Confidentiality is limited because of public interest in disclosure
Budgetary limits	Investment is constrained only by availability of attractive opportunities; funding can be found if prospects are good	Investment is constrained by externally imposed spending limits
Information exchange	Private sector buyers do not exchange information with other firms, because of confidentiality and competition	Public sector buyers are willing to exchange notes and use shared e-purchasing platforms, consolidate purchases etc.
Procurement policies/ procedures	Tend to be organisation-specific. Private sector buyers can cut red tape when speed of action is necessary	Tend to follow legislative directives. Public sector buyers are often constrained to follow established procedures
Supplier relationships	Emphasis on long-term partnership development where possible, to support value chain.	Compulsory competitive tendering: priority to cost minimisation and efficiency, at the expense of partnership development.

2.4 An article in *Procurement Professional* journal (CIPS Australia) noted that: 'Key issues for the procurement profession... are as relevant for the public sector as they are for the private sector... Work is currently underway in public sectors around the world to address these issues, centred on:

- Developing standards for the assessment and ongoing development of public procurement professionals
- The greater application of strategic sourcing principles to public procurement
- The introduction of e-procurement systems.'

2.5 It should be noted that there is increasing best practice sharing between sectors, with best practice models and recommendations published by public sector bodies in the UK such as the Organisation for Government Commerce (OGC) and Sustainable Procurement Task Force, and with commitment from the public sector to learn from private sector best practice (in areas such as closer supplier relationships, supply chain innovation and procurement professionalism).

2.6 Key priorities, such as corporate social responsibility, sustainability, customer service improvement and the reduction of cost inefficiencies, operate across sectoral boundaries.

10

3 Classifying industry sectors

3.1 It is common to distinguish between three major industry sectors, according to the type of process they perform.

- *Primary industries* are concerned with extracting natural resources or producing raw materials. This sector includes oil and mineral extraction (mining), agriculture and forestry.
- *Secondary industries* are engaged in transforming raw materials into end components, assemblies or finished products. This sector includes the manufacturing, engineering and construction industries, for example.
- *Tertiary industries* are those engaged in the development and provision of services. This sector includes professional services, financial services, transport, hospitality and so on.

3.2 This classification is neither clear cut nor exhaustive. Agriculture these days has some of the features of secondary industry, for example, and is often classified as such. The retail, energy and IT sectors do not fit clearly into any one category and are sometimes regarded as sectors in their own right. Nor is it helpful to separate the three types of activity when thinking about supply chains. The procurement function in a manufacturing organisation, say, might have to buy across a number of categories: raw materials, manufactured goods (such as components, or computers, tools, machinery and office furniture) and services (such as IT consultancy, insurance and transport).

3.3 It should not be surprising, however, to find that procurement priorities and practices do differ from one sector to another. Clearly, the organisational characteristics and operational challenges of an oil drilling company are likely to be very different from those of a management consultancy – and these differences are likely to be apparent at least to some extent within procurement and supply chain operations.

3.4 We will now look at some of the major industry sectors in more detail.

4 Primary industries

4.1 Primary industries are concerned with extracting natural resources from the earth. The primary sector includes oil extraction, mining and perhaps also agriculture (although these days, agriculture incorporates some of the features of manufacturing).

Extractive industries

4.2 The main procurement requirement for such businesses will be for extraction machinery, equipment, tools and spares – plus consumables (such as fuel and lubricants) for all of these, plus services such as transport of the extracted materials to a processing plant.

4.3 In an extractive industry such as mining, capital expenditure will be very high, because of the need to buy or lease large, specialised heavy-duty machinery: this usually gives the procurement function a relatively high-level role. There is less likely to be a continuous demand for supplies than in a manufacturing company, so procurement's focus may be less on swift response times, and more on ongoing support and service from suppliers. There may be particular transport and storage problems involved in supplying remote and difficult locations.

4.4 So what are the main objectives and challenges of procurement and supply chain management in this kind of industry?

- Procurement expenditure will typically be high, because of the need for large, specialised, heavy-duty machinery. One of the key objectives of the procurement function will be to secure the right machinery at the right price: this may involve complex investment and supplier appraisal, prior to the award of a major contract.

- Stocks of consumables and spares will be drawn on constantly – and will be critical to keep the process going. So another objective of procurement will be to maintain adequate 'emergency' or 'standby' stock levels of such items, in case of unforeseen needs or delayed deliveries – without having so much stock 'lying around' that it is a waste of money, or subject to deterioration, damage or theft.
- The specialist nature of most supplies means that procurement will need to liaise carefully with suppliers, engineers and users, in order to ensure that specifications are correct, and that they include provision for support and service from suppliers (eg ongoing maintenance and repair) where required. Pre-contract contingency planning and post-contract management will be particularly crucial, given the problems faced by suppliers in providing support services, responding swiftly to customer requirements, or replacing defective deliveries, in remote locations.
- The organisation has no choice about where it locates its operating facilities. (In the UK, for instance, no doubt it would be easier to build an oil rig in Lincolnshire than in the middle of the North Sea – but since the oil is in fact situated in the latter location, the easier option is not available.)

Remote and difficult locations make the provision of the right supplies in the right place at the right time much more difficult than it is for most other business types. Procurement staff will have to give careful consideration to issues such as: how to arrange transport of supplies to remote locations; how to optimise order quantities (bearing in mind the additional logistical problems involved); how to store materials safely once they are in place; and how to minimise the additional costs that all this gives rise to.

The agricultural sector

4.5   The agricultural sector is involved in the cultivation, harvesting and processing of plant crops and animal livestock, for use or consumption in other sectors such as the food and beverage sector, the textiles and clothing sector (using plant and animal fibres) and so on. Related 'agri-businesses' include manufacturers of agricultural machinery and chemicals and businesses working in the science and technology of 'agronomy' (producing and using plants, encompassing issues such as food production, genetic modification, sustainable agricultural methods, or developing renewable bio-fuels, biopharmaceuticals and other plant-based products).

4.6   The major products of the agricultural sector are foods (such as meat, dairy, cereals, vegetables and fruits), fibres (such as cotton, wool and silk), fuels (such as ethanol and biodiesel) and raw materials (such as wood/lumber, bamboo and resins). A typical agricultural supply chain might extend from input suppliers to producers of the raw commodities; intermediaries (eg agents, brokers or distributors); to processors (driers, canners, freezers and so on) – and thence into the retail or export supply chain, for supply to national and global markets.

4.7   Agricultural businesses vary widely from small, non-industrialised farms, mainly using pastoral herding or growing organic crops, to huge industrial agri-businesses (such as Monsanto). In general terms, however, the main procurement requirements for agricultural businesses will be:

- Agricultural machinery (tractors, harvesters, irrigation equipment and so on)
- Agricultural chemicals (such as pesticides and fertilisers)
- Start-up breeding stocks (seed, plant seedlings or breeding animals), for producers
- Feed (for livestock)
- Consumables (lubricants, fuel and electricity for equipment and machinery)
- Packaging or containers
- Support services (logistical, financial and technical).

4.8   The agricultural sector presents several key issues for procurement and supply chain management.

- The importance of maintaining volume and continuity of supply for local and national food security. This is so crucial that many governments subsidise agriculture (eg the production of key commodities such as wheat, corn, rice, soybeans and milk) to ensure an adequate food supply.

- A high degree of risk and uncertainty through the supply chain, resulting from eg: unpredictable weather and climate factors; the impact of pests and diseases; the unpredictable nature of biological processes; extreme seasonality of production; the frequent geographical distance between the points of production and end use or consumption (creating transport-related and supply chain management risk); and potential political and public intervention (eg in response to food scares, consumer trends and so on). In addition to the need for risk management, such uncertainties make the forecasting of production, and market supply and demand, difficult – which also affects the demand for inputs.

- Complex supply chains, involving physical flows, financial flows (credit terms and lending, insurance arrangements and so on), and information flows (communication). These may span other supply chains, geographic and political boundaries, and may involve a wide range of public and private sector institutions. Poor logistics and communications are a major source of risk in such supply chains!

- Logistical (transport and storage) challenges, arising from (a) the potential distance between the point of production and the point of use (in global markets); (b) the perishability of inputs and outputs, and associated health and safety risks and (c) the dangerous nature of some agricultural chemicals.

- Potentially high capital investment in machinery and start-up stock – and potential cashflow problems, given generally long time-to-market cycles and low profit margins

- Relatively low market power for producers in the supply chain (eg compared to major seed suppliers, and major customers such as supermarkets and grocery chains)

- Regulation to protect food hygiene, health and safety. Law, regulation and scrutiny may affect inputs (eg seed types), processes (slaughter and transport of livestock, production methods such as the pasteurisation of milk, ethical labour policies in relation to agricultural workers), product labelling and so on.

- Environmental sustainability issues. Recent decades have seen a growing awareness of the negative impacts of mainstream agri-business eg soil exhaustion; loss of biodiversity through monoculture; water depletion and contamination; the destruction of natural eco-systems and habitats (threatening biodiversity) to increase available agricultural land; the perceived risks of genetic modification; and cruelty to livestock (in living conditions and slaughter methods). There are pressures and incentives (eg from the European Union) to support organic and sustainable agriculture (changing input requirements for chemical fertilisers and pesticides, for example) and animal husbandry (changing input requirements for buildings and services).

5   Secondary industries

5.1   Secondary industries are engaged in manufacturing: that is, 'making' finished products out of raw materials and components. This sector used to be overwhelmingly the largest economic sector in the UK, for instance, and remains hugely important to the prosperity of the country, despite the fact that service industries now account for a larger slice of the economic cake. The purchasing literature reflects the fact that very many buyers are still employed in manufacturing companies.

Manufacturing and assembly

5.2   The main procurement requirement for manufacturing organisations is the inputs to the manufacturing process. These may be:

- Raw materials, which are processed in some way (eg by cooking, fermentation, refining or spinning) in order to create finished products for consumers or products for sale to other manufacturers (eg turning raw cotton into spun cotton, which is sold to the textile industry). *Processing industries* include plastics, steel, oil, gas, electricity, water, textiles, brewing, baking and food processing.

- Components (individual parts), which are *assembled* to create finished products for consumers (eg toys, shoes and television sets) or subassemblies or modules for incorporation into further assembly processes

- Subassemblies or modules, put together by another manufacturer and bought in for 'final assembly' and finishing (eg painting, varnishing and packaging) into finished products (eg gearboxes and bodies for cars, or hard drives for computers).

5.3   In addition, a manufacturing organisation may purchase: capital plant and machinery; support services (such as marketing, transport, IT, security or maintenance); and ongoing general supplies which keep the organisation operating. These non-production items are often called MRO (maintenance, repair and operational) supplies, and include things such as uniforms, safety equipment, lubricants, office supplies, cleaning supplies and so on.

5.4   So what are the main objectives and challenges of procurement in a manufacturing organisation?

- Procurement is a relatively advanced function in many manufacturing companies. Highly developed 'world class' techniques such as just in time (JIT), total quality management (TQM) and materials requirements planning (MRP) will often be used. Many inventory management and procurement processes are now likely to be computerised. While these are strategic issues – beyond the scope of this syllabus – it is important to remember the more complex framework within which procurement operations are carried out.

- Operations management is the focal point of the supply chain – and the key internal customer of procurement. The most important task is to ensure that production processes have materials of the right quality available in the right place at the right time in the right quantity to keep production going.

- Production machinery is 'hungry': it needs inputs to operate – and if it ceases operating, the organisation incurs costs of lost production, 'down time', restarting of the machinery and so on. Demand management is therefore key to maintaining service levels to internal customers: ensuring that stocks are reliably available and continually resupplied when needed to maintain the process.

- The sheer number and diversity of components which may go into a manufactured product places a burden on procurement to maintain records and follow procedures in order to achieve the 'five rights' effectively.

- Quality is a very important objective for manufacturing, because defective inputs can damage machinery, and cause waste. Procurement must know exactly what is required, convey this clearly to suppliers, and manage quality risks and issues throughout the supply chain.

- Because of the importance of inputs to the finished product, procurement expertise and contacts may be required throughout the process from new product design (which materials will be best to use, and most readily available?), through specification (how can the requirement most accurately be defined for suppliers?), inventory control (when will stock need to be replenished?) and so on.

- The cost of inputs is a very high proportion of manufacturing costs, so procurement will have the key objective of minimising costs – consistent with maintaining supply. The value of materials which are bought on a regular basis is a high proportion of total purchasing spend, so sourcing strategies typically focus on a slim supplier base, with close relations between buyers and suppliers (particularly for strategic items).

- Capital items (such as plant and machinery) are major, specialised and expensive purchases, and will require special procurement disciplines in investment appraisal, financing, leasing, supplier selection and contracting.

5.5   It is worth noting that procurement priorities may be subtly different according to how manufacture is organised.

- **Project work** is typically carried out in the construction and engineering industries. Each item of production (eg a railway bridge or office block) is individual and distinct from other projects undertaken by the same firm – and the size of the job can be vast. This makes 'timing' a priority for the procurement or supply chain function: supplies must be scheduled in a precise sequence, to meet the requirements for each stage of the process.

- **Jobbing production** is the term given to bespoke, one-off customer orders – but on a smaller scale to projects: for example, a bespoke furniture manufacturer or potter. Procurement will have to arrange for a constant stock of items that are used frequently – but will also need to order materials specially for each separate order.

- **Batch manufacturing** refers to the production of identical items in small or large batches: for example, this textbook has been printed in a batch of identical copies. Procurement will have to forecast demand, in order to provide the right quantities of materials for each batch.
- **Mass production** is typically carried out on a traditional 'production line', where items move steadily from one stage of the process to the next. It is important to avoid any interruption to the flow, which makes it vital to secure an uninterrupted supply of the necessary materials – although this is made easier by constant and predictable levels of demand.
- **Continuous process production** (eg oil refining or the supply of gas and electricity) is similar to mass production in the need to maintain an uninterrupted 'flow' of inputs. It is also important to secure standardised inputs – since the outputs must also be standardised.

5.6 Several writers have also noted that the structure and priorities of manufacturing supply chains will depend to a large extent on the complexity of the product manufactured, and the level of uncertainty and dynamism in its environment.

- For complex goods in dynamic environments (eg capital intensive industries such as aerospace, shipbuilding and construction), quality management and supply chain agility (flexibility and responsiveness) are a priority.
- For complex goods in stable environments (eg consumer durables or automotive), value for money and demand-driven supply may be a priority.
- For simple goods in dynamic environments (eg fashion, cosmetics, food and beverage), short cycle times may be key, in response to short product lifecycles: products are 'outdated' quickly by fast-changing consumer demand.
- For simple goods in stable environments (eg commodities), process efficiency and cost improvement are key, in response to price sensitivity.

The fast moving consumer goods (FMCG) sector

5.7 FMCG products include things such as confectionery, toiletries, soft drinks, mass fashion items and so on. The FMCG sector is a special example of the manufacturing sector, with the focus on production of goods for consumer mass markets, with the aim of high-volume sales.

5.8 FMCG manufacturers will share the purchasing priorities of any mass producer, as discussed above. However:

- There may be additional quality considerations arising from the need for FMCG producers to brand their goods, in order to differentiate them from the mass of competitors. Customers tend to expect higher quality from branded goods, and this must be reflected in the quality of their inputs.
- The FMCG sector is characterised by very short product lifecycles, due to intense competition and consumer fashions and fads. There is pressure to introduce new, adapted or improved products constantly – and this may impact on procurement by creating a constant need for new equipment purchases, re-specification of materials, short supplier lead times (supply chain responsiveness or 'agility') and so on.

The construction sector

5.9 The construction sector is broadly responsible for constructional works: projects such as the construction, alteration, repair, maintenance or demolition of buildings or structures (eg roads, power-lines, pipelines, bridges or industrial plant); the installation of fittings (eg for power supply, ventilation, water supply, fire protection); and so on.

5.10 As construction typically involves large-scale, complex projects, the procurement requirements are very varied. Input requirements may include: materials (such as bricks, stone or steel); equipment and machinery; fixtures and fittings (such as pipes and wiring); specialist project components (such as foundations, scaffolding, lifts or air-conditioning systems); specialist trades or services (such as surveying and architectural services, interior or exterior design, project management, plumbing, carpentry and electrical); and negotiated agreements with infrastructure providers (eg town planners, electricity, gas, water or sewage facilities).

5.11   Subcontracting and integrated project management are crucial factors in procurement for construction projects, enabling the prime contractor to access specialist expertise for incorporating specialist components (such as lifts or air-conditioning systems). An integrated project team approach is commonly used, bringing together multiple, integrated supply chains into one supply team (the primary or first-tier contractor) – which is then integrated with the client-side project team. This structure supports the management of the kinds of complex supply chains often employed in major construction projects.

5.12   Supply chain relationships are also crucially important, to support project working, co-ordination and co-operation over lengthy, complex projects. The UK's National Procurement Strategy for local government argued that: 'Construction spend is the biggest single area of local authority external expenditure [especially on roads]. It follows that getting the procurement of construction, repair and maintenance right is likely to bring huge benefits. Benefits such as getting the job done right first time, and delivering it defect and dispute free, also add real value. Many authorities have discovered that the best way they can secure those benefits is by developing long-term relationships with their contractors and the whole supply chain.'

5.13   The construction industry as a whole has faced a number of challenges in recent decades.

- A poor reputation for quality, delivery, cost control and health and safety. Positive reputation is a potential source of differentiation, competitive advantage – and therefore added value. Industry Codes of Conduct (such as the UK's Construction Commitment to: people; procurement and integration; client leadership; sustainability; design quality; and health and safety) have been developed to support the adequacy and consistency of service.

- Pressure to reduce its very high environmental impacts (such as energy and water usage and waste generation) and to contribute to sustainability targets – particularly in construction projects commissioned by the public sector. Procurement may have a role in developing sustainable materials and technologies, reducing the carbon footprint of haulage, and generally providing leadership in an industry that has so far been slow to embrace the sustainability agenda. The UK government's *Strategy for Sustainable Construction* (BERR, 2008), for instance, advocates 'achieving whole life value through the promotion of best practice construction procurement and supply side integration'.

- Downturn in the housing and commercial property market, due to global recession, creating pressures for cost reductions to support profitability.

- An adversarial supply chain climate, and fragmented supply chains (*Supply Management,* June 2007, 'Green building blocks'), due to entrenched competitive and transactional relationships with subcontractors and suppliers, and a trend towards contractors unilaterally imposing price reductions on suppliers, in order to keep bids competitive. This has created pressures for integrated project teamworking (to support more innovative, sustainable, buildable, client-focused solutions) and more integrated supply chains ('joined up thinking'), so that learning and development can be carried forward from one project to the next.

- The use of outsourced, subcontracted and casual labour, creating problems for health and safety (no time for ongoing training), capability development (no continuity) and sustainability (no opportunity to secure 'buy in'). This may also be a procurement issue, with the need to drill down through the supply chain to monitor and enforce ethical and safety standards.

5.14   Lysons & Farrington also identify a number of distinctive features of the procurement of supplies for construction, in comparison to manufacturing or service organisations.

- Construction sites (for which supplies and services are procured) may be far distant from the procurement unit, perhaps even in a different country.

- Many construction supplies (such as brick, stone or steel) have high bulk and high weight, despite relatively low value. The high costs of transportation and handling must therefore be minimised, eg by sourcing from close to the construction site.

- Security (theft, pilferage and damage) is often an issue on construction sites, which may lack storage facilities: delivery of supplies should be scheduled as close as possible to the time when they are required (just in time supply).
- Procedures for inventory management will have to be agreed with the site engineer or project manager, since the procurement officer may be off-site.
- Supplies may also need to be transferred from one site or construction project to another, putting further pressure on accurate stock management, tracking and control.
- Architects, site engineers or project managers may have discretion to arrange for the supply of materials and services, requiring strong communication, liaison and co-ordination with the project's procurement officer (or the contractor's procurement unit).
- Specification of construction supplies will often take the form of a 'bill of quantities': a document prepared by a quantity surveyor from drawings and specifications prepared by architects or engineers. The BOQ sets out the detailed requirements of the work and the quantities involved, as 'priceable items': items against which tenderers can quote a price per unit – so that the grand summary will provide the tender price for the contract. This should avoid large 'contingency' amounts (padding) built into tenders, and should assist in calculating price variations due to subsequent changes in design.
- The procurement function may be involved early in the procurement process, providing project estimators with prices for materials and subcontracted work, to help determine whether tenders are expensive or good value.

The technology sector

5.15 Important market segments in the technology sector include: hardware; software; telecommunications equipment and systems; and related services (systems design, systems maintenance and so on).

5.16 Different types of technology businesses share the procurement features and challenges of other types of business. For example, the manufacture of computer hardware is a mainstream manufacturing activity, sharing many of the characteristics discussed above. Technology-related services share the characteristics of the general services sector, discussed below.

5.17 Distinctive features of the technology sector, however, include the following.

- The value of bought-out materials, as a proportion of total expenditure, is typically high, which implies a significant role for the procurement function, often resulting in board level representation.
- The sector is characterised by large-scale research and development, which implies a large capital base for companies wishing to compete effectively. The results of R & D investment must be protected by appropriate patents and trade marks: intellectual property protection (IPP) is an important feature of the sector. (If you follow the business news, you may be aware of high-profile patent-related law-suits involving companies such as Apple, Samsung and Google, designed to protect patent-protected technologies, operating systems and design features.)
- Late customisation has become a source of competitive advantage for some technology brands, such as Dell. Products are modularised, and subassemblies manufactured for stock: finished computers can then be assembled swiftly to consumer specification, with the support of close supply chain collaboration. This is a textbook example of 'agile' supply – and its challenges for supply chain management.

6 The services sector

6.1 A service has been defined as 'any activity or benefit that one party can offer to another that is essentially intangible and does not result in the ownership of anything' (Philip Kotler). A wide range of services are offered by providers: financial services, banking and insurance; transport; entertainment, hospitality and catering; hairdressing; plumbing; education; healthcare; and so on.

6.2   Some of the services most commonly used by business organisations are categorised as follows.

- Personal (eg editing, translation)
- Professional (eg consultancy, legal, medical, insurance)
- Support (eg administrative, financial, IT management, procurement, logistics, waste management, catering, security)
- Personnel (eg recruitment and selection, training and development, welfare)
- Construction (eg building repair, alteration and maintenance).

6.3   Employment and wealth generation in many developed countries, such as the UK, depends very largely on the activities of the services sector. In the past decade the importance of this sector has outstripped that of manufacturing in terms of contribution to the country's gross domestic product or GDP: that is, the total value of goods and services produced by the country in a given year.

6.4   The relative importance of the three industry sectors in a country's economy varies according to the country's *economic development*, defined by the availability of resources, skills, capital (or finance) and advanced technology.

- In countries with little wealth and technology, most people will be employed in the primary sector, mainly in agriculture or fishery. These are known as 'developing' economies, or 'less-developed' countries: you might think of nations such as Ghana, Nigeria or Bolivia, for example.
- Greater availability of finance and technology supports the development of manufacturing. 'Advanced developing' countries such as South Africa, Brazil, Turkey, India and China (also called 'newly industrialised' countries) therefore divide employment and production between the primary and secondary sectors.
- In 'developed' economies, such as the UK, Western Europe and the USA, the highest proportion of employment – and of the total value produced by the economy – is in the tertiary sector.

Key features of service sector procurement

6.5   The major input of many service companies is staff time and expertise, generally sourced by the human resources (HR) function, rather than procurement. However, one impact of the growth of the service sector has been the corresponding growth in *outsourcing*: the practice of buying services from specialist external suppliers instead of performing them in-house. This tends to enlarge the role of procurement functions, which may have the responsibility of selecting and managing a larger number of external service providers.

6.6   Another noticeable trend is the growth in size of service companies, and the increased scale of their operations, often resulting from mergers and takeovers (or industry consolidation). Once operations reach a certain scale, a greater value may be given to procurement disciplines and expertise, in order to ensure consistency, efficiency and value.

6.7   The particular challenges of procuring services – as opposed to physical products – were discussed in Chapter 1, Section 6. Challenges such as intangibility, heterogeneity and perishability present a strong argument for procurement professionals to be involved in sourcing services – rather than users, who may lack expertise in demand forecasting, negotiation, specification, contracting and ongoing supplier management.

6.8   It should be remembered, however, that service organisations also procure office equipment and supplies, IT systems and support, motor vehicles, office maintenance services, advertising services and so on, but these sorts of items are often sourced by general managers or the users of the items: procurement may occupy a merely administrative or support role in the organisation.

6.9   Physical supply may be more important in some circumstances, however: the delivery of services may be based on the use of hard assets such as property (as in a hotel or fast food restaurant), vehicles (as in an airline or logistics company), machinery (as in a print works, cleaning service or internet café) or other physical items (eg lights, costumes and props for a theatrical production).

10

6.10   In addition, many service organisations attempt to overcome the intangibility of services, and the fact that customers don't own anything as a result of the purchase transaction, by providing physical or tangible symbols of the service offered. These may include staff uniforms, liveried transport fleets, merchandise for customers, brochures, vouchers and certificates – all of which may need to be procured.

6.11   The same basic principles of procurement will be important in a service setting, particularly where physical goods are concerned, but again, there are distinctive features.

- In service organisations, little of the procurement function's effort is directed at providing inputs for 'production', such as physical components and raw materials. The emphasis is more on capital purchases, MRO supplies and services – plus people (labour) and information. The 'internal customers' are therefore mainly the staff providing the service (who use equipment and supplies).
- People are a key element both in delivering services, and in differentiating one service provider from another. Training, motivation, empowerment and cultural values are important factors in service supply – and supply chain management is crucial to secure competitive advantage through service quality, cost efficiency and the integrated management of information.
- In service organisations, the value of bought-in materials is generally a low proportion both of sales output and total inputs: services are highly labour-intensive. As we noted above, therefore, procurement may occupy more of an administrative or support role in the organisation. However, some items (such as property and transport fleets) will be significant capital purchases, requiring specialist procurement disciplines.
- Services are increasingly being outsourced, as organisations focus on their core activities, and contract out functions such as security, catering, printing, IT, sales and customer service, fleet management, HR selection and training, logistics and facilities management. A service organisation may outsource its own service needs, and the procurement or supply chain function may have an important role in subcontracting and supplier management, in order to maintain 'the right quality' of services delivered on its behalf.
- Services increasingly involve the management and supply of information: financial services, information and research, entertainment, consultancy, design and so on. Many functions in this area have been automated, and can now be offered to consumers directly, through the internet, mobile 'apps', ATM machines and so on. Supply chains are thus shortening to direct interaction between the service provider and the consumer, increasingly on a self-service basis.
- The combination of automation and outsourcing has enabled the development of virtual service organisations and networks. Financial services are a good example: mortgages, insurance and investment products are often supplied by a network of providers, drawn on by brokers who interface with consumers.

The financial sector

6.12   The financial sector is made up of firms which provide a range of financial services to commercial and retail customers. It includes banks, building societies, credit unions and mortgage brokers; credit card companies; debt resolution and refinancing services; finance companies (eg venture capital or private equity firms); stock brokerages; investment funds (such as unit trusts and pension funds); and insurance companies.

6.13   As we suggested above, procurement in the financial services sector is fairly typical of service procurement in general, so we will not say much more about it here. Perhaps the most important points are:

- The extent to which both inputs and outputs take the form of information flows (eg advice or market information)
- The extent to which ICT is used in the procurement and delivery of financial services
- The extent to which the provision of financial services is commissioned or outsourced to a supply network

- The extent to which the financial services sector is regulated, for the protection of the market and consumers. Issues such as financial reporting, bank fees, stewardship, fraud, insider dealing, unauthorised supply of investment advice, and money-laundering (handling the proceeds of crime or terrorism) are the subject of detailed law and regulation.

7 The retail sector

7.1 The distinctive feature of retail supply chains is the direct relationship between the retailer and the final consumer. Retail buyers are purchasing finished goods for sale onwards to customers – with little or no work done on them by the organisation itself.

7.2 Retailers primarily buy the goods they intend to sell. This may include a wide range of different goods (as in a supermarket or department store); or a smaller range of speciality goods (as in a greengrocer, toy shop or consumer electronics store, say). The purchase 'package' may also include added value or service elements, such as sale-or-return arrangements; training for retail staff in the demonstration and handling of goods; or contribution to display and advertising costs.

7.3 In addition, the retailer will procure a range of goods and services to maintain the operations of the organisation: fixtures and fittings for retail outlets; transport and warehousing services; ICT systems (including electronic point of sale systems); office equipment and supplies; cleaning services; staff uniforms and so on.

7.4 Issues such as quality control, service levels and supplier relations will be important for retail purchasers – as they are in manufacturing environments – but some of the procurement or supply chain function's priorities will be different. Arjen van Weele (*Purchasing Management: Analysis, Planning and Practice*) summarises some distinctive features of retail procurement as follows.

- *Bottom line thinking.* Wholesalers and retailers are not in general adding much value to the products they sell, and their margins are therefore somewhat tight. Buyers must focus on buying what will sell at good profit margins.
- *Broad assortment.* One of the functions performed by wholesalers and retailers is to make available to customers a wide range of goods offered by many different manufacturers. The number of stock lines and the number of suppliers is typically very high – and this has implications for buyers attempting to monitor prices, quality and supplier terms and conditions.
- *Buying against supplier specifications.* In general terms, a manufacturing company specifies the materials and parts it requires for production, and sources suppliers who can meet its specifications. Retailers, on the other hand, will generally buy what is available on the market, as described by the suppliers. Changing suppliers is therefore easier for the retailer, and supplier relations tend to be less durable.
- *Short feedback loop.* In resale contexts, buying a product and selling it are close together in time. It very quickly becomes apparent which lines are selling and which are not: fast response to such information is a key requirement for procurement.
- *Technical complexity.* In retail organisations, the items purchased are usually of low technical complexity, whereas in industrial buying a procurement officer's technical knowledge may be indispensable.

7.5 We would highlight some further distinctive features, including the following.

- Buyers may have responsibility for selecting products that will appeal to external customers. This is much closer to marketing activity than conventional procurement activity: the decision on what to buy is crucially related to expectations of what will sell. Buyers will often be involved in market research and monitoring sales performance, in order to adjust their selection: their priority will be to anticipate and satisfy the needs of the external customer (consumer), not internal customers. External customer needs and perceptions will determine what is the 'right quality' – and the 'right quantity' (demand).

10

Because of the range of items which may be stocked, large diverse retailers (such as department stores and supermarkets) have specialist buying teams for different 'categories' of purchase: foods, household and electrical goods, clothing and so on.

- It will be important for buyers to secure products from suppliers at the 'right price', which will enable them to add a retail mark-up (to earn a profit on the transaction) and still be able to charge consumers a price they will be prepared to pay. This may be easy for a major retailer (such as a supermarket chain) which can use its large purchasing power to gain substantial retail discounts from suppliers. However, a small retailer dealing with a powerful supplier (eg a supplier of 'must-have' consumer brands) may face more of a challenge.
- The retailer may not have a choice of supplier, if consumers demand goods made by a particular manufacturer. This may expose the organisation to risk (if the supplier is unknown, unreliable or uncompetitive on price), which will need to be managed as far as possible by procurement managers.
- The control of stock ('the right quantity at the right time') will be a particular challenge. The retailer will want to maintain sufficient stock to avoid stockouts, because it may lose customer sales to competitors if a product is not available in store. On the other hand, it will want to avoid the cost (and space requirements) of holding excessive stock – particularly if goods are perishable (eg foodstuffs) or likely to become obsolete (or 'out of fashion') quickly. The solutions are accurate demand forecasting, responsive (perhaps just in time) stock replenishment systems and agile supply chains, capable of delivering on short lead times.
- Distribution (the 'right place') also comes into the stock management equation. Retail outlets rarely have space for handling and holding stock: deliveries may have to be made from suppliers to central warehousing facilities, which can then 'break bulk' and distribute small stocks, as required, to individual retail branches. A large supermarket, for example, would be faced with daily deliveries of thousands of items to hundreds of branches.
- Various forms of collaboration have been an increasing feature of retail buyer-supplier relationships, including training of retail sales and service staff by manufacturers, and supplier contribution to retailers' advertising and display costs (where this is of benefit to the supplier). Technological integration has also become widespread, in the form of computerised (EDI) purchasing, automated inventory control and replenishment, and the sharing of point of sale data (via EPOS systems) with suppliers for the purposes of demand forecasting.
- Because retail organisations often stock a wide range of suppliers' goods, and suppliers supply a wide range of retailers, retail supply more clearly corresponds to a network model than a chain model.

7.6 If the organisation sells 'own-brand' products (like many supermarkets, say), it may order goods made to its specification, as in other industrial procurement contexts. However, most retail buyers will focus more on product selection and availability: securing supply of ready-to-sell goods at a price that will allow them to be sold on at a profit.

7.7 It should be clear from the above discussion that procurement staff in the retail sector may become involved in many different aspects of the business – not traditionally considered within the scope of a procurement function. For example, they may be involved in:

- Market research activity – partly to establish what their customers wish to buy, but also to monitor the activities of competitors
- Setting expenditure budgets. Within a framework laid down by overall organisational budgets, individual buyers must typically negotiate their own spending limits, and other targets such as sales volume and profit margin to be achieved on particular products for which they are responsible.
- Selection of products (as well as suppliers), collaborating with other functions such as marketing and merchandising. Key decision variables include: market demand; quality; brand strength; purchase cost (including discounts and trade credit); reliability of supply; and the level of marketing support given by suppliers (eg consumer advertising, sales force training, or point-of-sale materials).
- Monitoring of promotional activity (to ensure stock availability to meet demand), and product sales performance.

Factoring and wholesaling

7.8   Factors and wholesalers are 'intermediaries' between manufacturers and retailers, or between manufacturers and an end customer.

- Wholesalers stock a range of products from different manufacturers, to sell on to other organisations, such as retailers. They get discounts from manufacturers for buying in bulk, then 'break bulk' (enabling retailers to buy smaller quantities) at a marked-up price, allowing them to make a profit.
- Factors are 'mercantile agents' or 'brokers' who purchase goods on behalf of a customer, and charge a 'factorage' fee for the service.

7.9   In many ways, intermediaries are similar to retailers, because they buy what they think will sell (or what they have been asked to acquire by a customer). Factors may, or may not, actually take possession of goods prior to their on-sale to customers: they may merely act as specialist buyers. Wholesalers, however, will face significant challenges of stock management and distribution.

Organisation of the procurement function

7.10   Two main structures are found in procurement functions in the resale sector.

- In some cases, the procurement function is a separate department. Working from sales forecasts and estimates of demand prepared by the sales and marketing functions, buyers plan their forward purchases.
- In other cases, the close link between procurement, sales and marketing is formalised in the organisational structure, to form a 'merchandising' department. In this structure, managers are appointed in respect of particular product lines and have responsibility for procurement, supply chain management and distribution.

7.11   Either way, it is common to find that the procurement (or merchandising) function is centralised, although this is not always possible for items with a very short shelf life (such as food products). A central team of buyers is often backed up by technical specialists such as technologists, quality controllers and researchers.

10

Chapter summary

- Organisations can be categorised by activity (industry sectors), structure and ownership (public, private), primary objective (profit and not-for-profit) or size (eg small medium enterprises).
- The private and public sectors differ in factors such as ownership, funding, primary objective, competition and stakeholder constituency. This creates some differences in purchasing objectives and constraints – although these should not be overemphasised.
- It is common to distinguish three major industry sectors: primary (extracting or producing raw materials), secondary (converting raw materials into products) and tertiary (developing and providing services). Different activities pose different purchasing challenges.
- The tertiary or service sector represents a major contributor to employment and gross domestic product in developed nations. As resources, skills, capital and technology become available, with economic development, the tertiary sector grows. There are particular challenges to purchasing in service organisations – and to purchasing services.
- The distinctive feature of the retail sector is the direct relationship between the retailer and the final consumer. Retail buyers must be as aware of marketing disciplines as of purchasing practice.

Self-test questions

Numbers in brackets refer to the paragraphs where you can check your answers.

1   List key differences between private and public sector organisations. (1.5, 1.6)

2   What are the functions of the public sector in a mixed economy? (1.11)

3   List areas of difference between private sector and public sector procurement. (Table 10.1)

4   Why do such differences not necessarily lead to differences in operational procedure? (2.3)

5   Distinguish between primary, secondary and tertiary industries. (3.1)

6   What are the distinctive issues faced by procurement staff in an extractive industry? (4.4)

7   What are the distinctive issues faced by procurement staff in the agricultural sector? (4.8)

8   What are the distinctive issues faced by procurement staff in the manufacturing sector? (5.4)

9   What is meant by the FMCG sector? (5.7)

10   What are the distinctive issues faced by procurement staff in the construction sector? (5.14)

11   What are the distinctive issues faced by procurement staff in the services sector? (6.11)

12   List the distinctive features of retail buying. (7.4, 7.5)

CHAPTER 11

Procurement in the Public Sector

Assessment criteria and indicative content

 Analyse the impact of the public sector on procurement or supply chain roles

- Objectives of public sector organisations such as improving services, communities and corporate social responsibility
- Regulations that impact on procurement and supply chain operations
- Need for competition, public accountability and value for money

Section headings

1 Public sector organisations
2 Responsibilities for public sector procurement
3 The regulation of public sector procurement
4 Key features of public sector procurement

Introduction

In this chapter we return to the public sector, and look at the particular requirements and considerations when undertaking procurement activities in that sector.

There is considerable variety in public procurement contexts, including different requirements for central government departments and agencies, and local government authorities. We endeavour to give a general overview of the procurement climate and structure in each context.

Since the learning outcome for this section of the syllabus focuses on 'the need for compliance', we focus specifically on key law and regulations in the area of public procurement: the EU Public Procurement Directives, and their enactment in UK law.

We also emphasise some of the key values and objectives of public sector procurement, such as competition, accountability and value for money – which have rather different connotations in the public sector than they do in the private sector.

1 Public sector organisations

Types of organisations in the public sector

1.1 There are several different types of public sector organisation in the UK, as an exemplar.

- **Government departments** (eg the Departments of Defence, Health, HM Treasury and the Foreign and Commonwealth Office) carry out the work of central government. They are financed by taxation revenue, although they also include trading organisations such as the Stationery Office.
- **Local government authorities** (eg County Councils, District Councils and Metropolitan District Councils) carry out the work of local service administration, financed by revenue raised predominantly from local sources.
- **Quasi-Autonomous National Government Organisations** (QUANGOs) are set up by the government

as independent (non-departmental) bodies, which are nevertheless dependent on the government for their existence. UK examples include the Environment Agency, the Competition and Markets Authority and the Equality and Human Rights Commission. (In the US, QUANGO stands for Quasi-Autonomous *Non* Governmental Organisation, and you may see this version used in some text books.)

- **Public corporations** (eg the BBC) are state-owned industrial and commercial undertakings. They are run by a board accountable to the Secretary of State of a sponsoring government department, with which they agree their strategic objectives, performance targets and funding. These public enterprises are an important part of the UK public sector, contributing significantly to national output, employment and investment. British Coal, British Energy, the Post Office and British Steel were among them in the UK, for example, but such industries have been progressively privatised (sold into private ownership) since the 1980s.
- **Municipal enterprises** are providers of goods and services (eg leisure services, museums, parks), run by local government authorities – often in competition with the private sector. Increasingly, local councils are creating separate companies or trusts to deliver such services, allowing partnership with private investors and providers.

Financing the public sector

1.2   All sources of public sector funding derive ultimately from the taxpayer. Funds are collected in various different forms: direct taxes (taxes on income, such as the corporation tax paid by companies and the income tax paid by individuals); indirect taxes (ie taxes on expenditure, such as value added tax and excise duties); and local taxes (such as council tax and business rates).

1.3   In the UK, most of this income is collected by central government (although some of it, such as council tax, is collected by local authorities). It is the task of government, and specifically the Treasury department, to distribute the income for use in the areas prioritised by government policy.

1.4   Government agencies (such as the Child Maintenance Service or the Health and Safety Executive) are provided with funds by central government for spending on their allotted responsibilities. In some cases, such agencies act as industry regulators, and when this happens, another source of their income comes from levies on the companies operating in that sector.

1.5   Where funds are collected locally, they are also spent locally, on services such as policing, rubbish collection, road maintenance and so on.

Objectives of public sector organisations

1.6   As we stated in distinguishing the public and private sectors in Chapter 10, the primary objectives of the public sector are *not* to make economic surplus or profits, but instead:

- To deliver essential public **services** (such as housing, healthcare, sanitation, transport, education, policing and defence) which the market might not otherwise provide equitably or fairly – to an acceptable level or quality (as expressed in government policies and targets)
- To encourage **national and community development**: developing education and skilling; stimulating economic activity and employment; developing technology and infrastructure (roads, communications, public spaces and so on); maintaining national security; preserving national and community heritage (both natural and human-made); supporting diversity and social inclusion (access to the benefits and opportunities offered by society); and so on
- To pursue **socio-economic goals** such as support for small and minority-owned businesses; the legislation of minimum standards for human, civil and labour rights; the promotion of work-life balance and public health; the pursuit of sustainable development, production and consumption (including sustainable procurement); environmental protection; and so on. This is often called 'corporate social responsibility' in the private sector.

1.7   The National Procurement Strategy for Local Government (published by the old Office of the Deputy Prime Minister in 2003) contained a procurement vision for local councils which included six key principles, reflecting these key objectives.

- Better quality services through sustainable partnerships (ie service commissioning)
- A mixed economy of service provision (ie partnering with the private and third sectors to deliver services), with ready access to a diverse and competitive range of suppliers
- Achieving continuous improvement by collaborating with partners
- Greater value from a corporate procurement strategy
- Realising community benefits
- Stimulating markets and driving innovation in the design, construction and delivery of services.

2   Responsibilities for public sector procurement

Central government procurement in the UK

2.1   The 1999 Gershon Efficiency Review recommended centralised co-ordination of central government procurement, through the Office of Government Commerce (OGC), which was established in 2000 (although it has since ceased to operate separately from the Cabinet Office). OGC's three main priorities were defined as: improving public services by working with departments to help them meet their efficiency targets; delivering savings in central government civil procurement; and improving the success rate of mission-critical programmes and projects. OGC therefore operated a wide-ranging programme supporting three significant activities: improving efficiency; programme and project management (PPM); and procurement.

2.2   OGC Buying Solutions was an executive agency of the OGC, providing procurement services to help public sector organisations and their private sector agents and contractors achieve value for money from procurement.

2.3   For those working in the public sector, the implications of the OGC included: greater pressure to achieve efficiency savings from procurement; greater emphasis on aggregating requirements and collaborative contracting; stronger focus on the status and role of procurement; stronger focus on professional and career development in procurement; increased involvement in contracting across the organisation; and increased involvement in cross-functional contracting teams.

2.4   In 2010 the OGC became part of the Efficiency and Reform Group (ERG) section of the Cabinet Office. The activities of the ERG emphasise in particular: combining the buying power of central government departments so they act as 'one customer'; delivering projects on time, within budget and to a high quality; using digital methods by default; allowing a wider range of UK businesses to bid for government contracts; using management information better. In 2014 the Crown Commercial Service was formed from the Cabinet Office to become the commercial and procurement function for the UK Government, responsible for procurement policy and providing expert commercial services and advice.

Local government procurement in the UK

2.5   There is less central co-ordination of local authority procurement in the UK. Functional departments and committees are influential, and procurement's role is often limited to advising on procedures and managing clerical processes. A 2002 Audit Commission report noted that: 'It is encouraging that some authorities are using procurement as a tool for improvement, and that there is evidence of good practice. However, many authorities still need to ensure that their approach to procurement makes full use of competition and challenges current services.'

2.6   In 2014 the Local Government Association (LGA) published a National Procurement Strategy for Local Government in England. Its vision is focused on four key outcomes.

- Making savings by using: category management; standard specifications; supplier analysis; partnering, collaboration and shared services; contract management and relationship management; performance monitoring and transparency; risk management; identifying and reducing fraudulent procurement practices in pre-contract and post-contract award and through the supply chain; demand management; reducing costs and oversupply
- Supporting local economies by: removing barriers to local businesses and charities bidding for council contracts; including economic, environmental and social value (sustainability) criteria in all contracts; reducing waste
- Improving leadership by: recognising the strategic importance of procurement; developing a commercially focused procurement culture; ensuring staff have the knowledge, training, and practical skills needed to derive maximum benefit from procurement
- Modernising procurement by: ensuring procurement staff are more commercially minded; encouraging supplier innovation; adopting e-procurement and e-invoicing; making council procurement processes quicker, simpler and less costly to run.

National Health Service (NHS) procurement in the UK

2.7   Until 2010, the Purchasing and Supply Agency (NHS PASA) acted as a centre of expertise, knowledge and excellence in purchasing and supply matters for the health service. It advised on policy and the strategic direction of procurement, and its impact on developing healthcare, across the NHS. It also contracted on a national basis for products and services which were strategically critical to the NHS, and where sectoral aggregation of demand was thought to yield greater savings than local or regional collaboration.

2.8   The agency was closed down in April 2010, and has been replaced by a more commercially focused regime. Its functions are now carried out by the Department of Health and other agencies, including NHS Supply Chain and regional CCGs (Clinical Commissioning Groups).

3   The regulation of public sector procurement

3.1   Spending in the public sector must comply with detailed legal regulations, and all spending decisions are subject to detailed scrutiny.

- Setting budgets for public spending begins with the Chancellor of the Exchequer, who sets overall revenue-raising and spending priorities. The budgets of public sector organisations must be set within the framework that this provides.
- Scrutiny of expenditure is carried out by the National Audit Office (which until 31 March 2015 dealt with central government departments and agencies) and the Audit Commission (which until 31 March 2015 dealt with local government authorities, from which date responsibility passed to the Local Government Association (LGA)).

3.2   There are also a number of other regulatory bodies operating in the public sector: eg Ofsted for educational standards and the General Medical Council for health care. The purpose of these regulators is to protect public welfare and national interest, to ensure compliance with institutionalised standards – and to ensure that taxpayers' money is well spent.

3.3   Regulators may be responsible for any or all of the following issues.

- Highlighting and advising on best practice, quality standards and service levels
- Reviewing and evaluating government strategies
- Receiving reports and returns on performance, and publishing evidence-based findings
- Monitoring and auditing organisational activity for compliance to standards
- Helping customers to make informed choices and, where necessary, complaints
- Communicating and promoting the work of the sector to the public.

The impact of regulation on public procurement

3.4   The impact of regulation on public sector procurement is, broadly:

- To ensure that bought-in materials, goods and services comply with defined public standards and specifications
- To ensure that all procurement exercises are compliant with public policies, standing orders and statutory procedures – with the general aim of securing competitive supply, value for money and ethical procurement
- To ensure that all supply chain operations are compliant with law, regulation and standards in areas such as health and safety (eg in regard to manual handling or transport of dangerous goods); sustainability (eg in regard to carbon emissions); employment rights (eg in regard to equal opportunity or employment protection); data protection and freedom of information.

3.5   Such regulations are common to both the public and private sectors. Public sector procurement is, however, subject to additional regulation and scrutiny.

- **EU procurement directives** were originally enacted in UK law as the Public Contracts Regulations 2006 and the Public Utilities Regulations 2006. Revised Directives were adopted by the EU in March 2014. There is a two-year deadline for the provisions to be enacted in UK law.
- **Anti-corruption law**, which broadly outlaws the offering and receiving of bribes and inducements which might influence, or be seen to influence, decision making by public officials (eg the Public Bodies Corrupt Practices Act 1989 and the Prevention of Corruption Act 1916)
- **Freedom of information** law (eg the Freedom of Information Act 2000), which gives the public the right to access information held by public authorities (including emails, the minutes of meetings, research and reports) – *unless* it is determined that the public interest in withholding the information is greater than the public interest in disclosing it: the 'public interest test'. Public authorities must respond promptly (within 20 days) to FOI requests, although they have 'reasonable time' to consider whether the disclosure would be in the public interest. Complaints and disputes are arbitrated by the Information Commissioner's Office
- Review by the **National Audit Office** (central government and public bodies) and the **Audit Commission** (local government authorities), whose job is to review public spending, efficiency and standards and publish reports and recommendations.

EU Public Procurement Directives

3.6   The EU Public Procurement Directives were originally implemented into UK law by the Public Contracts Regulations 2006, which apply to procurement by public bodies (above certain financial thresholds).

3.7   The purposes of the EU procurement directives are broadly as follows.

- To open up the choice of potential suppliers for public sector organisations and utilities, in order to stimulate competition and reduce costs
- To open up non-discriminatory and competitive markets for suppliers, while allowing achievement of value for money by authorities
- To ensure the free movement of goods and services within the European Union
- To ensure that public sector purchasing decisions are based on value for money (via competition) and that public sector bodies award contracts efficiently and without discrimination.

3.8   The main provisions of the regulations are shown in Table 11.1.

11

Table 11.1 *Public Contracts Regulations 2006 (Public Procurement Directive)*

Advertising	• Subject to certain exceptions, public bodies must use open tendering procedures: advertising the invitation to tender according to rules designed to secure maximum publicity across the EU.
Contract award procedures	• *Open procedure*: no requirement for pre-qualification of suppliers. Tenders must be issued within six days of request by a prospective bidder. Suppliers have 52 days (minimum) to submit bids. • *Restricted procedure*: suppliers may be pre-qualified, but there must be a pre-stated range of suppliers (5–20) to whom invitations will be sent. Prospective bidders have 37 days (maximum) to register interest and submit the required information for pre-qualification. • *Negotiated procedure*: with advertisement or without (eg in the case of urgency, exclusivity agreements, or no tenders being received under other procedures). Prospective bidders have 37 days (maximum) to register their interest to negotiate. A minimum of three parties must be selected to negotiate. • *Competitive dialogue* (for large, complex contracts): a process conducted in successive stages to identify potential solutions and gradually reduce the number of tenders to be negotiated.
Award criteria	• Contracts should be awarded on the basis of *objective* award criteria, ensuring transparency, non-discrimination, equal treatment, and competition. • Buyers are generally obliged to award contracts on the basis of *lowest price* OR *most economically advantageous tender* (MEAT). • If MEAT is used, buyers must make this known to tender candidates and must explain the criteria that will be used to assess 'economic advantage'. • All tenderers must have reasonable, equal and timely *information* about criteria and the weighting or ranking of non-price criteria (which may include environmental and social sustainability). • The buyer may exclude bidders if they fail to meet certain defined criteria in regard to suitability, financial standing and technical competence.
Right to feedback (debrief)	• The results of the tender must be notified to the Official Journal of EU. • Unsuccessful bidders have the right to a de-brief within 48 days of request. The focus should be on the weaknesses that led to rejection of the bid, as well as strengths. The de-brief should *not* be used to justify the award of the contract to the successful tenderer (and, in particular, confidential information about the successful bid should *not* be disclosed).
Other provisions	Contracting authorities may use: • Framework agreements (agreeing terms governing 'standing' contracts for defined periods of up to four years). • Electronic purchasing and tendering/auction systems: completely computerised systems for quotation submission, evaluation and contract award.

3.9   The main means by which a breach of the directives may be remedied are legal action by an aggrieved supplier or contractor against a purchaser, or an action against them by a member state in the European Court of Justice. Possible 'remedies' resulting from such an action include:

- Suspension of an incomplete contract award procedure
- Setting aside of a decision in a completed contract award procedure
- An award of damages (in cases where a contract has already been entered)

3.10   It is worth being aware that this regime of compulsory open tendering has certain disadvantages. All vendors are aware that a large number of bids are likely to be made, and this may deter some suitable applicants. Moreover, since very little pre-qualification of potential vendors is allowed, some may take risks in attempting to undercut potential rivals. The result may be a contract awarded at a price that gives no incentive to high quality performance. Additionally, open tendering imposes a great administrative burden on the procurement function, which is faced with a large number of tenders to evaluate! Some of these disadvantages have been addressed by the 2014 Directives.

3.11 The 2014 revised procurement directives affect the regime in the UK in the following areas.

- There are some exemptions from application of the main public procurement directive, in particular for: some 'public-public' contracts (contracts between two public bodies); contracts with defence or security implications; works and services concession contracts where the consideration consists in whole or in part in the right to exploit works or services (eg toll bridges, canteen services, outsourced leisure centres) and operating risk is transferred to the supplier (these are subject to the new, 'light touch' concessions directive)
- The 'light touch' regime also covers some services (mainly for social and health care) to reflect their limited cross-border interest (eg they relate to legal services in the context of national law) or the fact that they are sensitive (eg services to the person)
- Certain services contracts (mainly social, health and educational) can be reserved to sheltered workshops, or to mutual and social enterprises that meet defined conditions. Such contracts are awarded using the 'light touch' regime
- New rules to encourage greater access to contracts.
- New rules to streamline the EU procurement process.
- Rules for selection of suppliers are simpler and more flexible.
- Award criteria are clarified.

4 Key features of public sector procurement

Public sector supply chain drivers

4.1 In contrast to the profit focus of private sector concerns, public sector organisations have a primary orientation to achieving defined service levels: providing efficient and effective services (education, transport, healthcare) and utilities (water, power) to the public, often within defined budgetary constraints and environmental and sustainability strategies. This less intensely competitive environment allows greater information exchange, best-practice sharing and collaborative or consolidated buying and supply arrangements, such as shared e-procurement platforms and buying groups.

4.2 The range of stakeholders in public sector organisations is more diverse, including funding and user groups. This creates a more complex network of stakeholder expectations, relationships and accountabilities to be managed. A much wider diversity of items and services may also be purchased and supplied: consider a local government authority in the UK, which may be a purchaser of construction materials for use in housing or road maintenance, of dustbin lorries for refuse collection, of sporting equipment for a community leisure centre, and much more.

4.3 Public sector buyers are subject to a high level of accountability. They must ensure that appropriate processes have been followed to acquire best value for taxpayers' money; that a full 'audit trail' exists so that their actions and decisions can be vetted; and that appropriate service levels are achieved in the provision of services to members of the public. These objectives are thought to be best achieved by an insistence on competitive tendering, for contracts over a certain size (measured by contract value).

4.4 Public sector procurement (and therefore the dyadic relationships within the supply chain) are governed by EU Directives in areas such as the compulsory use of competitive bidding, the use of e-auctions, ethical requirements (eg in regard to gifts and hospitality) and public interest disclosure of information (limiting the confidentiality of the dealings between buyers and suppliers).

4.5 As we suggested earlier, the distinction between private and public sector procurement should not be over-emphasised, since both sectors deal with inputs and broadly aspire to good practice in terms of the 'five rights'. However, you should be aware that there are some distinctive challenges in public sector procurement.

- Public sector buyers generally have the overall objective of achieving defined service levels (rather than increasing profits, as in the private sector). 'Value' is thus defined by maintaining or improving service levels within value and cost parameters – rather than by minimising cost as part of a strategy of profit maximisation and competition.

- They are responsible ultimately to the general public, represented by the State (rather than to the shareholders of a private company, represented by its directors).
- They have to satisfy a wider range of stakeholders: managers, customers, beneficiaries of services, taxpayers, communities and so on. There will usually be a stronger emphasis on purchasing values such as ethics, social sustainability (eg using diverse, small and local suppliers), environmental protection and so on.
- They may have a wider range of activities, and therefore a wider range of purchasing requirements. (Think of the range of items required by a school, or a local government organisation, say.)
- They are subject to established procurement procedures, and legislative directives (including the EU Public Procurement Directives, enacted in UK law as the Public Contracts Regulations). This means, for example, that competitive tendering is compulsory for placing supply contracts, unless their value is small.
- They will often be subject to budgetary constraints, cash limits and/or efficiency targets, to maximise the value obtained from public funding.

4.6   The White Paper *Setting New Standards* recognised the strategic importance of public procurement and placed an increased emphasis on securing the benefits of best purchasing practice. Specific proposals were presented for improving practice in line with the best performing private sector companies, including: an emphasis on:

- Integrated lifecycle procurement processes (or whole life contract management)
- Better management of risk
- Use of cross-functional teams
- Information sharing and collaboration
- The development of supplier relationships and a supply chain management orientation (using influence over first-tier suppliers to manage their supply chains effectively and sustainably)
- Cost reduction (especially through efficiency and collaboration with suppliers)
- The development of professional skills (eg initiatives by the Office of Government Commerce to augment the number of CIPS-qualified staff in public sector departments).
- Performance measurement (especially using balanced efficiency/effectiveness approaches such as the Procurement Excellence Model).

4.7   Some of the distinctive features of public sector procurement are discussed below, focusing on areas highlighted by the syllabus: the need for competition, public accountability and value for money.

Competition

4.8   A key issue in the public sector is to ensure that suppliers are selected not on the grounds of political expediency, socio-economic goals, favouritism or fraud, but by transparent procedures which are open to audit and give all eligible suppliers an equal opportunity. There has been particular emphasis on ensuring that competitive procedures are followed, as part of developing the professionalism of the procurement function.

4.9   It has also been recognised that public procurement has an important role to play in ensuring the efficient use of public funds. Policy dictates that this is to be achieved wherever possible via competition, as the best guarantee of quality and value for money.

4.10   Some form of competitive tendering is therefore used within the public sector for almost all goods purchased. For small items this usually takes the form of written quotations from selected suppliers. However, the greater the value of goods purchased, the more formal the tendering procedure. EU public procurement procedures, as we have seen, are based on formal competitive tendering to ensure openness and equality of opportunity within a competitive framework.

4.11　It is important to note that the aim of procurement is not just 'competition' for its own sake, but its judicious use to achieve *competitive supply*: the extent to which a supply arrangement provides supply which matches or exceeds requirements at a cost which represents best value in relation to a given supply market. *Competitiveness* is the strength and intensity of competition within a market, which results in genuine customer choice and potential for gains in price, quality and innovation.

4.12　One key issue is whether levels of competitiveness in a supply market result in bids which represent competitive supply, or whether there is a need to *generate* greater competition eg through: encouraging new entrants or substitute products and processes; expanding the market (eg from regional to EU/global); collaborative buying to increase buyer power; making contracts more accessible/attractive to potential suppliers.

4.13　Compulsory competitive tendering is designed to ensure fair, non-discriminatory and competitive supplier selection, based on equality of access to tender information, selection of suppliers based on clear price (and non-price) criteria, and accountability for decisions (including feedback to unsuccessful bidders). It also supports value-for-money procurement – and procurement cost savings (as part of government efficiency targets) – by improving and maintaining the competitiveness of supply.

4.14　It has been recognised, however, that restrictive or inflexible use of competitive procedures may: discourage more innovative approaches; reinforce a risk-avoidance culture; provide an excuse for lack of expertise and professionalism; limit opportunities to achieve wider socio-economic goals through procurement; and place obstacles in the way of developing close relationships with suppliers.

4.15　The main focus in the UK has been on compliance with the EU Public Procurement Directives, emphasising the transparent use of competitive procedures, rather than necessarily the achievement of competitive supply or added value outcomes. An initial restrictive interpretation of the Directives by the UK government resulted in a negative view of the use of procurement for socio-economic purposes. EU rules have been seen not always to encourage best practice procurement, in areas such as sustainability, SME and minority business participation, longer-term supply partnership relations – or indeed competitive supply. Note that some, if not all, of these concerns have been addressed by the 2014 Directives.

4.16　One key challenge for public procurement is that inflexible use of competitive tendering may inhibit the development of the kinds of long-term collaborative relationships which underlie strategic procurement models. Consideration must be given to the benefits and feasibility of developing close supplier relationships within the regime.

4.17　It has long been recognised that there needs to be more constructive co-operation between customers and suppliers and that – particularly in highly specialised markets, and for complex and continuously developing requirements – longer-term partnering arrangements may be appropriate. Such partnerships will still be established by competitive tender and re-opened periodically to competition *(Treasury, 1995)*: a policy sometimes called 'partnership within competition.'

4.18　Whilst in principle 'partnership within competition' provides a viable alternative for the public sector, it risks undermining the principles of transparency, competitiveness and fraud prevention. Such risks need to be recognised and managed, eg through greater professionalisation of the procurement function, and through the development of procedures combining dialogue with potential suppliers and formal procedures for the submission of bids. Once competitive tendering processes have been completed, close relationships may be developed between clients and suppliers on the basis of continuing competitiveness, innovation, cost and quality improvement over the duration of the contract.

4.19　Another challenge has been the inflexible use of price and 'value for money' criteria in awarding competitive contracts – potentially at the expense of important criteria such as whole life costs, sustainability, or relational compatibility (eg potential for EDI links). Particular efforts have to be made to include such criteria in specifications – which is the latest stage at which non-price criteria can be introduced. Again, the 2014 Directives address some of these issues.

Public accountability

4.20   The existence of multiple stakeholder objectives (which Cox has called 'contested goals') makes it impossible to satisfy every legitimate aspiration of the public sector's 'customers'. Managers therefore need to prioritise, and they must do so in line with policy decided upon by government. In the UK, the government monitors the activities of public sector bodies to ensure that this is done.

- The National Audit Office scrutinises public spending on behalf of Parliament, with a programme of regular reviews covering central government departments and a wide range of other public bodies.
- The Audit Commission performs a similar role in relation to local government authorities.
- The Public Accounts Committee (PAC) also audits and scrutinises the probity of expenditure and value for money obtained. This is a powerful incentive for Accounting Officers to ensure that strict procedures are in place to avoid financial irregularities or lack of economy, efficiency and effectiveness in public procurement.

4.21   This level of accountability impacts strongly on public procurement. One key effect is an insistence on detailed procedures and record keeping: it may be difficult later to justify a course of action which breaches defined procedures or which is poorly documented.

4.22   Reports of the Public Accounts Committee illustrate the kinds of behaviour which are required by public accountability, in areas such as: the need to record the reasons for all decisions; the need for procurement officers to declare any personal interests in procurement decisions; the need to avoid conflicts of interest; the need to secure proper authorisations; and the need generally to monitor and manage fraud risk.

4.23   However, it is often argued that the scrutiny and accountability regime also creates a 'risk avoidance' culture among public sector officials. The National Audit Office has stated that a lack of flexibility and innovation, in seeking to minimise risks, may itself cause failure to achieve value for money. Here are some examples.

- Rigid application of procedures and use of the same terms and conditions for all contracts regardless of the nature of the requirement, market conditions and relationship with potential suppliers
- Reluctance to involve procurement at an early stage in working with clients, technical experts and users in cross-functional teams
- Reluctance to use innovative approaches such as early dialogue with suppliers over market availability and specification, visits to or presentations by potential suppliers
- Reluctance (usually by Finance) to expand the use or coverage of purchasing cards

4.24   The NAO recommends a more flexible approach, which may be adopted by procurement staff, including:

- A proportional risk management approach ('control risk, not obviate it')
- Engaging external and internal auditors in dialogue about the cost and risk of over-control
- Applying Directives and regulations creatively to meet customer needs
- Alerting the market to requirements early, engaging in dialogue with suppliers and improving the quality of information.

Value for money

4.25   Traditionally, measures based on VFM were based first on prices paid and cost savings. However, a more holistic concept of 'value for money' (VFM) was advocated in the UK Government's 1995 White Paper *Setting New Standards*. 'All public procurement of goods and services, including works, must be based on value for money . . . Value for money is not about achieving the lowest initial price: it is defined as *the optimum combination of whole life costs and quality*.'

4.26   This reflects an increased emphasis on:

- The importance of taking into account all aspects of cost over time, rather than lowest purchase price (discussed in Chapter 2)

- The importance of defining 'value' from the perspective of the customer, and meeting service level and quality requirements
- The importance of achieving efficiency (making best use of available resources) and effectiveness (accomplishing objectives) – in addition to economy (using the least possible resources).

4.27 Guidelines from Treasury and the NAO in 2004 identified a number of ways of achieving VFM in public procurement.

- More efficient processing of transactions and reduced processing overheads
- Getting better VFM for goods and services purchased
- Direct negotiation with suppliers
- Collaborative or consortium buyers
- Improving project, contract and asset management
- Making procurement decisions on the basis of long-term value
- Combining competition with innovative procurement methods (while managing risks effectively)
- Utilising e-procurement and good practice
- Using tools to promote and measure VFM gains

Public private partnerships

4.28 Public private partnerships (PPP) and Private Finance Initiatives (PFI) are schemes in which private sector firms and public authorities share capital and expertise, in various structured ways, with a view to building and operating major capital and infrastructure assets. Such structured partnerships have been used to create UK infrastructure such as the Channel Tunnel, the QEII bridge across the Thames at Dartford, the North Birmingham Relief Road, and the London Olympics facilities, as well as smaller projects such as hospitals, schools and barracks. Their use has declined since the 2009 global financial crisis and some well publicised scandals.

4.29 PPP projects may take various forms.

- A *Design-Build contract* means that the private partner designs and builds a facility, which the public authority (eg a council or NHS Trust) will operate once it is completed.
- A *Build-Operate contract* means that the private partner builds the facility (eg a toll road) and operates it for a period, in order to recoup its investment, then transfers ownership to the public sector body.
- A *Turnkey Operation* is where the public sector provides funding and retains ownership of the facility, but the private partner designs and builds it, and also operates it for a period.
- An *Operation and Maintenance contract* means that a private partner is simply contracted, on a tender basis, to operate and maintain a public facility (eg a prison or a waste disposal facility).
- A *Private Finance Initiative* typically means that a private consortium raises the capital finance to design and build a public sector project. It is also contracted to maintain the buildings while a public authority uses them: eg providing cleaning, catering and security services. Once construction is complete, the public authority begins to pay back the private consortium for the cost of the buildings and their maintenance, plus interest. The contracts typically last for 30 years, after which time the buildings belong to the public authority.

4.30 The advantages of a PPP scheme for the public sector are claimed to be as follows.

- It can lower public sector costs (owing to the way service charges paid to the private sector operator are accounted for) – and enable projects to be undertaken without having to cover capital costs from tax revenue.
- It can secure higher levels of capital expenditure and cashflow, owing to the potentially higher budget (and debt) capacity of the private sector partner. This may enable the public sector to undertake more large-scale projects than if they were prioritised under conventional public capital funding methods.
- It can tap into the creativity, expertise and existing capacity, capability and technology of private

sector organisations, allowing higher levels of service to be provided to the public (supporting the objectives of the public sector partner) – especially where service levels are secured by appropriate KPIs, or where the private sector partner is putting its own capital at risk.

- It can therefore represent excellent value for money, especially if the private partner has already invested in the required equipment, technology and so on.

- Overall, a PPP scheme can enable a public sector body to complete projects, upgrade facilities and improve public services much faster than would otherwise be possible. According to UK healthcare think tank the Kings Fund, for example, the physical condition of most hospitals is now 'vastly improved' thanks to such partnerships.

4.31   On the other hand:

- Critics of PPP argue that the public sector may be surrendering control of the project, with the risk of lower levels of service, public accountability and consideration of environmental and social sustainability objectives.

- PFI contracts can represent poor value for money and may saddle the public sector with unsustainable financial commitments for decades to come: some NHS trusts have found it too expensive to pay the annual charges to private sector contractors for building and servicing new hospitals, for example.

- The scheme may be unsustainably inflexible, because it ties public services into 20–30 year contracts – despite the fact that it is difficult to plan for changes in demand and service provision over such a long planning horizon.

- Trade unions such as Unison have claimed that some PPP structures lead to poorer services, because private companies maintain facilities as cheaply as possible in order to maximise their profits.

- The pay and conditions of cleaners, catering and security staff in facilities operated by the private sector are typically worse than their counterparts in the public sector.

4.32   From the private sector partner's point of view, the arrangement is only successful to the extent that it gains a reasonable return on its investment (and perhaps also enhanced political influence). Some PFI consortia have seen profits soar: Octagon, the private consortium that financed and built the Norfolk and Norwich Hospital, refinanced the PFI deal so that the partners could take early profits, for example. But other firms, such as engineering firm Amey (with PFI contracts in education and road building) were plunged into financial crisis.

Chapter summary

- Public sector organisations include: central government departments, local government authorities, QUANGOs, public corporations and municipal enterprises.
- Public sector funding ultimately derives from taxpayers. Funding is used to deliver essential public services, to encourage development, and to pursue socio-economic goals.
- All areas of the public sector are under pressure to achieve efficiency savings from procurement.
- The activities of procurement in the public sector are more tightly regulated than in the private sector.
- The EU procurement directives aim to foster competition as a stimulus to efficiency in public sector service provision.
- The objectives of public sector organisations differ from those of the private sector. In particular, the priority for the public sector is the achievement of defined service levels rather than the pursuit of profit.

Self-test questions

Numbers in brackets refer to the paragraphs where you can check your answers.

1   List different types of public sector organisation. (1.1)

2   What are the primary objectives of public sector organisations? (1.6)

3   How do the OGC and its successors impact on procurement in central government? (2.3–2.4)

4   Describe the main impacts of regulation on public procurement. (3.4)

5   What are the objectives of the EU procurement directives? (3.7)

6   The stakeholders in a public sector organisation are typically less diverse than in a private sector organisation. True or false? (4.2)

7   List some of the distinctive challenges of public sector procurement. (4.5)

8   What are the potential disadvantages of compulsory competitive tendering? (4.14)

9   List methods of achieving value for money in public procurement. (4.27)

10   List (a) advantages and (b) disadvantages claimed for public private partnerships. (4.30, 4.31)

11

CHAPTER 12

Procurement in the Private and Third Sectors

Assessment criteria and indicative content

4.3 Analyse the impact of the private sector on procurement or supply chain roles.

- Objectives of private sector organisations such as profitability, market share, shareholder value and corporate social responsibility
- Regulations that impact on procurement and supply chain operations
- The importance and role of branding

4.4 Analyse the impact of the not for profit or third sector on procurement or supply chain roles

- Objectives of the not for profit or third sector
- Regulations impacting on charities
- Need for regulated procurement exercises

Section headings

1 Private sector organisations
2 Objectives of private sector organisations
3 The regulation of private sector procurement
4 Key features of private sector procurement
5 Third sector organisations
6 Key features of third sector procurement

Introduction

In this chapter we continue our exploration of economic sectors, by focusing on the particular requirements of procurement in the private and third sectors.

Much of the good practice and generic processes discussed throughout this Course Book – as in the procurement literature in general – are drawn from the private sector. In this chapter, therefore, we merely draw out the additional points specified in the syllabus content. We also add some discussion of the regulation of private sector procurement, in line with the overall emphasis on 'compliance' in this section of the syllabus.

Finally, we give a brief overview of third sector procurement, focusing on the areas specified in the syllabus.

1 Private sector organisations

1.1 To get a handle on the numerous types of organisation in the private sector, there are various classifications we can use.

- We can distinguish on the basis of ownership and control – for example, sole traders, partnerships and limited companies.
- We can distinguish on the basis of size – for example, SMEs (small and medium-sized enterprises), to large, multinational corporations such as Unilever or Microsoft.
- We can distinguish on the basis of business activity – for example, **primary industries** engaged in the extraction of raw materials, **secondary industries** engaged in manufacturing, and **tertiary industries** engaged in services.

We will look at each of these classifications, and their impact on procurement.

The constitution of private sector organisations

1.2 Private sector organisations may be formed or 'constituted' in various different ways.

- An individual may carry on a business as a **sole trader**.
- A group of individuals may carry on a business together by legal agreement, as a **partnership**.
- A potentially very large number of people may carry on a business according to specific legal requirements for 'incorporation' as a **company**.

We will look at each of these types of organisation in turn.

Sole tradership

1.3 A sole tradership may be an appropriate business type for a tradesperson, say, or a shopkeeper or freelance designer. There is no legal distinction between the individual person and the business entity: the individual supplies all the capital for the business, and is personally liable for its debts. (This is *not* the case for a company, as we will see later...)

1.4 The advantages and disadvantages of sole tradership are summarised in Table 12.1.

Table 12.1 *Evaluating sole tradership*

ADVANTAGES	DISADVANTAGES
Few costs or legal requirements to establish the business	The proprietor is personally liable for the business's debts
No public accountability (though financial records are required for tax purposes)	It may be difficult to get finance for the business (eg a loan by personal guarantee)
The proprietor controls all decisions for the business – and enjoys all the profits	Resources are limited to what the proprietor can personally generate

Partnership

1.5 Many sole traders find that a logical way of expanding without the formalities of incorporation is to take on one or more partners, who contribute capital and expertise to the business, and who share the managerial and financial responsibilities. A partnership is usefully defined in UK law (Partnership Act 1890) as 'the relation which subsists between persons carrying on a business in common with a view of profit'. There must be at least two to a standard maximum of 20 partners, for a commercial partnership. (A professional practice, such as a firm of accountants or solicitors, can have any number of partners.)

1.6 Like a sole tradership (and *unlike* a company), a partnership does not have a separate legal identity from its members. This means, for example, that:

- Partners jointly own the assets of the partnership and are personally liable for its debts
- Partners are entitled to participate in management and act as agents of the firm (unlike in a company, where shareholders do not necessarily have this status)
- A change of partners usually terminates the old firm and begins a new one (unlike in a company, where shares can be transferred from one person to another).

1.7   The advantages and disadvantages of partnerships are summarised in Table 12.2.

Table 12.2 *Evaluating partnership*

ADVANTAGES	DISADVANTAGES
Partners contribute capital and expertise	Decision-making has to be shared/negotiated
Partners share managerial and financial responsibilities and liability	Profits have to be shared among the partners
With greater asset backing, it is often easier to raise loans than for a sole trader	Partners are generally personally liable 'without limit' for the partnership's debts
Suits professions, where members may be prohibited from practising as limited companies	

Limited company

1.8   By far the most common trading vehicle in the private sector is the *limited company*. A limited company is an 'incorporated' body: that is, it is considered a separate legal entity (or 'person') from its individual owners (shareholders).

- The company can own assets, enter into contracts and incur liabilities in its own name.
- If the company incurs a debt, payment will come from the assets owned by the company. The individual owners cannot be asked to contribute to the payment from their personal funds: their liability is *limited* to the amount they have invested in the company – usually by buying shares. (Hence, a 'limited company'.)

1.9   The people who pay for shares in a company are the shareholders, also known as the members of the company. These are the company owners. As time goes by, others may be invited to subscribe for shares in the company. Any money subscribed for shares belongs to the company. The company will not normally return the money to the shareholders, other than in exceptional circumstances (eg when the company ceases to trade and is wound up).

1.10   A company may be a *public company* (name ends in *'plc'* in the UK) or a *private company* (name ends in *'Ltd'* in the UK). The key differences are as follows.

- A *public* company may offer its shares to the general public. (A relatively small number of public companies – known as listed companies – trade their shares on investment exchanges, such as the London Stock Exchange.) This is not the case for a *private* company, whose shareholders are generally directors of the company, or connected to it in some way. This means that public companies are able to raise significantly larger sums of capital than private companies.
- A *public* company in the UK must have a minimum share capital (the value of shares the company is allowed to issue) of £50,000, with allotted shares of at least that value, and a minimum of one member and two directors. There are no minimum capital requirements for a private company, and the minimum number of directors is just one.
- A *public* company is subject to detailed company law requirements in regard to shares, directors, annual general meetings, accounting and so on. For *private* companies, there is much less red tape – because the owners and managers are generally the same people.

1.11   The advantages and disadvantages of incorporation as a company are summarised in Table 12.3.

Table 12.3 *Evaluating incorporation*

ADVANTAGES	DISADVANTAGES
Limited liability protects owners from personal liability for contracts and debts	Expense and red tape of incorporation, and the constraint of a written constitution
Shares are a stable source of finance: the amount of capital is unaffected by trading, and is not subject (like loans) to finance costs	Subject to regulation eg re public disclosure (in financial reports and accounts etc)
Directors provide the expertise the business needs, without 'diluting' ownership	Share trading can result in unwanted change of ownership

1.12   In the UK, limited companies are set up by filing documents including Articles of Association with the Registrar of Companies, who (for a small fee) issues the Certificate of Incorporation. All these documents are placed on file, maintained by the Registrar, and open to inspection by the public. The **Articles of Association** define the company's internal administration, rules and procedures: how shares will be issued and managed, the rights of shareholders, requirements for shareholder meetings, the powers and remuneration of directors, payment of dividends, and division of assets if the business is wound up.

Small and medium enterprises (SMEs)

1.13   From your own experience, you will have gathered that private sector organisations vary widely by size: from one-person operations to small businesses to vast global conglomerates. According to a 2005 European Union definition (used for grant-aid purposes):

- A 'micro' enterprise is one which has fewer than 10 employees and an annual turnover of less than 2 million euros.
- A 'small' enterprise is one which has 10–49 employees and an annual turnover of less than 10 million euros.
- A 'medium-sized' enterprise is one which has 50–249 employees and an annual turnover of less than 50 million euros.
- A 'large-scale' enterprise employs more than 250 employees, with an annual turnover of more than 50 million euros.

1.14   Particular attention has been given to small and medium enterprises (SMEs) in recent years, because (a) they are a significant contributor to economic activity (by the above definition, some 99% of enterprises in the EU in 2005, providing around 65 million jobs), and (b) because they require financial guidance and support in order to overcome lack of economic strength in competition with larger players.

1.15   Worthington and Britton *(The Business Environment)* ascribe the resurgence in the importance of the small-firm sector in the UK to a range of factors.

- The shift from manufacturing to service industry: many services are dominated by small firms
- Increasing consumer demand for more specialised and customised (as opposed to mass produced) products, to which small firms are better able to respond
- The growth of outsourcing, where non-core activities are contracted to small specialist firms
- Reorganisation and job cutting to reduce costs, creating 'downsized' organisations
- Government policy, with initiatives designed to support SMEs in creating economic activity and jobs
- More accessible technology, allowing small firms to reach global markets (via ICT) and eroding larger firms' technological edge and economies of scale

1.16   SMEs may have an advantage over large firms in clearly defined, small markets: it would not be worth large firms entering markets where there is no scope for cost-effective mass production. Such an advantage may apply in a geographically localised market, say, or in a 'niche' market for specialist, customised or premium-quality products. In addition, the entrepreneurial nature and speed of communication in small enterprises makes them particularly well suited to innovation and invention, and they may have an advantage over larger, less flexible firms in fast-changing, high-technology markets.

1.17 On the other hand, SMEs are at a disadvantage in areas such as: raising loan and share capital (because they are a greater risk); managing cashflow (being harder hard hit by late payment or non-payments); ability to take financial risks (including investment in research and development); and dealing with bureaucratic requirements.

1.18 Large organisations are able to take advantage of economies of scale.

- Technical economies, which arise in the production process. Large undertakings can afford larger and more specialised machinery, for example, and can take advantage of the cost efficiency of mass production.
- Commercial economies, such as purchasing economies (eg through bulk purchase discounts)
- Financial economies, such as obtaining loan finance at attractive rates of interest – or being able to raise large amounts of capital via the sale of shares to the public (as a public company).

A firm in an industry with a large consumer market may have to grow to a certain size in order to benefit from such economies of scale, and thus to be cost-competitive with larger players.

1.19 UK government support has focused on the problems and disadvantages of SMEs, in these areas, with initiatives designed to:

- Encourage on-time payment of bills by PLCs and public sector bodies
- Relax rules and regulations applicable to SMEs
- Reduce the tax burden (eg levels of corporation tax) on small business
- Provide grants to assist SMEs in rural areas or areas of industrial decline (eg the EU SME Initiative and the Enterprise Fund)
- Provide information, advice and support (eg through the Small Business Service and Business Link network).

1.20 From the above discussion, you may be able to identify particular challenges for the procurement or supply chain function in SMEs.

- A procurement officer in an SME will work within a limited expenditure budget and tight cost controls; will need to manage cashflow closely (eg securing long credit terms from suppliers); and may have to develop a supply chain which can respond to innovation, short product lifecycles and small-quantity, fast-turnaround requirements.
- A procurement officer buying *from* an SME will need to take into account the firm's limited capacity to handle volume; its potential financial instability (if it hits problems in the midst of a supply contract); and its cashflow issues (the ethical response to which would be to pay invoices on time in full).

Sources of finance in the private sector

1.21 There are a number of key sources of finance for private sector organisations.

- Initial capital investment by the owners of the business (eg in the case of a sole trader or partnership) or by venture capitalists
- Share capital: that is, the sale of shares in the company. A public company will, as we have seen, be able to sell shares to the general public on a Stock Exchange. A private company can raise finance by selling shares to investment syndicates and associates (eg friends and family members).
- Retained profits resulting from the profit-generating activities of the business, such as sales: that is, profits that are 'ploughed back' into the business (rather than being withdrawn by the owners or paid out to shareholders as dividends)
- Loan finance, such as bank overdraft facilities, or bank loans and debentures (usually secured against the assets of the business)

- The sale of unneeded assets
- Government grants (eg for small business development or other projects and capital purchases).

2 Objectives of private sector organisations

Profitability

2.1 As we have already seen, the primary objective for a private sector organisation is normally to maximise profits. Profit is the difference between the selling price of a product (or the total revenue earned from selling a product) and the cost of producing the product. In other words, it is the gain or surplus left over after the manufacturer or service provider has paid all its costs.

2.2 Both buyers and suppliers seek to make a profit for a number of reasons.

- Profit means that the business has covered its costs and is not 'bleeding' money in losses. This is important for the business to survive in the long term.
- Profit belongs to the owners or shareholders of the business, as a return on their investment: a share of profits is paid to them in the form of a 'dividend' on their shares. Strong and consistent profits are therefore important to encourage shareholders to continue to invest in the company, and to maintain the share capital of the company through a high share price (reflecting market demand for the shares).
- Profits which are not paid to shareholders ('retained profits') are available for reinvestment in the development of the business, enabling it to acquire assets, meet long-term borrowings, update plant and equipment, and build up reserves for future contingencies – without the cost and risk of borrowing funds for these purposes.

2.3 Procurement staff in a profit-seeking firm may well feel pressure to achieve the lowest possible cost when purchasing supplies – but this does not mean that they will sacrifice all other considerations in order to choose the lowest-cost option. Even in the short term this might not be the best way to achieve profits. For example, a more expensive material of higher quality might lead to lower levels of waste, rework and scrap: in the long run, it may work out cheaper than an inferior material.

2.4 More importantly, buyers must look to the longer-term benefit of their organisation, and more complex definitions of 'value'. This could mean an in-depth assessment of potential suppliers along a number of dimensions, not just price. For example, the long-term profitability of the organisation might be best served by a partnership relationship with a supplier offering technology sharing, just in time delivery, ongoing collaboration on cost reduction and process improvements – and/or other non-price advantages.

2.5 Procurement teams can, however, contribute measurably to profitability through savings on materials, inventory, and contracting and transaction costs (eg through effective negotiation and contract development, efficient management of the procurement process, and effective use of inventory management and e-procurement tools). These savings in turn contribute to bottom line profit.

2.6 If cost reductions are retained within the business, there is an immediate improvement in the bottom line. If the surplus resource is used up by budget holders, there is no direct impact on the bottom line – but there is added benefit.

Market share

2.7 One of the key features of the private sector is the very strong influence of competition. In nearly all cases, a private sector firm will be one of several, or many, firms offering goods or services of a particular type. Securing competitive advantage, in order to win *more* customers and *better quality* customers (higher lifetime value) is therefore a key focus of private sector strategy, including supply chain management.

2.8 Competitive advantage may be defined as the ability (gained through the development, protection and leverage of distinctive competencies and resources) to deliver value to customers more efficiently or effectively than one's competitors.

2.9 Strategy guru Kenichi Ohmae *(The Mind of the Strategist)* argued that: 'What business strategy is all about is, in a word, competitive advantage. The sole purpose of strategic planning is to enable a company to gain, as efficiently as possible, a sustainable edge over its competitors.' Ohmae argued that competitive advantage is achieved by matching the strengths and resources of the corporation with the needs of the market, in such a way as to achieve superior performance, relative to competitors in the market, in areas which are perceived as critical for success in the market.

2.10 Firms may measure the success of their competitive efforts in various ways: for example, sales volume growth, sales revenue growth, or growth in the number of customers. However, the most common measure of competitive success is market penetration or market share: the percentage of the total value of sales in a market (or market segment) which is accounted for by a given product or organisation. Market share may be defined in terms of either volume (units) or value (revenue).

2.11 Market share is a key indicator of performance for many private sector organisations in competitive markets. It enables firms to identify whether increases in their sales result from the market expanding – or from their capturing customers and sales from competitors.

Shareholder value

2.12 As we noted earlier, the purpose of securing or maximising corporate profitability is not just 'profitability' for its own sake. The aim of profitability is to generate a return on the value of shareholders' investment of capital in the business, in the form of:

- Dividends, through which a share of profits is distributed directly to shareholders
- Growth in the capital or equity value of shareholders' investment, through:
  - Retained profits being reinvested in the business
  - Maintaining or enhancing the value of the company's shares in the financial markets (eg due to positive market perceptions of the company's value, management and future prospects)
  - Maintaining or enhancing the value of the company's assets, such as land and buildings, plant, reputational capital, intellectual property (designs and patents), brand equity (the power of strong brands to command sales and profits) and so on – increasing the overall value or worth of the corporation.

Corporate social responsibility (CSR)

2.13 Corporate social responsibility is increasingly prioritised as a corporate objective in the private sector, owing to public, media and consumer pressure, and the risk of reputational damage as a result of the exposure of irresponsible corporate (and supply chain) behaviour.

2.14 We discussed the definition and issues of CSR in Chapter 4, in the context of stakeholder management: refresh your memory from Chapter 4 if you need to. However, it is worth noting that the value of CSR may be contested in the context of private sector organisations.

2.15 Milton Friedman and Elaine Sternberg have argued the view that 'the social responsibility of business is profit maximisation': to give a return on shareholders' investment. Spending funds on objectives not related to shareholder expectations is irresponsible: regard for shareholder wealth is a healthy discipline for management, providing accountability for decisions. The public interest is served by profit maximisation, because the State levies taxes. 'Consequently,' argued Friedman, 'the only justification for social responsibility is enlightened self interest' on the part of a business organisation.

2.16 So how does CSR serve the interest of the firm?

- Law, regulation and Codes of Practice impose certain social responsibilities on organisations (eg in relation to health and safety, employment protection, consumer rights and environmental care). There are financial and operational penalties for failure to comply (eg 'polluter pays' taxes).
- Voluntary measures (which may in any case only pre-empt legal and regulatory requirements) may enhance corporate image and build a positive brand. A commonly quoted example is the environmental and sustainability strategy adopted by The Body Shop.
- Above-statutory provisions for employees and suppliers may be necessary to attract, retain and motivate them to provide quality service and commitment – particularly in competition with other employers/purchasers.
- Increasing consumer awareness of social responsibility issues creates a market demand for CSR (and the threat of boycott for irresponsible firms)
- Social responsibility helps to create a climate in which business can prosper in the long term. In the same way, ethical sourcing helps to create a climate in which mutually-beneficial long-term relationships with suppliers can be preserved.

3 The regulation of private sector procurement

The influence of government

3.1 There are four main areas in which a nation's government influences private sector organisations (quite apart from its direct influence on public sector organisations).

- Governments influence the operation of organisations: what they can and cannot produce, and how they produce it (eg in laying down restrictions on production processes in order to protect the environment).
- Governments influence the costs and revenues incurred by organisations: by the application of taxes and duties on the production and sale of certain goods, and by the effect of taxes on the general level of consumer spending.
- Governments influence organisations by the actions they take in pursuing macroeconomic objectives (eg in establishing exchange rates and interest rates, by the extent to which they stimulate aggregate demand in the economy).
- Governments influence the values and norms that are regarded as acceptable within the national culture, and hence indirectly affect the outputs produced by organisations and the ways in which organisations behave.

3.2 Governments of all persuasions accept that some regulation of the private sector generally is desirable, for the following reasons.

- Governments wish to preserve a balance between consumers and firms. Consumers must be protected in terms of service, quality and price, while firms must be prevented from charging excessive prices for essential services.
- Governments wish to promote competition, eg by preventing mergers or acquisitions which result in monopolies or the abuse of a dominant market position.
- Governments wish to assist firms to prosper, because their prosperity makes for the prosperity of the nation generally.

- Governments wish to protect national interests, eg by protecting domestic companies from unfair competition from overseas companies.

Law and regulation

3.3 There is a wide variety of law and regulation affecting the conduct of business in a common law country, deriving (in the UK) from three main sources: regulations and directives issued by the European Union; statute law (Acts of Parliament) plus secondary legislation; and case law (law deriving from the decisions of judges in the courts, which set principles and precedents for future decisions). In addition, there are voluntary codes of practice developed by professions and industries, and scrutiny by various regulatory bodies.

3.4 This is a particularly important area for monitoring and management by procurement organisations, because:

- The organisation's response is not 'optional' or left to managerial discretion: compliance is required and enforced by various sanctions and penalties.
- The requirements are constantly changing, as courts and tribunals define them through their decisions, and as legislators and regulatory bodies issue new provisions and amendments.

3.5 Despite attempts to increase competition and innovation in markets through a process of de-regulation (eg in financial services), there are increasing legal and political constraints on managerial decision making, in areas such as the following.

- Restricting practices that tend to stifle competition, such as the formation of agreements between corporations (eg cartels) that would prevent, restrict or distort competition; and the control of monopolies, mergers which would result in monopolies, and the abuse of a dominant market position. UK legislation in this area includes the Competition Act 1998 and the Enterprise Act 2002 – and identical provisions apply in European law.
- Protecting the rights of minority groups in regard to equal opportunity and diversity in employment. This is covered by a range of equal opportunity law, which in the UK currently outlaws discrimination and harassment on grounds of sex, marital status, sexual orientation, race, colour, ethnicity, religious belief, disability and age.
- Protecting the rights of employees in the workplace and employment relationship. There is a wide range of employment law, embracing issues such as workplace health and safety; working hours and leave entitlements; family-friendly flexible working arrangements; rights of consultation for worker representative or trade unions; equal treatment of part-time and agency workers; and employee rights in the event of unfair dismissal, redundancies or transfer of undertakings.
- Protecting the rights and safety of consumers, through consumer protection law; the outlawing of unfair contract terms (eg limiting manufacturers' liability for faulty or unsafe goods); regulations on product health and safety; and so on.
- Enforcing environmental protection standards and commitments, which cover an increasing body of issues including: air and water quality, climate change and greenhouse gas emissions, agriculture, biodiversity and species protection, pesticides and hazardous chemicals, waste management, remediation of environmental impacts, impact review, and the conservation of public lands and natural resources.
- Restricting the types of products that firms can supply (eg forbidding the supply of dangerous goods) or materials and ingredients that can be used (eg forbidding the use of poisonous lead in paints used in toy manufacture)
- Restricting the uses to which firms can put personal data (eg the UK forbids firms from passing on customer details without their consent, under the Data Protection Act 1998).
- Enforcing good corporate governance: eg via corporate, finance and tax law (and voluntary regulation such as the London Stock Exchange UK Corporate Governance Code).
- Preventing corruption. In the private sector, this mainly concerns the prevention of money laundering: obtaining, concealing or investing funds or property known or suspected to be the proceeds of criminal conduct or terrorist funding (eg the UK's Money Laundering Regulations 2007).

Regulation of privatised firms

3.6 Privatised firms are those, such as BT in the UK, that used to be in public ownership but were sold by the government into private hands. In order to ensure that public services continue to be delivered (and priced) fairly, the government has imposed a regulatory regime on these firms.

3.7 The main power wielded by Ofcom (the UK telecommunications regulator) and similar bodies is concerned with limiting price rises. The regulator simply instructs the firm concerned that its price rises for a particular period must not exceed a certain percentage, which invariably is less than the general rate of inflation for that period.

3.8 Another important power arises from publicity. Naturally, the activities of an organisation such as BT affect very large numbers of people. There is widespread interest if Ofcom finds fault with any of those activities, which means that the regulator has no difficulty in gaining publicity in the media. This clearly puts pressure on the firm(s) in question to fall into line and pursue 'fair' policies.

3.9 Other powers include the following.

- Issuing and renewing licences for firms wishing to operate in the market. In exceptional circumstances the regulator may withdraw a licence to operate, but this would only be in extreme cases involving (for example) a threat to public safety or persistent and large-scale failure to comply with regulatory standards.
- Setting standards of good practice
- Monitoring the activities of firms operating in the market, responding to customer complaints, and seeking to ensure that firms operate to high standards.
- Communication and promotion of market activities to maintain consumer confidence.
- Making periodic reports to the government.

4 Key features of private sector procurement

The importance and role of branding

4.1 A 'brand' is defined by marketing guru Philip Kotler as 'a name, term, sign, symbol or design, or combination of them, intended to *identify* the goods or services of one seller or group of sellers, and to *differentiate* them from those of competitors [in the perceptions of customers]'.

4.2 By developing an identifiable and distinctive brand identity, branding allows customers to develop perceptions of the brand's values (eg prestige, quality, good value, style) which support purchase decisions and – ideally – foster customer loyalty. The task of the organisation marketing a brand is to ensure that the values associated with the brand, product – or organisation as a whole – are positive, attractive, and in line with how it wants to be seen, especially in relation to its competitors.

4.3 The term 'brand values', used in the syllabus, refers to what a product or corporate brand 'stands for' in the minds of customers and other stakeholders: the core values and characteristics associated with the brand. Brand values might include value for money (like Aldi Supermarkets), quality (like Rolls Royce cars), design (like Apple consumer electronics), technological innovation (like Dyson engineering products), corporate ethics (like The Body Shop), heritage and tradition (like Cadbury's chocolate), entrepreneurship (like the Virgin group) – and so on.

4.4 The term 'brand positioning' is given to the way consumers define or 'place' a brand on important attributes (like price, value, quality or trendiness), or how the brand is perceived or 'placed' relative to competing products and organisations. An organisation will often seek to determine – and influence – how its corporate image and products are perceived by customers in relation to its competitors.

4.5　The key point made by the mention of this topic in the syllabus is that procurement strategies, policies, practices and decisions will be concerned to *support* (or not undermine) the brand values and positioning created or desired by the organisation, as part of its marketing and competitive strategy.

4.6　So, for example:

- Procurement decisions should support any quality values attached to the brand, by securing high quality inputs and contributing to quality assurance processes.
- If the brand is competitively positioned on the basis of low price or value for money, procurement will have to support this by reducing or managing the costs of inputs and supply processes, so that the organisation can keep consumer prices down and maintain some kind of profit margin.
- If the brand's core values are corporate social responsibility, ethics or environmental responsibility, procurement will have to ensure that all inputs are ethical, fairly traded and environmentally friendly, and that the supply chain is managed in an ethical and responsible way.

And so on: you should be able to develop your own examples, from everything you have learned in this Course Book so far.

Alignment with suppliers

4.7　As we saw in Chapter 3, a key feature of private sector innovative procurement is the extent to which the interests of buyers and suppliers have become integrated or 'aligned'.

4.8　Dyadic supply relationships (with direct suppliers) have been replaced by supply chain relationships and supply chain management: an orientation which emphasises the continuous flow of value towards the customer from first producers to end users. Rather than firms competing, the modern view is that whole supply chains compete to offer customer value (and meet customer demand) more efficiently and effectively than their competitors. Suppliers are therefore seen as essential collaborators in value delivery, competitive advantage and business success.

4.9　For this reason, traditional adversarial, transactional (one-off, commercially driven) relationships have increasingly been replaced, for important and strategic procurements, by longer-term, collaborative relationships, or supply chain partnerships.

4.10　The interests of buyers and suppliers are no longer seen as mutually exclusive, or competitive – usually based around a win-lose battle to gain the advantage over the other party on price. Instead, the interests of buyers and suppliers are viewed as potentially 'aligned': that is, broadly compatible, or aiming towards the same goals. Everyone benefits from improved supply chain performance and competitive advantage. Supply chain management is often used to pursue mutual benefits, through mechanisms such as:

- Supplier development: enhancing the capacity and capability of suppliers to meet the buyer's needs – while at the same time enhancing their business development and earning potential with other (ideally non-competing) customers
- Collaborative waste and cost reductions through the supply chain: enhancing the efficiency of all parties' operations
- Collaborative process and quality improvements through the supply chain, or continuous improvement programmes: developing all parties' performance
- Collaborative efforts to improve labour and environmental management standards through the supply chain (eg through policy development, monitoring, or seeking certification under international standards schemes): improving all parties' sustainability, reputation and reputational risk management.

4.11　In addition to 'alignment', supply chains may also seek positive 'synergy', a state in which benefits are secured by collaboration, over and above what each party could secure on its own: a possibility sometimes summed up as '2 + 2 = 5'. While each party will want to maximise its own share of value gains (its 'slice of the pie'), this end can equally well be served by working together to 'enlarge the pie'. So, for example, buyers and suppliers may bring unique resources, competencies or technology to the relationship, to enhance the success of the supply chain as a whole. Meanwhile, the *pursuit* of supply chain alignment or integration may itself be synergistic, as it increases trust, information sharing and communication, joint problem-solving and other value-adding processes.

Innovative supply chain approaches

4.12   A number of supply chain approaches developed in the private sector have come to be regarded as innovative best practice which could benefit public sector procurement.

- **Early involvement of procurement**. Treasury (2007) argues that government departments and agencies should: 'ensure that procurement professionals are brought in at the earliest stages of projects, where their skills and knowledge are likely to have most impact.'
- **Early involvement of suppliers**. Treasury also makes it a general principle that the objectives of a procurement should be 'communicated to potential suppliers at an early stage, to gauge the market's ability to deliver and explore a range of possible solutions.' (We discussed early supplier involvement briefly in Chapter 5.)
- **The use of electronic procurement**. E-procurement has been identified as a significant opportunity to grasp savings across the public sector and the UK Treasury emphasised the successful adoption of a number of specific mechanisms in the private sector, such as e-auctions, e-marketplaces and procurement cards (discussed in Chapter 6).
- **Pro-active contract management**. The National Audit Office (1999) argued the need for 'active contract management' for high value and strategically important procurement. 'This involves ensuring that reliable and comprehensive information is available to monitor the performance of the contractor, and taking action quickly when delivery, price and quality is at risk. It also requires a clear understanding of shared responsibilities so that when the client department has agreed to provide facilities, support or other inputs essential for the supplier to meet the terms of the contract these are provided at the right time...' (Contract management was discussed in Chapter 5.)
- **Flexibility in the use of competition**. Formal competitive procedures are being adapted in a number of ways including: early procurement involvement; working more closely with suppliers; giving suppliers better access to information about contracts; greater use of e-procurement; explicit statement of non-price selection criteria and weightings; and improved supplier debriefing.

5   Third sector organisations

The not for profit (NFP) sector

5.1   The 'third sector' of an economy comprises non-governmental organisations (NGOs) which are operated on a not-for-profit (NFP) basis, generally reinvesting any 'surplus' from their activities to further social, environmental, cultural or other value-driven objectives. Such organisations include: charities, churches, political parties, museums, clubs and associations, co-operatives, interest, pressure and advocacy groups, trade unions and professional bodies such as CIPS.

5.2   Organisations in the NFP sector have typically been set up to achieve a defined objective (eg for a charitable or awareness-raising purpose, or to represent the interests of members) rather than to maximise profit.

5.3   NFP organisations usually derive their funding from voluntary donations, legacies (money left to the organisation in someone's will), sponsorships and government grants and subsidies. They may also have a profit-seeking trading arm to generate revenue (as in the case of 'charity shops', say).

5.4   They may be owned by their members (as in a club or association) or by a trust (as in a charity). They are typically managed by a board of trustees or directors.

The voluntary and subscription sectors

5.5   NFP organisations are sometimes subdivided into further sectors, according to their membership and funding.

- In the **voluntary sector** (eg churches, charities and interest groups), the organisations are generally controlled by a few individuals (eg trustees), but operate by voluntary contributions of funding (eg donations and grants, plus sales of product where relevant) and participation (volunteer labour). The funds are used to maintain the work.
- In the **subscription paid sector** (eg clubs, trade unions and professional bodies), the organisations are owned by the people who pay subscriptions to be members.

Objectives of third sector organisations

5.6   Obviously, the range of third sector organisations is very wide, and they may have a range of different specific purposes.

- Raising public awareness of a cause or issue (eg environmental or social pressure and interest groups)
- Political lobbying and advocacy on behalf of a cause, issue or group
- Raising funds to carry out activities (perhaps using commercial operations to generate profits, in addition to requesting grants, donations or subscriptions)
- Providing material aid and services to the public or specific beneficiaries (eg homeless or aged care charities, wildlife protection and conservation groups)
- Providing services to members (eg trade unions advocating employment rights, and professional bodies securing ethical and technical standards)
- Mobilising and involving members of the public in community projects, for mutual benefit (eg Volunteer Service Overseas).

5.7   As with public sector organisations, the range of an NFP organisation's stakeholders can therefore be wide, including: contributors (staff, volunteers, members, donors); funding bodies (sponsors, funding authorities); beneficiaries of the services or activities; the media (since activities are often 'in the public interest'); and regulatory bodies (such as the Charity Commission in England and Wales). This means that there will be multiple influences on organisational policy and decision-making.

5.8   In order to avoid loss of direction, or pressure to change direction from influential stakeholders (especially sponsors and donors), third sector organisations generally set out their objectives, policies, rules and regulations in some form of governing documents – similar to the Articles of Association of a corporation. These may take the form of a written constitution, charter, trust deed or memorandum and articles of association, setting out:

- The purpose and objectives of the organisation
- Governing principles, policies, rules and regulations for operation
- Responsibilities for management of the organisation (eg the board of trustees)
- Protocols for changing administrative provisions or ceasing operations.

12

5.9 Johnson, Scholes & Whittington (*Exploring Corporate Strategy*) summarise some of the key characteristics of the third sector as follows: Table 12.4.

Table 12.4 *Key characteristics of the third sector*

Objectives and expectations	• May be multiple service objectives and expectations • Expectations of funding bodies are usually very influential • May be subject to political lobbying • Multiple influences on policy: complicates strategic planning • Consultation and consensus-seeking becomes a major activity • Decision-making can be slow
Market and users	• Beneficiaries of services are not necessarily contributors of revenue or resources • Multiple stakeholders and customers • Service satisfaction is not measured readily in financial terms
Resources	• Multiple sources of funding • High proportion from sponsors and donors • Resources received in advance of service delivery, often with attached expectations • Tends towards strategic emphasis on financial or resources efficiency rather than service effectiveness • Strategies and communications may be addressed as much towards sponsors and donors as clients

5.10 You may like to browse the websites of some NGOs in areas that interest you, and see how clearly articulated their values and objectives are, and how these flow down to procurement, sourcing and corporate social responsibility policies.

6 Key features of third sector procurement

The need for regulated procurement exercises

6.1 A significant factor affecting procurement in NFP organisations is that they are seen as performing a 'stewardship' function. That is, they are spending money that has been derived not from the organisation's own trading efforts, but from someone else's donations or taxes. In fact, funding will often come from persons or organisations not themselves benefiting from the services provided.

6.2 Procurement functions are therefore more closely scrutinised and regulated than in the private commercial sector, with a strong emphasis on accountability and stewardship.

6.3 Johnson & Scholes *(Exploring Corporate Strategy)* argue that this may cause a focus on resource efficiency at the expense of service effectiveness. In other words, there is a danger that such organisations will be less concerned to identify and satisfy the needs of their 'customers' – and more concerned with demonstrating absence of waste in their use of sponsors' funds.

6.4 Third sector organisations generally establish clear governance structures for their management – and procurement – in order to provide clarity, accountability, checks and controls on the use of funds.

Regulations impacting on charities

6.5 Third sector organisations are subject to the same general laws and regulations as private and public sector enterprises, as discussed earlier. The syllabus therefore focuses here specifically on regulations impacting on charities.

6.6 The Charity Commission is the statutory regulatory body for charities in England and Wales. Its objectives are as follows.

• To register charities (like the registry of companies at Companies House)

- To ensure that charities meet the legal requirements for being a charity (in order to register with the Commission), and are equipped to operate properly and within the law
- To check that charities are run for public benefit, and not for private advantage
- To ensure that charities are independent and that their trustees take their decisions free of control or undue influence from outside agencies
- To detect and remedy serious mismanagement or deliberate abuse by or within charities
- To work with charities and other regulators, to enhance public confidence in charities and the work they do (in order to ensure continuing volunteer labour and funding).

6.7 The Commission has a range of responsibilities, including:

- Gathering and maintaining information about charities on the charities register, and making information available to the general public on request
- Offering advice and guidance to charities (via a help line and site visits) on governance and compliance
- Auditing charity activities to check governance and compliance arrangements
- Investigating complaints about charities, and – in the case of mismanagement or abuse – intervening to protect the charity's assets.

What do third sector organisations buy?

6.8 With such a wide range of activities, the range of items procured may be correspondingly wide.

- An NFP organisation may provide services – in which case, its requirements will be the same as those for other service organisations.
- An NFP organisation may have a retail arm, in order to help it raise funds – in which case, its requirements will be the same as those for other retail organisations.
- More generally, NFP organisations will have general operating requirements: office supplies and equipment, IT support, premises management services and so on.
- More specifically, NFP organisations may have requirements for specialist supplies related to their activities. A church will need premises, furniture and supplies for its religious services, say. A charity may need collecting tins, volunteer badges, merchandise for sale and so on.

Key drivers for third sector procurement policy

6.9 Key drivers for procurement policy in third sector organisations therefore include the following.

- The values of internal and external stakeholders (including founders, staff, voluntary workers, donors and supporters), which are often directly related to the mission and purpose of the organisation. The range of a third sector organisation's stakeholders can be wide, including: contributors (staff, volunteers, members, donors); funding bodies (sponsors, funding authorities); beneficiaries of the services or activities; the media (since activities are often 'in the public interest'); and regulatory bodies (such as the Charity Commission). This means that there will be multiple influences on procurement policy and objectives.
- The need to align procurement policies and procedures with the core values, cause, issue or theme promoted by the organisation (eg to support 'green' procurement, if the organisation is an environmental charity or lobbying group).
- The management of reputation and reputational risk. Public relations crisis, caused by some internal failure of policy or implementation, is both more likely for third sector organisations (because of the extent of scrutiny and high standards) and more significant in its impact (because of the dependence on volunteer labour, political support and discretionary funding – most of which will, in turn, be intentionally directed to the values for which the organisation purports to stand). One high-profile example of reputational damage, for example, concerned the exposure of labour exploitation practices in the supply chain for Oxfam's 'Make Poverty History' wristbands.
- The need to source inputs for a very wide range of activities, some of which pose significant logistical challenges (eg foreign aid and development work, disaster relief and so on).

- The need to act as retail or merchandise buyers, if goods are resold to raise funds. Procurement officers will therefore have to source goods of a quality, variety and distinctiveness which will appeal to consumers, at a price which allows them to make a significant 'surplus' on the sale. At the same time, there will often be ethical issues involved in dealing fairly with suppliers, and providing suppliers with a fair price for their goods (especially if, like Oxfam, for example, the organisation specifically obtains goods from developing countries and small rural suppliers, as part of their charitable activity).
- The need for differentiation (eg via best practice sustainable procurement policies, or distinctive merchandise for re-sale to raise funds) in order to compete for attention, volunteers and funding
- Limited resources. Some third-sector organisations (such as the International Red Cross) have very large procurement budgets. However, many have limited funds, and are anxious to devote as much as possible of their funding to the work for which they were formed: there is therefore a strong emphasis on cost control.
- The need for economic sustainability. The term 'non-profit' or 'not-for-profit' should not be interpreted as implying a disregard for commercial disciplines. On the contrary, such disciplines may be more important than in the private commercial sector, because of the scarcity of funds; pressure to devote as much as possible of their income to beneficiaries; or expenditure limits set by funding authorities (eg grant providers) or trustees. It is worth noting, too, that NFP organisations can enjoy a 'surplus' of income over expenditure, even if it is not described as a 'profit'. Procurement professionals therefore have a key role to play.
- The need for transparency, accountability and stewardship in the management of funds – and resulting oversight and regulation: as discussed earlier.

Chapter summary

- Private sector organisations include sole traders, partnerships and limited companies (both public and private). Many enterprises are now classed as small medium enterprises (SMEs), which face particular challenges and receive public sector support.
- Objectives of private sector organisations typically include maximisation of profits and shareholder wealth, and increase in market share. Increasingly, such organisations recognise objectives of corporate social responsibility.
- There are increasing legal and political constraints on the activities of private sector organisations.
- Private sector organisations frequently adopt a supply chain approach in which the interests of buyers and suppliers are aligned for mutual advantage.
- The third (not-for-profit) sector includes charities, churches, political parties, interest and pressure groups, clubs and associations. They may have a range of purposes and activities. The main challenges for purchasing will be limited funds and accountability in the use of those funds.

Self-test questions

Numbers in brackets refer to the paragraphs where you can check your answers.

1 In what ways may private sector firms be constituted? (1.2)

2 List advantages and disadvantages of incorporating a private sector firm. (1.11, Table 12.3)

3 What factors account for the resurgence in importance of the small-firm sector? (1.15)

4 Why is the lowest-cost option not always optimal even for a buyer pursuing profit maximisation? (2.3)

5 How does CSR serve the interests of private sector firms? (2.16)

6 How do governments influence private sector organisations? (3.1)

7 How are privatised firms regulated? (3.6–3.9)

8 Account for the growth in collaborative buyer-supplier relationships in recent years. (4.7–4.10)

9 Distinguish between the voluntary sector and the subscription paid sector. (5.5)

10 List key characteristics of the third sector in terms of objectives and expectations. (Table 12.4)

11 What are the objectives of the Charity Commission? (6.6)

Subject Index